Focus on Grammar

A
HIGH-INTERMEDIATE
Course for
Reference
and Practice

Marjorie Fuchs
Margaret Bonner

Sharon Hilles, grammar consultant

Longman

Focus on Grammar: A High-Intermediate Course for Reference and Practice

Copyright © 1995 by Addison-Wesley Publishing Company, Inc.

Editorial Director: Joanne Dresner
Senior Development Editor: Joan Saslow
Assistant Editor: Jessica Miller
Production Editorial: Lisa Hutchins
Text Design: Six West Design
Cover Design: A Good Thing, Inc.
Book Production: Circa 86, Inc.
Text Art: Linda Bladholm, Alex Bloch, Circa 86, Lauri Harden,
          Bobbie Moore, Ba Rea, Meryl Treatner

Library of Congress Cataloging-in-Publication Data
Fuchs, Marjorie, 1949–
    Focus on grammar. A high-intermediate course for reference and
practice / Marjorie Fuchs, Margaret Bonner; Sharon Hilles,
grammar consultant.
        p.   cm.
    Includes index.
    ISBN 0-201-65689-2
    1. English language—Textbooks for foreign speakers.   2. English
language—Grammar—Problems, exercises, etc.   I. Bonner, Margaret.
II. Title.
PE1128.F793   1995
428.2'4—dc20   94-39044
                                                              CIP

3 4 5 6 7 8 9 10-KE-99989796

*To the memory of my parents,
Edith and Joseph Fuchs—MF*

To my son, Luke Frances—MB

Contents

Focus on Grammar: A High-Intermediate Course for Reference and Practice

About the Authors

Marjorie Fuchs taught ESL for eight years at New York City Technical College and LaGuardia Community College of the City University of New York and EFL at the Sprach Studio Lingua Nova in Munich, Germany. She has authored or co-authored many widely used ESL textbooks, notably *On Your Way, Crossroads, Top Twenty ESL Word Games, Around the World: Pictures for Practice, Families: Ten Card Games for Language Learners, Focus on Grammar: An Intermediate Course for Reference and Practice*, and the *Workbooks* to the *Longman Dictionary of American English, The Longman Photo Dictionary*, and the *Vistas* series.

Margaret Bonner has been teaching and writing since 1978. She has taught at Hunter College, the Borough of Manhattan Community College, the National Taiwan University, and the Center for International Programs at Virginia Commonwealth University. Currently she is teaching at John Tyler Community College in Midlothian, Virginia. She worked for three years as a textbook author for the school system of the Sultanate of Oman, and she contributed to the *On Your Way* series and *Focus on Grammar: An Intermediate Course for Reference and Practice*. Her most recent text is *Step into Writing*.

Introduction

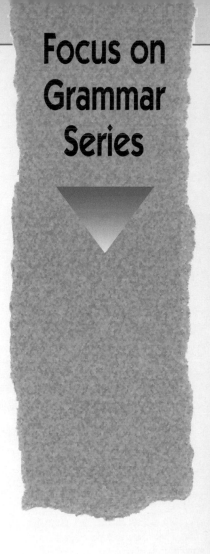

Focus on Grammar: A High-Intermediate Course for Reference and Practice is the third text in the four-level *Focus on Grammar* series. Written by practicing ESL professionals, the series focuses on English grammar through lively listening, speaking, reading, and writing activities. Each of the four Student's Books is accompanied by a Workbook, Cassettes, and a Teacher's Manual. Each Student's Book stands alone as a complete text in itself or can be used as part of the *Focus on Grammar* series.

Both Controlled and Communicative Practice

Research in applied linguistics suggests that students expect and need to learn the formal rules of a language. However, students need to practice new structures in a variety of contexts to help them internalize and master them. To this end, *Focus on Grammar* provides an abundance of both controlled and communicative exercises so that students can bridge the gap between knowing grammatical structures and using them. The many communicative activities in each unit enable students to personalize what they have learned in order to talk to each other with ease about hundreds of everyday issues.

A Unique Four-Step Approach

The series follows a unique four-step approach. The first step is **contextualization.** New structures are shown in the natural context of passages, articles, and dialogues. This is followed by **presentation** of structures in clear and accessible grammar charts and explanations. The third step is **focused practice** of both form and meaning in numerous and varied controlled exercises. In the fourth step, students engage in **communication practice,** using the new structures freely and creatively in motivating, open-ended activities.

A Complete Classroom Text and Reference Guide

A major goal in the development of *Focus on Grammar* has been to provide a Student's Book that serves not only as a vehicle for classroom instruction but also as a resource for self-study. The combination of grammar charts, grammar notes, and expansive appendices provides a complete and invaluable reference guide for the student at the high-intermediate level. Exercises in the Focused Practice sections of each unit are ideal for individual study, and students can check their work, using the complete answer key at the back of the book.

Thorough Recycling

Underpinning the scope and sequence of the series as a whole is the belief that students need to use target structures many times in many contexts at increasing levels of difficulty. For this reason new grammar is constantly recycled so that students will feel thoroughly comfortable with it.

Comprehensive Testing Program

SelfTests at the end of each of the ten parts of the Student's Book allow for continual assessment of progress. In addition, diagnostic and final tests in the Teacher's Manual provide a ready-made, ongoing evaluation component for each student.

PART AND UNIT FORMAT

Focus on Grammar: A High-Intermediate Course for Reference and Practice is divided into ten parts comprising twenty-seven units. Each part contains grammatically related units, each focusing on a specific grammatical structure. The first unit reviews and contrasts verb tenses already familiar to high-intermediate students (simple present tense and present progressive, simple past tense and past progressive, simple past tense and present perfect, present perfect and present perfect progressive). Each unit has one or more themes relating the exercises to one another. All units have the same clear, easy-to-follow format:

Introduction

The Introduction presents the grammar focus of the unit in a natural context. The Introduction texts, all of which are recorded on cassette, present language in various formats. These include newspaper and magazine excerpts, advertisements, reviews, interviews, and other formats that students encounter in their day-to-day lives. In addition to presenting grammar in context, the Introduction serves to raise student motivation and to provide an opportunity for incidental learning and lively classroom discussions. Topics are varied, ranging from people's names, friendship, and saving money to gun control, the new millennium, and possible encounters with visitors from outer space.

Grammar Charts

Grammar Charts follow each Introduction. These focus on the form of the unit's target structure. The clear and easy-to-understand boxes present each grammatical form in all its combinations. Affirmative and negative statements, *yes/no* and *wh-* questions, short answers, and contractions are presented for all tenses and modals covered. These charts provide a clear visual reference for each structure.

Grammar Notes

The Grammar Notes that follow the charts focus on the meaning and use of the structure. Each note gives a clear explanation of the grammar point and is always followed by one or more examples. Where appropriate, timelines help illustrate the meaning of verb tenses and their relationship to one another. *Be careful!* notes alert students to common ESL/EFL errors. Usage Notes provide guidelines for recognizing and understanding different levels of formality and correctness. Pronunciation Notes are provided when appropriate, and cross-references to other related units and the Appendices make the book easy to use.

Focused Practice Exercises

These exercises follow the Grammar Notes. This section provides practice for all uses of the structure presented in the notes. Each Focused Practice section begins with a "for recognition only" exercise called Discover the Grammar. Here, the students are expected to recognize either the form of the structure or its meaning without having to produce any language. This activity raises consciousness as it builds confidence.

Following the Discover the Grammar activity are exercises that practice the grammar in a controlled, but still contextualized, environment. The exercises proceed from simpler to more complex. There is a large variety of exercise types including fill-in-the-blanks, matching, multiple choice, question and sentence formation, sentence combining, and error analysis. As with the Introduction, students are exposed to many different written formats, including letters, journal entries, resumes, charts, schedules, advertisements, and news articles. Many exercises are art-based, providing a rich and interesting context for meaningful practice. All Focused Practice exercises are suitable for self-study or homework. A complete answer key is provided at the end of this book.

Communication Practice Exercises

These exercises are intended for in-class use. The first exercise is called Practice Listening. After having had exposure to and practice with the grammar in its written form, students now have the opportunity to check their aural comprehension. Students hear a variety of listening formats, including conversations, airport announcements, weather reports, and interviews. After listening to the tape (or hearing the teacher read the tapescript, which can be found in the Teacher's Manual), students complete a task that focuses on either the form or the meaning of the structure. It is suggested that students be allowed to hear the text as many times as they wish to complete the task successfully.

Practice Listening is followed by a variety of activities that provide students with the opportunity to use the grammar in open-ended, interactive activities. Students work in pairs or small groups in interviews, surveys, opinion polls, information gaps, discussions, role plays, games, and problem-solving activities. The activities are fun and engaging and offer ample opportunity for self-expression and cross-cultural comparison.

Review or SelfTest

At the conclusion of each part there is a review feature that can be used as a self-test. The exercises in this section test the form and use of the grammar content of the units in the part just concluded.

Appendices

The Appendices provide useful information, such as lists of common irregular verbs, common adjective-plus-preposition combinations, common phrasal verbs and their meanings, and spelling and pronunciation rules. The Appendices can help students do the unit exercises, act as a springboard for further classroom work, and serve as a reference source.

SUPPLEMENTARY COMPONENTS

All supplementary components of *Focus on Grammar*, the Workbook, the Cassettes, and the Teacher's Manual, are tightly keyed to the Student's Book, ensuring a wealth of practice and an opportunity to tailor the series to the needs of each individual classroom.

Cassettes

All of the Unit Introductions and the Practice Listening exercises are recorded on cassette. The symbol ▄▄ appears next to these activities. Listening scripts appear in the Teacher's Manual and may be used as an alternative way of presenting the listening activities.

Workbook

The Workbook accompanying *Focus on Grammar: A High-Intermediate Course for Reference and Practice* provides a wealth of additional exercises appropriate for self-study of the target grammar of each unit in the Student's Book. Most of the exercises are fully contextualized. Themes of the Workbook exercises are either a continuation or a spin-off of the corresponding Student's Book unit themes. There are also ten tests, one for each of the ten Student's Book parts. These tests have questions in the format of the Structure and Written Expression section of the TOEFL®. Besides reviewing the material in the Student's Book, these questions provide invaluable practice to those who are interested in taking this widely administered test.

Teacher's Manual

The Teacher's Manual, divided into three parts, contains a variety of suggestions and information to enrich the material in the Student's Book. The first part gives general suggestions for each section of a typical unit. The next part offers practical teaching suggestions and cultural information to accompany specific material in each unit. The Teacher's Manual also provides ready-to-use diagnostic and final tests for each of the ten parts of the Student's Book. In addition, a complete script of the cassette tapes is provided, as is an answer key for the diagnostic and final tests.

Software

The *Focus on Grammar* Software provides individualized practice based on each unit of the Student's Book. Fully contextualized and interactive, the activities broaden and extend practice of the grammatical structures in the reading, listening, and writing skill areas. The software includes grammar review, review tests, and all relevant reference material from the Student's Book. It can also be used alongside the *Longman Dictionary of American English* Software.

Acknowledgments

Writing a grammar book is an exhilarating but complex process. We couldn't have done it without the help of many people. We are grateful to:

Joanne Dresner, who initiated and oversaw the entire project. She made it possible for us to work full-time on the project and facilitated our long-distance collaboration. Her steady commitment helped keep a long endeavor always in focus.

Joan Saslow, who worked with unflagging energy, enthusiasm, diligence, speed, and efficiency. Her keen practical sense of what works in the classroom helped keep us grounded.

Sharon Hilles, who guided us on the remarkable linguistic journey from deep to surface structure. We appreciated her insight, candor, and humor.

Lisa Hutchins, who expertly guided the book through all stages of production. She kept a tight control of details while never losing sight of the project as a whole.

The Addison-Wesley staff, whose support we could always count on. Laura McCormick patiently and promptly answered our many questions about permissions. Polli Heyden painstakingly carried out the photo research. Jessica Miller expedited the reams of paperwork that the project generated and closely scrutinized the final pages.

Rick Smith, for his unswerving belief in us. His lively curiosity and remarkable collection of books were a never-ending source of inspiration and ideas.

Luke Frances, whose maturity enabled him to carry on with unruffled self-sufficiency during the writing of this book. His up-to-the-minute interests and candid criticism helped keep the book young.

To all these people and to the many students and teachers we have had, we say thank you!

Marjorie Fuchs
Margaret Bonner

Credits

Grateful acknowledgment is given to the following for providing photographs:

Page 2   photo by Molly Heron

Page 16   photo by Marjorie Fuchs

Page 19   photo by Marjorie Fuchs

Page 32   by permission of Harpo Productions, Inc.

Page 41   courtesy of New York Road Runners Club (NYRRC)

Page 78   photos of "Moffet, Aguirre" by Marjorie Fuchs

Page 79   photo of "Kato" by Richard M. Smith

Page 79   photo of "Wilson" by Marjorie Fuchs

Page 88   courtesy of William and Ruth Geen

Page 104   photo by Margaret Bonner

Page 115   Karen Preuss/Jeroboam, Inc.

Page 116   Laima Druskis/Jeroboam, Inc.

Page 144   courtesy of NASA

Page 167   Arthur Tress/Photo Researchers, Inc.

Page 175   Bates Littlehales, © National Geographic Society

Page 176   Thomas J. Abercrombie, © National Geographic Society

Page 204   photos by Marjorie Fuchs

Page 222   John Springer Collection/Bettmann Film Archive

Page 239   photo supplied by Marjorie Fuchs

Page 253   photo by Dutton Signet, a division of Penguin Books USA Inc.

Page 254   photo by Dianne Fong-Torres

Page 280   courtesy of National Archives

Page 291   Arthur Tress/Photo Researchers, Inc.

Page 312   courtesy of Magic Photo, White Plains, NY

PART

I

Present
and
Past

Review and Integration: Present, Past, Present Perfect

Section One
Simple Present Tense and Present Progressive

INTRODUCTION

▶ *Read and listen to this book review.*

What's in a Baby Name?

So, you**'re expecting** a baby, and you**'re** still **putting off** choosing a name. Perhaps you've read some of those studies that **claim** that teachers **give** better grades to David and Karen than to Elmer and Gertrude. Or that people **find** a Bertha less pretty than a Lisa—even when both women are equally attractive.

You**'re** right—it **is** a big decision, and you **don't want** to make a mistake. Now there**'s** help and solace for the anxious parent-to-be, in the form of Sue Browder's *The New Age Baby Name Book* (New York: Warner Books, 1987). Browder **explores** the psychological effects of names and **assures** us that those studies about teachers **are** probably flawed. On the other hand, she **believes** a distinctive name **helps** a child develop self-esteem. (Distinctive, not weird—a name like Ima Pigg **doesn't do** much for anyone's self-confidence.)

What are some of today's naming trends? Most Americans still **choose** names that already **exist,** but many **are taking** them from different sources. People **are using** yesterday's nicknames as today's formal given names. For example, Carrie **is becoming** more popular than Caroline. The distinction between male and female names **is blurring** somewhat, too. More and more people **are selecting** unisex names such as Dana, Leslie, or Marty. And many parents **are turning** to their roots and **choosing** names that **reflect** their ethnic background. Names like Kachina (Native American: "sacred dancer"), Lateef (North African: "gentle"), and Jonina (Hebrew: "dove") **are becoming** more and more common.

Whether you **are considering** traditional names like Mary and John, or you **prefer** more contemporary ones like Megan and Jared, this book **has** them all along with their place of origin, meaning, and—where necessary—pronunciation. *The New Age Baby Name Book* **presents** a wealth of information and **makes** fascinating reading—even if you **aren't becoming** a parent.

**The Most Popular Girls' and Boys'
Names in the United States**

Jessica	Ashley	Daniel
Jennifer	Tiffany	David
Stefanie	Samantha	Anthony
Melissa	✳ ✳ ✳ ✳	Joseph
Christina	Michael	Matthew
Nicole	Christopher	John
Amanda	Jonathan	Andrew

Source: *Guiness Book of World Records,* 1989.

SIMPLE PRESENT TENSE AND PRESENT PROGRESSIVE

SIMPLE PRESENT TENSE
People often **choose** relatives' names for their children.

PRESENT PROGRESSIVE
Today people **are choosing** names from different sources.

Grammar Notes

1. The present progressive describes what is happening right now or in the extended present. The simple present tense describes what generally happens (but not necessarily right now).

> I**'m reading** a book on baby names.

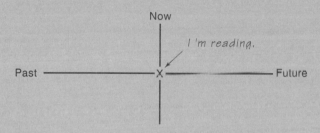

People often **read** baby-name books to help them choose a name.

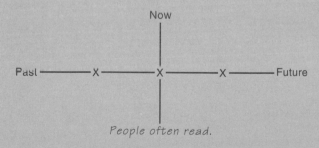

2. The simple present tense is used to talk about situations that are not connected to time—for example, scientific facts and physical laws.

> Water **freezes** at 39° F.

3. Remember that non-action verbs (also called stative verbs) are not usually used in the progressive even when they describe a situation that exists at the moment of speaking.

> I **want** to choose a distinctive name. NOT I'm wanting to choose a distinctive name.

Non-action verbs include: *hate, like, love, want, know, remember, suppose, think (=believe), understand, hear, see, smell, taste, feel, notice, seem, be, appear, sound, look, have, own, possess, belong.*

See Appendix 2 on page A4 for a list of non-action verbs.

4. The present progressive is often used with *always* to express a repeated action.

> She**'s always smiling.** That's why we call her "Sunshine."

Frequently we use this form to express a negative reaction to a situation.

> He**'s always calling** me "Sweetie." I wish he'd stop.

5. The simple present tense is often used in summaries, such as book or movie reviews.

> In her book, Browder **describes** the naming systems among different ethnic groups. She also **explores** the psychological effects of names.

FOCUSED PRACTICE

1. Discover the Grammar

Read this description, which appears in another baby-name book. Underline all the present progressive verbs and circle all the simple present tense verbs.

<u>Are</u> you <u>looking</u> for an original name for your baby . . . your pet . . . a character in your latest novel or short story?

From Adoración to Izzit, Maya, Naipaul, Ena, and Apollo, the names you (need) are here, organized alphabetically for quick cross-reference. . . . Whether you're waiting for a baby, giving birth to a novel, seeking a name for your newest pet, or looking for the perfect baby-shower gift, take a trip around the world with the book that has a name for everyone . . . *The International Baby Name Book* by Maxine Fields (New York: Pocket Books, 1985).

2. Party Talk

Complete the conversations with the correct form of the verbs in parentheses. Choose between the simple present and present progressive.

1. **Iantha:** Hi, I'm Iantha.

   Al: Nice to meet you, Iantha. I'm Alan, but my friends _____*call*_____ me Al.
   a. (call)

   Iantha: Nice to meet you, Al.

   Al: Iantha. That's an unusual name. Where _____ it _____ from?
   b. (come)

   Iantha: It's Greek. It _____ "violet-colored flower."
   c. (mean)

   Al: That's pretty. What _____ you _____, Iantha?
   d. (do)

   Iantha: Well, I usually _____ computer equipment, but right now
   e. (sell)

   I _____ at a flower shop. My uncle _____ it.
   f. (work)   g. (own)

   Al: You _____! I _____ it's true that names _____ our lives!
   h. (joke)   i. (guess)   j. (influence)

2. **Mario:** I _____ to find Greg Costanza. _____ you _____ him?
   a. (try)   b. (know)

   Bela: Greg? Oh, you _____ Lucky.
   c. (mean)

   Mario: Excuse me?

   Bela: It's his nickname. Everyone _____ him Lucky because he
   d. (call)

   _____ things.
   e. (always / win)

3. **Lola:** I _____ that you _____ a baby. Congratulations!
    <u>a. (hear)</u>   <u>b. (expect)</u>

    Vanya: Thank you.

    Lola: Have you decided on a name yet?

    Vanya: We _____ naming the baby Mangena. What _____ you
    <u>c. (think of)</u>
    _____ that?
    <u>d. (think about)</u>

    Lola: I've never heard the name before. How _____ you _____ it?
    <u>e. (spell)</u>

    Vanya: M-A-N-G-E-N-A. It's Hebrew.

    Lola: Oh. What _____ it _____?
    <u>f. (mean)</u>

    Vanya: "Song" or "melody."

    Lola: Mangena. I _____ it. It _____ pretty.
    <u>g. (like)</u>   <u>h. (sound)</u>

4. **Setsu:** _____ you _____ already? Don't go yet. They _____
    <u>a. (leave)</u>   <u>b. (make)</u>
    coffee.

    Mu Lan: Hm. It _____ good. OK. I'll stay a little longer.
    <u>c. (smell)</u>

    Setsu: Good. Besides, I _____ to introduce you to someone. _____ you
    <u>d. (want)</u>
    _____ Professor Wilson? He _____ freshman science this
    <u>e. (know)</u>   <u>f. (teach)</u>
    semester.

    Mu Lan: Oh. Nice to meet you. I _____ my friend Sammy _____ your
    <u>g. (believe)</u>   <u>h. (take)</u>
    class.

    Dr. Wilson: Sammy? What _____ he _____ like?
    <u>i. (look)</u>

    Mu Lan: Oh. It's not a he. Her real name is Samantha, but her friends always
    _____ her Sammy.
    <u>j. (call)</u>

5. **Rosa:** Would you like a cup of coffee, Dr. Wilson?

    Dr. Wilson: Oh. No, thanks. I _____ coffee. It _____ me too nervous.
    <u>a. (not drink)</u>   <u>b. (make)</u>

    Rosa: Well, how about a cup of tea, then? The water _____.
    <u>c. (boil)</u>

    Dr. Wilson: OK. Thanks.

    Rosa: You _____ science, Dr. Wilson. Can you explain something to me?
    <u>d. (teach)</u>
    Why _____ water _____ so quickly here?
    <u>e. (boil)</u>

    Dr. Wilson: Because we're in the mountains. At this elevation water _____
    <u>f. (boil)</u>
    at a lower temperature.

COMMUNICATION PRACTICE

3. Practice Listening

Listen to two classmates discuss these pictures. Then listen again and label each picture with the correct name from the box.

| Alex | Bertha | ~~"Bozo"~~ | Karl | Mehmet | "Sunshine" | Vicki |

a. _____

b. _____

c. _____

d. _____

e. _____"Bozo"_____

f. _____

4. Getting to Know You

Write down your full name on a piece of paper. Your teacher will collect all the names and redistribute them. Walk around the room. Introduce yourself to other students and try to find the person whose name you have on your piece of paper.

Example:
A: Hi. I'm Jelena.
B: I'm Eddy.
A: I'm looking for Kadin Al-Tattany. Do you know him?
B: I think that's him over there.

OR

Sorry, I don't.

When you find the person you are looking for, find out about his or her name. You can ask some of these questions:

What does your name mean?
Which part of your name is your family name?
Do you use a title? (Ms., Miss, Mrs., Mr. . . .)
What do your friends call you?
Do you have a nickname?
What do you prefer to be called?
How do you feel about your name?
Other: _____

Example:
A: What does Kadin mean?
B: It means "friend" or "companion." It's Arabic.

OR

I don't know what it means.

You can also ask some general questions such as:

Where do you come from?
Where are you living now?
Why are you studying English?
Other: _____

Finally, introduce your classmate to the rest of the class.

Example:
A: This is Henka Krol. Henka comes from Poland.
Her name means "ruler of the house or home." . . .

Section Two
Past Progressive and Simple Past Tense

INTRODUCTION

Read and listen to this excerpt from a journal article about naming systems.

Louisa Horvath **was following** tradition when she **named** her daughter Doris. "We **were going to name** her Amanda, but my great aunt Dorothy **died** just before she **was born,** so we **decided** to name the baby after her." Many cultures honor older family members by naming children after them. The Horvaths **were adhering** to an old Jewish custom which forbids naming a child after a living relative. However, in other western cultures, parents frequently name children after living relatives, especially parents and grandparents. "Before my son **was born,** the oldest boy was always named Walter," recalls one man. "As a boy, I **knew** I **was going to break** this tradition. I **was** just too uncomfortable with my father's name."

The practice of naming children after another person, living or deceased, has been frowned upon by different groups of people at different times. Believing that everyone should have a unique name, many Native American cultures even **kept** registers of available names and **appointed** officials who **gave** or **withheld** permission to use a name. As a result, Native Americans never **adopted** relatives' names. Instead, they often **used** names that **referred** to an event in someone's life. Sometimes they **chose** a name that **recalled** what **was happening** at the beginning of the mother's labor. A Miwok woman, for example, **was gathering** seeds for jewelry when her labor **began.** She **named** her child "Howotmila." (Howotu means "beads," and howotmila means "running hand down the branch of a bush to find seeds for beads.")

Incident naming, as this practice is called, is still used in many places, including modern Africa. "The sun **was shining** brightly when I **came** into the world," explains Ayadele. "In Swahili, my name means 'sunshine in the house.' "

The practice of incident naming may at first glance seem strange to Westerners. However, it is not unlike the derivation of some nicknames. One woman recalls: "In fourth grade, one of the boys **sneaked** a baby turtle into my lunchbox. It **crawled** out while I **was eating** lunch, and I **screamed** and **cried.** After that, everyone **called** me 'Turtle.' "

Incident naming and naming children after relatives are only two of many naming systems. Throughout history hopeful parents have also named children for some quality which they want their child to embody. This practice abounds all over the world. One East African man recalls: "My parents **named** me Jahi, which is a Swahili name meaning 'dignity.' They **wanted** me to get more education. Whenever I **was going to give up,** my name always **reminded** me of their hopes."

Name	Origin	Meaning
Abiona	Yoruba, Nigeria	"born during a journey"
Bo	Chinese	"precious"
Eva	Hebrew	"life-giving"
Helkimu	Miwok (Native American)	"hitting bushes with seed beater"
Margaret	Latin	"a pearl"
Palani	Hawaiian	"free one"
Paz	Spanish	"peace"
Richard	Old German	"powerful ruler"
Sharif	Arabic	"honest"
Taro	Japanese	"first-born male"

Source: Sue Browder, *The New Age Baby Name Book* (New York: Warner Books, 1987).

PAST PROGRESSIVE AND SIMPLE PAST TENSE

PAST PROGRESSIVE
I **was living** in Nigeria at the time.

SIMPLE PAST TENSE
I **moved** to Egypt in 1980.

PAST PROGRESSIVE AND SIMPLE PAST TENSE
I **was living** there when my son **was born**.

SIMPLE PAST TENSE AND SIMPLE PAST TENSE
We **moved** when my daughter **was born**.

PAST PROGRESSIVE AND PAST PROGRESSIVE
I **was working** while he **was studying**.

PAST INTENTIONS: *WAS/WERE GOING TO*
We **were going to name** her Amanda.

Grammar Notes

1. Use the past progressive (also called the past continuous) to describe an action that was <u>in progress</u> at a specific time in the past. The action began before the specific time and may or may not continue after the specific time.

> My wife and I **were living** on Tenth Street in 1990.

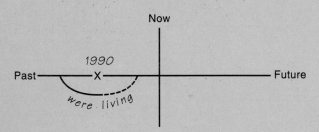

Use the simple past tense to describe an action or state that was <u>completed</u> at a specific time in the past.

> My wife and I **had** our first child in June.

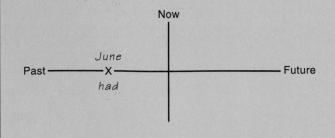

See Appendix 1 on page A1 for a list of irregular past-tense verbs.

Remember! Non-action verbs are not usually used in the progressive.

> I **had** a headache last night. NOT ~~I was having a headache last night.~~

2. Use the past progressive with the simple past tense to talk about an action that was <u>interrupted</u> by another action. Use the simple past tense for the interrupting action.

> I **was eating lunch** when the phone **rang**.
> OR
> While I **was eating** lunch the phone **rang**.

3. You can use the past progressive with *while* (or *when*) to talk about two actions in progress at the same time in the past. Use the past progressive in both clauses.

> While she **was eating** lunch, her classmates **were playing**.

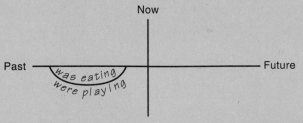

4. Be careful! Sentences with two clauses in the simple past tense have a very different meaning from sentences with one clause in the simple past tense and one clause in the past progressive.

> When he **came** home, I **was reading** the baby-name book. (First I was reading the book; then he came home.)

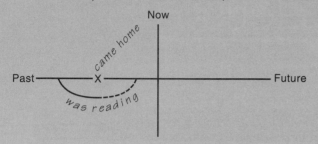

When he **came** home, I **read** the baby-name book. (First he came home; then I read the book.)

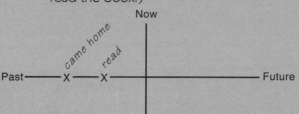

5. Use *was* or *were going to* to talk about future plans or expectations that you had in the past. (This structure is also known as <u>future in the past</u>.)

> It was 1980. I **was going to have** a baby.

Notice that we often use *was* or *were going to* when the things we expected to happen did not happen.

> We **were going to name** the baby Tom, but when it turned out to be a girl we named her Teresa instead.

FOCUSED PRACTICE

5. Discover the Grammar

Read these people's responses to an interview on names and nicknames. Then decide if the statements are true (T) *or false* (F). *If there isn't enough information to decide, put a question mark* (?).

1. **Lucky:** I was running home from school when I found a $100 bill.

   __F__ Lucky found the money before he started for home.

2. **Anna Danielson:** We were going to name our son Mark Allen. Then we realized that his initials would spell MAD.

   _____ The Danielsons named their son Mark Allen.

3. **Rod:** I was playing in the park when I got struck by lightning. I wasn't hurt, but my nickname "Rod" stuck.

   _____ Rod often played in the park.

(continued on next page)

4. **Amanda Smythe:** I was lying in my hospital bed in the maternity ward when the name

   Anesthesia just popped into my head. My daughter has never forgiven me.

   _____ Mrs. Smythe decided on a name for her daughter after she entered the hospital.

5. **Ana Ochoa:** My parents were going to name me Miguel. I spoiled their plans.

   _____ Mr. and Mrs. Ochoa expected a son.

6. **Alice Robinson:** How did we choose a name for our baby? Well, I read a book on how babies are

   named in different cultures. It gave us a lot of good ideas.

   _____ Mrs. Robinson finished the book.

7. **Tony Ortiz:** Why did we choose the name Consuela for our daughter? I was reading a book on

   baby names when I came across the name. I loved the way it sounded.

   _____ Mr. Ortiz finished the baby-name book.

8. **Lily Yang:** When our daughter was born, we were considering the name Jing-luh.

   _____ The Yangs knew what they were going to name their daughter when she was born.

9. **Greta Brooks:** When I got married I changed my name from Gertrude to Greta.

   _____ Ms. Brooks changed her name before she got married.

10. **Tom Saunders:** I had a great aunt named Nova. We were considering her name for our baby

   when she died. My daughter likes having an unusual name.

   _____ Mr. Saunders thought about the name Nova before his aunt died.

6. Reminiscing

Complete these conversations. Use the correct form of the verbs in parentheses—past progressive, simple past tense, or **was/were going to.**

1. **Lilith:** Someone _____called_____ you while you _____.
      a. (call)   b. (sleep)

   Kobe: _____ you _____ the name?
                           c. (write down)

   Lilith: Here it is—someone named Crackers.

   Kobe: Oh, yeah, Crackers. I _____ her at the restaurant when I _____
                                      d. (meet)   e. (work)

   evenings last summer.

   Lilith: Is Crackers her real name?

   Kobe: No, we _____ her that because she _____ saltine crackers. It
                         f. (nickname)   g. (always / eat)

   _____ a lot of noise.
       h. (make)

   Lilith: How annoying.

   Kobe: We _____ it.
                     i. (get used to)

2. **Aret:** Where _____ you _____ when your daughter _____?
a. (live)   b. (be born)

   Dede: We _____ a very small apartment on Euclid Street. After her birth we
c. (have)

   _____ to this one.
d. (move)

   Aret: What _____ you _____ at the time? Were you a teacher then?
e. (do)

   Dede: No. I was still a student. Actually, I _____ a course at the college when I
f. (take)

   _____ my husband, "Storm." We _____ the year after.
g. (meet)   h. (marry)

3. **Dennis:** Is "Storm" your husband's real name, or is it a nickname?

   Dede: It's his real name.

   Dennis: How _____ he _____ it?
a. (get)

   Dede: Well, before he _____, his parents _____ him after his father
b. (be born)   c. (name)

   and his father's father. But they never really _____ the idea. They
d. (like)

   _____ him to have a unique name. The night he _____, it
e. (want)   f. (be born)

   _____ very hard. In fact, it was a hurricane. So, they _____
g. (rain)   h. (change)

   their minds and _____ him "Storm."
i. (name)

   Dennis: And when _____ he _____ to become a meteorologist?
j. (decide)

   Dede: When he _____, his playmates _____ him, "Storm, how's the
k. (grow up)   l. (always / ask)

   weather up there?" (He was also tall for his age.) So he _____ to go to
m. (decide)

   school and really find out.

4. **Val:** Do you remember the time Terry _____ and _____ her knee?
a. (fall)   b. (hurt)

   Asmina: Uh-huh. She _____ in the schoolyard when some older kid
c. (play)

   _____ her. That's how she _____ her nickname, "Tumble."
d. (push)   e. (get)

5. **Mip:** Look at this photo. That's how my apartment _____ right after the 1994
a. (look)

   Los Angeles earthquake.

   Bob: That's terrible. What _____ you _____ when the earthquake
b. (do)

   _____?
c. (strike)

   Mip: I _____. It _____ early in the morning. When the bed
d. (sleep)   e. (happen)

   _____ to shake, I _____ and _____ over to the
f. (begin)   g. (jump up)   h. (run)

   doorway. That's supposed to be one of the safest places to be.

   Bob: Then what _____ you _____?
i. (do)

   Mip: When it _____, I _____ to my neighbor's. She _____.
j. (stop)   k. (run)   l. (still / sleep)

   I couldn't believe it! To this day I still call her Ms. Sleep-through-it-all.

COMMUNICATION PRACTICE

7. Practice Listening

 Listen to a woman explain how she got her nickname. Then listen again and circle the letter of the series of pictures that illustrate her story.

a.

b.

c.

8. Choose a Name

Choose a nickname for a classmate or your teacher based on the Native American method of naming people according to what they were doing the first time you saw them. Work in groups. Tell your classmates the nickname and have them guess who it refers to. Then explain your choice of nickname.

Example:

I gave Ms. Meyer the nickname "Chalk Eraser." The very first time I saw her she was erasing the board.

Now tell your class how you got your own name or nickname. How did you feel about your name?

Example:

A: When I was a kid, I had bright red hair, so my friends all called me "Carrot Top." I didn't like it.

B: One day I was answering a question in class when I mispronounced the word "computer," and called it "computter." From then on, all my classmates called me "the computer." I didn't mind it. I thought it was funny.

Section Three
Present Perfect and Simple Past Tense

INTRODUCTION

Read and listen to the newspaper advice column.

Times Have Changed

DEAR JOHN:

My son and his girlfriend **have been making** wedding plans. At first I **was** delighted, but last week I **heard** something that **changed** my feelings. It seems that our future daughter-in-law **has decided** to keep using her maiden name after the wedding. Her reasons: She doesn't want to "lose her identity." Her parents **named** her 21 years ago, and she**'s been** Donna So-and-so (I won't use her real name) since then. She sees no reason to change now. Secondly, she**'s been performing** with the Rockland Symphony Orchestra for eight years, and she**'s** already **become** known professionally by her maiden name.

Dr. John Sanders

John, when I **got** married, I **didn't think of** keeping my maiden name. I **felt** so proud when I **became** Mrs. "Smith" (not my real name). We **named** our son after my father, but our surname **showed** that we three **were** a family.

I**'ve read** several articles about this trend, and now I can understand her decision to use her maiden name professionally. But I**'ve been** worried about her using it socially. Why isn't she proud to show she's married to my son? **Has** she really **made** a commitment to this marriage? And what last name will their children use?

My husband and I **have been trying** to hide our hurt feelings, but it's getting harder. I want to tell her and my son what I think, but my husband says it's none of our business.

My son **hasn't said** anything, so we don't know how he feels. **Have** I **made** the right choice by keeping quiet?

HASN'T SAID A WORD YET

DEAR HASN'T:

Yes, you **have.** Since your son **hasn't indicated** his own feelings, you must assume he approves. Your husband is right: It's none of your business. The couple has a right to make this decision for themselves.

Don't take your daughter-in-law's decision personally. She **hasn't rejected** your family by keeping her own last name. The recent trend **has been** for women to keep their birth names after marriage—both osocially and professionally. According to studies, families **haven't suffered** because of this trend—love, not a surname, is the glue that keeps a family together.

As for the children's last names, couples **have been finding** their own solutions. Many parents **have been using** hyphenated surnames composed of the mother's and father's last name. (Readers: **Has** anyone **figured out** what to do when Roger Smythe-Sanders marries Julia Bernstein-Burke?) One couple I know **chose** the father's last name when their son **was born.** They **gave** the mother's last name to their daughter.

Social customs with regard to naming **have been changing** quickly, and right now almost anything goes. You and your husband **showed** a lot of self-control when you **decided** not to voice your opinion. Let the couple figure this one out themselves, and try to smile approvingly no matter what happens.

PRESENT PERFECT, PRESENT PERFECT PROGRESSIVE, AND SIMPLE PAST TENSE

PRESENT PERFECT
I**'ve read** several articles about names.

SIMPLE PAST TENSE
I **read** an article last night.

PRESENT PERFECT PROGRESSIVE
I**'ve been reading** an article about names.

Grammar Notes

1. The present perfect and present perfect progressive (also called the present perfect continuous) are used to talk about things that started in the past, continue up to the present, and may continue into the future.

> I**'ve lived** in Rockland my whole life.
>
> OR
>
> I**'ve been living** in Rockland my whole life. (I was born in Rockland, and I'm still living there.)

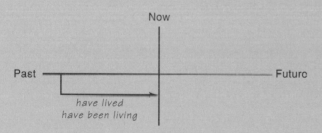

The present perfect progressive can indicate that the action is <u>temporary</u>.

> I**'ve been living** in Rockland for three years, but next month I'm moving to Los Angeles.

2. The simple past tense is used to talk about things that happened and were completed in the past.

> I **lived** in Rockland for two years. (I no longer live in Rockland.)

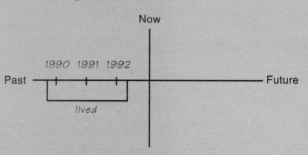

See Appendix 1 on page A1 for a list of irregular past participles used in forming the present perfect.

3. The present perfect is used to talk about things that happened at an <u>unspecified</u> time in the past.

> She**'s read** a book about baby names. (We don't know exactly when she read the book, or the time is not important.)

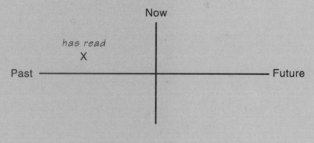

(continued on next page)

Be careful! *She's read a book* and *She's been reading a book* have very different meanings. The present perfect progressive shows that an activity or state is <u>unfinished</u>.

> I**'ve been reading** a book on baby names. (I'm still reading it.)

The present perfect (without *for* or *since*) refers to an activity or state that is <u>finished</u>.

> I**'ve read** a book on baby names. (I finished the book.)

4. The simple past tense is used to talk about things that happened at a <u>specific</u> time in the past. The exact time is known and sometimes stated.

> I **read** a book on baby names **last week**.

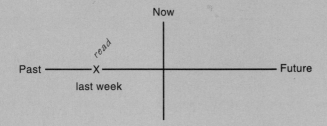

Be careful! Do not use specific past time expressions with the present perfect.

> She **changed** her name **last year**. NOT ~~She has changed her name last year.~~

5. Use the present perfect to talk about things that have happened in a period of time that is not finished, such as *today, this month, this year*.

> She**'s had** three cups of coffee **this morning**. (It's still this morning, and it is possible that she will have some more.)

Notice that we don't usually use the present perfect progressive to talk about how many times someone has done something or how many things someone has done.

> She**'s had** three cups of coffee this morning. NOT ~~She's been having three cups of coffee this morning~~.

6. Use the simple past tense to talk about things that happened in a time period that is finished, such as *yesterday, last month, last year*.

> She **had** three cups of coffee **yesterday**. (Yesterday is finished.)

Be careful! Some time expressions such as *this morning, this month*, or *this year* can refer to a finished or unfinished time period. Use the present perfect if the time period is unfinished. Use the simple past tense if the time period is finished.

> It's 10:00 A.M. She**'s had** three cups of coffee **this morning**. (The morning is not over.)
> It's 1:00 P.M. She **had** three cups of coffee **this morning**. (The morning is over. It is now afternoon.)

FOCUSED PRACTICE

9. Discover the Grammar

Read this marriage announcement from a newspaper. Underline all the present perfect verbs. Circle all the simple past verbs.

Weddings

Alison Anne Margolyes, Jason Barricelli

Alison Anne Margolyes, a daughter of Rosemary Peck-Margolyes and William J. Margolyes of San Marino, Calif. married Jason Barricelli, a son of Rose and Anthony Barricelli of Staten Island, N.Y. The Honorable Mary Riggens, a justice of the peace, performed the cere-mony at the Waterside Hotel yesterday in Greenville.

Ms. Margolyes, 29, has chosen to keep her own name. She has been an associate at the New York law firm of Miles, Shaker, & Lynch for two years. She graduated with honors from the University of California at Los Angeles and received a degree in law from Yale University. Her father owned and managed a video corporation for 15 years. Her mother has taught special education at the high-school level for 20 years.

Mr. Barricelli, 27, graduated from Ithaca College in 1992. He has been studying for a master's degree in social work at New York University. The groom's father has been a senior partner at a New York accounting firm, Poler & Co., since 1967. His mother, who is retired, worked as a rehabilitation nurse for 30 years. The groom's previous marriage ended in divorce.

Now read the statements and decide if they are true (T) *or false* (F).

___T___ 1. Alison Margolyes works for the law firm of Miles, Shaker, & Lynch.

_____ 2. Her father owns a video corporation.

_____ 3. Her mother teaches special education.

_____ 4. Jason Barricelli is attending Ithaca College.

_____ 5. He got his master's degree in 1992.

_____ 6. The groom's father works at an accounting firm.

_____ 7. The groom's mother works as a nurse.

_____ 8. This is the groom's first marriage.

_____ 9. The bride is changing her name.

10. Dear John

Complete this letter with the correct form of the verbs in parentheses—
simple past tense, present perfect, or present perfect progressive.

Yesterday I _____read_____ with interest the letter from "Hasn't." As an onomastician (a person
        1. (read)
who studies names), I _____ about the issue of name changes for many years. I agree with
            2. (think)
your answer that keeping a birth name (I don't like the term *maiden name*) is a very personal issue.
However, it isn't a new one. It _____ with us since our country _____.
                3. (be)   4. (begin)

Recently, many people _____ their names in order to make a statement about their
                5. (change)
ethnic identity. African Americans, for example, _____ their original names when they
                        6. (lose)
_____ to this country as slaves. Since the 1960s, however, many _____ African
    7. (come)   8. (adopt)
names in order to reflect their ethnic roots. In order to research his books, writer Alex Haley
_____ his ancestors back to their home in Africa. His story, *Roots,* _____ on
    9. (trace)   10. (appear)
television in 1977. Since then, Kinte, the name of the hero, _____ a popular African
                                                11. (become)
American surname.

In the nineteenth century, many immigrants to the United States _____ their names in
                                                        12. (change)
order to seem more "American." Often, immigration officials _____ that decision for them
                                13. (make)
and _____ names that the officials _____ pronounce. They _____
        14. (assign)   15. (can)   16. (create)
Pace from Pankratova and _____ Baratz into Barnes.
                17. (turn)
In this century, more and more families _____ their family's history by returning to
                                        18. (reclaim)
their original names. One famous recent example: David Wallenchinsky, son of Irving Wallace,
_____ under the family's original name for several years.
    19. (publish)
Sometimes the reasons for changing a name are simple. My friend, Boris Groans, _____
                                                            20. (always/hate)
his name, and who can blame him? He _____ about changing it to Travis Gray for some
                            21. (think)
time now, but _____ his mind yet. Apparently there's still a strong attachment to even a
        22. (not make up)
despised name.

Finally, there are pen names. From ancient times right up to the present, authors
_____ their identities with pseudonyms. One that comes to mind immediately is "Hasn't
    23. (disguise)
Said a Word Yet." The author of this letter clearly _____ a good reason when she
                                        24. (have)
_____ not to use her real name.
    25. (decide)

Ima X. Pert, Ph.D.

COMMUNICATION PRACTICE

11. Practice Listening

Alison and Jason have been planning a trip. Look at their To Do list and listen to their phone conversation. Then listen again and check the things that they've already done.

- ☐ renew passports
- ☑ pick up plane tickets
- ☐ read travel guide
- ☐ make reservations at Hotel Splendor
- ☐ stop mail for two weeks
- ☐ buy bathing suit (Alison)

12. Changes

Reread the advice column on page 16. Then discuss your own ideas with a partner.

Do you think the woman's daughter-in-law has made the right decision about keeping her birth name after marriage?
Why or why not?
Should the writer, Hasn't Said a Word Yet, express her feelings to her son?
When both parents have hyphenated last names, what last name should their children use?

Now think about a culture you know well and discuss these questions:

Under what circumstances does someone change his or her name?
Have customs regarding names changed or remained the same in recent years?
If they have changed, what changes have you noticed?

Integration

FOCUSED PRACTICE

13. Discover the Grammar

Read this newspaper article. Then answer the questions true (T) *or false* (F).

A Sign of the Times

Matt Rotell, 32, is working for the Los Angeles police department as an undercover detective while he pursues a degree in law from UCLA. In his jean jacket, he looks and speaks like a sensitive poet, but Matt is really a street-smart cop. Lately he's been trying to trap two suspected counterfeiters. He's trailed them on the freeway, sat a few seats away from them in movie theaters, and eavesdropped on them at McDonald's.

Matt wasn't going to fall in love until after graduation. He was just too busy. "I always thought that falling in love was going to be like jumping out of an airplane," he said recently. "But I just liked being with Nicole right from the start. I remember on our third date, we were walking down the street and she said, 'I like you.' I knew I was falling in love with her."

"Nicole" is Nicole Blanchard, a 45-year-old agent who works for StarGazers, a movie talent company in Hollywood. The complete show-biz professional, from her spiky hairdo to her spike heels, Nicole often arrives at work in a black suit, pearls, black stockings, and an old black leather jacket. The former singer grew up in Florida, lived in Paris in her twenties, and always believed that marriage was just fine for other people.

Matt and Nicole first laid eyes on each other four years ago when they were both attending the christening of a mutual friend's baby. "We talked nonstop the whole evening," Nicole recalled. "It was so fantastic. At that time in my life I was always meeting someone I liked and then finding out that he was a closed door. Or that maybe I wasn't interested in opening the door. With Matt, I thought: This looks promising."

Since Matt, friends say, everything about Nicole has mellowed, from her spikes to her attitude about commitment.

Matt and Nicole's afternoon wedding on June 19 was as sentimental as a love song. The two were married at a small traditional church ceremony. The bride was wearing a long, flowing summer dress as she walked down the aisle. The bridegroom was waiting for her in a casual suit and tie. When they kissed at the end of the ceremony, the crowd applauded.

Afterwards, the 30 guests walked to a friend's home for a

backyard barbecue that recalled Matt's Tennessee boyhood. A caterer served hamburgers, corn on the cob, grilled chicken sandwiches, and quesadillas. Guests strolled on the lawn or sat at picnic tables with red-and-white checkered tablecloths while a rock-and-roll band played love songs.

Jerry Daniels, a photographer who knew the bride in the early 1970s when they were both attending the University of Miami, was jubilant. "Times have really changed," he said. "Back then people thought it was silly to get married just because everyone expected it. Now everybody is happy that Nicki (that's what we called her back then) is getting married."

Just then, the bride grabbed the micro- phone and sang "We've Only Just Begun" to her new husband. Every time Nicole sang the line "We've only just begun to live," the crowd cheered and applauded. By the end of the song, a lot of guests were drying their eyes.

"It just seems like a vote of confidence in the future," Jerry sighed. This reporter agreed.

_T_ 1. Matt's job with the police is just temporary.

_____ 2. Matt is still trying to trap a pair of counterfeiters.

_____ 3. Matt's experience of falling in love is different from what he imagined it to be.

_____ 4. After Nicole told Matt that she liked him, they went for a walk.

_____ 5. Nicole still works at StarGazers.

_____ 6. Nicole and Matt went to the christening together.

_____ 7. Before she met Matt, Nicole was disappointed with the men she knew.

_____ 8. Nicole changed both her appearance and her views on marriage before she met Matt.

_____ 9. The bride wore a long summer dress.

_____ 10. The bridegroom wore a jean jacket at his wedding.

_____ 11. The crowd applauded during the marriage ceremony.

_____ 12. Nicole had a nickname in college.

_____ 13. According to Nicole's friend Jerry, people's attitudes toward marriage have changed since the 1970s.

_____ 14. Some of the wedding guests started to cry during Nicole's song.

14. At the Wedding

Complete these conversations by circling the correct words.

1. **Jason:** Listen! The bride <u>sings/(is singing)</u> a song to the groom.
   a.

   Alison: I think she <u>'s worked/worked</u> as a professional singer before she
   b.

   <u>started/was starting</u> at StarGazers.
   c.

   Jason: Wow. She <u>sings/'s sung</u> beautifully.
   d.

(continued on next page)

Alison: <u>Are you crying/Do you cry</u>?
                        e.

Jason: Of course not. That woman at the next table <u>wears/is wearing</u> flowers in her hair.
                                                                              f.

My eyes always <u>water/watered</u> around flowers.
                              g.

Alison: Oh sure.

2. **Yoshi:** What <u>are you eating/do you eat</u>? It <u>looks/'s looking</u> good.
                              a.   b.

Petras: A quesadilla.

Yoshi: I <u>haven't tried/haven't been trying</u> one. What's in it?
                        c.

Petras: Cheese, black beans, and some lettuce. It's delicious.

Yoshi: OK, I'll go try it. Your plate is empty. <u>Do you want/Have you wanted</u> another quesadilla?
                                                                        d.

Petras: No, thanks. I <u>have/'ve had</u> enough. I <u>'ve been eating/ate</u> them since we
                                    e.   f.

<u>got/were getting</u> here.
g.

3. **Taras:** How long <u>has Matt known/did Matt know</u> Nicole?
                                    a.

Anna: Let's see....They <u>were meeting/met</u> at my daughter's christening, and Sasha's three now.
                                          b.

So they <u>'ve been seeing/saw</u> each other for three years.
                    c.

Taras: So they <u>'ve started/started</u> dating right away?
                              d.

Anna: Oh, it was love at first sight. But it's funny. I <u>was asking/asked</u> Matt to come to the
                                                                        e.

christening at the last minute. I <u>didn't invite/wasn't going to invite</u> him at all.
                                                        f.

Taras: Why not?

Anna: Well, we <u>had/'ve had</u> a very small naming ceremony, and I <u>wasn't thinking/didn't think</u> he
                              g.   h.

and Nicole <u>can/could</u> get along together. They're so different.
                        i.

Taras: Funny.

4. **Eliza:** Hi, I'm Eliza Bacon, Nicole's cousin. Are you a friend of Matt's?

Joel: Hi, Eliza. I'm Joel Epstein. Yeah, I <u>work/'ve worked</u> with Matt for a long time.
                                                        a.

Eliza: Oh, right. He <u>'s mentioned/mentions</u> your name several times. <u>Do you do/Did you do</u>
                                    b.   c.

undercover work, too?

Joel: No. Actually, I <u>'m paying/pay</u> the bills. I'm in the accounting department.
                                    d.

Eliza: Oh. <u>Did you work/Have you worked</u> there long?
                              e.

Joel: Not that long....Listen. They <u>'re playing/play</u> "In the Still of the Night." Would you
                                                  f.

like to dance?

Eliza: Well, I'm not a great dancer, but I <u>'ve been taking/took</u> lessons, and my teacher says
there's still hope.

g.

5. **Noura:** Where <u>do you go/are you going</u>?

a.

Joel: To talk to the bride and groom.

Noura: They <u>'ve come/came</u> to our table a few minutes ago.

b.
<u>Didn't you talk/Haven't you talked</u> to them then?

c.

Joel: No. Eliza and I <u>danced/were dancing</u> when they <u>'ve come/came</u> over.

d.   e.

15. Name Autobiography

*Read this student's name autobiography. There are thirteen mistakes in the
use of verb tenses. Find and correct them.*

Name Autobiography: *Cynthia Lee Gordon-Hughes*

      I am born in 1960. My parents named me Cynthia Lee, after
my mother. (They named me John after my father, but I turned
out to be a girl.) I'm not sure what "Cynthia" means, but I think it
is coming from the Greek and has some connection to the moon.
When I was growing up, I found it hard to pronounce my name—
especially the *th*. Whenever I tried to say Cynthia, it came out
more like SIN-TEE. So as a little girl I have called myself Sinty.
When I got older, my younger brother nicknamed me "Kangaroo"
because I was always jumping on things. I hated the name and
called him "Stu" (short for "stupid") in return. In high school my
friends have started to call me "CiCi." I liked that because it was
sounding friendly—like the name of a girl who was popular.
However, when I got a little older, I prefer Cynthia. This pleased
my parents a lot. When I got married, I was deciding to use both
my last name and my husband's, so I became Cynthia Lee
Gordon-Hughes. My husband is calling me Cindy or occasionally
just "C." When he is annoyed at me, he calls me by my full name,
Cynthia. Now we expect our first child—a son. We don't decide
on a name for him yet. We don't want to name him after a
relative, so we have been looking through baby-name books for
ideas. At the moment we consider the names Forrest and Ian. We
also haven't been deciding yet which family name to use for our
son—mine, my husband's, or a combination of the two. Choosing
a name is very important, and we don't want to make a mistake.

COMMUNICATION PRACTICE

16. Practice Listening

Listen to these conversations that take place at a wedding reception. Then listen again and circle the letter of the pictures that illustrate the situations.

1. a.  b.

2. a.  b.

3. a.  b.

4. a.  b.

5. a.

b.

6. a.

b.

7. a.

b.

17. Name Survey

First complete this survey for yourself.

1. How did you get your first name?

   ☐ My parents named me after a relative.

   ☐ My parents named me after someone famous.

   ☐ My parents chose a name that they liked.

   ☐ Other: _____

2. How do you feel about your name?

   ☐ I like it.

   ☐ I don't like it.

   ☐ Neutral.

   ☐ Other: _____

3. Do you have a middle name?

   ☐ Yes

   ☐ No

   If yes, how many? _____

4. Do you have a nickname?

   ☐ Yes

   ☐ No

5. Have you ever changed your first name?

   ☐ Yes

   ☐ No

6. Have you ever changed your last name?

   ☐ Yes

   ☐ No

7. If you changed your name, how did you feel about it?

   ☐ Good

   ☐ Bad

   ☐ Neutral

   ☐ Other: _____

8. Do you own anything that has your name or initials on it (jewelry, dishes, towels, clothes)?

   ☐ Yes

   ☐ No

9. Are you wearing anything that has your name or initials on it?

   ☐ Yes

   ☐ No

10. Have you ever used a baby-name book?

☐ Yes

☐ No

Add your own question about names: _____

Now work in groups and discuss your answers. Report back to your class. Tally the class results.

Example:
Ten students have a nickname. Eight of the ten don't like their name.

18. Quotable Quotes

Work in small groups. Discuss these quotes about names. What do you think they mean? Give examples.

The glory and the nothing of a name.
—*Lord Byron (British poet, 1788–1824)*

Example:
A: What did Byron mean by that?
B: Well, think of a name like Rockefeller. It's a famous name because some people named Rockefeller have been important people. But just having that name doesn't really mean much unless someone achieves something.

A nickname is the hardest stone that the devil can throw at a man.
—*William Hazlitt (British essayist, 1778–1830)*

The name of a man is a numbing blow from which he never recovers.
—*Marshall McLuhan (Canadian educator, 1911–1980)*

What's in a name? That which we call a rose by any other name would smell as sweet.
—*William Shakespeare, from* Romeo and Juliet *(British playwright, 1564–1616)*

Consider the state of your life before you name a child.
—*Nigerian proverb*

The name given a child becomes natural to it.
—*Ancient proverb*

19. Name Autobiography

Write the history of your name. How did you get your name? What does it mean? Do you have a nickname? How do you feel about it? Have you ever changed your name? Use the name autobiography in excercise 15 as a model. Exchange papers with a classmate and discuss your histories.

20. Memorabilia

Look at the memorabilia in this family album. Work with a partner and talk about the couple's life. Use the verbs in the box and your own ideas.

attend	be	become	choose	drive	expect
go	graduate	live	marry	meet	move
read	reject	think	use		

Example:

A: This is Lynn's visa. She came to the United States in 1984.

B: Right. And look at this movie ticket. She and her husband met while she was attending the University of Miami.

Bring in pictures and other memorabilia to share with the class. Talk about what they are and the events around that time.

Example:

This is a newspaper article about me. When I was in high school, I won first prize in a spelling contest.

INTRODUCTION

Read and listen to this selection about talk-show host and actress Oprah Winfrey.

Oprah Winfrey began speaking publicly in church at the age of two. By the time she was twelve, she **had** already **decided** what she wanted to do for a living. She wanted to be "paid to talk." In fact, it wasn't too long afterward that she got her first radio job. Although she **hadn't had** any previous experience, she was hired to report the news.

When Winfrey got her own TV talk show in 1986, she **had** already **been** a TV news reporter and **had made** her acting debut in a major Hollywood movie, *The Color Purple*. Oprah's warm personality made her TV guests comfortable, and her human-interest stories on topics such as child abuse—Oprah, herself, **had been** a victim—touched the hearts of her viewing audience. "The Oprah Winfrey Show" quickly became one of the most popular shows in the United States, and by the late 1980s "Oprah Winfrey" **had become** a household word. When asked about her future, Winfrey says, ". . . it's so bright it burns my eyes."

PAST PERFECT

STATEMENTS		
SUBJECT	***HAD (NOT)* + PAST PARTICIPLE**	
I You He She We You They	**had (not) decided** on **had (not) chosen***	a career by then.
It	**had (not) been**	a difficult decision.

*See Appendix 1 on page A1 for a list of irregular past participles.

YES/NO QUESTIONS			
HAD	**SUBJECT**	**PAST PARTICIPLE**	
Had	I you he she we you they	**decided** on **chosen**	a career by then?
Had	it	**been**	a difficult decision?

SHORT ANSWERS		
AFFIRMATIVE		
Yes,	you I he she it you we they	**had.**

SHORT ANSWERS		
NEGATIVE		
No,	you I he she it you we they	**hadn't.**

WH- QUESTIONS				
WH- WORD	***HAD***	**SUBJECT**	**PAST PARTICIPLE**	
Why	**had**	she	**decided**	to be a talk-show host?

(continued on next page)

CONTRACTIONS		
I had	=	I'd
you had	=	you'd
he had	=	he'd
she had	=	she'd
we had	=	we'd
they had	=	they'd
had not	=	hadn't

Grammar Notes

1. Use the past perfect to show that something happened <u>before</u> a specific time in the past.

> By 1988 Oprah Winfrey **had become** famous.

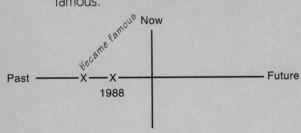

2. Use the past perfect with the simple past tense to show which of two events in the past happened first. The event in the past perfect took place <u>before</u> the event in the simple past tense.

> Oprah Winfrey **had acted** in a major Hollywood movie before she **got** her own TV show. (First she acted in a movie. Then she got her TV show.)

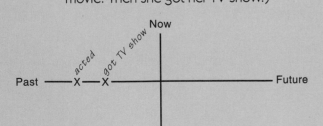

3. The relationship between the simple past tense and the past perfect is similar to the relationship between the simple present tense and the present perfect. In both cases, the event in the perfect form takes place <u>before</u> the event in the simple tense.

> She **wants** to see *The Color Purple* because she **has read** the book.
> She **wanted** to see *The Color Purple* because she **had read** the book.

4. Use the past perfect to talk about repeated actions in the past that took place <u>before</u> another event in the past.

> She **had spoken** in public on many occasions (before she got the TV job offer).

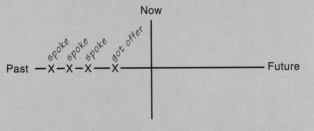

5. We often use the past perfect with *by* (a certain time).

> **By 1966** Oprah **had decided** on a career.
> **By the time I got home,** the show **had started.**

6. When the time relationship between two past events is clear (as with *before*, *after*, and *as soon as*), it is common to use the simple past tense for both events. The meaning remains clear.

> After Oprah **had appeared** in *The Color Purple*, she got a part in another movie, *Native Son*.
>
> OR
>
> After Oprah **appeared** in *The Color Purple*, she got a part in another movie, *Native Son*.

Be careful! Notice the different meanings of the following two sentences with *when*:

> When the show **ended**, she **left.**

This is similar in meaning to

> As soon as the show ended, she left.
> (First the show ended. Then she left.)

When the show **ended,** she **had left.**

This is similar in meaning to

> By the time the show ended, she had left.
> (First she left. Then the show ended.)

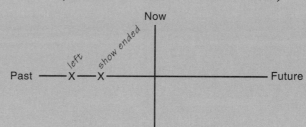

7. *Already*, *yet*, *ever*, and *never* are often used with the past perfect to emphasize the event which occurred first.

> I saw *The Color Purple* last night. I **had never seen** it before.
> John didn't go to the movies with us. He **had already seen** it.

FOCUSED PRACTICE

1. Discover the Grammar

Read each numbered sentence. Then circle the letter of the sentences whose meaning is similar.

1. When I got home, "The Oprah Winfrey Show" started.
   a. First I got home. Then the Oprah show started.
   b. First the Oprah show started. Then I got home.

2. When I got home, "The Oprah Winfrey Show" had started.
   a. First I got home. Then the Oprah show started.
   b. First the Oprah show started. Then I got home.

(continued on next page)

3. By the time Oprah's guest turned twenty, he had appeared in ten movies.
   a. First he turned twenty. Then he appeared in ten movies.
   b. He appeared in ten movies. Then he turned twenty.

4. He had saved $100,000 by the time he made his third movie.
   a. First he made his third movie. Then he saved $100,000.
   b. First he saved $100,000. Then he made his third movie.

5. He had already lost 100 pounds when Oprah interviewed him.
   a. First he lost 100 pounds. Then Oprah interviewed him.
   b. First Oprah interviewed him. Then he lost 100 pounds.

6. Oprah had him on her show because he had written a book.
   a. First he wrote a book. Then Oprah had him on her show.
   b. First he was on Oprah's show. Then he wrote a book.

7. By the end of the show, I had fallen asleep.
   a. First the show ended. Then I fell asleep.
   b. First I fell asleep. Then the show ended.

8. When I went to bed, I had turned off the TV.
   a. First I went to bed. Then I turned off the TV.
   b. First I turned off the TV. Then I went to bed.

2. Timeline

*Look at some important events in Oprah Winfrey's life. Then complete the sentences below. Use the past perfect with **already** or **not yet**.*

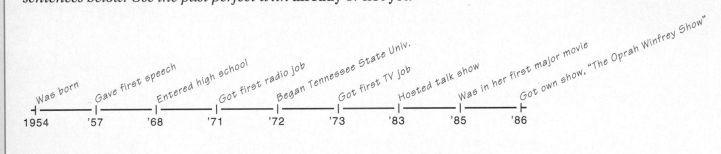

1. By 1958 Oprah _____had already given_____ her first speech.

2. By 1967 she _____ high school.

3. By 1971 she _____ her first TV job.

4. By 1971 she _____ her first radio job.

5. By 1972 she _____ in a major movie.

6. By 1973 she _____ classes at the university.

7. By 1985 she _____ her own TV show, "The Oprah Winfrey Show."

8. By 1986 she _____ in a major movie.

3.   Troubled Teen

Complete this psychologist's description of a patient who had appeared as a guest on "The Oprah Winfrey Show." Use the past perfect form of the appropriate verbs in the box.

arrest	become	bring	have	hurt
leave	lose	recommend	~~see~~	

I _____had seen_____ a hundred like him before. He sat on the couch and stared out the window.
_1._

He was only sixteen. His mother sat next to him. She _____ him to see me. She
_2._

_____ control of her son. Ever since his father _____ them four years
_3._   _4._

before, she _____ trouble with her son. He _____ more and more angry and
_5._   _6._

depressed. Recently he _____ someone in a school fight. The police _____
_7._   _8._

him and _____ psychological counseling. The mother was afraid that he was going to run
_9._

away from home.

4.   Runaway Children

A talk-show host is interviewing a teenager. Complete the interview. Determine the correct order of the sentences in parentheses and use the past perfect to express the event that occurred first.

Host: When did you decide to run away from home?

Guest: (I made up my mind to leave home. / I was ten.)

_____I had made up my mind to leave home_____ by the time _____I was ten_____.
_1._

Host: Why did you feel that you had to leave home?

Guest: (My father beat me for the third time. / I was afraid to stay there.)

After _____, _____.
_2._

Host: I see. Where did you go?

Guest: To Miami.

(I arranged to stay with a friend in Miami. / I left home.)

Before _____, _____.
_3._

Host: But what about money? I mean, you were just ten!

Guest: Well, my parents gave me a small allowance—about twenty dollars a month.

(I paid for my ticket. / I saved enough money from my allowance.)

As soon as I _____, _____.
_4._

(continued on next page)

Host: So what happened when you arrived in Miami?

Guest: (I got to Miami. / I already spent all my money.)

By the time _____, _____.
                               5.

(I hardly ate on the trip. / I had very little money.)

_____ because _____.
                       6.

Host: That's terrible. I want to hear more about that, but first we have to pause for these words.

5. Reporting the News

Look at this schedule for a TV news reporter.

10:00	arrive at studio
noon	see assignment editor
1:00	film main story for evening news
3:00	write story for evening news
5:30	makeup and hair
6:00	report news
7:00	meet with producer
9:00	dinner with Ella

Complete the questions about the reporter's schedule. Use the past perfect and give short answers.

1. At 11:00 the reporter was at his desk.

   A: _____ Had he seen _____ the assignment editor yet?

   B: _____ No, he hadn't. _____

2. At 1:00 he was filming the main story for the evening news.

   A: _____ the assignment editor by that time?

   B: _____

3. At 4:00 he took a coffee break.

A: _____ the story for the evening news yet?

B: _____

4. At 6:00 he reported the news.

A: _____ the producer yet?

B: _____

5. He met with the producer at 7:00.

A: _____ the evening news by then?

B: _____

6. He got home at 8:00.

A: _____ dinner yet?

B: _____

COMMUNICATION PRACTICE

6. Practice Listening

A talk-show host is interviewing a successful newspaper reporter. Listen to the reporter talk about some events in her life. Then read the list. Listen again and put the events in the correct chronological order.

_____ moved to Chicago

__1__ got married

_____ sold an article to a magazine

_____ got a job as a newspaper reporter

_____ found an apartment

7. Accomplishments

Think about what you did yesterday. Indicate whether it was or wasn't a busy day. Complete the sentences. Then compare your day with a classmate's.

Yesterday was/wasn't a busy day for me.

1. By 9:00 A.M., _____

2. By the time I got to work/school, _____

3. By the time I had lunch, _____

4. By the time I left work/school, _____

5. By the time I had dinner, _____

6. By 9:00 P.M., I _____

7. By the time I went to bed, I had done so much/little that I felt _____

> **Example:**
> **A:** By 9:00 A.M., I had made breakfast and taken the kids to school.
> **B:** By 9:00 A.M., I hadn't even gotten up!

8. There's Always a First Time

Think about things you had never done before you began living here (or before a certain year). Have a class discussion and write some of the results on the board. Possible topics: food, sports, clothing, entertainment, transportation.

> **Example:**
> Before I moved here (or before this year), I had never eaten pizza or popcorn.

9. What about You?

Look at the timeline in exercise 2. Complete this timeline with some important events in your own life. Discuss them with a classmate. Use **already, yet, ever,** *and* **never** *when appropriate. Possible topics: school, employment, marriage, children, moving.*

Year: _____

Event: _____

> **Example:**
> **A:** By the time I was 18, I had already lived in three different countries.
> **B:** Oh. Where had you lived?

Read and listen to this part of a newspaper sports column.

A Dream Finally Comes True

By A. L. SOTOMAYOR

Yesterday, along with an estimated 2 million other spectators, I attended New York City's 23rd annual marathon. It was a beautiful fall day. It **had been raining** hard the night before, but that morning the weather was clear and cool—perfect for the 26.2-mile run.

I found my usual spot in Central Park, three miles before the finish line. This is where experienced runners give their best effort, and exciting things have often happened here. I wasn't disappointed. As I watched, 28-year-old Willie Mtolo from South Africa overtook front-runner Andrés Espinosa of Mexico. By the time he passed Espinosa, Mtolo **had been running** for almost two hours, but he still looked fresh and confident. With just a short distance more to run, Mtolo was sure the race was his. The crowd **had been gathering** at this spot for hours, and as Mtolo came through the tunnel of spectators, the cheers were deafening.

Mtolo finished first out of 26,000 runners representing more than 90 different countries. He finished the race in just 2 hours, 9 minutes, and 29 seconds.

Yesterday's race fulfilled a lifelong dream for Willie Mtolo of South Africa. Because of its policy of apartheid, his country had been banned from international races for 21 years. Several of Mtolo's well-known compatriots had emigrated to the United States and the United Kingdom because they wanted to continue their athletic careers, but Mtolo had stayed in South Africa and had worked to improve conditions there. For years before this event, he **had been waiting** for this chance to compete internationally. The ban was lifted this year, and yesterday Mtolo found himself running in—and winning—the world's largest marathon.

41

PAST PERFECT PROGRESSIVE

STATEMENTS		
SUBJECT	HAD (NOT) BEEN + BASE FORM OF VERB + -ING	
I You He She It We You They	had (not) been running	for hours.

YES/NO QUESTIONS			
HAD	SUBJECT	BEEN + BASE FORM OF VERB + -ING	
Had	I you he she it we you they	been running	for hours?

SHORT ANSWERS		
AFFIRMATIVE		
Yes,	you I he she it you we they	had.

SHORT ANSWERS		
NEGATIVE		
No,	you I he she it you we they	hadn't.

CONTRACTIONS		
I had	=	I'd
you had	=	you'd
he had	=	he'd
she had	=	she'd
we had	=	we'd
they had	=	they'd
had not	=	hadn't

WH- QUESTIONS			
WH- WORD	HAD	SUBJECT	BEEN + BASE FORM OF VERB + -ING
How long	had	he	been running?

Grammar Notes

1. Use the past perfect progressive (also called the past perfect continuous) to talk about an action that was in progress <u>before</u> a specific time in the past. Remember that the progressive emphasizes the <u>process</u>, not the end result.

It was 2:00 P.M. The runners **had been running** since 10:48 A.M.

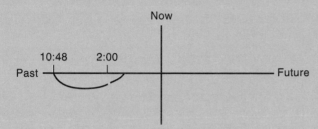

Willie **had been running** for 2 hours, 9 minutes, and 29 seconds when he crossed the finish line.

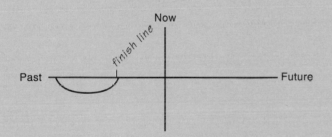

Notice that the context tells you if the past perfect progressive action continued or not.

Be careful! Non-action (stative) verbs are not usually used in the progressive.

He **had had** a headache all day. NOT ~~He had been having a headache all day.~~

2. Use the past perfect progressive to express <u>repeated</u> actions in the past that took place <u>before</u> another event in the past.

The telephone **had been ringing** for several minutes before she answered it.

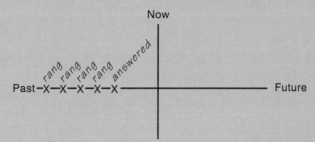

Be careful! Notice the difference in meaning between the past progressive and the past perfect progressive.

When the race started, it **was raining** and the streets were wet. (It was still raining during the race.)

When the race started, it **had been raining,** and the streets were wet. (It wasn't raining during the race. It had already stopped.)

3. We often use the past perfect progressive to draw conclusions based on evidence.

She was out of breath. It was clear that she **had been running.**

FOCUSED PRACTICE

1. Discover the Grammar

Underline the past perfect progressive forms in this interview with a marathon runner.

1. **Q:** What was the best part of the race for you?

   A: Around three o'clock I had this burst of energy. I'd been feeling tired for about half an hour, and I was even thinking of dropping out of the race. I was so happy that I could continue running.

2. **Q:** Did anything worry you before you started?

   A: Yes. The weather. It had been raining, and when the race started the air was very humid. I don't usually run very well in that kind of weather.

3. **Q:** Why did you take up running?

   A: In 1992, my doctor told me I'd better find a sport. At that time I'd been working at a desk job for fifteen years, and I hadn't been exercising at all. So I started jogging, and I loved it. I've been running every day for years now.

4. **Q:** What made you decide to run a marathon?

   A: I missed my husband. He'd been training for the New York Marathon, so he hadn't been spending much time with me. One day I decided to join him on his morning run. After a few weeks, we decided to run the marathon together.

5. **Q:** Had your husband been running marathons for a long time before you joined him?

   A: Oh, yes. Many years. He'd been selling sports equipment, and his customers always wanted to know about his own experience with the products. Running had just become popular in New York, and he started running to try out the shoes. Now he owns the store, but he still loves to run.

Now decide if each statement is true (T) *or false* (F).

__F__ 1. The runner felt tired after three o'clock.

_____ 2. It was raining when the race started.

_____ 3. In 1991 this runner didn't get any exercise.

_____ 4. The runner and her husband don't spend much time together.

_____ 5. Her husband used to be a salesperson.

2. Counting the Miles

Complete the sentences with the past perfect progressive form of the
appropriate verbs in the box. Refer to the chart for some of the answers.

lead	~~race~~	run	trail*	train	try	wait

*Trail means follow behind.

Ⓜ = Mtolo   Ⓔ = Espinosa

Miles: 20   21   22   23   24   25   Finish line

Ⓜ   Ⓔ   Ⓜⓔ   ⓂⒺ   ⒺⓂ   ⒺⓂ   Ⓔ   Ⓜ Ⓔ   Ⓜ

1. By the time Mtolo passed the finish line, he __had been racing__ for more than two hours.

2. Before he reached the 22-mile mark, Mtolo _____ Espinosa.

3. Mtolo _____ to pass Espinosa for several miles.

4. When Mtolo passed Espinosa, he _____ for almost 23 miles.

5. Both runners _____ for a long time for this event.

6. Until the time they reached the 22-mile mark, Espinosa _____ the race.

7. The crowd _____ at the finish line for hours.

3. An Interview

It's the day after the marathon. Complete this interview with one of the
runners. Use the words in parentheses to ask questions with **how long** *and*
the past perfect progressive.

A: Was that your first New York Marathon?

B: Yes, but I'd been training for it for a long time.

A: Really? _____ How long had you been training? _____

                                    1. (train)

B: For more than four years. First in Madrid, then in Rome. I'm from Rome originally.

A: _____

                                    2. (live)

in Madrid when you moved back to Rome?

B: About two years.

A: And what did you do when you got back to Rome—besides train, that is?

B: Oh. I was studying at the university. Then I quit and joined a rock band.

A: _____

                                    3. (study)

at the university when you quit?

(continued on next page)

B: Just a year. But I'm glad I did. I met my husband in the band. It was love at first sight.

A: _____ when
                                      4. (date)
you got married?

B: About a month.

A: A month! That's fast!

B: Yes. The marathon seemed to take longer!

A: I bet it did. _____ when
                                    5. (run)
you finally crossed the finish line?

B: Four hours, twenty minutes, and fifty-seven seconds.

4. Run for Your Life

Complete this story from a magazine called Run for Your Life. *Use the past perfect progressive form of the verbs in parentheses.*

On October 23 I ran the Boston Marathon. I ran it with a partner, Marcia Davis.

We _____ had been training _____ together since last year, and
                    1. (train)

we _____ to enter the race for years before that. The marathon meant a
        2. (plan)

lot to us. We didn't care about winning, but we both wanted to finish.

The start of the race was very dramatic. A few minutes before the gun went off, everyone got very

quiet. Up to that point, we _____, but when we lined up, we all felt very
                               3. (joke and laugh)

solemn. There were thousands of us starting the race. I was so nervous I nearly cried when the gun

went off.

At the beginning, Marcia and I did very well. We _____ on those same
                                    4. (practice)

streets for a couple of weeks, and I felt very confident. By the time we got to Heartbreak Hill, we

_____ for about four hours, and I really believed we could finish. That
        5. (run)

whole time, I _____ a little behind Marcia, but I could always see her.
                6. (trail)

Halfway up the hill, Marcia suddenly stopped—she just couldn't run anymore. We

_____ to this race for so long I didn't want to go on without her, but she
        7. (look forward)

really wanted me to finish.

I finished the race in about seven hours. When I got to the finish line, I saw Marcia with some

other friends. They _____ for me for almost three hours. We started
                 8. (wait)

talking about next year's marathon right away.

COMMUNICATION PRACTICE

5. Practice Listening

Two friends had been at a post-marathon party the night before. Listen to their conversation the next day. Then read the sentences. Listen to the conversation again and mark each sentence true (T) or false (F).

___T___ 1. Alice looked unhappy.

_____ 2. Alice started crying as soon as she got to the party.

_____ 3. Alice's husband was all wet.

_____ 4. Alice and her husband argued during the party.

_____ 5. They lived in California before.

6. Drawing Conclusions

*Work in pairs. Read these descriptions of people who had been at the party the night before. Say what you think had been happening **before** the party. Use your imagination. Compare your answers with those of the rest of the class.*

Example:
Alice's eyes were red.
  A: Maybe she'd been crying.
  B: Or maybe she'd been cutting onions.
  A: I think her eyes were red because she'd been rubbing them.

1. Caryn was out of breath.

2. Mr. and Mrs. Jackson were frowning.

3. Carlos greeted everyone in a foreign language.

4. Margot's hair was all wet.

5. Jack couldn't walk straight.

6. Angela arrived an hour late.

7. Ben's shirt had a red stain on it.

7. Information Gap: Driving All Night

Complete the story. Work with a partner. You are each going to read a version of the same story. Each one is missing some information. Your task is to get the missing information from your partner.

Student A, read the story below. Get information from Student B. Ask questions and fill in the information. Answer Student B's questions.

Student B, turn to the Information Gap for Unit 3 on page IG 1 in the back of the book. Follow the instructions there.

Example:
  A: What had the woman been doing?
  B: She had been driving all night.
     What had the woman been drinking?
  A: She'd been drinking coffee.

She was tired. She had been _____driving_____ all night. She had been drinking cup after cup of coffee, but it hadn't helped. The radio was on loud. She had been listening to music when they interrupted the program with a special news bulletin. The police had been looking for a man since _____. The man had robbed a bank. He was dangerous.

The woman shivered. The streets were slippery and wet. It had been snowing for more than _____. She wasn't sure where she was. She had been looking for her map when suddenly she saw something ahead on the road. It was a man. She hadn't noticed him at first because he had been standing behind a _____. The woman stepped on the brakes. The man opened the door and got in. The woman smiled and breathed a sigh of relief. She had been expecting him.

When you are finished, compare your two versions. Are they the same?

Now discuss the following questions: Who do you think the woman was? Who was the man? What do you think their relationship was?

8. The Night Before

Look at the picture. Work with a partner. Make guesses about what had been happening the night before. Compare your guesses with those of another pair of students.

Example:
I think someone had been eating popcorn the night before.

I. *Complete this magazine article by circling the correct verb forms.*

It's June. Nice weather <u>had finally/has finally arrived</u>. And along
with it, thoughts of barbecues. <u>Are you thinking/Do you think</u> of having
one? Have you ever wondered about the origin of the term? According
to Jeff Smith, author of *The Frugal Gourmet Cooks American,* the
term *barbecue* is not strictly an American one, but Americans
"… <u>barbecue/are barbecuing</u>. The rest of the world simply
<u>cooks/is cooking</u> meals over a fire." People <u>dispute/are disputing</u> the
origin of the name. Smith <u>continues/is continuing</u>: "Some researchers
<u>claim/are claiming</u> that the word <u>comes/is coming</u> from Spanish and
Haitian origins, and *barbaco* <u>refers/is referring</u> to a framework of sticks
set upon posts." In the past, people <u>used/were using</u> this rack to roast
meat or simply dry it. Other researchers <u>believe/are believing</u> that
the origin of the term is the French phrase *barbe à queue,* which
<u>means/is meaning</u> "from whisker (*barbe*) to tail (*queue*)." In the
eighteenth century, people <u>roasted/have roasted</u> whole animals
outdoors as well as indoors. Native Americans, too, used this method
of cooking outdoors. Whatever the origin of the term, a barbecue
<u>is/has been</u> now not only a means of cooking, but an event. According
to Smith, by 1733 the process <u>had become/had been becoming</u> a party.
People <u>stood/have stood</u> around the fire and <u>drank/had drunk</u> until the
food <u>was/had been</u> ready. That, with the addition of barbecue sauce,
<u>sounds/is sounding</u> pretty much like what a barbecue <u>is/has been</u> today.

Source: Smith, Jeff. *The Frugal Gourmet Cooks American.* New York: William Morrow and
Company, 1987.

II. *Complete these conversations that take place at a barbecue.*

1. **A:** George! How are you? <u>I haven't seen/haven't been seeing</u> you for
   a long time. What <u>happens/'s been happening</u>?
   B: Oh. <u>Haven't you heard/Don't you hear</u>? Betty and I
   <u>moved/have moved</u> last month. We <u>bought/were buying</u>
   a house.

50

A: Congratulations! I didn't know you <u>had looked/had been looking</u> for one. So, where are you now?
                                            f.

B: In Rockport County. We <u>were going to move/moved</u> to Putnam County, but we
                                        g.
    <u>have decided/decided</u> on Rockport instead.
           h.

A: Oh, how come?

B: The school district <u>is/has been</u> better here. <u>Have you ever been/Had you even been</u> to Rockport?
                                i.   j.

A: No. It's near Putnam, isn't it?

B: Uh-huh. Listen we <u>have/'re having</u> a barbecue almost every weekend. You'll have to come to one.
                                k.

A: Thanks. I'd love to.

2. **A:** Have you <u>tried/been trying</u> the hot dogs? They're delicious.
                    a.

   B: Yes. I<u>'ve already eaten/'ve been eating</u> four! The hamburgers <u>smell/are smelling</u> good, too.
                 b.   c.
    I<u>'m thinking/think</u> of having some of those.
        d.

   A: Well, just save some room for dessert. When I <u>saw/see</u> Betty in the kitchen a few minutes ago,
                                              e.
    she was taking some pies out of the oven. They <u>looked/were looking</u> great.
                                         f.

3. **A:** <u>Have you met/Have you been meeting</u> Jack's new wife?
               a.

   B: No. What's her name?

   A: Alice, but everyone <u>calls/is calling</u> her Al.
                      b.

   B: <u>What does she do/What is she doing</u>?
           c.

   A: Well, she's "between jobs." She <u>was working/worked</u> for a health insurance company when they
                                   d.
    <u>laid off/had laid off</u> a lot of employees. She was one of the people who <u>lost/was losing</u> their jobs.
       e.   f.

   B: A lot of health insurance companies <u>have been cutting/had been cutting</u> their staff. That's too bad.
                                              g.

   A: Yes. And she really <u>likes/liked</u> her job. Now she's <u>trying/tries</u> to change careers.
                        h.   i.

4. **A:** <u>Have/Had</u> Al and Jack left for their honeymoon yet?
      a.

   B: Yes. As a matter of fact, I <u>got/'ve gotten</u> a postcard from them yesterday. They <u>stay/'re staying</u>
                                  b.   c
    at the Hotel Splendor. It <u>sounds/'s sounding</u> great.
                    d.

   A: Well, they really <u>need/are needing</u> a vacation. They <u>hadn't been/haven't been</u> away since they
                        e.   f.
    <u>met/were meeting</u> each other.
      g.

   B: I know. What <u>are they doing/do they do</u> there?
                    h.

   A: Well, they<u>'re taking/take</u> scuba diving lessons, and they also
                i.
    <u>have been learning/had been learning</u> to water-ski.
          j.

   B: Sounds like fun.

(continued on next page)

5. **A:** Barbecues are such fun.

   B: I Know. In fact we<u>'ve been considering/consider</u> having one for Tashina's birthday next
   a.
   month. But we <u>don't decide/haven't decided</u> yet.
   b.

   A: For how many kids?

   B: We're not sure. We <u>were going/'re going</u> to invite all the kids in her class, but twenty
   c.
   seems like a lot. What <u>have you been doing/are you doing</u> for Jamal's parties for the last
   d.
   few years?

   A: Up until last year, we<u>'d been having/'re having</u> birthday parties at Pizza Hut. But by the time
   e.
   Jamal <u>turned/was turning</u> seven, that<u>'s getting/had gotten</u> a little old. Last year we
   f.   g.
   <u>gave/were giving</u> him his party at a miniature-golf place.
   h.

   B: That<u>'s sounding/sounds</u> better than having it at home. That way, when the party's over, you
   i.
   <u>don't/didn't</u> have to clean up.
   j.

6. **A:** These gnats <u>drove/are driving</u> me crazy. I<u>'m finding/found</u> two in my iced tea a
   a.   b.
   minute ago.

   B: I know. I<u>'ve been swatting/'m swatting</u> them away all afternoon.
   c.

   A: I think it's our perfume. Scent <u>is attracting/attracts</u> gnats and mosquitoes.
   d.

   B: I <u>didn't/don't</u> believe it. Where <u>do you read/did you read</u> that?
   e.   f.

   A: I <u>heard/'ve heard</u> it on the radio yesterday. When I <u>was turning on/turned on</u> the news at
   g.   h.
   6:00 they <u>interviewed/were interviewing</u> someone about summer health issues.
   i.

   B: What else <u>were you learning/did you learn</u>?
   j.

   A: Just that.

III. *Complete the conversation with the correct form of the verbs in parentheses.*

A: Hi, I _____'m_____ Matt Rotell, a friend of Alice's.
           1. (be)

B: Oh, yes. Alice _____ you the other day. Gee, you _____ like a detective.
                      2. (mention)   3. (not look)

A: Well, that's good, I _____.
                           4. (guess)

B: Tell me, how _____ you _____ to become an undercover cop?
                              5. (decide)

A: Well, when I _____ a kid, I _____ to read detective novels. By the time I
                   6. (be)   7. (love)
_____ ten, I _____ every book in the Hardy Boys series. I _____ then that
8. (be)   9. (read)   10. (know)
I _____ into law enforcement when I _____.
   11. (go)   12. (grow up)

B: But, according to Alice you _____ law school nowadays.
                                   13. (attend)

A: Right. I _____ married last month. I _____ being on the police force when I
              14. (get)   15. (not mind)
_____ single, but ever since I _____ Nicole (that's my wife) I _____ to do
16. (be)   17. (meet)   18. (want)
something less dangerous.

B: I _____. By the way, _____ you _____ any luck yet with those counterfeiters?
19. (understand)   20. (have)

A: Well, I _____ them for more than a month now, but so far I _____ catch them in the
21. (follow)   22. (not be able to)

act. Sometimes I _____ that by the time they're caught, I'll have my law degree.
23. (worry)

B: Well, just think. Then you'll be able to defend them!

IV. *Read this letter from Al. There are ten mistakes in verb tenses. Find and correct them.*

Dear Nicole,

        have been staying
    Jack and I ~~are staying~~ at the Splendor for almost a week already. We've been spending a lot of time

at the beach swimming and water-skiing, and I was taking scuba lessons in the hotel pool for several

days now. Yesterday, I am going to take my first dive from a boat. Unfortunately, by the time we left

shore, the weather has changed. We had to cancel the dive. This morning it was still a little cloudy, so

we did something different. We were deciding to visit the Castle, an old pirate stronghold in Hideaway

Bay. We had both read about it before we left, and it sounded fascinating. So we've rented a motorbike

and took off. They aren't having any road signs here outside of town, so by the time we found the

Castle, we've been driving for about an hour. It was fun, though. When we were first seeing the Castle,

dark clouds were drifting over it. It really looked spooky and beautiful.

    Well, the weather has cleared, and Jack gets ready to go for a dive. I think I'll join him. See you

soon.

        Love,

        Al

II

Future

Read and listen to this magazine article about what the new millennium will bring.

PRESENTING— THE FUTURE!

JANUARY 2000

A new millennium is dawning and with it the powerful feeling that a new era has begun. Where **will** we **be working** in this new era? How **will** we **be traveling?** What **will** we **be wearing?** Here's what futurists predict.

WORK. Futurists see a breakdown in the division between home and office. In the twenty-first century, more and more people **will be telecommuting**—working at home with telephones, faxes, and computers. They**'ll be** spending much less time in offices. This development will allow people to spend more time with their families as well as cut down on pollution from automobiles.

HOME. Who**'ll be cleaning** house while Mom and Dad are sending faxes? Robots—tiny insectlike ones that hang around in corners and eat the dust. One Massachusetts Institute of Technology designer predicts that in just a few years, small, intelligent robots **are going to be doing** all the household chores.

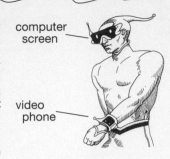

computer screen

video phone

TRANSPORTATION. You**'ll** still **be driving** the family car to the grocery store—at least for a while. However, for middle-distance travel, high-speed mass transit like Japan's Bullet Train will probably replace individual cars.

CLOTHING. Like a *Star Trek* officer, the well-dressed millenarian **will be wearing** a body suit. Made of high-tech materials, the suit will be cool in summer and warm in winter. Most likely, we**'re going to be wearing** our technology as well—wrist video phones and sunglasses with computer screens etched onto the lenses.

ENTERTAINMENT. Before the end of the new century, people **will be watching** life-size images on TV—ones that they can see, hear, feel, and smell. Called "virtual reality," this technology creates powerful images that audiences experience as real. The new entertainment will also be interactive. Viewers **won't be sitting** passively watching the explorer shoot the rapids; they **will be guiding** the raft themselves.

EDUCATION. Virtual-reality technology will transform instruction as well as entertainment. On a typical school day, the geography class **will be experiencing** life in a rain forest, while the history class next door shudders at the sights, sounds, and smells of the Battle of Waterloo.

The line between education and employment will blur. Our grandchildren **will** probably **be dividing** their time between the classroom and an apprenticeship. However, job skills will quickly become obsolete in the new era, so they**'ll** also **be updating** their skills and knowledge continually throughout their lives.

THE NEW SUBURBS. In 1992, radio antennas in California and Puerto Rico began a systematic search for signs of life in the universe. For the next several years, astronomers **will be scanning** the heavens for other civilizations. Meanwhile, the Mars Underground, a group of visionary scientists, has already planned the first real-estate development project on Mars. The shuttles **will be leaving** as soon as they iron out a few transportation problems.

Many of these changes have already begun, and we**'ll be seeing** others, such as changes in school systems, very soon. The future **will be arriving** any minute. Are you ready for it?

FUTURE PROGRESSIVE

STATEMENTS			
SUBJECT	**WILL (NOT)/ BE (NOT) GOING TO**	**BE + BASE FORM + -ING**	
People	will (not) are (not) going to	be working	at home.

YES/NO QUESTIONS				
WILL/BE	SUBJECT	GOING TO	BE + BASE FORM + -ING	
Will	you		be working	at home?
Are	they	going to		

SHORT ANSWERS		SHORT ANSWERS	
AFFIRMATIVE		NEGATIVE	
Yes,	I will. they **are**.	No,	I won't. they're **not**.

WH- QUESTIONS					
WH- WORD	WILL/BE	SUBJECT	GOING TO	BE + BASE FORM + -ING	
When	**will**	you		be working	at home?
	are	they	**going to**		

Grammar Notes

1. Use the future progressive with *will* or *be going to* to talk about actions that will be in progress at a specific time in the future.

   > **I'll be taking** the Bullet Train tomorrow afternoon.

   > OR

   > **I'm going to be taking** the Bullet Train tomorrow afternoon.

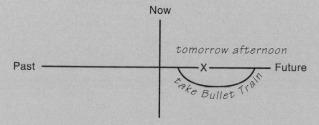

   Remember that non-action (stative) verbs are not usually used in the progressive.

   > We'll **have** our own video phone next year. NOT ~~We'll be having our own video phone next year.~~

2. Remember that if the sentence has a time clause, use present, not future, in the time clause.

   > I'll **be working** in the kitchen while the robot **cleans** the office. NOT ~~I'll be working in the kitchen while the robot will clean the office.~~

3. People often use the future progressive to hint that they would like someone to do them a favor.

   > A: **Will** you **be going** by the post office tomorrow?
   > B: I plan to. Why? Do you need stamps?
   > A: Yes. If you remember, could you buy some for me?

FOCUSED PRACTICE

1. Discover the Grammar

Professor Granite is a futurist. Look at her plans for the next month and mark the statements true (T) or false (F).

AUGUST 2020						
Sun.	Mon.	Tues.	Wed.	Thurs.	Fri.	Sat.
						1
2	3	4	5	6	7	8
	← attend conference of World Future Society in Tokyo →					
9 take Bullet Train to Osaka	10	11 ← free days sightseeing	12 →	13	14	15 fly to Denver
16	17	18	19	20	21	22 fly home
	← attend seminar on energy at the university → stay with Mom and Dad					
23	24	25 ← work at home →	26	27	28	29
30 shop for kids' school clothes	31					

1. Professor Granite will be attending a conference during the first week of August. ___T___

2. She'll be flying to Osaka on the 9th. _____

3. She'll be working on a paper during her visit to Osaka. _____

4. She'll be traveling to Denver the weekend of the 15th. _____

5. She'll be staying with her friends while she attends the seminar in Denver. _____

6. She'll be flying home on the 22nd. _____

7. She'll be commuting to work the week of the 23rd. _____

8. She'll be shopping on the 30th. _____

2. Robo's Schedule

Dr. Granite's family uses a robot for household chores. Look at Robo the Robot's schedule for tomorrow. Make sentences, using the words in parentheses and the future progressive.

Tomorrow

8:00	make breakfast
9:00	pay bills
10:00	vacuum
11:00	dust
12:00	do laundry
12:30	make lunch
1:00	shop for food
2:00	recycle garbage
3:00	give Mr. Granite a massage
5:00	make dinner
6:00	play chess with Karen and Danny

1. _____At 8:00 Robo won't be paying bills. He'll be making breakfast._____
 (8:00 / pay bills)

2. _____
 (9:00 / pay bills)

3. _____
 (10:00 / vacuum)

4. _____
 (11:00 / do laundry)

5. _____
 (12:00 / make lunch)

6. _____
 (12:30 / make lunch)

7. _____
 (1:00 / shop for food)

8. _____
 (2:00 / recycle garbage)

9. _____
 (3:00 / give Mr. Granite a massage)

10. _____
 (5:00 / make dinner)

11. _____
 (6:00 / play cards with Karen and Danny)

3. On Campus

Complete the conversations. Use the future progressive form of the words in parentheses or short answers where appropriate.

1. **Student:** _____Will_____ you _____be having_____ office hours today? I'd like to
   (Will / have)
   talk to you about my term paper.

   Prof. Granite: I _____ to lunch at two o'clock. But stop in any time
   (will / go)
   before then.

2. **Prof. Gupta:** _____ you _____ us for lunch? Dr. Russ from the Mars Underground
   (Will / join)
   is going to be there.

   Prof. Granite: _____. I've been looking forward to meeting him.

3. **Mr. Granite:** When _____ you _____ the office?
   (be going to / leave)

   Prof. Granite: At two o'clock. Why? Do we need something?

   Mr. Granite: Would you mind picking up some salt? I forgot to put it on Robo's list.

   Prof. Granite: OK.

4. **Reporter:** I'm calling from the *Times-Dispatch*. We've heard that the Mars Underground
   _____ a shuttle service to Mars soon. Is that true?
   (will / start)

   Prof. Granite: I can't comment now. But I think we _____ a lot more
   (be going to / hear)
   about it in the next few weeks.

5. **Prof. Granite:** Dr. Russ, _____ you _____ an announcement
   (be going to / make)
   about the Mars Shuttle soon? Everyone is very curious.

   Dr. Russ: _____. We've decided not to say anything until our
   plans are more developed.

4. Leaving Earth

Complete this ad for the Mars Shuttle. Use the correct form—the future progressive or the simple present tense—of the verbs in parentheses.

The Sky's Not the Limit

Leave all your earthly problems behind. Call today and in just one week you ___'ll be flying___ on the new Shuttle to Mars! Imagine—
1. (fly)
while everyone _____ stuck back here on Earth,
2. (be)
you _____ gravity in our spacious, comfortable, modern
3. (defy)
spaceship. You _____ in your own compartment when
4. (float)
one of our friendly flight robots _____ you a freshly
5. (offer)
reconstituted meal. You _____ your complimentary copy of
6. (read)
Star Magazine while the gentle swaying of the spacecraft
_____ you to sleep. And before you know it,
7. (rock)
you _____ to land on the planet of your dreams. So don't
8. (get ready)
delay! Call for a reservation. Once aboard, we guarantee it—
you _____ about anything except returning again and again
9. (not think)
and again....

COMMUNICATION PRACTICE

5. Practice Listening

Four members of the Mars Underground are trying to arrange a conference on Venus. Listen to their conversation. Then listen again. Mark the chart below to help you figure out when they are all available.

x = not available								
	JULY				**AUGUST**			
Weeks:	1	2	3	4	1	2	3	4
Jennifer							x	x
Brian								
Lorna								
Tranh								

The time that they're all available: _____

6. Let's Get Together

First fill out the schedule below. Write in all your plans for next week. Then work with a partner. Without showing each other your schedules, find a time to get together by asking and answering questions with the future progressive.

Example:
A: What will you be doing at 11:00 on Tuesday?
B: I'll be taking a history test.

	Monday	Tuesday	Wednesday	Thursday	Friday
9:00					
11:00					
1:00					
3:00					
5:00					
7:00					

7. Robots of the Future

Computerized robots will be doing many things in the near future. Look at the list of activities and decide which ones you think robots will or won't be doing. In small groups, share and explain your opinions. Do you think robots will be doing too much for humans? Why?

make dinner	plant gardens
go shopping	take a vacation
write letters	answer the phone
teach English	clean house
take care of children	paint walls
sew clothes	knit sweaters
read books	drive a car

Example:
Robots will be cleaning houses, but they won't be taking care of children. Children need human contact to help them develop emotional security.

INTRODUCTION

●● *Read and listen to this newsletter about saving money.*

THE PENNY-PINCHING TIMES

Volume 5, Number 1   January

From the Editor's Desk:

In our New Year's issue, we traditionally talk about savings goals for the coming year. But is it possible to save money in these hard times? This question has been on the minds of many of our subscribers. Let's turn to one of our readers for the answer.

Janice Bedford's goal is to buy a car by the end of the year. Janice works as a word processor and takes home about $20,000 a year. About $15,000 of that goes to pay essential costs—food, clothing, rent. Another $5,000 goes for optional expenses such as books, movies, and gifts. Janice has figured out that if she saves just $15.00 a week, by the end of the year, she **will have met** her savings goal of $780—enough for the down payment on a good used car.

How will she do it? Well, to begin with, Janice, an avid reader who usually buys three paperback books a month, will become reacquainted with her local library. By borrowing instead of buying, Janice **will have saved** about $200 by the end of the year. And with no sacrifice—she**'ll** still **have been keeping up** with all those best sellers while she saves. If she continues her new habit, by the year 2001, Janice **will have put away** an impressive $1,200. And that's just one of many painless ways that Janice, and you, can save money for the things you want and need. Read on for more. . . .

Happy penny pinching!
Mary Dobbs, Editor

$ $ $ $ $ $ $ $ $ $ $ $ $ $ $ $ $ $
$ $
$ Sayings worth saving . . . $
$ $
$ The safest way to double your money is to fold $
$ $
$ it over once and put it into your pocket. $
$ $
$ (Frank McKinney Hubbard, 1868–1930) $
$ $ $ $ $ $ $ $ $ $ $ $ $ $ $ $ $ $

A Penny Saved . . .
Tips from our Readers

•A year ago, Anne Marie DuPont wanted her daughter Jennifer to start studying piano, but she just couldn't afford the lessons. By packing four inexpensive lunches a week for Jennifer and herself, Anne Marie saved the $60 a month she needed for private lessons. On the 15th of this month, Jennifer **will have been studying** piano for six months, and Anne Marie will have the pleasure of attending her daughter's first recital. Happy New Year, Anne Marie!

•Don Caputo wants to pay off a costly credit-card debt. By writing letters to his relatives instead of making expensive long-distance phone calls, he can pay an additional $50 a month on his card. By June, Don figures, he**'ll have cut** the debt in half—just by putting pen to paper. By a year from June, he**'ll have paid off** the whole thing. This seems like a long haul, but remember that all along, Don **will** also **have been saving** on the costly 20% that the credit-card company charges for the unpaid balance.

•Tom Lu has wanted a CD player for a long time. A student with very little disposable income, Tom had to look hard for places to save. Recently, Tom has started hanging his clothes up to dry instead of putting them in the dryer at his local laundromat. Considering that it costs him $1.50 a machine, and he needs to do two loads a week, Tom **will have accumulated** an extra $156 by the time the holidays are here again. That's enough to buy himself the present he wants—a used CD player.

$ $

Write to us with your own penny-pinching tips. If we publish yours, you'll receive a FREE copy of our popular booklet, *More Bang for the Buck*—AND you**'ll have helped** others pinch a penny.

$ $

$ $

Here's this month's Penny-Pincher Problem: A ten-ounce box of Boast Cereal costs $1.59. The same brand costs $2.29 for eighteen ounces. Which is the better buy? If you buy two boxes a month of the better buy, how much **will** you **have saved** by the end of twelve months?

Answer: The eighteen-ounce box at 13 cents an ounce is a better buy than the ten-ounce box at 16 cents an ounce. By buying the eighteen-ounce box, you'll **have saved** $12.96 by next January.

$ $

FUTURE PERFECT

STATEMENTS			
SUBJECT	***WILL (NOT)***	***HAVE + PAST PARTICIPLE***	
I You He She We They	**will (not)**	**have saved**	enough by then.
It	**will (not)**	**have earned**	interest by then.

YES/NO QUESTIONS			
WILL	**SUBJECT**	***HAVE + PAST PARTICIPLE***	
Will	I you he she we they	**have saved**	enough by then?
Will	it	**have earned**	interest by then?

SHORT ANSWERS		
AFFIRMATIVE		
Yes,	you I he she we they	**will (have).**
	it	

SHORT ANSWERS		
NEGATIVE		
No,	you I he she we they	**won't (have).**
	it	

WH- QUESTIONS				
WH- WORD	***WILL***	**SUBJECT**	***HAVE + PAST PARTICIPLE***	
When	**will**	she	**have saved**	enough?

FUTURE PERFECT PROGRESSIVE

STATEMENTS			
SUBJECT	**WILL (NOT)**	**HAVE BEEN + BASE FORM + -ING**	
I You He She We They	**will (not)**	**have been living**	there for ten years.
It	**will (not)**	**have been earning**	interest for ten years.

YES/NO QUESTIONS			
WILL	**SUBJECT**	**HAVE BEEN + BASE FORM + -ING**	
Will	I you he she we they	**have been living**	there for ten years?
Will	it	**have been earning**	interest for ten years?

SHORT ANSWERS		
AFFIRMATIVE		
Yes,	you I he she we they	**will (have).**
	it	

SHORT ANSWERS		
NEGATIVE		
No,	you I he she we they	**won't (have).**
	it	

WH- QUESTIONS				
WH- WORD	**WILL**	**SUBJECT**	**HAVE BEEN + BASE FORM + -ING**	
How long	**will**	she	**have been living**	there?

Grammar Notes

1. Use the future perfect to talk about a future action that will already be completed by a certain time in the future.

> By June, he**'ll have paid** his debt.

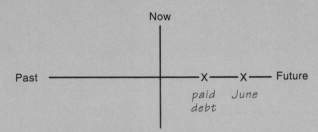

2. Use the future perfect progressive to talk about an action that will still be in progress at a certain time in the future. The action may have already started, or it may start sometime in the future.

> They're going to move into their new apartment next month. By 2001, they **will have been living** in their apartment for ten years.

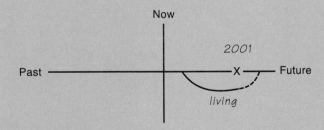

> They moved to Chicago five years ago. By 2001 they **will have been living** there for fifteen years.

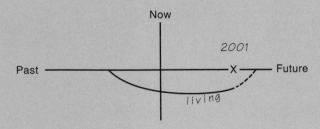

Remember that non-action (stative) verbs are not usually used in the progressive.

> By the spring, he**'ll have owned** that car for five years. NOT ~~he'll have been owning that car for five years.~~

3. Use the future perfect or the future perfect progressive with the simple present tense to show the relationship between two future events. The event that will take place first uses the perfect. The event that will take place second uses the simple present tense.

> By the time you **arrive,** I **will have finished** dinner. NOT ~~By the time you will arrive, I will have finished dinner.~~

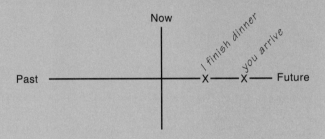

> When my daughter **turns** eight, we **will have been living** here for ten years.

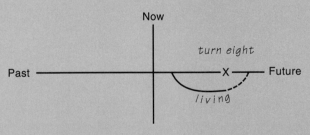

4. We often use *already* and *yet* with the future perfect to emphasize which event takes place first.

> By the time he graduates, he**'ll have already saved** $1,000.
> By the time he graduates, he **won't have saved** $5,000 **yet.**

FOCUSED PRACTICE

1. Discover the Grammar

Read each numbered sentence. Then circle the letter of the sentence whose meaning is similar.

1. By this time tomorrow, I'll have decided which car to buy.
   a. I know which car I'm going to buy.
   (b.) I haven't decided yet.

2. By the time you get home, we'll have finished the grocery shopping.
   a. You will get home while we are shopping.
   b. You will get home after we finish shopping.

3. By next year, Mary will have been working at *Penny-Pinching Times* for five years.
   a. Next year, Mary will no longer be working at *Penny-Pinching Times*.
   b. Next year, Mary can celebrate her fifth anniversary at *Penny-Pinching Times*.

4. She won't have finished writing her column by ten o'clock.
   a. She will still be writing at ten o'clock.
   b. She will finish writing at ten o'clock.

5. By the year 2010, we will have moved to a larger office.
   a. We will move to a larger office before the year 2010.
   b. We will move to a larger office after the year 2010.

6. They will have finished mailing the newsletter by five o'clock.
   a. They'll be finished by five o'clock.
   b. They'll still be working at five o'clock.

2. Future Plans

Look at the timeline. Write sentences describing what Tom Lu will have done or won't have done by the year 2010.

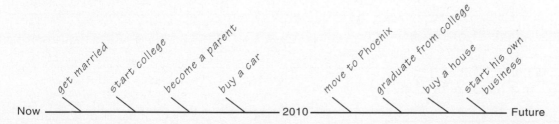

(continued on next page)

1. (start college)

   By 2010 Tom will have started college.

2. (graduate from college)

   _____

3. (get married)

   _____

4. (become a parent)

   _____

5. (buy a car)

   _____

6. (buy a house)

   _____

7. (move to Phoenix)

   _____

8. (start his own business)

   _____

3. By the Time . . .

*Look again at the timeline in exercise 2. Now relate two events in the future. What will or won't have happened by the time the first event occurs? Use **already** and **yet.***

1. start college/get married

   By the time Tom starts college, he'll have already gotten married.

2. graduate from college/become a parent

   _____

3. buy a car/graduate from college

   _____

4. move to Phoenix/graduate from college

   _____

5. buy a house/get married

   _____

6. move to Phoenix/start his own business

   _____

7. start his own business/graduate from college

   _____

4. Accomplishments

Ask and answer questions about these people's accomplishments. Choose between the future perfect and the future perfect progressive. Use the calendar to answer the questions.

	January							Feburary							March					
S	M	T	W	T	F	S	S	M	T	W	T	F	S	S	M	T	W	T	F	S
					1	2		1	2	3	4	5	6		1	2	3	4	5	6
3	4	5	6	7	8	9	7	8	9	10	11	12	13	7	8	9	10	11	12	13
10	11	12	13	14	15	16	14	15	16	17	18	19	20	14	15	16	17	18	19	20
17	18	19	20	21	22	23	21	22	23	24	25	26	27	21	22	23	24	25	26	27
24	25	26	27	28	29	30	28							28	29	30	31			
31																				

	April							May							June					
S	M	T	W	T	F	S	S	M	T	W	T	F	S	S	M	T	W	T	F	S
				1	2	3							1			1	2	3	4	5
4	5	6	7	8	9	10	2	3	4	5	6	7	8	6	7	8	9	10	11	12
11	12	13	14	15	16	17	9	10	11	12	13	14	15	13	14	15	16	17	18	19
18	19	20	21	22	23	24	16	17	18	19	20	21	22	20	21	22	23	24	25	26
25	26	27	28	29	30		23	24	25	26	27	28	29	27	28	29	30			
							30	31												

	July							August							September					
S	M	T	W	T	F	S	S	M	T	W	T	F	S	S	M	T	W	T	F	S
				1	2	3	1	2	3	4	5	6	7				1	2	3	4
4	5	6	7	8	9	10	8	9	10	11	12	13	14	5	6	7	8	9	10	11
11	12	13	14	15	16	17	15	16	17	18	19	20	21	12	13	14	15	16	17	18
18	19	20	21	22	23	24	22	23	24	25	26	27	28	19	20	21	22	23	24	25
25	26	27	28	29	30	31	29	30	31					26	27	28	29	30		

	October							November							December					
S	M	T	W	T	F	S	S	M	T	W	T	F	S	S	M	T	W	T	F	S
					1	2		1	2	3	4	5	6				1	2	3	4
3	4	5	6	7	8	9	7	8	9	10	11	12	13	5	6	7	8	9	10	11
10	11	12	13	14	15	16	14	15	16	17	18	19	20	12	13	14	15	16	17	18
17	18	19	20	21	22	23	21	22	23	24	25	26	27	19	20	21	22	23	24	25
24	25	26	27	28	29	30	28	29	30					26	27	28	29	30	31	

1. On January 1, Jennifer DuPont started saving $5.00 a week.

   QUESTION: (By February 19/how long/save?)

   By February 19, how long will Jennifer have been saving?

   ANSWER: _By February 19, she'll have been saving for seven weeks._

2. On January 1, Valerie Morgan started saving $5.00 a week.

   QUESTION: (By February 18/how much/save?)

   ANSWER: _____

3. On March 3, Tom Lu began reading a book a week.

   QUESTION: (By June 16/how many books/read?)

   ANSWER: _____

4. On September 1, Janice Bedford started losing two pounds a week.

   QUESTION: (lose ten pounds by October 6?)

   ANSWER: _____

(continued on next page)

5. On November 24, Don Caputo began running two miles a day.

QUESTION: (How long/run/by December 29?)

_____

ANSWER: _____

6. On November 24, Tania Zakov began running two miles a day.

QUESTION: (How many miles/run/by December 29?)

_____

ANSWER: _____

7. On May 6, Rick Gregory began saving $10.00 a week.

QUESTION: (save $100 by July 1?)

_____

ANSWER: _____

8. On October 4, Tim Rigg began painting two apartments a week.

QUESTION: (How many apartments/paint/by October 25?)

_____

ANSWER: _____

9. Tim's building has twelve apartments.

QUESTION: (finish/by November 15?)

_____

ANSWER: _____

COMMUNICATION PRACTICE

5. Practice Listening

Don and Thea Caputo want to save for a summer vacation with their two children. Listen to their conversation about how to cut back on their spending. Then listen again and write the amount they will have saved in each category by next summer.

Amount They Will Have Saved by Next Summer

food _____ $500.00 _____

clothing _____

transportation _____

entertainment _____

Total all the categories. How much will they have saved by the end of the year?

Total: _____

With their savings, where can they go for a two-week vacation?

1. ☐ a car trip to British Columbia, camping on the way $800.00

2. ☐ a car trip to British Columbia, staying in motels $1,450.00

3. ☐ a trip to Disneyland $2,300.00

4. ☐ a trip by airplane to Mexico and two weeks
    in a hotel $3,800.00

6. Goals

Work in a small group. Conduct a survey to find out how many of your classmates will have done the following things by a year from now. Fill out this chart. In groups, report back to the class.

Event	Number of People
1. take a vacation	
2. get married	
3. become a parent or grandparent	
4. move	
5. buy a new car	
6. graduate	
7. get a new job	
8. turn sixty	
9. decide on a career	
10. start a business	

Example: None of the students in our group will have moved. Three
of the students will have gotten new jobs by next year.

7. Savvy Consumers

Write down some tips for saving money and then share your tips with a group. Choose the best tips for yourself and figure how much you will have saved by the end of the year if you use the tips. Tell your group.

Example: I can save $10 a week by parking farther from my office.
By the end of the year I'll have saved $500.

I. *Circle the correct words to complete the conversation.*

A: Graduation ceremonies were this afternoon. I can't believe this year is over already.

B: Me neither. Do you realize that in September we <u>'ll live</u>/<u>'ll have been living</u> in this apartment for two years?
1.

A: Amazing. And you <u>'ll have been studying</u>/<u>'ll be studying</u> here for four years.
2.

B: I know. Next year at this time <u>I'll have been graduating</u>/<u>'ll have graduated</u> already.
3.

A: So, what <u>'ll you be doing</u>/<u>'ll you have done</u> next June? Any plans?
4.

B: That's easy. Next June I <u>'ll be looking</u>/<u>'ll have been looking</u> for a job. How about you?.
5.

A: I <u>won't have graduated</u>/<u>'ll have graduated</u> yet. I plan to go home
6.
at the beginning of July next year, so during June, I guess
<u>I'm going to be getting ready</u>/<u>'ll have gotten ready</u> to travel
7.
to Greece.

B: Lucky you. Next summer you <u>sit</u>/<u>'ll be sitting</u> on beautiful beaches
8.
while I <u>still sit</u>/<u>'ll still be sitting</u> through job interviews.
9.

A: But just think. By the time I <u>'ll be getting</u>/<u>get</u> back, you
10.
<u>'ll find</u>/<u>'ll have found</u> a good job. So while I<u>'m learning</u>/<u>will learn</u>
11.   12.
about verb tenses, you <u>start</u>/<u>'ll be starting</u> your career.
13.

II. *Complete the conversations with the correct words.*

1. **A:** I'm going to study tonight. I have a lot to do.
   B: That's too bad. The NBA playoffs are on at nine.
   A: Oh, I _____ 'll have finished _____ by nine.
       a. finished   c. finish
       b. 'll have finished   d. 'll have been finishing

2. **A:** Could you pick up my brother at the airport for me? I'm working overtime today.
   B: No problem. But how will I know who he is?
   A: He has short dark hair, and he _____
   a black leather jacket.
       a. 'll be wearing   c. 'll have been wearing
       b. wore   d. 'll have worn

3. **A:** Do you think Mustafa should take the TOEFL® this spring?

   B: Sure. The test is in June. By that time, he _____ for more than six months.
   | a. 'll prepare | c. 's prepared |
   | b. prepared | d. 'll have been preparing |

4. **A:** My mother loves Jack Francis novels. She's afraid she'll finish them all and there won't be any more for her to read.

   B: Impossible. Francis writes fast. By the time your mother _____ this one,
   | a. 'll have read | c. reads |
   | b. 'll have been reading | d. read |

   he _____ two more.
   | a. 'll have written | c. wrote |
   | b. 'll have been writing | d. writes |

5. **A:** These roller-blades are getting too tight. I'm going to need new ones by the time school's over.

   B: Why don't you try saving for them? You can make an extra five dollars a week on chores. By the end of May, you _____ enough for a new pair.
   | a. 'll have been saving | c. 'll have saved |
   | b. saved | d. save |

6. **A:** The conductor just told me we're going to be delayed here in Boston for about an hour.

   B: I'll go call Anna and tell her not to pick us up until six.

   A: Too late. By the time you find a telephone, she _____ for the train station.
   | a. 'll have left | c. 'll have been leaving |
   | b. 'll leave | d. left |

7. **A:** When we get there, let's take Anna out to dinner.

   B: Good idea. She _____ for us for over an hour.
   | a. waited | c. 'll have been waiting |
   | b. 'll wait | d. waits |

8. **A:** Did she ever finish painting the house?

   B: Not yet. She can only work on it on weekends. She says it'll take her at least two more weeks.

   A: Gosh. I remember when she started. At the end of this month, she _____ for three months.
   | a. 'll have painted | c. 'll have been painting |
   | b. 'll paint | d. painted |

III. *Complete the conversation with the future progressive, future perfect, or future perfect progressive form of the verbs in parentheses.*

A: It says in this article that by the year 2020, scientists _____will have perfected_____ an
   1. (perfect)
electric car. That means we _____ gasoline-powered cars in just
   2. (not drive)
another few years.

B: Too bad. We _____ paying for our gasoline-powered car by then.
   3. (finish)
Just in time to sell it and buy another one.

A: Oh, come on. Think of the benefit to the environment. We _____
   4. (not pollute)
the atmosphere the way we do now. And we _____ all that money
   5. (not spend)
for fuel every year.

B: I guess you're right. Speaking of driving, _____ you _____ by
   6. (go)
the post office tomorrow?

(continued on next page)

A: Probably. Why? Do you need stamps?

B: No, but I promised to get this report in this week. I _____ on it
7. (work)
all night tonight. With luck, I _____ it by the time you leave for
8. (finish)
work tomorrow.

A: I can send it overnight mail for you. No problem.

B: You know, this is an anniversary for me. I _____ for five years
9. (telecommute)
as of tomorrow.

A: I'll be home at seven. Let's go out for dinner and celebrate.

B: I've got to work all night tonight. I'm afraid I _____ by seven
10. (sleep)
tomorrow evening.

A: OK. The next day then.

IV. *Read this thank-you note. There are six mistakes with the future.*
Find and correct them.

Dear Aisha,

We decided to take an earlier flight, so by the time you ~~will~~ read this, we'll already have left.
We'll be travel for a couple of days, but we'll call you as soon as we get home. We had a wonderful
time—it was great seeing you again. Let's try to visit each other more often. Next year, we'll
staying in Barcelona for the summer, and we'd love for you to visit us. I finished school by then,
so my schedule should be very flexible. And you'll been studying Spanish for three years, so
you'll be speaking like a native! We'll be having a great time.

Thanks again for a wonderful visit. See you next year!

Love,

Carla and Alberto

Tag Questions, Additions, and Responses

INTRODUCTION

Read and listen to these on-the-street interviews reported in a popular magazine.

AROUND TOWN
It's a Nice Place to Live, **Isn't It?**

La Costa: Excuse me. I'm conducting a survey to find out how people feel about living in L.A. Would you mind answering a few questions?

TOM MOFFET: *"I'm a screenplay writer. Hollywood's the only place to be."*

Moffet: Hey, you're Jackie La Costa from Channel 7, **aren't you?**

La Costa: That's right.

Moffet: I watch you all the time!

La Costa: Thanks. You're not originally from California, **are you?**

Moffet: No. I moved here two years ago from New York. You could tell by my accent, **couldn't you?**

La Costa: So, how do you like it here?

Moffet: Well, I'm a screenplay writer, and so Hollywood's the place to be.

La Costa: But it's gotten harder to sell scripts, **hasn't it?**

Moffet: Uh-huh. It's not like a few years ago when . . . I'm sorry. Will you excuse me? I think I see my agent over there. . .

La Costa: No problem. Thanks.

* * * * * * * *

La Costa: Excuse me, ma'am. Can I ask a few questions?

Aguirre: Sure.

La Costa: Are you from L.A.?

Aguirre: No. I'm from New York.

MARTA AGUIRRE: *"Two hundred and fifty-eight days of sunshine a year. You can't beat that, **can you?**"*

La Costa: Oh. How long have you been in L.A.?

Aguirre: Almost twenty years.

La Costa: That's a pretty long time, **isn't it?** Why did you move here?

Aguirre: The weather. Two hundred and fifty-eight days of sunshine a year. You can't beat that, **can you?**

La Costa: Not if you don't mind the smog!

Aguirre: Well, New York has its problems with air pollution, too.

La Costa: That's true.

* * * * * * * *

La Costa: So, why did you move to L.A.?

Kato: I work in the computer industry. My company does a lot of business in Asia, and I have to fly to Japan at least once a month.

La Costa: L.A. *is* a lot closer to Japan, **isn't it?**

Kato: Yes, it is. I save a lot of time traveling. And our customers come here, too.

La Costa: L.A. has really become an international center, **hasn't it?**

Kato: It really has.

KAZUHIKO KATO: *"I have to fly to Japan at least once a month."*

* * * * * * * *

La Costa: Excuse me, ma'am. You're not from L.A., by any chance, **are you?**

ROBERTA WILSON: *"It's a nice city to live in, **isn't it?**"*

Wilson: I'm from L.A.

La Costa: Oh. I was beginning to think that no one was born here! I'm trying to find out how people feel about living here.

Wilson: That's funny.

La Costa: Funny?

Wilson: Yes. I've lived here all my life, but I'm moving next month. I just got laid off, so I'm moving east. I got a job in New York.

La Costa: It seems like everyone I speak to is either going to or coming from New York.

Wilson: Small world, **isn't it?**

La Costa: Well, how *did* you like living in L.A.?

Wilson: Except for the traffic on the freeway, I liked it a lot. I'm not even going to have a car in New York.

La Costa: Will you miss L.A.?

Wilson: Sure. It's a nice city to live in, **isn't it?**

TAG QUESTIONS FOR STATEMENTS WITH *BE* AS THE MAIN VERB

AFFIRMATIVE STATEMENT	NEGATIVE TAG		NEGATIVE STATEMENT	AFFIRMATIVE TAG
SUBJECT + *BE*	*BE NOT* + SUBJECT		SUBJECT + *BE NOT*	*BE* + SUBJECT
You're from L.A.,	aren't you?		**You're not** from L.A.,	are you?

TAG QUESTIONS FOR STATEMENTS WITH AN AUXILIARY VERB

AFFIRMATIVE STATEMENT	NEGATIVE TAG		NEGATIVE STATEMENT	AFFIRMATIVE TAG
SUBJECT + AUXILIARY	AUXILIARY + *NOT* + SUBJECT		SUBJECT + AUXILIARY + *NOT*	AUXILIARY + SUBJECT
You're moving, **He's** been here before, **They can** move tomorrow,	aren't you? hasn't he? can't they?		**You're not** moving, **He hasn't** been here before, **They can't** move tomorrow,	are you? has he? can they?

TAG QUESTIONS FOR STATEMENTS WITH OTHER VERBS

AFFIRMATIVE STATEMENT	NEGATIVE TAG		NEGATIVE STATEMENT	AFFIRMATIVE TAG
SUBJECT + VERB	*DO NOT* + SUBJECT		SUBJECT + *DO NOT* + VERB	*DO* + SUBJECT
You live here, **They decided** to move,	don't you? didn't they?		**You don't** live here, **They didn't** decide to move,	do you? did they?

Grammar Notes

1. Tag questions consist of a statement and a tag.

Statement   **Tag**
You're not from California, are you?

We often use tag questions in conversations when we expect the person we're talking to to agree with us or when we want to check if some information is correct. The forms for tag questions vary, but their meaning is always similar. A tag question means *Isn't that true?* or *Right?*

You're Jackie La Costa, **aren't you?**
(You're Jackie La Costa, right?)

2. In most tag questions, the voice rises and then falls on the tag.

It's a beautiful day, **isn't it?**

Notice that the example is really more like a statement or a comment than a question. The listener doesn't even need to answer. The listener can just nod or say *uh-huh* to show that he or she is listening and agrees.

A: Nice day, **isn't it?**
B: Uh-huh. Seems more like spring than winter.

3. Tag questions can also be used to get real information. In this kind of tag question, you don't expect the listener to just agree with you. You're not sure of the answer, and you really want to confirm your information. It is more like a *yes/no* question.

You're not moving, **are you?** (Are you moving?)

Like a *yes/no* question, the voice rises at the end, and you usually get an answer.

A: You're not moving, **are you?**
B: Yes, we are. We're moving next month.

4. Like *yes/no* questions, tags always use a form of *be*, or an auxiliary verb (a form of *be, do, have,* or *will,* or modal verbs such as *can, could, should* or *would*).

a. If the statement uses the verb *be*, use a form of *be* in the tag, too.

It**'s** a nice day, **isn't** it?

b. If the statement uses an auxiliary verb, use the auxiliary in the tag, too.

You**'ve** lived here a long time, **haven't** you?
You **can** drive, **can't** you?
You**'ll** be here tomorrow, **won't** you?

c. If the statement does not use the verb *be* or an auxiliary, you must use the appropriate form of *do* in the tag.

You **come** from New York, **don't** you?
He **lives** nearby, **doesn't** he?
They **moved** here years ago, **didn't** they?

5. If the verb in the statement is affirmative, the verb in the tag is negative. If the verb in the statement is negative, the verb in the tag is affirmative.

Affirmative   **Negative**
You **work** on Fridays, **don't you?**

Negative   **Affirmative**
You **don't work** on Fridays, **do you?**

Be careful! Only use pronouns in the tag:

Tom works on Fridays, **doesn't he?** NOT
~~Tom works on Fridays, **doesn't Tom?**~~

Notice that when the subject of the statement is *that*, the subject of the tag is *it:*

That's a good idea, **isn't it?** NOT ~~That's a good idea, **isn't that?**~~

6. Answer all tag questions the same way you answer *yes/no* questions.

A: You're from L.A., aren't you?
OR
You're not from L.A., are you?
(Are you from L.A.?)

B: Yes, I am. I've lived here all my life.
OR
No, I'm not. I'm from New York.

FOCUSED PRACTICE

1. Discover the Grammar

Read the conversation between Tom and a friend. Underline all the tags.

Kay: Hi, Tom. Nice day, <u>isn't it?</u>

Tom: Sure is. Not a cloud in the sky. How are you doing?

Kay: Pretty good, thanks. You don't know of any vacant apartments, do you? My son is looking for one.

Tom: He is? I thought he was staying with you.

Kay: Well, he just got a new job, and he wants a place of his own. Do you know of anything?

Tom: As a matter of fact, I do. Some friends of mine are moving to New York next month.

Kay: They are? What kind of apartment do they have?

Tom: A one-bedroom.

Kay: It's not furnished, is it?

Tom: No. Why? He doesn't need a furnished apartment, does he?

Kay: Well, it would be better. He doesn't have much furniture. But I guess he can always rent some, can't he?

Tom: Why don't you give your son my number, and I'll give him some more information.

Kay: Will you? Thanks, Tom.

2. Getting Ready to Move

Roberta and her husband are talking about their move. Match the statements with the tags.

	Statement		Tag
__i__	1. You've called the movers,	a.	can we?
_____	2. They're coming tomorrow,	b.	do we?
_____	3. This isn't going to be cheap,	c.	is he?
_____	4. You haven't finished packing,	d.	isn't it?
_____	5. We don't need any more boxes,	e.	aren't they?
_____	6. Paul is going to help us,	f.	have you?
_____	7. We can put some things in storage,	g.	isn't he?
_____	8. Jack isn't buying our bookcases,	h.	is it?
_____	9. We need to disconnect the phone,	i.	haven't you?

_____ 10. The movers aren't packing the books for us,   j. don't we?

_____ 11. We can't turn off the electricity yet,   k. can't we?

_____ 12. Moving is hard,   l. are they?

3. A TV Interview

Complete the interview with appropriate tags or tag questions.

Host: You've lived in Hollywood for many years, _____ haven't you _____?
                                                                      1.

Guest: Since I was eighteen and came here to write my first screenplay. Seems like ages ago. Looking back now, I can't believe I just packed one suitcase and got on a plane.

Host: You didn't know anyone here either, _____?
                                                                  2.

Guest: No. And I didn't have a cent to my name. Just some ideas and a lot of hope. It sounds crazy,

_____?
     3.

Host: Not when you look at all the movies you've done. Things have sure worked out for you,

_____? You've already written four major hits, and you've done
     4.

some work for television as well. You're working on another screenplay now,

_____?
     5.

Guest: Yes. It's a comedy about some kids who become invisible.

Host: Sounds like a good movie for the whole family. I know I'll certainly take my kids to see it.

Speaking of kids, you have some of your own, _____?
                                                                     6.

Guest: Two boys and a girl—both very visible!

Host: I know what you mean. Do you ever wish they were invisible?

Guest: Hmmm. That's an interesting thought, _____?
                                                                    7.

4. L.A. People

Read the information about film director Tim Burton. Imagine you are going to interview him, and you are not sure of the underlined information. Write tag questions to check that information.

1. Tim Burton: Film director, screenplay writer, <u>cartoonist</u> (?)

2. born and <u>grew up in Burbank</u> (?), a suburb of L.A.

3. made home movies as a child, <u>has always loved horror films</u> (?)

4. worked for Disney Studios, but <u>they didn't like his work</u> (?) It was too unusual for them.

5. directed Batman in 1989 — it was a huge success, but Burton <u>wasn't satisfied with</u> Batman (?) He was too rushed to do a good job.

6. finished Batman Returns in 1992. Burton <u>liked</u> Batman Returns <u>better</u> (?)

7. enjoys making films, but <u>doesn't like publicity</u> (?) and hates the way Hollywood does things

8. <u>isn't planning to leave the business</u> (?) — just opened his own company.

1. _____ You're a cartoonist, aren't you? _____
2. _____
3. _____
4. _____
5. _____
6. _____
7. _____
8. _____

COMMUNICATION PRACTICE

5. Practice Listening

Listen to these people ask questions. Notice if their voices rise or fall at the end of each question. Listen again and decide in each case if they are really asking a question (and expect an answer) or if they are just making a comment (and don't expect an answer). Check the correct column.

Expect an Answer	Don't Expect an Answer
1. ☐	☑
2. ☐	☐
3. ☐	☐
4. ☐	☐
5. ☐	☐
6. ☐	☐
7. ☐	☐
8. ☐	☐

6. Who Knows Better?

How much do you know about your classmates? Work with a partner. Complete these ten tag questions. Then check your answers with your partner. Check all the information that you got correct. Count the number of checks. Which one of you knows the other one better?

1. _____, aren't you?

2. _____, can you?

3. _____, don't you?

4. _____, haven't you?

5. _____, did you?

6. _____, do you?

7. _____, are you?

8. _____, will you?

(continued on next page)

9. _____, didn't you?

10. _____, can't you?

Add your own questions.

11. _____, _____?

12. _____, _____?

> **Examples:**
> **A:** You're from Venezuela, aren't you?
> **B:** That's right.
>
>   OR
>
> No, I'm from Colombia.
>
> **A:** You can't speak Portuguese, can you?
> **B:** No, I can't.

7. Information Gap: Los Angeles and New York

Work with a partner.

Student A, look at the questions below. What do you know about Los Angeles? Circle the correct words and complete the tag questions.

Student B, turn to the Information Gap for Unit 6 on pages IG 1 and 2 in the back of the book. Follow the instructions there.

> **Example:**
> **A:** Los Angeles is one of the (largest)/smallest cities in the United States, (isn't it?)
> **B:** That's right.

1. Los Angeles <u>is/isn't</u> the capital of California, _____?

2. Los Angeles is located on the <u>Pacific/Atlantic</u> Ocean, _____?

3. There <u>are/aren't</u> a lot of famous movie studios in L.A., _____?

4. The city <u>has/doesn't have</u> a problem with air pollution, _____?

5. There <u>are/aren't</u> a lot of cars in L.A., _____?

Ask Student B the same questions. He or she will read a paragraph about Los Angeles and tell you if your information is correct or not.

Now read about New York City and answer Student B's questions.

New York City

New York is the largest city in the United States. Located at the mouth of the Hudson River, New York consists of five separate "boroughs," or parts: the Bronx, Brooklyn, Manhattan, Queens, and Staten Island. With its ninety-four universities and colleges, it is one of the major educational centers in the country. New York's historical importance, as well as its fine cultural life, make it a major tourist attraction.

8. It's a Nice Place to Live, Isn't It?

Work in small groups. Role-play an on-the-street interview like the one beginning on page 78. Ask how people feel about life in your city or town. Use tag questions.

Example:
A: You're not originally from here, are you?
B: No, but I've lived here for five years.

Additions
and
Responses
with *So, Too,
Neither,
Not either,*
and *But*

INTRODUCTION

▶️ *Read and listen to this magazine article about identical twins.*

THE TWIN QUESTION: NATURE OR NURTURE?

Mark and Gerald are identical twins. Mirror images of each other, they also share many similarities in lifestyle. Mark hasn't ever been married, and **Gerald hasn't either.** Mark is a firefighter, and **so is Gerald.** Mark likes hunting, fishing, going to the beach, eating Chinese food, and watching John Wayne movies. **Gerald does too.**

These similarities might not be unusual in identical twins, except for one fact: Mark and Gerald were separated when they were five days old and grew up in different states with different families. Neither Mark nor Gerald knew that he had a twin. The two men found each other accidentally when they were thirty-one, and they discovered their almost identical lifestyles at that time.

Average people are fascinated by twins like Mark and Gerald. **So are serious researchers.** Identical twins share the same genes. Therefore, they offer researchers the chance to study the effect of genetic inheritance on disease, length of life, and personality.

However, identical twins who grow up together also experience the same influences from their environment. How can researchers separate environmental factors from genetic factors? Identical

twins who are separated at birth and grow up in different environments offer researchers a way to investigate the age-old question: Which has more effect on our lives, heredity (the genes we receive from our parents) or environment

(the social influences in our childhood)?

Some startling coincidences have turned up in recent studies of identical twins separated at birth. Perhaps the most astonishing twins of all are the Springer and Lewis brothers, who were adopted by different families soon after they were born. The Springer family named their adopted son Jim. **So did the Lewis family.** When the two Jims met for the first time as forty-year-old adults, they discovered that their similarities went way beyond their identical names and looks. Jim Lewis had worked as a gas station attendant and a law enforcement agent. **So had Jim Springer.** Lewis chewed his fingernails when he was nervous, and **Springer did too.** Both men had had dogs. Lewis had named his Toy; **so had Springer.** And believe it or not, Lewis had married a woman named Linda, divorced her, and later married a woman named Betty. **So had Springer.**

Do our genes really determine our names, the people we marry, the jobs we choose, even the pets we adopt? The lives of other twins indicate that the question of nature or nurture is more complicated than that.

Identical twins Andrea and Barbara, for example, were born in Germany and separated shortly after birth. Andrea stayed in Germany, **but Barbara didn't.** She moved to the United States with her adoptive American family. The twins grew up in different cultures, speaking different languages. Barbara didn't know she had a twin, **but Andrea did,** and she searched for her sister until she found her. When they met they discovered some amazing similarities. Each had a scar on her lip from an accident. Each had had a tonsillectomy—on the same day!

Nevertheless, their personalities and life histories were quite different. Andrea is outgoing and expressive, **but Barbara** **isn't,** despite her identical genetic heritage. Both sisters got married and had two children. Andrea stayed married to the same man, **but Barbara didn't.** In fact, Barbara married and divorced several times.

Clearly, heredity isn't the only force that governs our lives, and **neither is environment.** The lives of twins separated at birth suggest that we have a lot to learn about the complex role these two powerful forces play in our lives.

ADDITIONS WITH *SO, TOO, NEITHER, NOT EITHER*

WITH *BE* AS THE MAIN VERB

SUBJECT + *BE*	*(AND) SO + BE +* SUBJECT	SUBJECT + *BE + NOT*	*(AND) + NEITHER + BE +* SUBJECT
Andrea **is** a twin,	**and so is** Barbara.	Andrea **isn't** very tall,	**and neither is** Barbara.

SUBJECT + *BE*	*(AND) +* SUBJECT + *BE + TOO*	SUBJECT + *BE + NOT*	*(AND) +* SUBJECT + *BE + NOT EITHER*
Andrea **is** a twin,	**and** Barbara **is too.**	Andrea **isn't** very tall,	**and** Barbara **isn't either.**

WITH AUXILIARY VERBS

SUBJECT + AUXILIARY	*(AND) + SO +* AUXILIARY + SUBJECT	SUBJECT + AUXILIARY + *NOT*	*(AND) NEITHER +* AUXILIARY + SUBJECT
Andrea **has** had two children,	**and so has** Barbara.	Andrea **can't** speak Chinese,	**and neither can** Barbara.

SUBJECT + AUXILIARY	*(AND) +* SUBJECT + AUXILIARY + *TOO*	SUBJECT + AUXILIARY + *NOT*	*(AND) +* SUBJECT + AUXILIARY + *NOT EITHER*
Andrea **has** had two children,	**and** Barbara **has too.**	Andrea **can't** speak Chinese,	**and** Barbara **can't either.**

(continued on next page)

WITH OTHER VERBS

SUBJECT + VERB	(AND) + SO + DO + SUBJECT
Andrea **has** a scar,	**and so does** Barbara.

SUBJECT + DO NOT + VERB	(AND) + NEITHER + DO + SUBJECT
Andrea **doesn't** have her tonsils,	**and neither does** Barbara.

SUBJECT + VERB	(AND) + SUBJECT + DO + TOO
Andrea **has** a scar,	**and** Barbara **does too.**

SUBJECT + DO NOT + VERB	(AND) + SUBJECT + DO NOT + EITHER
Andrea **doesn't** have her tonsils,	**and** Barbara **doesn't either.**

ADDITIONS WITH *BUT*

WITH *BE* AS THE MAIN VERB

SUBJECT + BE	BUT + SUBJECT + BE NOT
Andrea **is** outgoing,	**but** Barbara **isn't.**

SUBJECT + BE NOT	BUT + SUBJECT + BE
Andrea **isn't** quiet,	**but** Barbara **is.**

WITH AUXILIARY VERBS

SUBJECT + AUXILIARY	BUT + SUBJECT + AUXILIARY + NOT
Andrea **has** stayed with her husband,	**but** Barbara **hasn't.**

SUBJECT + AUXILIARY + NOT	BUT + SUBJECT + AUXILIARY
Andrea **couldn't** speak English,	**but** Barbara **could.**

WITH OTHER VERBS

SUBJECT + VERB	BUT + SUBJECT + DO NOT
Andrea **lives** in Germany,	**but** Barbara **doesn't.**

SUBJECT + DO NOT	BUT + SUBJECT + DO
Andrea **doesn't** speak English,	**but** Barbara **does.**

Grammar Notes

1. Use *so*, *too*, *neither*, and *not either* to join or add to statements of similarity.

> Mark is a firefighter, **and so is Gerald.**

> OR

> Mark is a firefighter, **and Gerald is too.**

Both of these sentences mean *Mark is a firefighter, and Gerald is a firefighter, too.*

> Mark isn't married. **Neither is Gerald.**

> OR

> Mark isn't married. **Gerald isn't either.**

Both of these pairs of sentences mean Mark and Gerald are both unmarried.

In the examples above, note that *so*, *too*, *either*, and *not either* can "attach" a clause of similarity or can add a second sentence of similarity.

2. These additions always use a form of *be* or an auxiliary verb (a form of *be, have, do,* or *will* or modal verbs such as *can, could, should,* or *would*).

   a. If the first statement uses the verb *be*, use *be* in the second statement, too.

   > **I'm** a twin, and so **is** my cousin.

   b. If the first statement uses an auxiliary verb, use the auxiliary verb in the second statement, too.

   > Jim Lewis **had** worked in a gas station, and so **had** Jim Springer.
   > I **can't** drive, and neither **can** my brother.

   c. If the first statement doesn't use the verb *be* or an auxiliary verb, you must use the appropriate form of *do* in the attached statement.

   > Jim Lewis **bought** a Chevrolet, and so **did** his brother.
   > Jim Lewis **owns** a dog, and so **does** his brother.

3. Use *be* or the auxiliary with *so* and *too* if the first statement is affirmative.

   > Mark **is** a firefighter, and **so is Gerald**.

   > OR

   > Mark **is** a firefighter, and **Gerald is too**.

4. Use *be* or the auxiliary with *neither* or *not . . . either* if the first statement is negative.

   > Mark **didn't** get married. **Neither did Gerald.**

   > OR

   > Mark **didn't** get married. **Gerald didn't either.**

Be careful! Notice the word order after *so* and *neither*. The verb comes before the subject.

> So **is Gerald**. NOT ~~So Gerald is~~.
> Neither **did Gerald**. NOT ~~Neither Gerald did~~.

5. Use *but* to join or add statements of contrast.

   > Andrea **lived** in Germany, **but Barbara didn't.**
   > Andrea's family **didn't speak** English, **but Barbara's did.**

Notice that you can use *but* if the first statement is affirmative or negative.

6. In conversation, you can use short responses with *so*, *too*, *neither*, and *not either* to express agreement with another speaker. These short responses are sometimes called "rejoinders."

   > A: I **have** a twin sister.
   > B: **So do I.**
   >> OR
   > **I do too.**

   > A: **I don't** have any brothers or sisters.
   > B: **Neither do I.**
   >> OR
   > **I don't either.**

(continued on next page)

Usage note: In informal speech people say *Me too* to express agreement with an affirmative statement and *me neither* to express agreement with a negative statement.

> A: I think twin studies are fascinating.
> B: **Me too.**

> A: I've never heard of the Jim twins.
> B: **Me neither.**

7. In conversation, use short responses with *but* to express disagreement with another speaker.

> A: I **wouldn't like** to have a twin.
> B: Oh, **but I would.**

Notice that you can often omit *but*.

> A: I **wouldn't like** to be a twin.
> B: **I would.**

FOCUSED PRACTICE

1. Discover the Grammar

Read these short conversations between reunited twins. Decide if the statement that follows each conversation is true (T) *or false* (F).

1. **Mark:** I like Chinese food.

   Gerald: So do I.

   _T_ Gerald likes Chinese food.

2. **Andrea:** I don't want to go out tonight.

   Barbara: Neither do I.

   _____ Barbara wants to go out tonight.

3. **Amy:** I didn't understand that article.

   Kerrie: Oh, I did.

   _____ Kerrie understood the article.

4. **Jean:** I'm not hungry.

   Joan: I'm not either.

   _____ Jean and Joan are hungry.

5. **Andrea:** I was born in Germany.

   Barbara: So was I.

   _____ Barbara was born in Germany.

6. **Amy:** I've always felt lonely.

    Kerri: So have I.

    _____ Kerrie has felt lonely.

7. **Mark:** I'm ready to get married.

    Gerald: I'm not.

    _____ Gerald is ready to get married.

8. **Dewayne:** I can meet at eight o'clock.

    Paul: I can too.

    _____ Paul can meet at eight o'clock.

9. **Jim:** I have a headache.

    Jim: So do I.

    _____ Both Jims have headaches.

10. **Dewayne:** I'm not looking forward to the TV interview.

    Paul: I am.

    _____ Paul isn't looking forward to the TV interview.

2. We Have So Much in Common

Two twins are talking. They agree on everything. Complete their conversation with responses.

Marta: I'm so happy we finally found each other.

Carla: So _____*am I*_____. I always felt like something was missing from my life.
        1.

Marta: So _____. I always knew I had a double somewhere out there.
        2.

Carla: I can't believe how similar we are.

Marta: Neither _____. It's like always seeing myself in the mirror.
        3.

Carla: I know what you mean. Not only do we look identical, we like and dislike all the same things.

Marta: Right. I hate lettuce.

Carla: I _____. And I detest liver.
      4.

Marta: So _____. I love pizza, though.
       5.

Carla: So _____. But only with tomato and cheese. I don't like pepperoni.
       6.

Marta: Neither _____.
        7.

Carla: This is amazing! I wonder if our husbands have so much in common.

Marta: So _____!
       8.

3. The Two Bobs

Look at this chart about the twins' husbands. Then complete the sentences about them. Add statements with **so, too, neither, not either,** *and* **but.**

	Bob Bowen	Bob Phillips
Age	42	42
Height	6'2"	5'8"
Weight	180 lbs.	180 lbs.
Color hair	blond	blond
Color eyes	blue	brown
Hobbies	tennis	tennis
Military service	yes	no
Education	graduate degree	graduate degree
Job	lawyer	engineer
Brothers or sisters	none	none

1. Bob Bowen is 42, _____ and so is Bob Phillips. _____

   OR

   _____ and Bob Phillips is too. _____

2. Bob Bowen is 6'2", _____

3. Bob Bowen weighs 180 pounds, _____

4. Bob Bowen has blond hair, _____

5. Bob Bowen doesn't have green eyes, _____

6. Bob Bowen plays tennis, _____

7. Bob Bowen served in the military, _____

8. Bob Bowen has attended graduate school, _____

9. Bob Bowen became a lawyer, _____

10. Bob Bowen doesn't have any brothers or sisters, _____

4. My Brother and I

Read this student's composition. There are five mistakes in sentence additions. Find and correct them.

My Brother and I

My brother is just a year older than I am. We have a lot of things in common. We look alike. I am 5' 10", and so ~~he is~~ *is he*. I have straight black hair and dark brown eyes, and so does he. We share some of the same interests, too. I love to play soccer, and he too. Both of us swim every day, but I can't dive, and either can he.

Although there are a lot of similarities between us, there are also many differences. For example, he likes eating all kinds of food, but I don't. Give me hamburgers and fries every day! My brother doesn't want to go to college, but I don't. I believe it's important to get as much education as possible, but he wants to get real-life experience. Our personalities are quite different. I am quiet and easy-going, but he not. He has lots of energy and talks a lot. When I think about it, we really are more different than similar.

COMMUNICATION PRACTICE

5. Practice Listening

A couple is out on a first date. Listen to their conversation. Then listen again and complete the chart.

	✓ = Yes	X = No
	Man	**Woman**
1. loves Italian food	✓	✓
2. cooks	☐	☐
3. eats out a lot	☐	☐
4. enjoys old movies	☐	☐
5. reads biographies	☐	☐
6. enjoys fiction	☐	☐
7. plays sports	☐	☐
8. watches sports on TV	☐	☐
9. watches news programs	☐	☐
10. wants to see the documentary	☐	☐

6. Let's Eat Out

Work in pairs. Look at these two restaurant ads. What do the two restaurants have in common? In what ways are they different? Discuss these questions and agree upon the restaurant you want to go to.

Luigi's
Italian Restaurant

Family-style eating since 1990

Open Tuesday–Sunday, 12:00–9:00

EARLY-BIRD SPECIAL
(full dinner for $10.95 if ordered before 6:00)

No reservations necessary
No credit cards

875 Orange St.

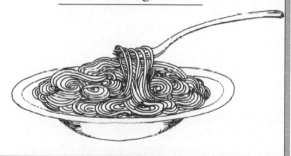

Antonio's
Ristorante Italiano

Established in 1990

Relaxed dining in a romantic atmosphere

open seven days a week—dinner only
reservations suggested

all credit cards accepted

1273 Orange Street 453-3285

one free beverage with this ad

Example:
A: Luigi's serves Italian food.
B: So does Antonio's.

7. A Good Match?

Work in pairs. Look at the chart in exercise 5. Do you think that the man and woman are a good "match"? Discuss your reasons. How important is it for couples to have a lot in common?

Example:
The man and woman have a lot in common.
He loves Italian food, and so does she.

8. How Compatible Are You?

Complete these statements. Then read your statements to a classmate. He or she will give you a short response. Check the items the two of you have in common.

Example:
A: I like to walk in the rain.
B: So do I.
OR
Oh, I don't. I like to stay home and watch TV.

I Have These Things in Common with:

	(Classmate 1)	(Classmate 2)
1. I like to _____	✓	☐
2. I never _____	☐	☐
3. I get angry when _____	☐	☐
4. I hate _____ (name of food)	☐	☐
5. I love _____ (name of food)	☐	☐
6. I can _____	☐	☐
7. I can't _____	☐	☐
8. I believe that people _____	☐	☐
9. I would like to _____	☐	☐
10. I have never _____	☐	☐
11. When I was younger, I didn't _____	☐	☐
12. I will never _____	☐	☐
13. I should _____	☐	☐
14. I have to _____	☐	☐

Now work with another classmate. Count the number of checks for each of the two classmates. Which classmate do you have more in common with?

9. Michael and Matthew

Work with a partner. Look at the picture of these twins. How many things do they have in common? How many differences can you find? You have eight minutes to write your answers. Then compare your answers with those of another pair.

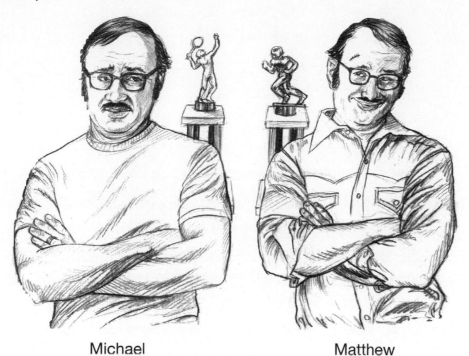

Michael   Matthew

Example:
Michael has a mustache, and so does Matthew.

10. Twins

Do you know any twins? If so, write about them. What do they have in common? What are their differences? If you don't know any twins, write about two people who are close (siblings, cousins, friends, spouses, etc.). Use the composition in exercise 4 as a model.

11. Nature or Nurture?

Reread the article beginning on page 88. Which is more important, nature or nurture? Have a class discussion. Give examples to support your views.

I. *Complete these question tags.*

1. Mr. Chen comes from China, ___doesn't he___?

2. He's staying with the Carsons, _____?

3. The Carsons don't speak Chinese, _____?

4. They've been to China before, _____?

5. They didn't meet each other in China, _____?

6. They got to know him in school, _____?

7. Mr. Chen was studying English, _____?

8. He hadn't known them before, _____?

9. We're having dinner with them Saturday night, _____?

10. We should bring something, _____?

11. It probably won't be a late evening, _____?

12. We'll have a lot of questions to ask, _____?

II. *Complete the questions with an appropriate form of the verbs in parentheses. Choose between affirmative and negative.*

1. The population of China _____is_____ over a billion, isn't it?
   (be)

2. In land area, it _____ much bigger than the United
   (be)
   States, is it?

3. China _____ a lot of rice, doesn't it?
   (export)

4. The Yangtze Delta _____ 25 percent of China's rice
   (produce)
   crop, doesn't it?

5. To stop erosion, the Chinese _____ now _____
   (plant)
   millions of trees, aren't they?

6. Beijing _____ always _____ the capital of China,
   (be)
   has it?

7. Marco Polo _____ Beijing, did he?
   (build)

8. Kublai Khan _____ Beijing Dadu, didn't he?
   (name)

9. The Chinese language _____ an alphabet system, does
   (use)
   it?

10. The Chinese _____ different dialects, don't they?
    (speak)

III. *Circle the letter of the appropriate response.*

1. John lives in L.A.
   - (a.) So does Alice.
   - b. Neither does Alice.
   - c. But Alice does.
2. He used to live in New York.
   - a. Neither did Alice.
   - b. But Alice didn't.
   - c. Alice didn't either.
3. Alice got married two years ago.
   - a. John didn't either.
   - b. So did John.
   - c. But John did.
4. Alice has been to China.
   - a. So has John.
   - b. Neither has John.
   - c. But John has.
5. John works for A. Linden & Co.
   - a. Alice can too.
   - b. So does Alice.
   - c. But Alice isn't.
6. Alice has been there for five years.
   - a. But John hasn't.
   - b. John hasn't either.
   - c. John is too.
7. Alice is looking for a new job.
   - a. So is John.
   - b. But John doesn't.
   - c. John isn't either.
8. He has an interview tomorrow.
   - a. But Alice does.
   - b. Alice does too.
   - c. Alice doesn't either.
9. John should look at the employment ads.
   - a. But Alice should.
   - b. Neither should Alice.
   - c. So should Alice.
10. Alice was going to speak to her boss.
    - a. So did John.
    - b. So was John.
    - c. So will John.

IV. *Complete these conversations with responses.*

1. **A:** I've never eaten here before.

   B: I _____haven't either_____. But it's supposed to be very good.

2. **A:** I don't like cabbage.

   B: _____ my husband. He never eats the stuff. Maybe they have another vegetable.

3. **A:** My dish tastes very salty.

   B: _____ mine. We're going to be really thirsty later.

4. **A:** My mother used to make this dish.

   B: My mother _____. It was always one of my favorites.

5. **A:** I was going to invite Alice to join us.

   B: That's funny. _____ too. Maybe next time.

6. **A:** I'd love some dessert.

   B: _____ I. The chocolate cake looks good.

7. **A:** I'm full.

   B: I _____. I can't eat another bite.

8. **A:** Luigi's doesn't accept credit cards.

   B: This restaurant _____. But don't worry. I have enough cash on me.

9. **A:** I shouldn't have any more coffee.

   B: _____ I. I won't be able to sleep.

10. **A:** I'm glad we did this.

    B: _____ I. It was a lot of fun.

V. *Read this letter. There are five mistakes in sentence additions and tag questions. Find and correct them.*

Dear Stacy,

How are you? Things here are pretty good. You're still rooming with Marta, aren't you? Well, I just got a new roommate. Her name is Rafaella, and we have a lot in common. She's 18, and so ~~I am~~ *am I*. She used to live in Chicago, and, of course, I did too. She likes old movies, but so do I. We have the same study habits, too. She doesn't stay up late, and neither don't I.

Luckily, there are some important differences, too. As you may remember, I'm not very neat, but Rafaella is. I don't like to cook, but she does either. So life is improving. You have a break soon, do you? Why don't you come for a visit? I know the three of us would have a good time.

Write soon.

Love,

Mona

IV

▼

Gerunds
and
Infinitives

Gerunds and Infinitives: Review and Expansion

INTRODUCTION

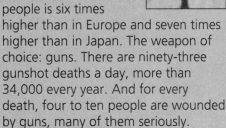

Read and listen to this editorial about gun control from a U.S. magazine.

·········· VIEWPOINT ··········

STOP LIVING IN FEAR

GERARD TAYLOR

Some shocking statistics: In the United States, the rate of murders per 100,000 people is six times higher than in Europe and seven times higher than in Japan. The weapon of choice: guns. There are ninety-three gunshot deaths a day, more than 34,000 every year. And for every death, four to ten people are wounded by guns, many of them seriously.

Americans have long had an international reputation **for being** in love with their guns. But it seems like they are finally getting **fed up with becoming** victims of a growing epidemic of gun violence. In fact, according to recent opinion polls, a majority of voters are now **in favor of Congress's passing** more laws **to control** handguns, the most frequently used firearms.

The Brady law, passed in 1994 after years of debate, seemed like a victory for gun control at the time. This law **requires would-be gun owners to wait** five days **before purchasing** a handgun. The purpose of the waiting period is **to give police time to check** that the prospective customer does not have a criminal record. It also prevents people **from committing** impulse crimes. (The waiting period gives people time to **stop to think** things through **before acting** rashly.) Now some critics realize that the law doesn't go far enough **in curbing** gun violence. For one thing, criminals easily succeed **in getting** hold of the more than 200 million firearms already out there.

What else can be done **besides imposing** waiting periods on the purchase of guns? One senator has suggested "bullet control." **Banning** certain kinds of ammunition would make it harder **to stand** on top of buildings and **spray** bullets at crowds of people below. The same senator has also **proposed taxing** ammunition at a rate of 10,000%. Others **suggest making** it more difficult **to get** a license **to sell** guns. One social critic points out that it is much harder **to get** a California driver's license than it is **to obtain** a license that **enables you to acquire** a whole arsenal of weapons and **to have** them shipped right to your home.

The biggest opponent of gun control is, of course, the National Rifle Association. Its 2.5 million members have succeeded **in defeating** national gun-control legislation for years. Their position: "Guns don't kill people. People kill people."

A recent study, however, of two cities now goes far **in providing** an answer to the NRA. Seattle in the United States and Vancouver in Canada are similar economically, ethnically, socially, and culturally. Their crime statistics are also similar except for one: You are eight times more **likely to get** shot in Seattle than in Vancouver. The only factor that explains the large difference in their murder rates is the widespread availability of guns in the United States compared to Canada, which practices strict gun control. Clearly, people with guns kill people much more frequently than people without guns.

People around the world think our gun culture is crazy, and they are right. We must **stop thinking** of ourselves as noble frontierspeople who need weapons **to survive**—or the already shocking statistics will get worse. According to a recent Harvard School of Public Health Survey, 59 percent of children in the sixth to twelfth grade said it was easy for them **to get** handguns. Gun control may not be the entire answer, but it is a start.

What about our constitutional **right to bear** arms, ask members of the National Rifle Association. This "right" is undermining the very freedom our constitution **meant to protect:** freedom from fear. **Locking** oneself behind closed doors and **staying** off the streets out of fear **of being** shot at does not constitute freedom. Do we want to **stop living** in fear? If so, **restricting** guns is a small **price to pay.**

Gun Murders in a Recent Year

1,582	New York City, U.S.A.
67	London, England
1,480	Miami, U.S.A.
16	Manchester, England
666	Chicago, U.S.A.
61	Toronto, Canada
695	Detroit, U.S.A.
75	Munich, Germany

GERUNDS AND INFINITIVES

GERUNDS
Banning guns is necessary.
They **recommend banning** handguns.
Voters **started supporting** gun control.
She **remembered locking up** the gun.
We're tired **of reading** crime statistics.
We're shocked at **his voting** against it.

INFINITIVES
It's necessary **to ban** guns.
They **refuse to ban** handguns.
Voters **started to support** gun control.
She **remembered to lock up** the gun.
We were **surprised to read** the statistics.
We urged **him to vote** against it.
It's **time to take** action.

Grammar Notes

1. The gerund is often used as the subject of a sentence.

   > **Reducing** the number of handguns is essential.
   > **Not admitting** the problem is foolish.

   You can also reverse the order of the sentence and use *it* + adjective + the infinitive to make general statements.

   > **It** is **essential to reduce** the number of handguns.
   > **It**'s **foolish not to admit** the problem.

2. The gerund is often used after certain verbs as the object of the verb.

   > I **dislike owning** a gun.
   > The teachers **discussed not allowing** toy weapons in school.

   Use a possessive (*Anne's, the boy's, my, your, his, her, its, our, their*) before the gerund when necessary.

   > I dislike **John's owning** a gun.
   > I dislike **his owning** a gun.
   > (John owns a gun. I dislike it.)

   Usage note: In informal spoken English, many people use object pronouns instead of possessives before the gerund.

   > I dislike **him owning** a gun.

   See Appendix 3 on page A4 for a list of verbs that can be followed by the gerund.

3. Some verbs can be followed by the infinitive. These verbs fall into three patterns:

   a. Verbs followed directly by the infinitive.

      > The president **hopes to pass** new gun-control laws.
      > He **swore not to give up** on the issue of gun control.

   b. Verbs followed by an object plus the infinitive.

      > The president **urged Congress to pass** legislation.
      > He **urged them to pass** legislation.
      > He **urged them not to delay.**

   c. Verbs with or without an object plus the infinitive.

      > The president **wants to control** guns.
      > The president **wants the police to control** guns.

   See Appendices 4 and 5 on page A5 for a list of these verbs.

   Usage note: In formal written English, it is considered incorrect to "split" an infinitive by placing a word between *to* and the base form of the verb. However, many people do not follow this rule.

> He wants to ban the sale of handguns immediately. NOT ~~He wants to immediately ban the sale of handguns.~~

4. Some verbs can be followed by either the gerund or the infinitive.

> I **started collecting** signatures of people in favor of gun control.

> OR

> I **started to collect** signatures of people in favor of gun control.

See Appendix 6 on page A5 for a list of these verbs.

Be careful! A few verbs (for example, *stop, remember,* and *forget*) can be followed by either the gerund or the infinitive, but the meanings are very different.

> He **stopped buying** guns. (He doesn't buy guns anymore.)
> He **stopped to buy** a gun. (He stopped another activity in order to buy a gun.)

> She **remembered registering** her gun. (First she registered the gun. Then she remembered that she did it. She can picture it in her mind.)
> She **remembered to register** her gun. (First she remembered. Then she registered the gun. She didn't forget.)

> She **forgot to sign** the petition. (She didn't sign.)
> She **forgot signing** the petition. (She signed, but afterward she didn't remember the event.)

5. Remember that there are certain verb + preposition and adjective + preposition combinations that must be followed by the gerund and not the infinitive.

> I don't **approve of allowing** people to carry guns.
> We're **interested in banning** civilian use of assault weapons.

Be careful! *To* can be part of an infinitive or it can be a preposition. Use the gerund after the preposition *to*.

> We look forward **to seeing** new gun legislation. NOT ~~We look forward to see new gun legislation~~.

See Appendices 7 and 8 on page A6 for lists of common verb-plus-preposition and adjective-plus-preposition combinations.

6. Use the infinitive to explain the purpose of an action.

> She keeps a gun at home **to protect herself.**

7. The infinitive can often follow an adjective. Many of these adjectives express feelings or attitudes about the action in the infinitive.

> She was **eager to hear** the president's speech.
> I was **glad to learn** that he supported gun control.
> Congress is **ready to vote** on the proposal.

See Appendix 9 on page A6 for a list of common adjectives that can be followed by the infinitive.

8. The infinitive can also follow certain nouns.

> It's **time to ban** all guns.
> We have a **right to bear** arms.
> They made a **decision to wait.**
> It's a small **price to pay** for freedom.
> She has **permission to carry** a gun.

FOCUSED PRACTICE

1. Discover the Grammar

Read this survey and petition on gun control. Underline the gerunds and circle the infinitives.

Opinion Survey on Gun Control

Please take a few minutes (to answer) these questions.

1. Stopping gun violence should be a priority for the U.S. Congress.

   ☐ Yes   ☐ No

2. Are you in favor of requiring a one-week waiting period between the time a person applies for a gun and the time it is sold?

   ☐ Yes   ☐ No

3. Are you against allowing people to carry concealed weapons?

   ☐ Yes   ☐ No

4. Each year, 25,000 people in the United States are killed by guns. Which statement below comes closest to your opinion about this fact?

   ☐ It's sad, but it's the price we must pay for living in a free society.

   ☐ It isn't possible to prevent the violence.

   ☐ We just need to make a greater effort to keep guns away from criminals.

5. Do you support banning civilian use of assault weapons (military-style guns that can hold up to 100 bullets)?

   ☐ Yes   ☐ No

6. Should we require the police to enforce current gun laws more strictly?

   ☐ Yes   ☐ No

7. Many people die from gun accidents each year. Should it be necessary to pass a course on handling a gun before purchasing one?

   ☐ Yes   ☐ No

National Petition to the U.S. Congress

Dear Representative:

Whereas gun violence is a national problem, stopping gun violence should be a priority for the U.S. Congress.

Whereas assault weapons and concealed handguns are the types of guns used most often in violent crimes, it is necessary to ban these weapons completely.

Whereas we should not allow criminals to purchase 5, 10, or 20 guns a month, gun purchases should be restricted to one a month.

I respectfully urge the members of Congress to work for this crucial legislation. We need to stop the tide of violent bloodshed in this country.

Sincerely,

_____

☐ **Yes,** I'm for controlling gun violence. And I want the politicians to pass sensible gun-control laws! That's why I have remembered to complete my survey, to sign my petition to Congress, and to enclose my contribution in the amount of:

   ☐ $25   ☐ $35   ☐ $50   ☐ $100   ☐ $1,000

(Your contribution will help us to get this message to Congress.)

Source: *Designed after a survey conducted by the Coalition to Stop Gun Violence.*

2. The Real Problem

This reader doesn't agree with the opinion in the editorial about gun control. Complete the letter with the correct form (gerund or infinitive) of the verbs in parentheses.

To the Editor:

With the laws we already have, it should be harder for criminals

___*to obtain*___ guns than ever before. As we all know, this is not true.
1. (obtain)

Who, then, is affected by these laws? Sportspeople, who enjoy

_____, _____, and _____ at targets.
2. (hunt)   3. (collect)   4. (shoot)

Law-abiding people, anxious _____ their homes, businesses,
5. (protect)

and families.

Let's look at the record for gun-control legislation. New York City

has some of the strictest gun-control laws in the United States, yet it

also struggles _____ one of the worst problems with illegal
6. (control)

guns. If you are a criminal in New York, it is easy _____ a
7. (buy)

gun. But law-abiding citizens find it almost impossible _____
8. (get)

permission _____ a gun for protection. In essence, New
9. (carry)

York laws prevent its honest citizens from _____ themselves.
10. (protect)

Until we solve the problem of crime in our streets, we must resist our

lawmakers' _____ stricter controls on guns for personal
11. (impose)

protection. Instead, we should challenge them _____ the real
12. (find)

causes of violence. Unfortunately, social problems such as drug dealing,

violence in the media, and the decline of family values are complex. It

takes time, effort, and money _____ them. _____
13. (solve)   14. (blame)

guns is the easy way out.

We are fortunate _____ the protection of the U.S.
15. (have)

Constitution, which guarantees U.S. citizens the right _____
16. (bear)

arms. Before _____ with the basic law of the land, we need
17. (interfere)

_____ other ways _____ gun violence. Some
18. (seek)   19. (curb)

remedies are fairly obvious: We can teach gun owners _____
20. (handle)

guns safely. We can remind them _____ firearms at home.
21. (lock up)

Remember, guns don't kill people; people do.

Al Richards

Richmond, Virginia

3. Under Fire

Read what was said at an emergency meeting about violence in one troubled urban high school. Then complete the summary statements with the appropriate verbs from the box and the gerund or infinitive form of the verbs in parentheses.

~~admit~~	agree	appreciate	consider	deny
hesitate	promise	stop	suggest	volunteer

1. **Parent:** I think we have a major problem on our hands.

    Principal: I can't deny it. Violence *is* on the rise in our school.

    SUMMARY: The principal _____admitted having_____ a big problem in the school.
    (have)

2. **Parent:** I'm not sure if I should ask this, but…

    Principal: Please, go ahead. Ask anything you want.

    Parent: Is this school really safe enough to stay open?

    SUMMARY: The parent _____ the question.
    (ask)

3. **Parent:** Why were two students suspended?

    Principal: They were suspended (cough, cough). Excuse me. I need to have a sip of water before I continue. . . .

    SUMMARY: The principal _____ some water.
    (drink)

4. **Parent:** Why aren't any students present at this meeting?

    Principal: Well, I *thought* about it but decided we should meet alone first. Maybe we can have some students attend our next meeting.

    SUMMARY: The principal _____ the students.
    (invite)

5. **Reporter:** I'm from the *City News*. Do you mind answering a few questions for the press?

    Principal: Not at all.

    SUMMARY: The principal _____ the reporter's questions.
    (answer)

6. **Reporter:** Is it true that you wear a bullet-proof vest?

    Principal: Absolutely not. That is simply not true.

    SUMMARY: The principal _____ a bullet-proof vest.
    (wear)

7. **Parent:** What about metal detectors at the door? Don't you think they might help?

    Principal: We may do that. I'm looking into it.

    SUMMARY: The parent _____ metal detectors.
    (have)

8. **Parent:** Can't we hire some more security guards?

    Principal: Yes, we *will* hire more guards. You have my word.

    SUMMARY: The principal _____ more guards.
    (hire)

9. **Parent 1:** Well, I can help patrol the halls in the afternoon.

    Parent 2: And I can put in some hours in the morning.

    SUMMARY: Two parents _____ the halls.

(patrol)

10. **Principal:** We've run out of time. I'd like to thank you all for coming to the meeting.

    SUMMARY: The principal _____ the parents'

    _____ the meeting.

(attend)

4. Problem Solving

Readers of a parents' magazine commented on violence. Summarize their comments, using the correct form of the words in parentheses.

1. My kids always acted violent after they watched cartoons on TV. They still want to watch them, but I won't tolerate that anymore.
MARY ANN PALERMO
She won't tolerate their watching cartoons on TV.
(tolerate / they / watch)

2. I wrote to my Congress member yesterday. In my letter I told her, "It's very important to vote for stricter gun-control legislation."
JIM VINCENT
_____
(urge / she / vote)

3. In our neighborhood association, we talked about inviting a police officer to our next meeting. We want the officer to teach personal safety.
SANDRA KRAMER
_____
(discuss / officer / teach)

4. Our son wanted to take up hunting as a sport. We talked to him about it, and he finally agreed to try rock climbing instead.
LISA AND TOM LIN
_____
(convince / he / take up)

5. My upstairs neighbor was robbed a few weeks ago, and now he keeps a handgun in his apartment. It makes me very nervous.
GARY KOVAC
_____
(feel nervous about / he / keep)

6. Yesterday I left my keys in the door. The letter carrier told me about it. I appreciated that.
NADIA HASSAN
_____
(appreciate / he / tell)

7. Two of my co-workers have been arguing in the office. This morning, my boss told them to resolve their problems right away. If they don't, he may fire them.
PAMELA LECLERC
_____
(warn / they / resolve)

8. Senator Lombard doesn't support gun control. This surprises me.
DAVE KASKY
_____
(surprised at / he / support)

5. In My Opinion

Read this student's opinion essay on gun control. There are ten mistakes in the use of gerunds and infinitives. Find and correct them.

banning
At this time, ~~ban~~ guns completely is a good idea. Guns don't have any useful purpose for the average citizen anymore. Two hundred years ago, when the U.S. Constitution was written, it was necessary own a gun for hunting. People also needed weapons to defending this new country. However, those reasons do not hold true now.

The NRA argues that we need keeping guns for protection from criminals. However, half of the victims of violence are attacked by acquaintances and family members, not strangers. The police can use guns to fight criminals. The rest of us should stop to use violence as a way of solving social and personal problems.

I recommend start with children. In order to prevent they learning a violent lifestyle, networks should stop broadcasting violent TV programs for children. I remember to watch violent shows for hours when I was younger. Afterwards, my brother and I would act them out. In addition, schools should start a program in resolving conflicts.

Violence costs the United States $60 billion in medical and legal expenses. Banning all guns for private citizens and learning new ways solving problems will save us billions of dollars and thousands of lives. I hope this happens. I'm in my second year of high school now, and I'm eager graduating into a peaceful society, not a violent one.

COMMUNICATION PRACTICE

6. Practice Listening

Listen to a radio talk-show debate on gun control. Then listen again and check the issues the debaters are in favor of.

	Sen. Lois Blake	Sen. Tom Wilson
1. Banning handguns	☐	✔
2. Banning assault weapons	☐	☐
3. Prohibiting hunting	☐	☐
4. Limiting the number of guns an individual may buy within a specific time period	☐	☐
5. Making the production of real-looking toy guns illegal	☐	☐
6. Holding parents responsible if their children find and use a gun	☐	☐
7. Applying the death penalty for criminals who use a gun to commit a crime	☐	☐

7. Survey

Look again at the survey on page 108. Answer the questions. Discuss your answers with your classmates. Then tally the results.

Example:
Fifteen students agree that stopping gun violence should be a priority.

8. Troubleshooting

Work in small groups. For each of the problems below, brainstorm as many solutions as you can in five minutes. Then compare your answers with those of another group. You can use some of the following expressions.

I'm in favor of...	I'm opposed to...
I support...	I'm against...
I suggest...	What about...
I go along with...	We need...
I advise...	I recommend...
We should start/stop...	I urge...

1. In the United States, more than 40,000 people die in car accidents per year. How can this number be reduced?

   Example:
   A: How about requiring people to retake the road test every year?
   B: I'm in favor of passing stricter traffic laws.
   C: We need to build safer cars.

2. Cigarette smoking is responsible for thousands of deaths and many illnesses. What can we do about it?

3. Many adults can't read or write well enough to function in society. What can be done about this problem?

4. There are millions of homeless people living in the streets and parks. How can we help solve this problem?

5. Other social problems: _____

9. A Letter to the Editor

Write a short editorial about a social problem. You can use one of the topics in exercise 8 or choose your own. Express your opinions and give reasons for your ideas.

   Example:
   I'm in favor of requiring people to take a road test every time they renew their license. By polishing their skills and knowledge every few years, people will become better drivers. . . .

Exchange editorials with a classmate. After you read your classmate's editorial, write a letter to the editor explaining why you agree or disagree with your classmate's viewpoint.

   Example:
   To the Editor:
   I go along with requiring additional road tests for drivers. People's eyesight and reflexes can change a lot in five years. . . .

🎞 *Read and listen to part of an article on teaching.*

Two Teaching Styles

All teachers want to help their students learn. There are, however, different teaching approaches. Currently, student-centered teaching has become more popular. Teachers who use this approach believe **you should let students choose** their own curriculum. In other words, allow students to decide what they want to learn. In the student-centered classroom, the teacher is viewed as a facilitator who assists students in reaching their educational goals.

If you have only experienced teacher-centered learning, you would be surprised if you walked into the student-centered classroom of Sandra Jacobson, who teaches writing at a community college. For one thing, her classroom is noisy. **Ms. Jacobson usually has her students work** in groups or pairs, and often they are all talking at once. For another, it's hard to find the teacher. Ms. Jacobson often sits in on the groups, and she looks like a student herself.

Ms. Jacobson's methods also differ from those of the traditional teacher-centered course. Ms. Jacobson doesn't assign topics or cover the students' papers with red ink. Instead, **she has her students keep** journals, and she gets her students to select their own topics from interests that emerge in their journal writing. She also uses cooperative-learning techniques such

as peer tutoring and group discussion. Her class publishes a newsletter with student writing, and a committee of students selects the writing to be published. **The committee** (not the teacher) **makes the writers revise** their writing several times, and a lot of peer tutoring occurs naturally as students do their revisions.

Although Ms. Jacobson's student-centered teaching is quite popular for some courses, many teachers still pursue a teacher-centered approach quite successfully. In this approach, the teacher controls what is taught and how it is taught. The students usually work from a textbook that has been assigned by the teacher.

Right down the hall from Ms. Jacobson is Mrs. Quintana's writing class. When you walk into this classroom, there is no mistaking who Mrs. Quintana is. At 8:05 she is standing in front of her class. The students are all at their desks. Everyone is quiet, eyes directed toward their teacher. **Mrs. Quintana has everyone turn** to page 51, an introduction to paragraph development. **She has students read** passages aloud from the book. **She makes them stop** several

times while she explains points or corrects a mispronounced word. When she finishes the presentation, she asks questions. One student can't answer, so **she has him go back and find** the answer in the material they have just read. Mrs. Quintana is well prepared, and her students are attentive. At the end of the class, she assigns the rest of the chapter for homework and announces a test for the next Wednesday. Both homework and test papers will be corrected (in red) before they are returned.

Both of these teaching approaches have many followers, but it is unclear **which approach makes students learn** more

effectively. Ms. Jacobson's student-centered approach seems more exciting, but how will students learn if **the teacher doesn't make them correct** their mistakes immediately? Do students really know enough about the subject matter to decide what they want to learn? Mrs. Quintana seems in complete control of her class, but can students learn to write just by reading about it and taking tests? By choosing topics, **is she making them write** about things that don't interest them?

Of course, such pure examples of each philosophy are not usually found. Rarely is a class totally student-centered or totally teacher-centered. **Many traditional teachers have students work** in groups. Many student-centered teachers structure their courses with a textbook, though they may use it less often than Mrs. Quintana. Most experienced teachers realize that students and situations differ, and they wisely choose the appropriate mixture of philosophies and techniques for each class.

VERBS FOLLOWED BY OBJECTS AND THE BASE FORM: *MAKE, HAVE, LET, HELP*

SUBJECT	VERB	OBJECT	BASE FORM	
They	(don't) make have let help*	us students	do	homework.

*Help can also be followed by the infinitive.

Grammar Notes

1. Some verbs can be followed by an object plus the base form of the verb. Use *make, have,* and *let* plus the base form of the verb to talk about things that someone can require, cause, or permit another person to do.*

   They **make** their students **do** homework every night. (They require them to do homework.)

   They **have** them **take** responsibility for their own learning. (They cause them to take responsibility.)

   They **let** them **choose** their own curriculum. (They permit them to choose their own curriculum.)

2. *Help* can be followed by an object and either the base form of the verb or the infinitive. The meaning is the same.

   She **helped** me **understand** the homework.

   OR

   She **helped** me **to understand** the homework.

   The first example, with the base form of the verb, is more common.

3. Be careful! *Get* is followed by an object plus the infinitive, not the base form of the verb.

   The teacher **got** us **to stay** a little later. (After some effort the teacher succeeded in persuading us to stay.) NOT ~~The teacher got us stay a little later.~~

   Several other verbs with a similar meaning (*force, cause, order*) follow the same pattern.

4. You can also use *make* to mean *cause to.*

   This will **make** you **become** a better student. (This will cause you to become a better student.)

*Make and *have* are causative verbs. In this unit they are grouped together with *let* and *help* because all four verbs are related in meaning and structure.

FOCUSED PRACTICE

1. Discover the Grammar

Read the first sentence in each set. Then circle the letter (a) *or* (b) *of the sentence that is true.*

1. My teacher made me rewrite the report.
   (a.) I wrote the report again.
   b. I didn't write the report again.

2. Ms. Trager let us use our dictionaries during the test.
   a. We were allowed to use our dictionaries.
   b. We had to use our dictionaries.

3. Mr. Goldberg had us translate a short story.
   a. Mr. Goldberg translated a short story for us.
   b. We translated a short story.

4. Paulo helped Meng do her homework.
   a. Paulo did Meng's homework for her.
   b. Both Paulo and Meng worked on her homework.

5. Ms. Bates got the director to arrange a class trip.
   a. Ms. Bates arranged a class trip.
   b. The director arranged a class trip.

6. Professor Washington let us choose our own topic for our term paper.
   a. We chose our own topic.
   b. We didn't choose our own topic.

2. Who's the Boss?

Students in an English conversation class are talking about their experiences with authority figures. Complete the sentences by circling the correct underlined verbs. Then match each situation with the person in authority.

Situation	Authority Figure
g 1. I didn't really want to work overtime this week, but she made/let me work late because some of my co-workers were sick.	a. my teacher

Situation	Authority Figure
_____ 2. I forgot to turn on my headlights before I left the parking lot a few nights ago. She <u>made/let</u> me pull over to the side of the road and asked to see my license.	b. my doctor
_____ 3. At first, we didn't really want to write in our journals. He explained that it would help us. Finally, he <u>had/got</u> us to try it.	c. my father
_____ 4. My check was delayed in the mail. I told him what had happened, and he <u>had/let</u> me pay the rent two weeks late.	d. a police officer
_____ 5. I needed to get a blood test for my school physical. He <u>got/had</u> me roll up my sleeve and make a fist.	e. the judge
_____ 6. We're a big family, and we all have our own chores. While she washed the dishes, she <u>helped/had</u> me dry. My brother swept.	f. my landlord
_____ 7. I'm an only child, and when I was young I felt lonely. He <u>let/got</u> me sleep over at my friend's house.	g. my boss
_____ 8. I wasn't paying attention, and I hit a parked car. He <u>let/made</u> me tell the court what happened.	h. my mother

3. In Class

Read these short conversations that take place in Ms. Allen's English class. Complete the summary sentences, using the correct form of the verbs in parentheses.

1. **Pablo:** Ms. Allen, do I have to rewrite this composition?

    Ms. Allen: Only if you want to.

    SUMMARY: She _____didn't make him rewrite_____ his composition.

(make / rewrite)

2. **Ms. Allen:** OK, now. Please get into groups of six.

    Class: Groups of six?

    Ms. Allen: That's right.

    SUMMARY: She _____ in groups.

(make / work)

(continued on next page)

3. **Masami:** Can we use our dictionaries during the test?

   Ms. Allen: No. You should be able to guess the meaning of the words from the context.

   SUMMARY: She _____ their dictionaries.
   (let / use)

4. **Ms. Allen:** Fernando, could you do me a favor and clean the board before you leave?

   Fernando: Sure.

   Ms. Allen: Thank you.

   SUMMARY: She _____ the board.
   (have / clean)

5. **Yasuko:** Can I leave the room?

   Ms. Allen: Of course. The key to the ladies' room is hanging next to the door.

   SUMMARY: She _____ the room.
   (let / leave)

6. **Ms. Allen:** OK. Now repeat after me: "thorn."

   Uri: "Torn."

   Ms. Allen: Try putting the tip of your tongue between your teeth like this: "th, thorn."

   Uri: "Thorn."

   Ms. Allen: That's it! Great!

   SUMMARY: She _____ an English *th*.
   (got / pronounce)

7. **Hector:** What does *intractable* mean?

   Ms. Allen: Why don't you see if one of your classmates can explain it to you?

   SUMMARY: She _____ his classmates for help.
   (have / ask)

8. **An-ling:** Do you mind if we record the class?

   Ms. Allen: Not at all. In fact I think it's an excellent idea.

   SUMMARY: She _____ the class.
   (let / record)

9. **Greta:** *Bitte, was bedeudet* telecommute? *Ich kann das Wort nicht verstehen.*

   Ms. Allen: In English, please, Greta!

   Greta: Sorry. What does *telecommute* mean?

   SUMMARY: She _____ in English.
   (make / speak)

10. **Jean-Paul:** Ms. Allen, can you recommend a video in English for us to watch?

    Ms. Allen: Sure. I have a list of recommended ones right here.

    SUMMARY: She _____ an appropriate video to rent.
    (help / find)

4. All Work and No Fun

Read this student composition. There are six mistakes.
Find and correct them.

When I was a teenager, my parents were very strict with me. They never let me ᶜᵒ play until I had finished all my homework. They even made me helping my brothers and sisters with their homework before I could have any fun.

On the one hand, I believe their discipline was good for me. By being so demanding, they certainly got me to learn a lot more. As a result I always got good grades in school. But I wish they had let me to have a little more fun. I was much too serious. I think parents should help their children learn to enjoy life. There is plenty of time for adult responsibility later on.

If I become a parent, I hope to find a good balance between discipline and permissiveness. I would want to have my child learns responsibility, but also I would want to let he or she have fun. I agree with Ben Franklin, who said that all work and no play makes Jack to become a dull boy. I want to avoid that mistake.

COMMUNICATION PRACTICE

5. Practice Listening

You are going to hear a conversation about school between a mother and her son. Before you listen, read the statements. Then listen again and write true (T) or false (F) next to each statement.

_____T_____ 1. The teacher allowed the students to choose a play to perform.

_____ 2. The teacher let the students eat cake in class.

_____ 3. The teacher is going to make the costumes for the play.

_____ 4. The mother made her son help cook dinner.

_____ 5. The son has to learn part of the play for the next day.

_____ 6. The mother is going to make her son eat dinner before he does his homework.

6. Bringing up Teenagers

Look at this list. Check the things you think are important to make and let a teenager do. Compare and discuss your list with a partner.

☐ stay out until midnight on weekends   ☐ take care of younger children

☐ stay over at a friend's house   ☐ learn to drive

☐ travel alone to a foreign country   ☐ study every day, including weekends

☐ get a part-time job   ☐ exercise

☐ dye his or her hair another color   ☐ go to the dentist every year

☐ smoke   ☐ learn another language

☐ drink alcohol   ☐ pay part of the bills

Example:
A: I think it's important to make your kids come home before midnight—even on weekends.
B: I'm not so sure. I think parents should let their children stay out late one night a week. It gives them a sense of responsibility. . . .

7. What Should You Do?

Work in small groups. Read the following situations and discuss what you should do about each one. Begin with **I think you should(n't) let/make/have/help/get . . .**

1. You are a parent. Your twelve-year-old-daughter asks permission to go to a school dance with a boy from her class who you do not know. She wants to buy a new dress and wear makeup.

    Example:
    A: I think we should let her go.
    B: Yes, but we should make her introduce the boy to us first.
    C: . . .

2. You are married. Your husband or wife wants to buy a very expensive watch. You don't think a new watch is necessary. In addition, you are saving money for a car that you both need very badly.

3. You have been dating someone for a year. Your boyfriend or girlfriend now wants to go out with other people but still continue to see you. You were hoping to marry this person.

8. Textbook Survey

Complete this survey. Then work in small groups. Compare answers. Do you and your classmates have the same perception of your textbook?

Does this textbook . . .	Always	Often	Sometimes	Rarely	Never
1. make you think?	☐	☐	☐	☐	☐
2. help you learn?	☐	☐	☐	☐	☐
3. have you use your first language in class?	☐	☐	☐	☐	☐
4. have you work in pairs and groups?	☐	☐	☐	☐	☐
5. get students to speak in class?	☐	☐	☐	☐	☐
6. let you take responsibility for your own learning?	☐	☐	☐	☐	☐
7. get you to practice outside of class?	☐	☐	☐	☐	☐
8. help you ask questions?	☐	☐	☐	☐	☐
9. let you find and correct mistakes?	☐	☐	☐	☐	☐
10. help you to speak accurately?	☐	☐	☐	☐	☐
11. make learning fun?	☐	☐	☐	☐	☐
12. let you test your own progress?	☐	☐	☐	☐	☐
13. let you choose your own topics for discussion?	☐	☐	☐	☐	☐

9. What Do You Think?

Reread the article about teaching on pages 115 and 116. In small groups discuss your own opinions about education. What should or shouldn't teachers make students do? What should or shouldn't teachers let students do? Compare your answers with those of the rest of the class.

I. *Complete these sentences by circling the correct letter.*

1. My friend Sue has just succeeded in _____ her driver's license.
   a. get
   b. getting
   c. to get

2. We all celebrated _____ passing her road test.
   a. she
   b. her
   c. hers

3. She took lessons _____ prepare for it.
   a. for
   b. in
   c. to

4. When Sue was first learning to drive, she avoided _____ left turns.
   a. make
   b. making
   c. to make

5. At first she was terrible at _____.
   a. park
   b. parking
   c. to park

6. _____ is important, so we all told her to keep trying.
   a. Drive
   b. Driving
   c. To drive

7. I helped her _____ for the test.
   a. practice
   b. practicing
   c. practiced

8. A lot of people are afraid of _____ with new drivers, but I'm not.
   a. drive
   b. driving
   c. to drive

9. Now Sue and I are thinking _____ taking a long car trip.
   a. of
   b. to
   c. for

10. It's important _____ a lot of driving experience.
    a. get
    b. getting
    c. to get

11. Would you like _____ for a ride with us?
    a. go
    b. going
    c. to go

 (continued on next page)

12. We enjoy _____ in the country.
   a. drive
   b. driving
   c. to drive

13. We're eager _____ Sue's new car.
   a. try out
   b. trying out
   c. to try out

14. Please buckle up. Some people dislike _____ seatbelts, but they do save lives.
   a. wear
   b. wearing
   c. to wear

15. That was nice. That driver _____ me go ahead of her.
   a. let
   b. got
   c. made

16. I can't afford _____ a higher insurance premium, so I'm always very careful.
   a. pay
   b. paying
   c. to pay

17. Once, a police officer had me _____ at the side of the road.
   a. stop
   b. stopping
   c. to stop

18. I couldn't understand his _____ me.
   a. stop
   b. stopping
   c. to stop

19. He _____ me show him my license.
   a. made
   b. let
   c. got

20. Then he advised me _____ another route because of road problems ahead.
   a. take
   b. taking
   c. to take

II. *Complete this letter to the editor of a newspaper. Use the correct form of the verbs in parentheses.*

Dear Editor:

   Cars are essential in today's society. We need them _____*to get*_____ from place to place.
                                                              1. (get)

However, _____ is a privilege, not a right. I'm in favor of _____ licenses
            2. (drive)   3. (suspend)

for serious moving violations. Furthermore, if someone has his or her license suspended more

than once, that person should not be permitted _____ at all.
                                                    4. (drive)

   I learned _____ when I was sixteen. I remember _____ very happy
               5. (drive)   6. (be)

when I first got my license. In fact, my friends and family even celebrated my _____ the
                                                                                    7. (pass)
road test. But my parents cautioned me _____ this new responsibility lightly. In order
                                              8. (not take)
_____ in me a sense of responsibility, they made me _____ my own car
     9. (instill)   10. (pay)
insurance from the start. They expected me _____ a cautious and courteous driver at all
                                                   11. (be)
times. They insisted on my _____ all rules and regulations.
                                 12. (obey)

    Some of my friends objected to _____ wear seatbelts. They couldn't stand
                                              13. (have to)
_____ "confined." Seatbelts save lives and help _____ serious injuries.
     14. (feel)   15. (prevent)
It's irresponsible _____ them, and if my friends refused _____, I didn't even
                        16. (not use)   17. (buckle up)
let them _____ with me.
              18. (ride)

    I believe that too many people consider _____ a sport. Stricter laws, and the
                                                       19. (drive)
enforcement of those laws, will force people _____ more carefully on the road, and that,
                                                     20. (behave)
in turn, will result in _____ lives. It's time _____ our roads safer.
                             21. (save)   22. (make)

Sally McKay

Detroit

III. *Read these conversations. Write a summary statement using the appropriate form of the verbs in the box.*

afford	deny	invite	let	make
offer	persuade	~~postpone~~	quit	suggest

1.   **Caryn:** It's raining. Maybe we shouldn't take the class on the field trip today.

    Jason: You're right. Let's wait for a nicer day.

  SUMMARY: Caryn and Jason just _____ *postponed taking the class on* _____ the field trip.

2.   **Caryn:** Can I use the new car tomorrow? I'm driving students on a field trip, and my seatbelts
             aren't in good shape.

    Dan: OK. But please be sure to bring it back by five.

  SUMMARY: Dan _____ the new car tomorrow.

3.   **Dan:** Why didn't you buy that van? I thought you liked it.

    Caryn: I do like it. But it's too expensive. I don't have the money for it now.

  SUMMARY: Caryn can't _____ the van.

(continued on next page)

4.   **Jason:**   You need a break. You're working too hard.

       Caryn: I really have to finish this report.

       Jason: You'll feel better if you take a break.

       Caryn: Oh, all right. I suppose you're right.

    SUMMARY: Jason _____ a break.

5.   **Dan:**   Would you like to join us? We're going to Monticello, and it's supposed to be a beautiful day.

       Jason: Thanks. It would be nice to get out of the city.

    SUMMARY: Dan _____ them.

6.   **Jason:**   Oh, no. I forgot to bring my lunch.

       Caryn: Why don't you share ours? We have fruit and some cheese sandwiches.

       Jason: Oh, thanks a lot. I'll just have some fruit, but I don't eat cheese anymore. I'm trying to lower my fat intake.

    SUMMARY: Jason _____ cheese.

7.   **Caryn:**   I can't lift the cooler into the van. Can you give me a hand?

       Jason: Sure. Just leave it. I'll do it.

    SUMMARY: Jason _____ the cooler.

8.   **Caryn:**   It's hot in here.

       Dan: I know. Why don't we turn on the air conditioner?

    SUMMARY: Dan _____ the air conditioner.

9.   **Officer:**   Your license, sir.

       Dan: Here it is, officer. What's the problem?

    SUMMARY: The officer _____ his license.

10.   **Caryn:**   Did you call me last night at 11:00 P.M.?

       Jason: No, I wouldn't call you that late. Besides, I was tired from our trip. I fell asleep at eight.

    SUMMARY: Jason _____ at eleven.

IV. *Complete these sentences, using the correct form of the words in parentheses.*

1. My daughter's teacher _____ *wants her to work* _____ harder.

(want / she / work)

2. She _____ questions when she doesn't understand.

(urge / Alicia / ask)

3. The teacher always _____ after class to ask questions.

(let / students / stay)

4. She _____ the class.

(not mind / my daughter / tape)

5. Alicia _____ patient.

(appreciate / the teacher / be)

6. All the students _____ a lot from them.

(be used to / Ms. Allen / demand)

7. She _____ responsibility for their own learning.

(make / they / take)

8. She often _____ each other.

(get / they / help)

9. She really _____ well.

(want / they / do)

10. The students _____.

(be happy with / she / teach)

V. *Read this letter to a newspaper editor. There are seven mistakes in the use of verbs. Find and correct them.*

        I believe that ~~to smoke~~ *smoking* in public areas should be prohibited by law. If people don't want to stop to smoke, that's their right. Let them smoke at home. As a nonsmoker, I object to have to breathe in their cigarette smoke in restaurants, trains, and even on the streets. Studies show that inhaling second-hand smoke is dangerous. You can't help breathing it in even in a large room. And just imagine to work in such conditions! I'm a waiter in a restaurant that accommodates smokers. I have to endure dealing with customers in the smoking section. If I refuse working in that section, I may lose my job. Making smoking illegal in public places would protect my job *and* my health. Maybe it would even make more smokers to give up to smoke.

V

Passive

INTRODUCTION

 *Read and listen to this advertisement for "the world's most widely read magazine."*

The World Keeps Informed With Reader's Digest.

Reader's Digest **was founded** in 1922. Today it **is read** by people in every country in the world. It **is published** in eighteen languages and forty-six editions. Each foreign-language edition **is** especially **tailored** to fit the needs and interests of its international audience. Last year *Reader's Digest* **was read** by 100 million people. Shouldn't you be one of them? Subscribe today.

Reader's Digest

We make a difference in 100 million lives worldwide.

Courtesy of the *Reader's Digest Association, Inc.*

131

THE PASSIVE

ACTIVE	PASSIVE
Millions of people **buy** it.	It **is bought** by millions of people.
Someone **published** it in 1920.	It **was published** in 1920.

PASSIVE STATEMENTS				
SUBJECT	BE (NOT)	PAST PARTICIPLE	(BY + OBJECT)	
It	is (not)	bought	by millions of people.	
It	was (not)	published		in 1920.

YES/NO QUESTIONS			
BE	SUBJECT	PAST PARTICIPLE	
Is Was	it	sold	in Ukraine?

SHORT ANSWERS		
AFFIRMATIVE		
Yes,	it	is. was.

SHORT ANSWERS		
NEGATIVE		
No,	it	isn't. wasn't.

WH- QUESTIONS			
WH- WORD	BE	SUBJECT	PAST PARTICIPLE
Where	is was	it	sold?

Grammar Notes

1. Active and passive sentences often have similar meanings, but a different <u>focus</u>.

   Active: Millions of people **read** the magazine. (The focus is on the people.)

   Passive: The magazine **is read** by millions of people. (The focus is on the magazine.)

2. Form the passive with a form of *be* + the past participle.

   It **is written** in eighteen different languages.
   It **was published** in 1920.

3. Use the passive when it is not important or when you do not know who the person or thing doing the action (the agent) is.

   Reader's Digest **was founded** in 1920. (I don't know who founded it.)

4. Use the passive when the identity of the agent is clear from the context.

   The magazine **is printed** in many languages. (It is assumed that a magazine is printed by a machine so it is unnecessary to mention it.)

5. Use the passive when you want to avoid mentioning the agent.

   Some mistakes **were made** in that article on Bolivia. (I know who made the mistakes, but I don't want to blame the person who made them.)

6. Use the passive with *by* if you mention the agent.

   That article was written **by a world-known psychologist.**

Mention the agent:

a. When you introduce necessary new information

   John Delgado is a famous sports writer. Recently, he was hired **by International Sports** to write a monthly column.

   (The name of John's employer is necessary new information.)

b. When the agent is the name of someone such as an artist, writer, or inventor who created something

   The soccer article was written **by John Delgado.**
   The cotton gin was invented **by Eli Whitney.**

c. When the agent is surprising

   Our windows are washed **by a household robot.**

Be careful! In most cases, you do not need to mention an agent in passive sentences. Do not include an agent unnecessarily.

   John Delgado completed a good soccer article recently. It was written last month, but it won't appear until next spring.
   NOT John Delgado completed a good soccer article recently. It was written last month ~~by him~~.

FOCUSED PRACTICE

1. Discover the Grammar

Read the sentences and decide if they are active (A) or passive (P).

1. *Reader's Digest* was founded in 1922. __P__

2. It was founded by DeWitt Wallace and Lila Acheson Wallace. _____

3. Millions of people read it. _____

4. It is translated into many other languages. _____

5. A large-type edition is also printed. _____

6. It is also recorded. _____

7. Proofreaders are hired to correct mistakes. _____

8. They look for mistakes in spelling and grammar. _____

9. *Reader's Digest* is sold at newsstands. _____

10. It is published once a month. _____

11. Many of the articles are condensed from other sources. _____

12. Many readers subscribe to *Reader's Digest*. _____

13. I bought a copy last week. _____

14. One of the articles was written by a famous scientist. _____

15. It was translated from Spanish into English. _____

2. Many Tongues

Look at the chart. Then complete the sentences. Decide between the active and passive.

Language	Number of Speakers (in Millions)
Arabic	214
Cantonese (China, Hong Kong)	65
English	463
Ho (Bihar and Orissa States, India)	1
Japanese	126
Spanish	371
Swahili (Kenya, Tanzania, Zaire, Uganda)	47
Tagalog (Philippines)	43

Source: *The World Almanac* (1994).

1. Japanese _____ is spoken by 126 million people _____.

2. One million people _____.

3. _____ by 43 million people.

4. Spanish _____.

5. _____ Cantonese.

6. _____ 214 million people.

7. More than 400 million people _____.

8. _____ in Uganda.

3. An Interview

Jill Jones is writing an article about Bolivia. Use the passive form of the verbs in parentheses and short answers to complete her interview with a Bolivian cultural attaché.

Jones: I'm writing an article about Bolivia, and I'd like to check my information.

Attaché: Certainly. How can I help you?

Jones: First, I'd like to find out about the early history of Bolivia. __Was__ the area first __inhabited__ by the Inca?
1. (inhabit)

Attaché: _____. There was a great civilization on the shores of Lake Titicaca long
2.
before the Inca flourished. That civilization _____ probably _____ by
3. (create)
ancestors of the Aymara, who still live in Bolivia.

Jones: That's fascinating. Changing the topic, though, let me ask about the agriculture of your
country. I know potatoes are an important crop in the mountains. _____ corn
_____ in the Andes as well?
4. (grow)

Attaché: _____. The climate is too cold and dry. But quinoa is. Quinoa is a traditional
5.
grain that grows well in the mountains.

Jones: Quinoa? How _____ that _____, with a *k*?
6. (spell)

Attaché: No, with a *q*—q-u-i-n-o-a.

Jones: OK. Thanks. Now, I know our readers will want to read about llamas. How _____ they
_____?
7. (use)

Attaché: They have many uses—fur, meat, transportation. But only in the highlands.

Jones: Really? Why _____ they _____ there and not in the lowlands?
8. (raise)

Attaché: They're suited to the mountain climate and terrain. They don't do well in the lowlands.

Jones: I see. I understand that tin is an important resource. Where _____ it _____?
9. (mine)

Attaché: The richest deposits are in the Andes.

(continued on next page)

Jones: Let's talk about some other resources. How about the eastern part of the country—the Oriente. What crops _____ there?
10. (grow)

Attaché: The most important crop is rice. We also raise cattle there.

Jones: Are there any other natural resources in the lowlands?

Attaché: Yes. Oil. Petroleum _____ there.
11. (find)

Jones: OK, let's talk about languages for a moment. I know that Spanish is the official language of Bolivia. But _____ any other languages _____?
12. (speak)

Attaché: _____. Actually, more people speak Native American languages than Spanish—especially Quechua and Aymara.
13.

Jones: I've heard that naturalists love to visit Bolivia. _____ condors still _____ in the mountains?
14. (see)

Attaché: _____. They live in the highest regions. And in the rain forests there are a lot of fascinating animals—parrots, boa constrictors, jaguars—many, many species.
15.

Jones: Well, thank you very much. You've been really helpful. By the way, I'm planning to visit La Paz next month. I've heard that Bolivian textiles are very beautiful.

Attaché: Yes, that's true. They _____ still _____ by hand. And be sure to listen to some traditional music, too.
16. (made)

4. Changes

There were a lot of changes at Modern Reader Magazine *this year. Read the notes for an article for the employee newsletter and then complete the article. Use the passive form of the words in the box.*

Last Year	*This Year*
20 employees	*40 employees*
10 computers	*20 computers*
one floor	*two floors*
English only	*English, Spanish, and Japanese*
print and recorded editions	*print only*
John Crandon, managing editor	*Nora Gilbert, managing editor*
hours: 9:00–6:00	*hours: 9:00–5:00*
vacation: 10 days	*vacation: 14 days*

| appreciate | build | buy | discontinue | ~~hire~~ |
| increase | publish | reduce | replace | |

We have many exciting changes to celebrate at *Modern Reader* this year. During the year, twenty new employees ___*were hired*___, and ten new computers _____ for the new staff.

1.   2.

Of course, this meant we needed more room, so in July, new offices _____ for us on

3.

the second floor.

What started this growth spurt? Partly the success of *Modern Reader* with English-speaking readers, and partly our new foreign-language editions. As most of you know, our first Spanish and Japanese editions of *Modern Reader* _____ this year, and they have already found a large

4.

audience. Unfortunately, our recorded edition _____ last month because of lack of interest.

5.

In November, we were sad to say good-bye to John Crandon, who decided to retire. In December, John _____ by Nora Gilbert, our new managing editor, and we give her a warm welcome.

6.

Finally, some changes in our workday. Working hours _____, and vacation days

7.

_____ this year.

8.

I know these changes _____ by our families, who got to see us more. We look forward

9.

to seeing what exciting changes next year will bring.

5. Checking Facts

After reading Jill Jones's article, a copyeditor has several questions. Reread the interview in exercise 3. Then correct each of the nine factual mistakes in the article. Use the passive in each pair of sentences.

Visitors to Bolivia are amazed by the contrasts and charmed by the beauty of this South American country's landscapes—from the breathtaking Andes in the west to the tropical lowlands in the east.

Two-thirds of Bolivia's five million people are concentrated in the cool western highlands or Altiplano. Today, as in centuries past, corn? and kuinoa (*spelling?*) are grown in the mountains. Llamas are raised only for transportation.? And tin, Bolivia's richest natural resource, is mined in the high Andes.

The Oriente, another name for the eastern lowlands, is mostly tropical. Rice is the major food crop, and llamas? are raised for meat in the lowlands. Rubber? is also found in this region.

Bolivia is home to many fascinating forms of wildlife. The colorful parrot? is seen in the highest mountains. Boa constrictors, jaguars, and many other animals are found in the rain forests.

Hundreds of years before the Inca flourished, a great civilization was created on the shores of the Pacific,? probably by ancestors of Bolivia's Aymara people. The Aymara were defeated by the Inca in the 1500s, but their descendants still speak the Aymara language. Today, Native American languages are still widely spoken in Bolivia. Although Portuguese? is spoken in the government, Quechua and Aymara are used more widely by the people. Beautiful traditional textiles are woven by machine.? Music is played on reed pipes that are made by the musicians themselves. Their tone resembles the sound of the wind blowing over high plains in the Andes.

1. _____ Corn isn't grown in the mountains.

   _____ Potatoes are grown in the mountains.

2. _____

   _____

3. _____

4. _____

5. _____

6. _____

7. _____

8. _____

9. _____

6. Did You Know?

John Delgado wrote a soccer trivia column for International Sports.
*Complete the information with the correct form of the verbs in the first set of
parentheses. Only include the agent (from the second set of parentheses) if
absolutely necessary.*

- Soccer is the most popular sport in the world. It ___is played by more than 20 million people___.

1. (play) (more than 20 million people)
- It ___is called___ football _____ in 144 countries.

2. (call) ~~(people)~~
- Except for the goalie, players _____ _____ to use their hands. Instead,

3. (not allow) (the rules)
  the ball _____.

4. (control) (the feet, the head, and the body)
- Soccer _____ in the United States very much until twenty years

5. (not play) (people)
  ago. The game _____ in the 1970s.

6. (make popular) (Pelé and other international stars)
- Soccer has a long history. A form of soccer _____ in China

7. (enjoy) (Chinese people)
  2,000 years ago.
- It _____ in 1365--his archers spent too much time playing,

8. (ban) (King Edward III of England)
  and too little time practicing archery.
- Medieval games _____ for entire days, over miles of territory.

9. (play) (players)
- Today, the World Cup games _____ every four years.

10. (hold) (The World Cup Association)
  The best teams in the world compete.

COMMUNICATION PRACTICE

7. Practice Listening

Listen to the conversations between editors at Modern Reader. *Then listen again and circle the letter of the sentence you hear from each pair.*

1. a. Jill hired Bob.
   b. Jill was hired by Bob.

2. a. I trained Minna.
   b. I was trained by Minna.

3. a. It's published just six times a year.
   b. It was published just six times a year.

4. a. Tony fired Jill.
   b. Tony was fired by Jill.

5. a. She interviewed Jay.
   b. She was interviewed by Jay.

6. a. He was laid off.
   b. Was he laid off?

8. Translations

These are some non-English titles of Reader's Digest.* *Work in small groups. Try to guess which language each title is written in and where it is sold.*

1. 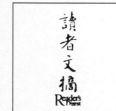 讀者文摘 Reader's Digest

4. Seleções *do* Reader's Digest

7. Reader's Digest Ридерз Дайджест

10. Sélection *du* Reader's Digest

5. सर्वोत्तम रीडर्स डाइजेस्ट

8. Reader's Digest Válogatás

11. Valitut Palat *from* Reader's Digest

2. Das Beste *aus* Reader's Digest

6. 리더스 다이제스트

9. Det Bästa *ur* Reader's Digest

12. Výběr Reader's Digest

3. Selecciones *del* Reader's Digest

*Courtesy of *The Reader's Digest Association, Inc.*

Example:
A: I think number 2 is written in German.
B: Right. And it's probably sold in Germany and Austria.
C: It's probably also sold in Switzerland.

9. Information Gap: The Philippines

The Philippines consist of many islands. The two largest are Luzon in the north and Mindanao in the south.

LUZON

MINDANAO

Work with a partner. You and your partner will be looking at different maps. The maps show some of the many important products found and made in the Philippines. Your task is to find out about each other's maps.

Student A, look at the map of Luzon. Complete the chart for Luzon. Answer Student B's questions. Then ask Student B questions about Mindanao. Write Y for yes and N for no.

Student B, turn to the Information Gap for Unit 10 on page IG 2 in the back of the book. Follow the instructions there.

Example:
  A: Is tobacco grown in Mindanao?
  B: No, it isn't.
     Is it grown in Luzon?
  A: Yes, it is. It's grown in the north and central
     part of the island.

			Mindanao	Luzon
G R O W	🍃	tobacco	N	Y
	🌽	corn		
	🍌	bananas		
	☕	coffee		
	🍍	pineapples		
	🌾	sugar		
R A I S E	🐄	cattle		
	🐖	pigs		
M I N E	G	gold		
	M	manganese		
P R O D U C E	🌿	cotton		
	🍁	rubber		
	🪵	lumber		

LUZON

N
W   E
S

Now compare charts with Student B. Are they the same?

10. Trivia Quiz

Magazines often have games and puzzles. Work in pairs. Complete this quiz. Then compare your answers with those of your classmates.

1. Urdu is spoken in _____.

    a. Ethiopia   b. Pakistan   c. Uruguay

2. Air conditioning was invented in _____.

    a. 1911   b. 1950   c. 1980

3. The X ray was discovered by _____.

    a. Thomas Edison   b. Roentgen   c. Marie Curie

4. The World Trade Center in New York was designed by _____.

    a. Minora Yamasuki   b. Frank Lloyd Wright   c. I. M. Pei

5. The 1988 Olympics were held in _____.

    a. Germany   b. Japan   c. Korea

6. A baby _____ is called a cub.

    a. cat   b. dog   c. lion

Now, with your partner, make up your own questions with the words in parentheses. Ask another pair to answer them.

7. _____ _____ by _____.
    (paint)
    a. _____ b. _____ c. _____

8. _____ _____ by _____.
    (invent)
    a. _____ b. _____ c. _____

9. _____ _____ by _____.
    (compose)
    a. _____ b. _____ c. _____

10. _____ _____ by _____.
    a. _____ b. _____ c. _____

11. Said around the World

Reader's Digest *often has a page of famous quotations or sayings like these.*
What do you think they mean? Discuss them in small groups.

Rome wasn't built in a day. (English)

He who was bitten by a snake avoids tall grass. (Chinese)

As fast as laws are devised their evasion is contrived. (German)

The torch of love is lit in the kitchen. (French)

He ran away from the rain and was caught in a hailstorm. (Turkish)

The stitch is lost unless the thread is knotted. (Italian)

Never promise a fish until it's caught. (Irish)

12. A Country You Know Well

Complete the table with information about a country that you know well.
Then write an essay about the country, using the information you have
gathered. Use the article in exercise 5 as a model.

geographical areas _____

_____

crops grown in each area _____

_____

animals raised in each area _____

_____

natural resources found in each area _____

_____

wildlife found in each area _____

_____

languages spoken _____

_____

art, handicrafts, or music created _____

_____

INTRODUCTION

Read and listen to this article about an international space project.

CLOSE QUARTERS

Japanese astronauts fear that decisions **will be made** too fast, while Americans worry that in an emergency, they **might not be made** quickly enough. The French and Dutch worry that dinner **won't be taken** seriously, and Italians suspect that their privacy **may not be respected.**

The focus of all this apprehension is the space station *Freedom,* a major international project that **will be launched** from the Space Shuttle in the very near future. By the end of the century, *Freedom* **will be operated** by a crew of astronauts from Europe, Japan, Canada, and the United States. At first, the crew **will be replaced** every ninety days, but the stay **could be lengthened** to prepare for a two-year trip to Mars.

How **can** an international group of astronauts **be expected** to get along during long periods in this "trapped environment"? To find out, anthropologist

Mary Lozano and engineer Clifford Wong have begun to ask astronauts from around the world about their concerns. The two scientists hope that many cross-cultural problems **can be avoided** by what they learn.

Besides the concerns already mentioned, all the astronauts worry about language. English will be the official language of the station, and, of course, a great deal of technical language **must be mastered** by everyone. However, on a social level, some part-

ners fear that they **might be treated** like outsiders because they won't know American slang. Another concern is food. What time **should meals be served?** How **should** preparation and cleanup **be handled? Can** religious dietary restrictions **be observed** on board?

To deal with cross-cultural differences like these, Lozano and Wong feel strongly that astronauts **should be taught** interpersonal skills as well as **given** technical and survival know-how. They have interviewed participants in each country, and they hope that what they learn from them **will be applied** in training. Ultimately, they believe, cross-cultural training will save money and reduce errors caused by misunderstanding, ranging from misreading a facial expression to incorrectly interpreting data.

Often qualities like sensitivity and tolerance **can't be taught** from a textbook; they **must be observed** and **experienced**. Lozano and Wong say that the necessary model for space station harmony **can be found** in the TV series *Star Trek*. The multicultural *Enterprise* crew has been getting along in space for eons now, and the scientists suggest that watching the show might be helpful for future astronauts. Since cross-cultural harmony **could be imagined** by the *Star Trek* creators, perhaps it **can be achieved** by the crew of *Freedom.*

Source: Judith Stone, "It's a Small World after All, " *Discover Magazine*, February 1992, pp. 23–25.

The Passive with Modals

STATEMENTS				
Subject	**Modal***	**Be**	**Past Participle**	
The space station	will (not) should (not)	be	launched	next year.

*Modals have only one form. They do not have *-s* in the third-person singular.

YES/NO Questions				
Modal	**Subject**	**Be**	**Past Participle**	
Will Can	it	be	launched	next year?

SHORT ANSWERS		
Affirmative		
Yes,	it	will. can.

SHORT ANSWERS		
Negative		
No,	it	won't. can't.

Grammar Notes

1. After a modal, form the passive with the base form of *be* + the past participle.

> The shuttle **will be used** to launch the space station.
> The launch **won't be postponed.**
> The crew **must be given** cross-cultural training.
> Decisions **shouldn't be made** too quickly.

2. Use *will* with the passive to talk about the future.

> It **will be launched** very soon.
> They'**ll be notified** as soon as we know the launch date.
> He **won't be appointed** until next year.

3. Use *can* and *could* with the passive to express present or past ability.

> The blastoff **can be seen** for miles.
> It **could be seen** very clearly last year.
> It **couldn't be avoided.**

4. Use *could, may, might,* and *can't* with the passive to express future possibility or impossibility.

> It **could be launched** very soon.
> French scientists **may be invited** to participate.
> The effects of weightlessness **might be studied** extensively.
> It **can't be done.**

5. Use *have (got) to* and *had better* (modal-like expressions), *should, ought to,* and *must* with the passive to express advisability, obligation, and necessity.

> The crew **should be prepared** to deal with cultural differences.
> Crew members **ought to be given** communication training.
> Privacy **had better be respected** on board.
> Everyone **must be consulted** before decisions are reached.

FOCUSED PRACTICE

1. Discover the Grammar

Read this article about comfort in space. Underline all the examples of the passive with modals and modal-like expressions.

Ten former astronauts were recently asked about what <u>could be done</u> to improve comfort in space. Here are some of the issues they raised.

• FOOD Wherever you are, mealtime is important for your sense of well-being. The astronauts feel they should be able to enjoy what they eat, but food just doesn't taste good in zero gravity. This problem can be overcome by making the food spicier. A little pepper or mustard could go a long way in making meals more palatable.

• CLOTHING The temperature on board a space station can vary from one part to the other. To stay comfortable, the astronauts suggested layered garments. The top layer could be removed in warmer sections of the station. Astronauts could also be provided with different uniforms for different occasions. Having a choice of style and color might boost morale.

• PRIVACY Living in tight quarters doesn't allow for much privacy. All agreed that this might pose a serious problem on long trips. No one had any answers, but they felt strongly that solutions to this issue should be investigated.

• SLEEPING Because of weightlessness and other factors, sleep is often interrupted in space. One astronaut feared that there might be long-term effects as a result of never getting a good night's rest.

• DEATH No one likes to think about this issue, but it is possible that an astronaut could die while aboard the space station. What should be done if this happens? One astronaut suggested that the body could be frozen and then brought back to Earth.

• EMOTIONAL NEEDS Many of the astronauts pointed out that people have the same needs in space as they do on Earth. They believe that time should be provided for relaxation, and that everything possible ought to be done to make the astronauts feel happy and at home.

Source: Willian K. Douglas, *Human Performance Issues Arising from Manned Space Station Missions* (prepared for Ames Research Center, National Aeronautics and Space Administration, 1986).

2. After the Flight Simulation

Some astronauts are talking about problems they experienced during a flight simulation. Complete their conversations, using the passive form of the words in parentheses.

1. **A:** These flight simulations are useful.

   B: Yes. They really give you a feeling of what it'll be like out there in space.

   A: There are still a lot of problems, though. I just hope that they _____ can be solved _____ before the real thing.
   (can / solve)

   B: I'm sure they will be.

2. **A:** It was uncomfortably warm in there. What was the temperature?

   B: I don't know. But it _____ at 68°.
   (should / keep)

   A: Well, that's still warm for some of us.

   B: Don't forget—they say our space suits _____ so that the top
   (will / design)
   layer _____.
   (can / remove)

3. **A:** What did you think of the food?

   B: I didn't like it very much.

   A: Me neither. Maybe we _____ more of a choice.
   (could / give)

   B: That would be good. And I think we _____ plates. I really
   (should / give)
   don't like eating out of a plastic bag.

4. **A:** Shaving was a strange experience.

   B: You're not kidding! The whisker dust keeps flying back in your face!

   A: I wonder if it's harmful to inhale.

   B: Me too. Some experiments _____ on the long-term effects.
   (ought to / carry out)

5. **A:** We didn't deal with the issue of garbage disposal during this simulation. What
   _____ with all the trash that's produced? We don't want to
   (will / do)
   litter outer space!

   B: I'm not sure, but I think it _____ on board and then
   (may / store)
   _____ and _____ back to Earth by
   (remove)   (bring)
   the Space Shuttle. They're still working on the problem.

   A: Well, it _____ before we go up there.
   (have to / solve)

   B: Absolutely.

3. Zero-G

Complete the interview with aerospace engineer Dr. Bernard Kay.

Interviewer: Dr. Kay, I'd like to ask how daily life _____will be conducted_____ in a space
          1. (will / conduct)
station.

Dr. Kay: Sure. What would you like to know?

Interviewer: First, about food. _____ it _____ on board or
        2. (Will / prepare)
_____ out of tubes?
3. (squeeze)

Dr. Kay: Neither. Gourmet meals _____ on Earth and then they
      4. (will / prepackage)
_____ just _____ on board in microwave ovens.
      5. (will / warm up)

Interviewer: The space station will have an international crew. In your opinion, how _____
food _____ to suit everyone's taste?
    6. (should / select)

Dr. Kay: Foods from all participating countries _____. I think a
        7. (have to / offer)
food preference form _____ by each new member.
      8. (should / fill out)
Then, foods _____ from the forms.
    9. (can / select)

Interviewer: _____ dishes _____ on board?
      10. (Will / use)

Dr. Kay: Possibly. We're also considering throw-away bags.

Interviewer: I know that sleep is really important on space missions. _____ sleeping
quarters _____ by several crew members?
    11. (Will / share)

Dr. Kay: We hope not. We've learned from other programs that privacy is very important. In
my opinion, each crew member _____ with private
      12. (must / provide)
sleeping quarters. Everyone needs space for family pictures and personal items.

Interviewer: What else _____ from other space programs?
    13. (can / learn)

Dr. Kay: Astronauts really enjoy watching the Earth. Earlier vehicles didn't provide enough
windows for viewing.

Interviewer: _____ more windows _____?
      14. (Could / provide)

Dr. Kay: Sure. And some windows even _____ in the
      15. (ought to / place)
astronauts' private quarters as well.

Interviewer: Thanks, Dr. Kay. You've given us an intriguing picture of how human needs
_____ aboard a space station.
    16. (can / meet)

4. Space Journal

Read an astronaut's journal notes. There are six mistakes in the use of future and modal passives. Find and correct them.

Oct. 4

6:15 A.M.
I used the sleeping restraints last night, so my feet and hands didn't float around as much. I slept a lot better. I'm going to suggest some changes in the restraints though—I think they ought to be ~~make~~ *made* more comfortable. I felt really trapped. And maybe these sleeping quarters could be designed differently. They're too small.

10:45 A.M.
My face is all puffy, and my eyes are red. Exercise helps a little—I'd better get on the exercise bike right away. I can be misunderstanding very easily when I look like this. Sometimes people think I've been crying. And yesterday Max thought I was angry when he turned on Star Trek. Actually, I love that show.

1:00 P.M.
Lunch was pretty good. Chicken Teriyaki. It's nice and spicy, and the sauce can actually been tasted, even at zero gravity. Some more of it had better be flown in on the Shuttle pretty soon. It's the most popular dish in the freezer.

4:40 P.M.
I'm worried about Kristen. Just before I left on this mission, she said she was planning to quit school at the end of the semester. That's only a month away. I want to call her and discuss it. But I worry that I might get angry and yell. I might be overheard. They really should figure out some way to give us more privacy.

10:30 P.M.
The view of Earth is unbelievably breathtaking! My favorite time is spent looking out the window—watching Earth pass below. At night a halo of light surrounds the horizon. It's so bright that the tops of the clouds can see. It can't be described. It simply have to be experienced.

11:30 P.M.
I'm glad I took some time out just to watch the Earth. Some of my crewmates were beginning to get on my nerves. It's hard to spend so much time together in such close quarters. The shower has become a popular way of getting some time to be alone. (We're all going to be really clean if we keep this up!) They're beginning to be aware of the problem, though. I think the next crews will be better train to deal with this kind of stress.

COMMUNICATION PRACTICE

5. Practice Listening

Some crew members aboard the space station are watching television. Listen and read the script below. Then listen again and circle the underlined words you hear.

Picarro: Spaceship Endeavor calling Earth. . . . This is Captain Picarro speaking. We've been hit by a meteorite.

Earth: Is anyone hurt?

Picarro: No, everyone is safe.

Earth: You'd better start repairing the damage immediately.

Picarro: It can/can't be repaired out here.
1.

★　　★　　★　　★　　★　　★　　★

Picarro: We'll be approaching Planet CX5 of the Delta solar system in a few hours. Is their language on our computer, Dr. Sock?

Sock: I'm checking now. . . . We don't have a language for CX5 on the computer, but we have one for CX4. Shall we try it?

Picarro: We'd better be very careful. Our messages could/should be misunderstood.
2.

★　　★　　★　　★　　★　　★　　★

Lon: OK. I'm ready. Let's go.

Ray: What about oxygen?

Lon: Isn't the atmosphere on CX5 just like Earth's?

Ray: I think you've been in space too long. Read your manual. Oxygen must/must not be used on all other planets.
3.

★　　★　　★　　★　　★　　★　　★

Picarro: I've lost contact with Lon and Ray. I hope their electronic equipment works on CX5.

Sock: Don't worry. They'll pick up the radar/They'll be picked up by the radar pretty soon.
4.

★　　★　　★　　★　　★　　★　　★

Lon: Look at those plants. I want to take some back to the ship.

Ray: But they're huge!

Lon: Well, let's try. I bet they can be grown/thrown on board.
5.

★　　★　　★　　★　　★　　★　　★

(continued on next page)

CX5 Leader: What do you want to ask us, Earthlings?

Ray: Our vehicle was hit by a meteorite. We have to get it ready to return to Earth.

CX5 Leader: What do you want of us?

Ray: It must be <u>prepared/repaired</u> on the ground. May we have permission
6.
to land on your planet?

★   ★   ★   ★   ★   ★   ★

6.   Close Quarters

Work in small groups. Imagine that in preparation for a space mission, you and your classmates are going to spend a week together in a one-room apartment. You will not be able to leave the apartment for the entire time. Make a list of rules for yourselves. Use passive modals. Compare your list with that of another group.

Some Issues to Consider:

Food
Clothes
Room temperature
Noise
Neatness
Cleanliness
Privacy
Language
Entertainment
Other: _____

Example:
Dinner will be served at 6:00 P.M.
The dishes must be washed after each meal.

7. | What Should Be Done?

Work in small groups. Look at the picture of a classroom. You are responsible for getting it in order, but you have limited time and money. Agree on five things that should be done.

Example:

A: The window has to be replaced.
B: No. That'll cost too much. It can just be taped.
C: That'll look terrible. It should be replaced.
D: OK. What else should be done?

8. | Money for Space

Sending people to the space station is going to cost about $16,000 an hour. Should money be spent for these space projects, or could it be spent better on Earth? If so, how? Discuss these questions with your classmates.

INTRODUCTION

▼

●● *Read and listen to this TV news report.*

Department of the Treasury—Internal Revenue Service

Form
1040EZ

**Income Tax Return for Single and
Joint Filers With No Dependents** (o) **1995**

OMB No. 1545-0675

**Use the
IRS label**
(See page 10.)
Otherwise,
please print.

L
A
B
E
L

H
E
R
E

Print your name (first, initial, last)

If a joint return, print spouse's name (first, initial, last)

Home address (number and street). If you have a P.O. box, see page 11.   Apt. no.

City, town or post office, state and ZIP code. If you have a foreign address, see page 11.

Your social security number

Spouse's social security number

See instructions on back and in Form 1040EZ booklet.

**Presidential
Election
Campaign**
(See page 11.)

Note: *Checking "Yes" will not change your tax or reduce your refund.*
Do you want $3 to go to this fund?   ▶
If a joint return, does your spouse want $3 to go to this fund? ▶

Yes   No

**Filing
status**

1 ☐ Single   ☐ Married filing joint return
                                (even if only one had income)

**Report
your
income**

**Attach
Copy B of
Form(s)
W-2 here.**
Attach any tax
payment on
top of
Form(s) W-2.

Note: *You
must check
Yes or No.*

2 Total wages, salaries, and tips. This should be shown in
   box 1 of your W-2 form(s). Attach your W-2 form(s).   2

3 Taxable interest income of $400 or less. If the total is
   over $400, you cannot use Form 1040EZ.   3

4 Add lines 2 and 3. This is your **adjusted gross income.**   4
5 Can your parents (or someone else) claim you on their return?
   ☐ **Yes.** Do worksheet   ☐ **No.** If **single**, enter 6,050.00.
   on back; enter   If **married**, enter 10,900.00.
   amount from   For an explanation of these
   line G here.   amounts, see back of form.   5

6 Subtract line 5 from line 4. If line 5 is larger than line
   4, enter 0. This is your **taxable income.**   6

7 En... ...deral income tax withheld f...

Dollars   Cents

Anchor: Your time is running out. If you haven't yet mailed your
              tax return, you have just a little more than half an hour
              to **have it postmarked** by midnight tonight. We turn now
              to Ken Watanabe, reporting live from Manhattan. Ken,
              what's happening?

Reporter: I'm standing in Manhattan's Main Post Office on West
              33rd Street and Eighth Avenue. It's 11:25 P.M. on April 15,
              the deadline for mailing in federal income tax returns.
              As you can see, the place is mobbed—there's a carnival
              atmosphere here. People are selling t-shirts, food, and
              drinks. You can even **get your back rubbed** while you
              wait on line.
              Let's go find out why some of these people are mailing
              their returns in at the eleventh hour.
              Excuse me. Is that your federal income tax you're filing?

Woman: Yes, it is.

Reporter:	Do you always file at the last minute like this?
Woman:	Oh, no. I've always **had my taxes prepared** by an accountant, but this year I decided to do them myself. It took a lot longer than I thought it would. Right up until about an hour ago, as a matter of fact.
Reporter:	Why are *you* here at the eleventh hour?
Man:	Well, I **got my taxes done** by R. H. Brock a couple of weeks ago. Then I lost them.
Reporter:	You *lost* your taxes?
Man:	Yeah. I **was having my apartment painted** at about that time, and I was moving stuff around a lot. I guess I just slipped them into the wrong folder.
Reporter:	But you did find them in time.
Man:	Right. Just in time.
Reporter:	And you, sir? What's your excuse?
Man:	The dog ate my W-2 form.
Reporter:	Oh, come on. You can do a lot better than that!
Man:	No, it really happened.
Reporter:	What did you do when you found out?
Man:	Well, I had moved, and this employer was in another state, so I called and **got another W-2 sent.** That took about a week.
Reporter:	So you waited until last week.
Man:	Yeah.
Reporter:	What do you plan to do next year?
Man:	First, I think I'll get my dog trained.
Reporter:	Sounds like a good idea. Well, there's probably a story behind every tax return here tonight. These folks may be filing at the last minute, but the bottom line is, they got it done. Reporting live from Midtown, I'm Ken Watanabe, Channel 7 News.

PASSIVE CAUSATIVES

STATEMENTS					
SUBJECT	**HAVE/GET**	**OBJECT**	**PAST PARTICIPLE**	**(BY + OBJECT)**	
I	**get**	**my taxes**	**done**		at R. H. Brock.
She	**has**	**her hair**	**cut**	**by** André	every month.

(continued on next page)

YES/NO QUESTIONS					
AUXILIARY VERB	**SUBJECT**	***HAVE/GET***	**OBJECT**	**PAST PARTICIPLE**	***(BY* + OBJECT)**
Do	you	**get**	**your taxes**	**done?**	
Does	she	**have**	**her hair**	**cut**	by André?

WH- QUESTIONS						
***WH-* WORD**	**AUXILIARY VERB**	**SUBJECT**	***HAVE/GET***	**OBJECT**	**PAST PARTICIPLE**	***(BY* + OBJECT)**
Why	do	you	**get**	**your taxes**	**done?**	
How often	does	she	**have**	**her hair**	**cut**	by André?

Grammar Notes

1. Form the passive causative with the appropriate form of *have* or *get* + object + past participle. The passive causative can be used in all tenses and with modals.

> I always **have my taxes done** at R. H. Brock.
> Last year I **got my hair cut** only twice.
> Next week I'm going to **have my windows washed.**
> I **had them washed** a long time ago.
> You **should get the car checked.**

2. Use the passive causative to talk about services that you arrange for someone to do for you.

> I used to do my own taxes, but now I **get them done.**

Be careful! Do not confuse the simple past causative with the past perfect.

> Simple past causative: I **had it done** last week. (Someone did it for me.)
> Past perfect: I **had done** it before. (I did it myself.)

3. As with the passive, use *by* only when it is necessary to mention the agent.

> Where do you get your taxes done?
> NOT Where do you get your taxes done by an accountant?

But:

> This year I'm having them done **by a new accounting firm.**

See Unit 10, page 133 for information on when to include the agent.

4. Usage note: *Get something done* and *have something done* have the same meaning. However, in formal writing, we usually use *have*.

5. Be careful! Do not confuse the expression *to get something done* (= to finish something) with the passive causative. The context will usually make the meaning clear.

> I had a lot of homework. But I worked hard and got it done before midnight. (I finished my homework before midnight.)
> I got my taxes done at R. H. Brock. (R. H. Brock did my taxes for me.)

FOCUSED PRACTICE

1. Discover the Grammar

Read the conversations. Then decide if the statements are true (T) *or false* (F).

1. **Deborah:** The lines at the post office were terrible last night.

   Jake: Well, it won't happen again. Next time, we'll have our taxes done.

   Deborah and Jake are going to do their own taxes next year. ___F___

2. **Jake:** Did you see John at the post office?

   Deborah: No, he's in California. Remember?

   Jake: Oh that's right.

   Deborah: Anyway, he had his taxes done just before he left.

   John did his own taxes this year. _____

3. **Jake:** I'm glad that's over. Now we can start catching up on other things.

   Deborah: Right. I'm going to get my hair cut after work tomorrow.

   Deborah cuts her own hair. _____

4. **Deborah:** Speaking about hair—Sally, *your* hair's getting awfully long.

   Sally: I know, I'm cutting it tomorrow.

   Sally cuts her own hair. _____

5. **Sally:** Mom, why didn't you get your nails done last time you went to the hairdresser?

   Deborah: Because I had done them just before my appointment.

   Deborah did her own nails. _____

6. **Jake:** I think you'd better start on that book report, Tommy. It's eight o'clock already.

   Tommy: I can get it done in an hour.

   Tommy plans to ask someone else to do his book report. _____

7. **Jake:** I'm going to watch some TV and then go to bed. What's on the agenda for tomorrow?

   Deborah: I have to get up early. I'm getting the car washed before work.

   Someone is going to wash Jake and Deborah's car for them. _____

8. **Deborah:** You know, I think it's time to change the oil, too.

   Jake: You're right. I'll do it this weekend.

   Jake works on the family car. _____

2. Essential Services

It's April 19, and Art is moving into a new house at the end of the month. Look at his April calendar and write sentences about when he had things done, and when he is going to have things done before he moves in.

				April			
S	**M**	**T**	**W**	**T**	**F**	**S**	
	1	2 R. H. Brock taxes	3	4 fly to CA	5 locksmith	6	
7	8 painters	9	10	11	12 →	13	
14	15 TAX deadline!	16 carpet cleaner	17	18	19	20 plant trees	
21	22 electrician- hall light	23	24 change address	25	26 shelves	27	
28	29 furniture	30					

1. have/his taxes/prepare

   He had his taxes prepared on the second.

   _____

2. get/his address/change at the post office

   _____

3. get/the carpet/clean

   _____

4. get/his locks/change

   _____

5. have/his shelves/put up

   _____

6. get/the hall light/repair

_____

7. have/the house/paint

_____

8. have/furniture/move in

_____

3. Getting Things Done

Deborah and Jake are hosting a family reunion on Mother's Day. Complete the conversations with the passive causative and the appropriate verbs in the box.

clean	color	cut	deliver	develop
dry clean	make	paint	repair	~~shorten~~

1. **Sally:** I bought a new dress for the party, Mom. What do you think of it?

   Deborah: It's pretty, but it's a little long. Why don't you _____ get it shortened _____?

   Sally: OK. They do alterations at the cleaner's. I'll take it in tomorrow.

2. **Sally:** By the way, what are _you_ planning to wear?

   Deborah: My blue dress. I'm glad you reminded me. I'd better _____.

   Sally: I can drop it off at the cleaner's with my dress.

3. **Deborah:** I think the house is all ready, don't you?

   Jake: Except for the windows. They look pretty dirty.

   Deborah: Oh, you're right. When was the last time we _____?

4. **Deborah:** Sally, your hair is getting really long. I thought you were going to cut it.

   Sally: I decided not to do it myself this time. I _____ by

   Elise's hairdresser tomorrow.

5. **Deborah:** My hair's getting a lot of gray in it. Should I _____?

   Jake: It looks fine to me, but it's up to you.

   Deborah: Well, maybe I'll go with Sally to the hairdresser tomorrow.

6. **Tommy:** Mom, someone's at the door!

   Sally: It's only twelve o'clock.

   Tommy: No, it's not.

   Sally: Don't tell me the clock stopped again.

   Jake: I don't believe it! I _____ already _____ twice this

   year, and it's only May.

(continued on next page)

7. **Guest:** The house looks beautiful, Jake. _____ you _____?

   Jake: No, actually we did it ourselves last summer.

   Guest: I like the color.

8. **Deborah:** I have one shot left in the camera. Come on, everyone! Say "cheese"!

   Guests: Cheese!

   Deborah: Great. We took three rolls of pictures today. Maybe we can _____ before Mom and Dad go back to Florida.

9. **Guest 1:** That was a nice party. Why don't I order some flowers for Jake and Deborah tomorrow?

   Guest 2: Good idea. _____ after three o'clock, though. That's when Deborah gets home.

10. **Sally:** That last picture of everyone turned out great.

    Deborah: You're right. Maybe we can _____ into a holiday greeting card.

    Sally: Good idea.

COMMUNICATION PRACTICE

4. Practice Listening

It's a year later, and Art is having his taxes done. Listen to the conversation between Art and his new accountant. Then listen again and check the correct column.

	Art Did the Job Himself	Art Hired Someone to Do the Job
1. converted garage into a workshop	☐	☑
2. painted the workshop	☐	☐
3. installed second telephone line	☐	☐
4. set up computer	☐	☐
5. rewired garage	☐	☐
6. built shelves	☐	☐
7. printed business cards	☐	☐

5. Home Improvements

Work with a partner. Look at the pictures of this house. You have five minutes to find and write down all the things the owners had done to their home.

Before

After

Example:
They got the roof repaired.

When the five minutes are up, compare your list with that of another pair. Then look at the picture again to check your answers.

6. Making Plans

Work in groups. Imagine that you are taking a car trip together to another country. You'll be gone for several weeks. Decide where you're going. Then make a list of things you have to do and arrange before the trip. Use the ideas below and your own.

Passport and visas
Car (oil, gas, tires, seatbelts)
Home (pets, plants, mail, newspaper delivery)
Personal (clothing, hair)
Medical (teeth, eyes, prescriptions for medicine)
Other: _____

Example:
A: I have to get my passport renewed.
B: Me too. And we should apply for visas right away.

Now compare your list with that of another group. Did you forget anything?

I. *Circle the active or passive form of the verbs to complete the conversation with a travel agent.*

Lindsay: This is Lindsay Boyle from AL Metals. I

(didn't receive)/wasn't received my airline tickets today, and I
1.

leave/'m left for Jamaica in two days.
2.

Agent: Let me check. Hmmm. That's strange. The tickets

mailed/were mailed a week ago. You should be had/have
3.   4.

them by now.

Lindsay: How about my hotel reservations?

Agent: Those made/were made for you last week. They
5.

confirmed/were confirmed by the Hotel Mariel today.
6.

Will you need/be needed a car when you arrive?
7.

Lindsay: Not right away. I'll be met/meet at the airport by my client.
8.

I'll probably rent/be rented a car later on. Oh, the
9.

receptionist was just handed/just handed me a note.
10.

The tickets are here. They were sent/sent to the wrong floor.
11.

Agent: Sorry about that.

Lindsay: Never mind. We have them now, so no harm did/was done.
12.

II. *Complete the conversations with the modal and the passive form of the verbs in parentheses.*

Lindsay: _____Will_____ the reports ___be printed___ by the end of
1. (Will / print)

next week?

Ted: Sure. In fact they _____ to the office by Tuesday.
2. (might / deliver)

Lindsay: Good. I hope they turn out well. They _____ by a
3. (will / read)

lot of people.

Ted: Don't worry. This company always does nice work. I'm sure

you _____ when you see them.
4. (will / satisfy)

Lindsay: Oh, by the way, those reports _____ for shipment
5. (have to / pack)

as soon as they arrive. I'm taking them with me to Jamaica.

Ted: I didn't know you planned to bring them. I _____
6. (ought to / tell)

things like that. So how long are you staying?

Lindsay: About a week. But my stay _____. It depends on
7. (could / extend)

how things go.

Ted: You know, your office _____ while you're gone. And your computer
8. (should / paint)
_____. So maybe you should stay another week.
9. (have to / service)

Lindsay: I think that _____. I hear it's a pretty nice place.
10. (can / arrange)

III. *Complete the information about Jamaica with a passive form of the verbs in parentheses.*

Visitors love Jamaican culture and scenic beauty. Reggae music _____is performed_____ at the
1. (perform)
Island's Sunsplash festival every year, attracting music lovers from all over the world. The Mardi Gras
festival, another yearly event, _____ with colorful street pantomimes and
2. (celebrate)
traditional costumes. Jamaica's beautiful beaches _____ by swimmers, divers, and
3. (enjoy)
sunbathers.

But Jamaica isn't just fun and games. The country has strong traditions of education. The
University of the West Indies _____ there in 1948. Thousands of students have
4. (establish)
received university degrees since then. Today, Jamaica's high schools _____ by
5. (attend)
more than 50 percent of primary school graduates.

Jamaica also has important deposits of bauxite. This ore _____ to produce
6. (use)
aluminum. Most of Jamaica's bauxite _____ to other countries. However, some
7. (export)
aluminum _____ on the island as well.
8. (produce)
Jamaica _____ by people from Africa, England, France, and Spain. English is
9. (settle)
the official language, but Creole _____ by many people on the island. Creole is a
10. (speak)
mixture of the languages that _____ to the island by these settlers.
11. (bring)
Jamaica _____ by thousands of tourists and business people every year.
12. (visit)
Wouldn't you like to be one of them?

IV. *Complete the memo with **have** or **get** and the correct form of the verb in parentheses.*

I'd like to ____have____ some work _____done_____ in my office, and this seems like a good time
1. (do)
for it. Please _____ my carpet _____ while I'm gone. And while you're at it, could
2. (clean)
you _____ my computer and printer _____? It's been quite a while since they've
3. (look at)
been serviced. Ted wants to _____ my office _____ while I'm gone. Please tell him
4. (paint)
any color is fine except pink.

Last week, I _____ some new brochures _____. Please call the printer and
5. (design)
_____them _____ directly to the sales reps. And could you _____ more
6. (deliver)
business cards _____ too? We're almost out.
7. (make up)

(continued on next page)

When I get back, it will be time to plan the holiday party. I think we _____ it

_____ this year. While I'm gone, why don't you call around and get some estimates
　　　8. (cater)

from caterers? _____ the estimates _____ to Ted.
　　　　　　　　　　　　　　　　　9. (send)

See you in two weeks!

Lindsay

V. *Complete these facts about Jamaica with a passive form of the verbs in the box. Include the agent in parentheses only where necessary.*

~~discover~~	employ	export	grow	listen to	popularize	strike

1. Jamaica _____was discovered by Europeans_____ on May 4, 1494, during Columbus's second
　　　　　　　　　　　　(Europeans)

  voyage.

2. Some of the best coffee in the world _____ on the slopes of
　　　　　　　　　　　　　　　　　　　(coffee growers)

  Jamaica's Blue Mountains.

3. About 50,000 people _____.
　　　　　　　　　　　　　(the sugar industry)

4. Sugar _____ to many countries.
　　　　　　　(sugar producers)

5. The island _____ about once every eight years, but few have
　　　　　　　　　(hurricanes)

  caused severe damage.

6. Reggae music originated in Jamaica. It _____ in the 1970s.
　　　　　　　　　　　　　　　　　　(Bob Marley)

7. Now it _____ everywhere.
　　　　　　　(people)

VI. *Read Ted's fax to Lindsay. There are six mistakes with passives. Find and correct them.*

Dear Lindsay,

  I hope you're enjoying your trip.

  　　　　　　　　　　　　　　　　sent
  The reports arrived late, so I had them ~~send~~ on a flight this morning. Did you get them?

Please let me know. I checked the new brochure today. It looks very nice, but some mistakes were

made in the text. They will corrected before it's printed by the printer.

  A funny thing was happened yesterday. The painters came to paint your office, and guess

what color they brought? Luckily we saw it before your office was painted pink. It's a nice off-

white now.

  Several estimates from caterers was left on my desk today. I think decisions about the party

should make by all of us, so I'll hold the estimates until you get back.

Ted

VI

▼

Modals

UNIT

13

Advisability
and Obligation
in the Past:
*Should have,
Ought to have,
Could have,
Might have*

▼

INTRODUCTION

◾◾ *Read and listen to this article from a popular psychology magazine.*

Useless Regrets

For all sad words of tongue or pen
*The saddest are these: "It **might have been**."*

John Greenleaf Whittier

Not only the saddest, but perhaps the most destructive. According to recent ideas in psychology, our feelings are mainly the result of the way we *think* about reality, not reality itself. Take Paul, for example. Talented in school, he decided not to go on to college. Here's what Paul thinks about this decision now:

> I **ought to have applied** to college.
> I **could have become** a doctor.
> My parents **might have encouraged** me more.
> I **shouldn't have missed** that opportunity.
> I **could have been** rich and famous by now.

According to Nathan S. Kline, M.D., it's not unusual to feel deep regret about things in the past that you think you **should have done** and did not do—or the opposite, about things you did do and feel you **should not have done.** In fact, we learn by thinking about past errors.

However, dwelling too much on past mistakes and missed opportunities can create such bad feelings that people become paralyzed and can't move on with their lives. Arthur Freeman, Ph.D. and Rose DeWolf have labeled this process "woulda/coulda/shoulda thinking," and they have written an entire book about this type of disorder.

In *Woulda/Coulda/Shoulda: Overcoming Regrets, Mistakes, and Missed Opportunities* (New York: William Morrow, 1989), Freeman and DeWolf suggest challenging regrets with specifics. "Instead of saying, 'I **should have done** better,'" they suggest, "write down an example of a way in which you **might have done** better. Exactly what **should you have done** to produce the desired result? Did you have the skills, money, experience, etc., at the time?"

When people examine their feelings of regret about the past, they often find that many of them are simply not based in fact. A

166

*Paul: **I could have become** a doctor.*

mother regrets missing a football game in which her son's leg was injured. She blames herself and the officials. "I **should have gone**," she laments. "I **could have prevented** the injury. They **might** at least **have telephoned** me as soon as it happened." Did she really have the power to prevent her son's injury? **Should** the officials **have called** her before they had looked at the injury? Probably not.

Once people realize how unrealistic their feelings of regret are, they are more ready to let go of them. Cognitive psychologist David Burns, M.D., suggests specific strategies for dealing with useless feelings of regret and getting on with the present. One amusing technique is to spend ten minutes a day writing down all the things you regret. Then say them all aloud (better yet, record them), and listen to yourself. Here's a typical session:

I **shouldn't have told** that joke in the office. My career is ruined.

I **ought to have cleaned** the house instead of going out this weekend. My mother's right. I'm just lazy.

My boyfriend **could have told** me he was going out of town this weekend. He's an inconsiderate jerk. I **should** never **have started** going out with him.

Once you listen to your own "woulda/coulda/shoulda" thoughts, it's easier to see their illogic. For example, it's unlikely that your entire career is in ruins because of one joke. You're an adult and you can choose to go out instead of cleaning house. That doesn't make you a lazy person. Nor is your boyfriend a jerk for making a single mistake.

After you recognize how foolish most feelings of regret sound, the next step is to let go of them and to start dealing with life in the present. For some, this might be harder than sighing over past errors. An Italian proverb notes, "When the ship has sunk, everyone knows how she **could have been saved**." The message from cognitive psychology is similar. It's easy to speculate about the past; the real challenge is to solve the problems you face right now.

ADVISABILITY AND OBLIGATION IN THE PAST: *SHOULD HAVE, OUGHT TO HAVE, COULD HAVE, MIGHT HAVE*

STATEMENTS				
SUBJECT	MODAL*	*HAVE*	PAST PARTICIPLE	
He	**should (not)** **ought (not) to** **could (not)** **might (not)**	**have**	**told**	her.

Should, ought to, could, and *might* are modals. Modals have only one form. They do not have -s in the third-person singular.

YES/NO QUESTIONS				
SHOULD	SUBJECT	*HAVE*	PAST PARTICIPLE	
Should	he	**have**	**told**	her?

SHORT ANSWERS			
AFFIRMATIVE			
Yes,	he	**should**	**have.**

SHORT ANSWERS			
NEGATIVE			
No,	he	**shouldn't**	**have.**

WH- QUESTIONS					
WH- WORD	*SHOULD*	SUBJECT	*HAVE*	PAST PARTICIPLE	
When	**should**	he	**have**	**told**	her?

CONTRACTIONS		
should have	=	should've
could have	=	could've
might have	=	might've
should not have	=	shouldn't have

Grammar Notes

1. Use the modals *should have, ought to have, could have,* and *might have* to talk about actions that were advisable in the past. When we use these modals, we often communicate a sense of regret or blame.

> I **should've applied** to college. (I didn't apply to college. I'm sorry that I didn't do it.)
>
> I **ought to have taken** the job at the bank. (I didn't take the job. That was a mistake.)
>
> She **could've gone** to a much better school. (She didn't go to a good school although it was possible for her.)
>
> You **might've let** me know sooner. (You didn't let me know. That was impolite.)
>
> A: You **should've told** me first.
> B: I told you yesterday. Remember?
> A: Oh, that's right. You did tell me. Sorry.
>
> He **shouldn't have talked** to me that way. (He talked to me that way, but it was wrong of him.)

2. We rarely use *ought to have* in negative statements or questions. Instead we use *should have*.

Rare:
He **ought not to have missed** the final exam.
Ought he **to have called** the teacher?

More Common:
He **shouldn't have missed** the final exam.
Should he **have called** the teacher?

Pronunciation note: In informal speech, *have* in modal phrases is often pronounced like the word *of,* for example:

could have / k ʊ d ə v /

Be careful! Do not write *of* instead of *have* with these past modals.

> I should **have** gone. NOT ~~I should of gone.~~

Do not write *a* instead of *to* with *ought*.

> I **ought to** have gone. NOT ~~I ought a have gone.~~

Could have and *might have* are also used to express assumptions about the past. See Unit 14.

FOCUSED PRACTICE

1. Discover the Grammar

Read the first sentence of each set. Circle the letter (a) *or* (b) *of the sentence that is true.*

1. I shouldn't have called him.
   (a.) I called him.
   b. I didn't call him.
2. My parents ought to have moved away from that neighborhood.
   a. They're going to move, but they're not sure when.
   b. Moving was a good idea, but they didn't do it.

(continued on next page)

3. I should have told them what I thought.
    a. I didn't tell them, and now I regret it.
    b. I told them, and that was a big mistake.
4. We could have told you that movie was no good.
    a. We didn't know you were planning to go, so we didn't tell you.
    b. We haven't seen the movie yet, so we can't tell you about it.
5. He might have warned us about the traffic.
    a. He didn't know, so he couldn't tell us.
    b. He knew, but he didn't tell us.
6. Felicia could have been a vice president by now.
    a. Felicia didn't become a vice president.
    b. Felicia is a vice president.
7. I ought to have practiced more.
    a. I practiced enough.
    b. I didn't practice enough.
8. They shouldn't have lent him their car.
    a. They refused to lend him their car.
    b. They lent him their car.

2. Ethics Discussion

A class is discussing an ethical question. Complete the discussion with the correct form of the verbs in parentheses or short answers.

> Problem: Greg, a college student, worked successfully for a clothing store for a year. He spent most of his salary on books and tuition. One week he wanted some extra money to buy a sweater to wear to a party. He asked for a raise, but his boss refused. The same week, Greg discovered an extra sweater in a shipment he was unpacking. It was very stylish and just his size. Greg "borrowed" it for the weekend and then brought it back. His boss found out and fired him.

Teacher: ___Should___ Greg's boss _____have given_____ him a raise?
                                          1. (Should / give)

Student A: Yes, he _____ . After all, Greg had worked there for a whole year.
                            2.

His boss _____ at that point.
              3. (should / refuse)

Student B: But maybe his boss couldn't afford a raise. Anyway, Greg still

_____ the sweater. It wasn't his.
      4. (should / take)

Teacher: What _____ he _____ instead?
                                    5. (should / do)

Student C: He _____ his boss to sell him the sweater. Then he
                      6. (might / ask)

_____ for it slowly, out of his salary.
      7. (could / pay)

Student A: He _____ his old clothes to the party. A new sweater just wasn't
                      8. (ought to / wear)
worth all this trouble.

Teacher: Well,_____ Greg's boss _____ him?
                                          9. (should / fire)

Student B: No, he _____. Greg had been a good employee for a year.

10.
And he did bring the sweater back.

Teacher: How _____ he _____ the situation?

11. (should / handle)

Student C: He _____ him. He _____ just _____ him

12. (ought to / warn)   13. (should / fire)
without any warning.

3.   Ron Regrets

Read the things Ron is complaining about. Rewrite all the things he regrets about the past, using the modals in parentheses.

1. I didn't go to college. Now I'm unhappy with my job.
(should)

   _____ I should have gone to college. _____

2. My brother quit a good job, and now he's sorry. I knew it was a mistake, but I didn't warn him. How inconsiderate of me.
(might)

   _____

3. I feel sick. I ate all the chocolate.
(should)

   _____

4. Christina didn't come over. She didn't even call.
(might)

   _____

5. I didn't have enough money to buy the shirt. Why didn't Richard offer to lend me some?
(could)

   _____

6. I jogged five miles yesterday, and now I'm exhausted.
(should)

   _____

7. The supermarket charged me for the plastic bag. They used to be free.
(should)

   _____

8. I didn't do the laundry yesterday, so I don't have any clean socks. Everyone else gets their laundry done on time. Why can't I?
(ought to)

   _____

9. I didn't invite Cynthia to the party. Now she's angry at me.
(should)

   _____

4. Mistakes

An employee is writing in a journal about a work problem. Find and correct six mistakes with modals.

About a week ago, Jennifer was late for work again, and Doug, our boss, told me he wanted to get rid of her. I was really upset. Of course, Jennifer shouldn't ~~had~~ *have* been late so often, but he might has talked to her about the problem before he decided to let her go. Then he told me to make her job difficult for her so that she would quit. I just pretended I didn't hear him. What a mistake! I ought a have confronted him right away. Or I could at least have warned Jennifer. Anyway, Jennifer is still here, but now I'm worried about my own job. Should I of told his boss? I wonder. Maybe I should handle things differently last week. The company should never has hired this guy.

COMMUNICATION PRACTICE

5. Practice Listening

▣▣ *Jennifer is taking some of Dr. David Burns's advice by recording all the things she regrets at the end of the day. Listen to her recording. Then listen again and check the things she did.*

To Do

- ☐ Homework
- ☑ Walk to work
- ☐ Make $100 bank deposit
- ☐ Buy coat
- ☐ Call Aunt Rose
- ☐ Call Ron
- ☐ Go to supermarket
- ☐ Finish David Burns's book

6. S.O.S.

How strong is your sense of obligation? Take this test and find out.

Sense of Obligation Survey (S.O.S.)

Instructions: Read each situation. Circle the letter of your most likely response.

1. You want to lose ten pounds, but you just ate a large dish of ice cream.

    a. I shouldn't have eaten the ice cream. I have no willpower.

    b. I deserve to enjoy things once in a while. I'll do better tomorrow.

2. Your daughter quit her job. Now she's unemployed.

    a. Maybe she was really unhappy at work. It's better that she left.

    b. She shouldn't have quit until she found another job.

3. You had an appointment with your doctor. You arrived on time but had to wait more than an hour.

    a. My doctor should have scheduled better. My time is valuable, too.

    b. Maybe there was an emergency. I'm sure it's not my doctor's fault.

4. You bought a coat for $140. A day later you saw it at another store for just $100.

    a. That was really bad luck.

    b. I should have looked around before I bought the coat.

5. Your brother didn't send you a birthday card.

    a. He could have at least called. He only cares about himself.

    b. Maybe he forgot. He's really been busy lately.

6. You just got back an English test. Your grade was 60 percent.

    a. That was a really difficult test.

    b. I should have studied harder.

7. You just found out that an electrician overcharged you.

    a. I should have known that was too much money.

    b. How could I have known? I'm not an expert.

8. You forgot to do some household chores that you had promised to do. Now the person you live with is angry.

    a. I shouldn't have forgotten, I'm irresponsible.

    b. I'm only human. I make mistakes.

9. You got a ticket for driving five miles per hour above the speed limit.

    a. I ought to have obeyed the speed limit.

    b. The police officer could've overlooked it and not given me the ticket. It was only five miles per hour.

10. You went to the movies but couldn't get a ticket because it was sold out.

    a. I should've gone earlier.

    b. Wow! This movie is really popular!

Scoring

Give yourself one point for each of these answers:

1. a	6. b
2. b	7. a
3. a	8. a
4. b	9. a
5. a	10. a

The higher your score, the stronger your sense of obligation.

Compare your survey results with those of a classmate.

Example:

A: What did you answer for question 1?

B: I said I shouldn't have eaten the ice cream. What about you?

7. Dilemmas

Work with a group. Read and discuss each case. Did the people act properly
or should they have done things differently?

Case 1.   Sheila was in her last year of college when she decided to run for student council president. During her campaign, a school newspaper reporter asked her about something from her past. In high school, Sheila had once been caught cheating on a test. She had admitted her mistake and repeated the course. She never cheated again. Sheila felt that the incident was over, and she refused to answer the reporter's questions. The reporter wrote the story without telling Sheila's side, and Sheila lost the election. Her reputation at school was also damaged, and she's afraid she won't find a job easily when she graduates.

Example:
A: Should Sheila have refused to answer questions about her past?
B: I don't think so. She should've told her side of the story.

Case 2.   Mustafa is a social worker who cares very deeply about his clients. A few months ago, there was a fire in his office building. After the fire, the fire department declared that the building was no longer safe, and Mustafa's supervisor forbade anyone to go back for any reason. Mustafa became worried because all his clients' records were in the building. The records included names, addresses, telephone numbers, and other information Mustafa needed to help his clients. He decided it was worth the risk, and he entered the building to get them. His supervisor found out and fired Mustafa. Now he is unemployed, and his clients have a new social worker who is not as familiar with their problems as Mustafa was.

Case 3.   Pierre's wife had been sick for a long time. One day, the doctor told him that there was a new medication that might save his wife. However, he warned Pierre that the medicine was very expensive. Since it was still experimental, Pierre's insurance would not pay for it. The doctor wrote a prescription, and Pierre immediately went to the pharmacy to buy the medication. He discovered that it was so expensive that he just didn't have enough money to buy it. The pharmacist would not agree to give Pierre the medication and let him pay later. Pierre decided to look for extra work on nights and weekends to pay for the medicine. However, the extra work prevented him from taking care of his wife as carefully as he had before.

8. Hindsight

Use exercise 4 as a model and write about a dilemma that you have faced.
Discuss what you and others should have, might have, or could have done
in the situation. When you finish writing, exchange paragraphs with
another student and discuss your ideas.

INTRODUCTION

▼

The great achievements of ancient cultures fascinate modern people. Read and listen to one writer's theories regarding these achievements.

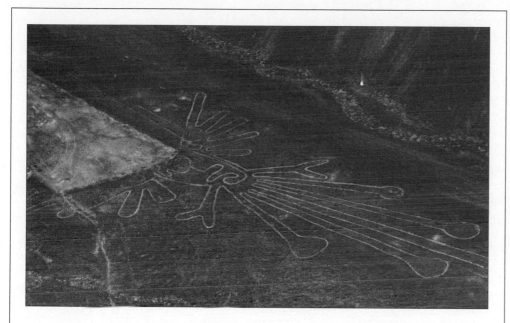

Close Encounters

In 1927, a Peruvian surveyor **must have been** astonished to see lines in the shapes of huge animals and geometric forms on the rocky ground below his airplane. Created by the ancient Nazca culture, these beautiful, clear-cut forms (over 13,000 of them) are too big to be recognized from the ground. However, seen from about 600 feet in the air, the giant forms take shape. Toribio Mexta Xesspe **may have been** the first human in almost a thousand years to have recognized the designs.

Since their rediscovery, many people have speculated about the Nazca lines. Without airplanes, how **could** an ancient culture **have made** these amazing pictures? What purpose **can** they **have served?**

One writer, Erich von Däniken, has a theory as amazing as the Nazca lines themselves. According to von Däniken, visitors from outer space brought their civilization to the Earth thousands of years ago. When these astronauts visited ancient cultures here on Earth, the people of those cultures **must have believed** that they were gods. Since the Nazcans **could have built** the lines according to instructions from an aircraft, von Däniken concludes that the drawings **might have marked** a landing strip for the spacecraft of the ancient astronauts. Von Däniken writes, "The builders of the geometrical figures **may have had** no idea what they were doing. But perhaps they knew perfectly well what the 'gods' needed in order to land."

In his book *Chariots of the Gods?* (New York: Bantam, 1972),von Däniken offers many other "proofs" that ancient cultures had contact with astronauts from advanced civilizations in outer space. Giant statues on Easter Island provide von Däniken with strong evidence of the astronauts' presence. Von Däniken estimates that the island **could** only **have supported** a very small population. After examining the tools that the islanders probably used, he concludes:

> Even 2,000 men, working day and night, would not be nearly enough to

carve these colossal figures out of the steel-hard volcanic stone with rudimentary tools—and at least part of the population **must have tilled** the barren fields, **gone** fishing, **woven** cloth, and **made** ropes. No, 2,000 men alone **could not have made** the gigantic statues.

Von Däniken finds no resemblance between the statues and human beings, and he suggests that islanders **may have modeled** them after the space visitors.

In a later book, *In Search of Ancient Gods* (New York: Putnam, 1974), von Däniken points to creation myths to support his theory of contact from another solar system. He notes, "All the stories of creation assert, with variations, that man was

created by gods from the cosmos, after they had come down to earth from heaven." These mythological gods **must** actually **have been** space creatures, according to von Däniken. He believes that ancient pictures of creatures with wings record the visits of these space beings. Arriving on Earth millennia ago, these beings brought amazing scientific and technological information to primitive cultures. The cultures **couldn't have been able** to understand or use this knowledge, but they preserved it in their art. Von Däniken sees rocket ships, robots, and wristwatches in the art of many different cultures.

Von Däniken also finds touching evidence of gifts from these wise astronauts in the map of a sixteenth-century Turkish admiral, Piri Reis. Dated 1513, the

map (several copies of which exist) was compiled from a number of other charts. Von Däniken believes that in 1513 cartographers **couldn't** possibly **have had** the information shown in this map. He insists, "Whoever made it **must have been able** to fly and to take photographs." According to von Däniken, only one con-clusion is possible:

To me it is obvious that extraterrestrial spacemen made the maps from space stations in orbit. During one of their visits, they made our ancestors a present of the maps.

Obvious? Well, perhaps not to everyone. Scientists, among others, remain skeptical and prefer to look for answers closer to home. However, von Däniken's theories continue to fascinate millions of readers, both believers and nonbelievers. And even nonbelievers must admit that space visitors **might have contributed** to human culture. After all, no one can prove that they didn't. . . .

SPECULATIONS AND CONCLUSIONS ABOUT THE PAST: MAY HAVE, MIGHT HAVE, COULD HAVE, MUST HAVE, HAD TO HAVE

AFFIRMATIVE STATEMENTS				
SUBJECT	MAY/MIGHT COULD/MUST/* HAD TO	HAVE	PAST PARTICIPLE	
They	may might could must had to	have	seen	the statues.

NEGATIVE STATEMENTS					
SUBJECT	MAY/MIGHT COULD/MUST*	NOT	HAVE	PAST PARTICIPLE	
He	may might could must	not	have	found	much support.

May, might, could, and *must* are modals. Modals have only one form. They do not have *-s* in the third person singular.

(continued on next page)

CONTRACTIONS		
may have	=	may've
might have	=	might've
could have	=	could've
must have	=	must've
could not	=	couldn't

Note: We usually do not contract *may not have*, *might not have*, and *must not have*.

QUESTIONS
Did they carve statues?

SHORT ANSWERS		
SUBJECT	**MODAL**	**HAVE**
They	**may (not)** **might (not)** **could (not)** **must (not)** **had to**	**have.**

YES/NO QUESTIONS: *COULD*				
COULD	**SUBJECT**	**HAVE**	**PAST PARTICIPLE**	
Could	he	**have**	**been**	in Peru?

SHORT ANSWERS WITH *BEEN*		
SUBJECT	**MODAL**	**HAVE BEEN**
He	**may (not)** **might (not)** **could (not)** **must (not)** **had to**	**have been.**

WH- QUESTIONS				
WH- WORD	**COULD**	**HAVE**	**PAST PARTICIPLE**	
Who	**could**	**have**	**built**	the statues?

Grammar Notes

1. We often make assumptions, or "best guesses," about past situations based on information that we have. A logical guess based on facts is a conclusion. Use *must have* and *had to have* to state conclusions based on facts.

Facts	Conclusions
The Easter Island statues are made of stone.	The islanders **must have had** sharp tools.
	The stone **must not have been** too hard for the tools they had.
The statues are very big.	The islanders **had to have moved** them with ropes.

2. When we are less certain, we speculate, or express possibilities. Use *may have, might have,* and *could have* to speculate, or express possibilities about a past situation.

Fact	Possibilities
Archaeologists found pictures of winged creatures.	Space beings **may have visited** that culture.
	Local artists **might have recorded** visits by space beings.
	Von Däniken **might not have understood** mythology.
	The pictures **could have shown** mythological creatures and not visitors from outer space.

Pronunciation note: In informal speech, *have* in modal phrases is often pronounced like the word *of*, for example:

could have /kʊdəv/

Be careful! Do not write *of* instead of *have* with these past modals.

> They must **have** been very skillful.
> NOT They ~~must of been~~...

3. *Couldn't have* often expresses a feeling of disbelief or impossibility.

> He **couldn't have drawn** that map! He didn't have enough information.

4. We do not usually use *may have* or *might have* in questions about possibility. We use *could have*.

> **Could** the Nazca people **have drawn** those lines?
> **Could** they **have known** about hot-air balloons?

5. Use *been* in short answers to questions that include a form of *be*.

Was Xesspe surprised when he saw the Nazca lines?	He **must have been.** No one knew about them at that time.
Could von Däniken have **been** wrong?	He certainly **could have been.** There are more plausible explanations.

However, use only the modal + *have* in short answers to questions containing other verbs.

Did archaeologists **measure** the drawings?	They **must have.** They studied them for years.
Did Reis **make** many copies of his map?	He **might have.** They've found several copies of it already.

Could have and *might have* are also used to express past advisability and obligation. See Unit 13.

FOCUSED PRACTICE

1. Discover the Grammar

Match the facts with the conclusions.

Facts

_____ *e* 1. The original title of *Chariots of the Gods?* was *Erinnerungen an die Zukunft*.

_____ 2. Von Däniken visited every place he described in his book.

_____ 3. In 1973, he wrote *In Search of Ancient Gods*.

_____ 4. He doesn't have a degree in archaeology.

_____ 5. *Chariots of the Gods?* was published the same year as the Apollo moon landing.

_____ 6. In the early 1900s, Annie Besant, another writer, said that beings from Venus helped develop culture on Earth.

_____ 7. Von Däniken's books sold millions of copies.

_____ 8. As soon as von Däniken published his book, scientists attacked him.

Conclusions

a. He must have traveled a lot.

b. He may have known about her ideas.

c. He could have learned the subject matter on his own.

d. He must have made a lot of money.

e. He must have written it in German.

f. This scientific achievement must have increased sales of the book.

g. They must not have believed his theories.

h. He might have written other books too.

2. On Their Own

Complete the review of Erich von Däniken's book, Chariots of the Gods? *with the verbs in parentheses.*

Who ____could have made____ the Nazca lines? According to Erich von Däniken, author of this
　　　　　1. (could / make)

runaway best-seller, ancient human achievements like these present a great mystery. Our ancestors

_____ these structures on their own, he believes. Their cultures were too primitive.
2. (could / not erect)

Von Däniken's solution: They _____ help from space visitors.
　　　　　　　　　　　　　　　3. (had to / get)

　　　Von Däniken's many readers may not realize that practical experiments have shed light on

several of these "mysteries." Von Däniken asks: How _____ the Nazcans _____
　　　　　　　　　　　　　　　　　　　　　　　　　　　　　　　　　　　4. (could / plan)

the lines from the ground? Archaeologists now believe that this civilization _____
　　　　　　　　　　　　　　　　　　　　　　　　　　　　　　　　　　5. (might / develop)

flight. They think that ancient Nazcans _____ a picture of a hot-air balloon on a piece
　　　　　　　　　　　　　　　　　　6. (may / draw)

of pottery discovered in a Nazcan grave. To test their theory, archaeologists were able to build a similar balloon, using only Nazcan cloth and ropes similiar to ones found in Nazcan graves. The balloon soared high into the air, high enough to view the Nazca lines. The experiment shows that Nazcans _____ the pictures from the air, using only the materials and skills of their
7. (could / design)
own culture.

But what about the Easter Island statues? _____ islanders _____ the huge
8. (Could / cut)
statues from hard rock with primitive tools? And how _____ only 2,000 people

_____ them around the island? When he wrote his book, von Däniken
9. (could / move)

_____ about the Easter Island experiments of 1955. Working with ancient stone tools,
10. (must / not know)
seven Easter Islanders carved the rough shape of a statue in just three days. Only two hundred men were able to move a twelve-ton statue across the island. These experiments proved that the ancient

islanders _____ and _____ these statues without any help from alien
11. (could / carve)   12. (transport)
visitors. Not only that, but the island's population _____ much larger than von
13. (might / be)
Däniken believes. One scientist speculates that Easter Island _____ a population of
14. (may / support)
20,000 or more.

_____ space aliens _____ Erich von Däniken write his book? After all, von
15. (Could / help)
Däniken started with no formal education and very little money. How _____ he

_____ the world's great archaeological sites and _____ an
16. (could / visit)   17. (write)
international best-seller? Of course, we believe that von Däniken _____ these sites
18. (could / explore)
and _____ his ideas without help from other worlds. In fact, we give von Däniken a
19. (develop)
lot more credit than he gives our ancestors. A wiser response to the mysterious achievements of the

past might be to say, "Our forebears _____ great skill, intelligence, and strength to
20. (must / have)
create these wonderful things."

3. Nature Puzzles

Read about these puzzling events and the speculations on their causes. Then rewrite the sentences. Substitute a modal phrase for the underlined words or phrases.

 Beginning two hundred million years ago, dinosaurs existed on the Earth. Then, about sixty-five million years ago, these giant reptiles all died in a short period of time. What could have caused the dinosaurs to become extinct? Here's what scientist say.

1. <u>It's likely that</u> the Earth became colder. (must)

   The Earth must have become colder.

2. <u>Probably,</u> dinosaurs didn't survive the cold. (must not)

   _____

   _____

3. <u>It's been suggested that</u> a huge meteor hit the Earth. (might)

   _____

   _____

4. <u>It's possible that</u> dust from the impact blocked the sun for a long time. (may)

   _____

   _____

 In 1924, Albert Ostman went camping alone in Canada. Later, he reported that a Bigfoot (a large, hairy creature that looks human) had kidnapped him and taken him home, where the Bigfoot family treated him like a pet. Ostman escaped after several days. What do you think happened? Could a Bigfoot really have kidnapped Ostman?

5. A Bigfoot didn't kidnap Ostman—<u>that's impossible.</u> (couldn't)

   _____

   _____

6. Ostman <u>probably</u> saw a bear. (must)

   _____

7. <u>It's possible that</u> Ostman dreamed it. (may)

   _____

8. <u>It could be that</u> he thought his dream was real. (could)

   _____

 In 1932, a man was taking a walk around Scotland's beautiful Loch Ness. Suddenly, a couple hundred feet from shore, the water bubbled up and a huge monster appeared. The man took a picture. When it was developed, the picture showed something with a long neck and a small head. Since then, many people have reported similar sightings. What do you think? Did the man really see the Loch Ness monster?

9. <u>Most likely</u> the photograph was a fake. (must)

   _____

   _____

10. <u>Perhaps</u> the man saw a large fish. (might)

    _____

11. <u>It's possible that</u> it was a dead tree trunk. (may)

    _____

12. <u>It's very unlikely that</u> he saw a dinosaur. (couldn't)

    _____

    _____

4. Archaeology 101

Some archaeology students are asking questions in class. Use the modals in
parentheses to write short answers.

1. **A:** Do you think the people on Easter Island built the giant statues themselves?

    B: _____They could have_____. They had the knowledge and the tools.

(could)

2. **A:** Were the Nazcans really able to fly?

    B: _____. There's some evidence that they had hot-air balloons.

(might)

3. **A:** Is it possible that the Nazcan lines were ancient streets?

    B: _____. Some of them just lead to the tops of mountains and

(could not)
    then end abruptly.

4. **A:** What about ceremonial walkways? Do you think the Nazcans used "the streets" during

    religious rituals?

    B: _____. But we have no proof.

(might)

5. **A:** Did the sixteenth-century Turkish admiral, Piri Reis, know about Antarctica?

    B: _____. Antarctica wasn't discovered until 1842.

(could not)

6. **A:** Von Däniken says that many ancient artifacts show pictures of astronauts. Could these

    pictures have illustrated anything closer to Earth?

    B: _____. It's possible that the pictures show people dressed in

(may)
    local costumes.

7. **A:** Was von Däniken upset by all the criticism he received?

    B: _____. After all, it created more interest in his books.

(might not)

8. **A:** Do you think von Däniken helped increase general interest in archaeology?

    B: _____. Just look at how many of you are taking this class!

(must)

COMMUNICATION PRACTICE

5. Practice Listening

Some archaeology students are discussing artifacts they have found at various sites. Look at the pictures. Then listen to the students speculate and draw conclusions about what each item is. Listen again and match the pictures with the appropriate conversation.

1. ____

4. ____

2. ____

5. ____

3. ____

6. _a.8_

6. Useful Objects

Work in small groups. Look at the objects that archaeologists have found in different places. Discuss what they are and how people might have used them. Give reasons for your opinions. After your discussion, compare your group's ideas with those of the rest of the class.

1. Archaeologists found this object in the sleeping area of an ancient Chinese house. It's about the same diameter as a basketball.

   Example:
   I think people might have used this as a foot stool. The floor must have been cold at night, and people could have rested their feet on this thing. It's about the right height.

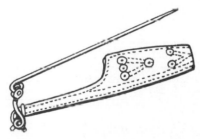

2. Archaeologists have found iron objects like these with men's and women's clothing. This one is about the size of a pocket comb.

3. Objects like these were made of plant fiber or animal skin. They were covered with chalky paste and then painted with figures like these. What could this picture have represented?

(continued on next page)

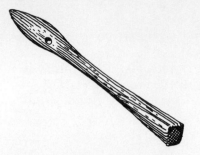

4. This smooth wooden artifact was used by ancient Egyptians. It's about the size of a pencil.

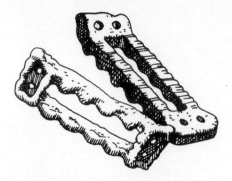

5. These are made of ivory, and they were found in Alaska. Each one is about the length of a cassette tape. They always come in pairs.

Now turn to page AK 15 in the Answer Key and read what archaeologists believe about the objects.

7. Unsolved Mysteries

Work in small groups. Read about some famous unsolved mysteries. Speculate on what happened. Think of as many explanations as possible. Then compare your answers with those of another group.

1. The Maya once inhabited the northern Yucatán in what today is Mexico. They had a very advanced civilization. In about A.D. 600, for no known reason, the entire Maya population suddenly left their large and well-built cities. The jungle soon covered the entire area. The Maya never returned. Why did they leave? Why did they never return?

   Example:
   Their source of food may have failed. They might have moved to find new food sources.

2. On June 30, 1908, a gigantic object headed toward Earth and exploded in a great ball of fire near the Yenisey River in Siberia. The explosion was one of the strongest ever recorded on Earth. Almost twenty years passed before scientists studied the area. They found miles of burnt land, but absolutely no sign of what had caused the explosion. What could it have been?

3. On October 23, 1947, at about 7:30 A.M. in a small U.S. town, it suddenly started raining fish. The town's bank director reported that hundreds of fish had fallen into his yard, and townspeople were hit by the falling fish as they walked to work. The fish were only the kinds found in local rivers and lakes, and they were all very fresh. Nothing else—no frogs, turtles, or water plants—fell that morning, only fish. How could this have happened?

8. Chariots of the Gods?

Reread the introduction to this unit. Then discuss your opinion about Erich von Däniken's theory with a partner. Afterward, have a class discussion. How many students think space creatures might have visited the Earth? How many think space creatures couldn't have affected human culture?

I. *Complete the conversation by circling the correct words.*

A: You (must have)/should have been up late last night. You look tired.
1.

B: I couldn't sleep. My boss passed me up for a raise. He

could have/couldn't have given me one. After all, I've been there a
2.

whole year.

A: Did anyone else get one?

B: Ann got a raise and a promotion. He

shouldn't have/may not have promoted her. She's terrible. By the
3.

way, your friend Amy also got a promotion.

A: Really? She had to have/might have been pleased about that. But,
4.

getting back to you—you should have/shouldn't have called me if
5.

you were upset. I might have/must have been able to help.
6.

B: I did call you. You were out.

A: I wasn't out. I must not have/could not have heard the phone.
7.

I might have/ought to have been in the shower.
8.

B: Well, I ended up calling Sam. That was a mistake.

I should have/shouldn't have called him.
9.

A: Why not?

B: He repeated everything to Ann.

A: That's terrible. He certainly ought not to have/must not have
10.

done that.

II. *Complete the conversation with the correct forms of the verbs in
parentheses. Choose between affirmative and negative.*

A: What's the matter? You look kind of upset.

B: Oh, I just got back my math test. I only got a C. I

should have done better.
1. (should / do)

A: Don't be so hard on yourself. It _____ entirely
2. (may / be)

your fault. It just _____ a more difficult test than
3. (might / be)

usual.

B: No, I don't think so. It _____ that difficult. The rest
4. (could / be)

of the class did pretty well on it.

A: Well, did you study for it?

B: Yes, but apparently I _____ harder.
5. (should / study)

A: What _____ you _____ differently?
6. (could / do)

B: Well, I guess I _____ my notes more carefully. And I _____ that
7. (could / read)   8. (should / miss)
day of class.

A: You missed a day? Did you get the notes?

B: No. I _____ them. Some of the problems I got wrong _____
9. (ought to / copy)   10. (must / come)
from that day.

III. *Summarize these sentences. Use the past form of the modals in parentheses. Choose between affirmative and negative.*

1. It was a mistake to stay up so late.

   (should) _____ I shouldn't have stayed up so late. _____

2. I regret not watching the show about von Däniken.

   (should) _____

3. I'm sure it was very interesting.

   (must) _____

4. I was surprised that the library didn't have his books.

   (ought to) _____

5. I'm annoyed at Sara for not reminding me about it.

   (should) _____

6. I wish that John had told me about it.

   (could) _____

7. I'm sure he didn't remember our conversation about it.

   (must) _____

8. I feel bad that my roommate didn't invite me to the party.

   (might) _____

9. It's possible that John didn't get an invitation.

   (might) _____

10. I'm sure he didn't forget our date.

    (could) _____

IV. *Read this journal entry. There are four mistakes in the use of past modals. Find and correct them.*

                                               stayed

What a day! I guess I shouldn't have ~~stay~~ up so late last night. That way I could of gotten up earlier this morning and had an earlier start. By the time I got to the post office, the lines were already really long. I must have waited at least a half an hour for my turn. Of course, then I was really late to work, and my boss was angry. I guess I could have called. It really didn't matter that much, though, because the computers weren't working. We must have lost three hours that way. While the system was down, some of us went out to lunch. Afterwards we all felt sick. It had to has been the food—we all ate the same thing. On the way home, I got stuck in a traffic jam. A trip that should have taken only twenty minutes wound up taking forty-five. I just should have stay in bed.

VII

Conditionals

INTRODUCTION

Read and listen to this informational brochure containing advice for travelers.

Know Before You Go

High-speed air travel is usually fast and efficient. However, it has its special hassles, and **these can cause delay and discomfort if you don't know how to avoid them.** Know before you go and enjoy your journey more.

RECONFIRMING. **If you are traveling internationally, you should reconfirm your flight 72 hours ahead of time.** In spite of electronic reservation systems, many airlines rely on your telephone call to reserve your seat.

CHECKING IN. A good travel agent can often get you a boarding pass in advance. However, even with a previously issued boarding pass, you should still check in at the gate. **You could be bumped from a flight if you don't.**

MEALS. **If you need a low-calorie, low-sodium, or low-cholesterol meal, order it in advance from the airline.** You can also order vegetarian and kosher meals ahead of time. **If you hate airplane food** (and many people do), **then it's a good idea to order one of these special meals anyway.** It will be fresher and taste better than the standard meal.

COMFORT. One common cause of discomfort on a plane is dehydration, caused by traveling in a pressurized cabin. To avoid this problem, drink a glass of juice or water every hour you are on the plane. Sitting in one place for too long is another cause. **If you move around the cabin every hour, you can avoid stiffness.** We also suggest doing stretching exercises in your seat.

JET LAG. When you get to your destination, jet lag will catch up with you. There's no way to avoid it. **If you travel across time zones at high speeds, your internal clock doesn't keep up with the time changes.** That's why your body thinks it's midnight when it's really 9:00 A.M. To minimize the discomfort, reset your watch for the time zone of your destination before you leave home. Also, arrange to arrive late in the day. **You are psychologically prepared to sleep at the right time if it's evening when you get to your destination.**

WHEELCHAIR FLYERS. Airline wheelchairs are heavy, and someone must push you from behind. **You have much more mobility if you store your own wheelchair in the cabin.** Terry Winkler, a physician who is also a paraplegic, gives this advice: "**If my wheelchair can't be stored on board, I insist that they bring it from the baggage compartment as soon as the plane lands.**" If you have a disability, be aware of your rights as a passenger. Most airlines cannot bar you except under very special circumstances. **If you do not require special equipment, you do not even have to notify the airline of your disability in advance.**

FLYING WITH CHILDREN. **If you are traveling with children, your big challenge is to stay together on the plane.** Ask for seats as early as possible (30 days before your flight). **If you get scattered seats, preboard and ask the flight attendant to help you.** He or she may be able to reassemble the family before the flight. Always try to get a direct flight. **If you must make a connecting flight, you might be able to arrange for an electric car to drive you from one gate to the next.** Ask your flight attendant to radio ahead for one.

FACTUAL CONDITIONALS: PRESENT

STATEMENTS		
	IF CLAUSE	**MAIN CLAUSE**
If	air **heats,**	it **expands.**
	it**'s snowing,**	the airports **could close.**
	you **need** a special meal,	**call** in advance.

YES/NO QUESTIONS		
MAIN CLAUSE	**IF CLAUSE**	
Does air **expand** **Could** the airports **close**	**if**	it **heats?** it**'s snowing?**

SHORT ANSWERS	
AFFIRMATIVE	
Yes,	it **does.** they **could.**

SHORT ANSWERS	
NEGATIVE	
No,	it **doesn't.** they **couldn't.**

WH- QUESTIONS	
MAIN CLAUSE	**IF CLAUSE**
Why **does** air **expand**	**if** it **heats?**

Grammar Notes

1. Use present factual conditional sentences to talk about general truths and scientific facts. The *if* clause talks about the condition, and the main clause talks about the result if the condition occurs. Use the simple present tense in both clauses.

If Clause (Condition)	Main Clause (Result)
If air **expands,**	it **becomes** lighter.

2. You can also use factual conditional sentences to talk about habits and things that recur (happen again and again). Use the simple present tense in both clauses.

If Clause (Condition)	Main Clause (Result)
If Bob **flies,**	he **orders** a special meal.
If the flight **is** bumpy,	I **keep** my seat belt buckled.

3. You can begin conditional sentences with the *if* clause or the main clause. The meaning is the same.

> If the seat belt light goes on, buckle your seat belt.
> OR
> Buckle your seat belt if the seat belt light goes on.

Be careful! Use a comma between the two clauses only when the *if* clause comes first.

4. Use modals in the main clause to express ability, advisability, or possibility.

> If you practice your Chinese, you **can improve** quickly.
> If you shop in open-air markets, you **shouldn't get dressed up.**
> If you dress up, shopkeepers **might charge** you more.

5. Use the imperative in the main clause to give instructions, commands, and invitations that depend upon a certain condition.

> If you want good weather, **travel** in October.
> If you shop in open-air markets, **don't get dressed up.**
> If you come to Hong Kong, **stay** with us.

6. We sometimes use *then* to emphasize the result in factual conditional sentences with modals or imperatives.

> If you shop in open-air markets, **then** you shouldn't dress up.
> If you want good weather, **then** travel in October.

7. You can negate either or both clauses of conditional sentences.

> If I'm traveling a long distance, I fly.
> If I'm **not** traveling a long distance, I drive.
> If I'm traveling a long distance, I **don't** drive.
> If I'm **not** traveling a long distance, I **don't** fly.

8. You can often use *when* or *whenever* instead of *if*. This is especially true when you talk about general truths, habits, and recurring events.

> **When** air expands, it becomes lighter.
> **Whenever** Bob flies, he orders a special meal.
> **Whenever** the flight is bumpy, I keep my seat belt buckled.

FOCUSED PRACTICE

1. Discover the Grammar

In each factual conditional sentence, underline the main clause once.
Underline the clause that expresses the condition twice.

<u>If you run into problems on your journey</u>, <u>know your rights as a passenger.</u> Often the airline company is required to compensate you for delays or damages. For example, the airline provides meals and hotel rooms if a flight is unduly delayed. However, the airline owes you a lot more if the delay is caused by overbooking. This occurs mostly during holidays, when airlines often sell more tickets than there are seats. If all the passengers actually show up, then the flight is overbooked. Airlines usually award upgrades or additional free travel to passengers who volunteer to take a later flight. However, if no one volunteers, your flight may be delayed. In that case, the airline must repay you 100 percent of the cost of your ticket for a delay of up to four hours on an international flight. Whenever the delay is over four hours, you receive 200 percent of the cost of your ticket.

(continued on next page)

Suppose you arrive on time, but your suitcase doesn't. Ask for funds to buy clothing or toiletries if your luggage is delayed. The airline should award you twenty-five to fifty dollars. If the airline actually loses your suitcase, then it must pay you the value of its contents. The limit is $1,250 for a domestic flight and nine dollars a pound for an international flight.

2. If It's Tuesday, This Must Be Hong Kong

Read the conversations about Hong Kong. Summarize the advice with conditional sentences.

1. **Q:** I hate hot weather.

   A: The best time to go to Hong Kong is November or December.

   If you hate hot weather, the best time to go to Hong Kong is November or December.

   The weather is cooler then.

2. **Q:** I'm traveling with my children.

   A: Take them to Lai Chi Kok Amusement Park in Kowloon.

   _____

   They'll enjoy the games, shows, and rides.

3. **Q:** We need a moderate-priced hotel.

   A: I suggest Harbour View International House.

   _____

   It's a good hotel, and it's fairly inexpensive.

4. **Q:** We like seafood.

   A: There are wonderful seafood restaurants on Lamma Island.

   _____

   You can take the Star Ferry there.

5. **Q:** I'm fascinated by Chinese opera.

   A: You might like the street opera in the Shanghai Street Night Market.

   _____

   Opera is also performed at City Hall.

6. **Q:** I'd like to get a good view of Hong Kong.

   A: You should take the funicular to the Peak.

   _____

   From the top you can see Hong Kong harbor, the outer islands, and the New Territories.

7. **Q:** I'm interested in buying some traditional Chinese crafts.

   A: Then you ought to visit the Western District on Hong Kong Island.

   _____

   You can find craftspeople making fans, mahjong tiles, and a lot of other traditional articles.

8. **Q:** I'm looking for a good dim sum restaurant.

   A: Try Luk Yu Teahouse on Stanley Street.

   _____

   It's an historical monument as well as a restaurant. The early-twentieth-century decor is beautiful.

3. Frequent Flyer

Complete the interview with a Skyways flight attendant. Combine the two sentences in parentheses to make a factual conditional sentence. Keep the same order and decide which clause begins with **if**. Make necessary changes in capitalization and punctuation.

Interviewer: How long are you usually away?

Attendant: It depends.

   1. _____ If I go to the Bahamas, I have a two-day layover. _____
            (I go to the Bahamas. I have a two-day layover.)

Interviewer: What do you do for two days?

Attendant: 2. _____ I spend a lot of time at the pool if I stay at a hotel. _____
            (I spend a lot of time at the pool. I stay at a hotel.)

   3. _____
            (I stay with friends. I spend time with them.)

Interviewer: Sounds nice.

Attendant: 4. _____
            (It's not so nice. I get a Dracula.)

Interviewer: A Dracula?

Attendant: That's when you fly to Pittsburgh at midnight, spend four hours in the airport, and then fly back to New York.

Interviewer: I see what you mean. Who walks the dog and waters the plants when you're away for several days?

Attendant: I share an apartment with three other flight attendants.

   5. _____
         (You have three roommates. You don't have trouble finding dogwalkers.)

Interviewer: Most people think this is a very glamorous job.

Attendant: Actually, it's a very physically demanding job. But

   6. _____
         (it's very rewarding. You don't mind hard work.)

Interviewer: What do you like most about it?

Attendant: The travel. I can write my own ticket for any destination on a Skyways route.

   7. _____
         (A flight has an empty seat. I ride for free.)

(continued on next page)

Interviewer: Where have you been so far this year?

Attendant: Tokyo, Honolulu, Hong Kong, San Francisco. It's wonderful—except when you can't get back.

Interviewer: What do you mean?

Attendant: 8. _____
(A flight is completely booked. You can't get on it.)

Interviewer: Has that ever happened to you?

Attendant: Sure. I've been stranded in some of the most beautiful cities in the world.

4. In the Air

Read Pietro's notes about experiments with air. Then write a sentence stating a general truth about each situation.

Cover a burning candle with a jar.

The flame goes out.

1. _____ If you cover a burning candle with a jar, the flame goes out. _____

Heat the air in a balloon.

The balloon rises.

2. _____

Boil water.

The water evaporates.

3. _____

Put an empty glass upside down in a basin of water.

The air in the glass keeps the water out.

4.

Attach an object to a parachute.

The object falls slowly.

5. _____

Suck on a straw.

Liquid replaces the air that has been sucked out.

6. _____

COMMUNICATION PRACTICE

5. Practice Listening

You and your nephew, Pietro, are flying to Hong Kong by way of Los Angeles. Listen to the announcements. Then read each situation. Listen to the announcements again and check the appropriate box.

	True	False

1. You have two pieces of carry-on luggage

   and Pietro has one.

   You can take them on the plane.   ☑ ☐

2. These are your boarding passes:

   ✈✈✈✈✈✈✈✈✈✈✈✈✈✈

   UPAir *Boarding Pass*

   01 of 02

   NAME OF PASSENGER
   DI MARCO/PIETRO

   FROM X/O
   NYC

   TO X/O
   LOS ANGELES/LAX

   CARRIER
   UPAIR

   CODE   FLIGHT   CLASS   DATE   TIME
   UP   398   V 13AUG1020A

   GATE   BOARDING TIME   SEAT   SMOKING
   ADVANCE   16A   ⊘✈

   1   037   2171281950   2

   ✈✈✈✈✈✈✈✈✈✈✈✈✈✈

   ✈✈✈✈✈✈✈✈✈✈✈✈✈✈

   UPAir *Boarding Pass*

   02 of 02

   NAME OF PASSENGER
   DI MARCO/PAT

   FROM X/O
   NYC

   TO X/O
   LOS ANGELES/LAX

   CARRIER
   UPAIR

   CODE   FLIGHT   CLASS   DATE   TIME
   UP   398   V 13AUG1020A

   GATE   BOARDING TIME   SEAT   SMOKING
   ADVANCE   16B   ⊘✈

   1   037   2171281950   2

   ✈✈✈✈✈✈✈✈✈✈✈✈✈✈

   You can board now.   ☐ ☐

3. Look at your boarding passes again.

   You can board now.   ☐ ☐

4. Pietro is a child.

   You should put on his oxygen mask first.   ☐ ☐

5. You're sitting in a left window seat.

   You can see the Great Salt Lake.   ☐ ☐

6. You need information about your connecting flight.

   You can get this information on the plane.   ☐ ☐

6. Travel Tips

Work with a partner. Imagine that you are preparing a travel brochure for your city or town. Use factual conditional sentences and write tips for visitors. Compare your brochure with another pair's.

Examples:

If you enjoy swimming or boating, you should visit Ocean Park.
If you like to shop, Caterville has the biggest mall in this part of the country.

7. What Happens If...

Write your typical daily schedule. Exchange schedules with a partner. Ask each other what you do if there are special situations.

Examples:

How do you get to work if the bus is late?
What do you do if there's no food in the house and you don't have time to shop?
Where do you go if your class is canceled and you have some extra time?
Who takes care of your daughter if she gets sick and can't go to school?

8. Experiments

Work in small groups and do these experiments with air and gravity. Try each one several times and then state a general truth about each one. Discuss the reason for this result with your group. Then check your ideas on page AK 16 in the Answer Key.

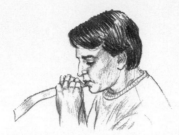

1. Hold a strip of paper to your mouth. What happens if you blow across the top of the strip? Does it rise or fall?

   Example:
   If you blow across the top of a strip of paper, the strip (<u>rises/falls</u>).

2. Pinch a plastic drinking straw tightly and push it into a crisp apple. Can you drive the straw into the apple?

3. Take a small, dense object such as an eraser, and a larger, heavier object such as a book. If you drop them from the same height at the same time, which one hits the floor first?

4. Hold two sheets of paper to your mouth with about two inches between the sheets. What happens if you blow between them?

9. Quotable Quotes

Read these proverbs and quotations about traveling. Discuss them with a partner. Use factual conditional sentences to explain what each one means.

If you travel by boat, prepare to get wet.
—*Chinese proverb*

Example:
I think this means if you travel, you have to accept whatever conditions you find.

If you are traveling, even a straw is heavy.
—*English proverb*

If a donkey goes traveling, he doesn't come home a horse.
—*U.S. proverb*

If you wish to be thoroughly misinformed about a country, consult a man who has lived there for thirty years and speaks the language like a native.
—*George Bernard Shaw (Irish playwright, 1856–1950)*

If you reject the food, ignore the customs, fear the religion, and avoid the people, you might [as well] stay home. You are like a pebble thrown into water; you become wet on the surface, but you are never part of the water.
—*James Michener (U.S. novelist, 1907–)*

Own only what you can carry with you: know language, know countries, know people. Let your memory be your travel bag.
—*Alexander Solzhenitsyin (Russian novelist, 1918–)*

A journey of a thousand miles begins with the first step.
—*Lao Tzu (Chinese philosopher, 6th cent., B.C.)*

INTRODUCTION

▷ ⊙ ⊙ *Two candidates are running for mayor of a large city. Read and listen to their statements from a voter's guide.*

★ ★ M A Y O R ★ ★

Daniel Baker
Party: Democrat
Occupation: Mayor
Background: City Clerk, State Assembly member, attorney
Education: Yale Law School, LL.B.; Howard University, B.S. cum laude

Gabriela Ibarguen
Party: Republican
Occupation: City Comptroller
Background: City Comptroller, District Attorney, member U.S. House of Representatives, lawyer
Education: U.C.L.A. Law School, LL.B.; U.S.C., B.A.

Statement supplied by the candidate:

Four years ago, I promised to create a government that you could count on. Today, after four years as mayor of this great city, I am proud to say that we have come a long way. But the job is not finished. **If I am reelected, together we will finish the work we started four years ago.**

The backbone of our effort must be education. In the next ten years, there will be 16 million new jobs in the United States. **A lot of those jobs will be filled by citizens of our city if we prepare them. But they won't be ready unless we improve our school system now.**

My second priority is housing. **It won't do any good to provide jobs if people continue to live in bad conditions.** We must continue to rebuild housing in our city neighborhoods. My opponent talks about waging a war on crime and drugs. I agree that violent crime is a problem. But **we're not going to solve the social problems in this city unless we house people better.**

If our city offers an educated work force, business will thrive here. And as business thrives, we will have more money to rebuild housing. **If our citizens have decent homes, then our neighborhoods will become healthy again.** I'm not going to pretend that these problems will go away quickly. But **if we work together, we will solve them.**

I urge everyone to get out and vote on election day. **Unless you vote, you will not have a say in the future of our great city.**

Statement supplied by the candidate:

Our streets are plagued by crime, and many people are afraid to go out of their homes. **If I am elected, my highest priority will be to give the neighborhoods back to the citizens.** A lot of this violence is being committed by very young offenders. My administration will say to these young people: **If you want to stay out of trouble, we will help you do that.** But **if you do the crime, you'll do the time. If you commit a violent crime, you will go to jail, and you will serve your full sentence.**

If I become mayor, I will help citizens protect their neighborhoods. I will put more police on the streets, demand mandatory prison sentences for drug dealers, and set up a cooperative program between police and communities. **If I am elected, I will help you fight for every street, for every house.** Together we will win.

But **our young people won't have a reason to avoid crime unless they have some hope for their futures.** That's why my second priority as mayor will be to bring businesses back to our city. My opponent raised taxes as soon as he took office four years ago. As a result, businesses left in droves—we have lost over 100,000 jobs in the last four years. **If we lower taxes, businesses will return. If businesses return, our youth will have jobs to look forward to and some reason to hope. And if they have hope, they will not turn to a life of crime.**

I urge you to vote for me next Tuesday. **If I am elected, we'll hang out a sign:** "Open for business again."

★ C A N D I D A T E S ★

FACTUAL CONDITIONALS: FUTURE

STATEMENTS	
IF CLAUSE: PRESENT	**RESULT CLAUSE: FUTURE**
If she **wins,**	she**'ll lower** taxes. she**'s going to fight** crime.

YES/NO QUESTIONS	
IF CLAUSE: PRESENT	**RESULT CLAUSE: FUTURE**
If she **wins,**	**will** she **lower** taxes? **is** she **going to fight** crime?

SHORT ANSWERS	
AFFIRMATIVE	
Yes, she	**will.** **is.**

SHORT ANSWERS	
NEGATIVE	
No, she	**won't.** **isn't.**

WH- QUESTIONS		
RESULT CLAUSE: FUTURE		**IF CLAUSE: PRESENT**
What	**will** she **do** **is** she **going to do**	**if** she **wins?**

Grammar Notes

1. Use factual conditional sentences with the future to talk about what will happen under certain conditions. The *if* clause states the condition; the main clause states the probable or certain result.

   If Ibarguen wins, she'll lower taxes.
   (It's a real possibility that Ibarguen will win.)

   Be careful! Even though the *if* clause refers to the future, use the simple present tense.

   If Ibarguen **wins**… NOT If Ibarguen will win…

2. You can also use *be going to* in the result clause to express the future result of a condition.

   If Ibarguen wins, she**'s going to lower** taxes.

3. You can begin any conditional sentence with the *if* clause or the result clause. The meaning is the same.

   If you vote for Baker, you won't regret it.

   OR

   You won't regret it **if you vote for Baker.**

   Be careful! Use a comma between the two clauses only when the *if* clause comes first.

4. *If* and *unless* can both be used in conditional sentences, but their meanings are very different. Use *unless* to state a negative condition.

   If Baker wins, the Democrats will remain in control.
   Unless Baker wins, the Republican party will gain control. (If Baker doesn't win, the Republican party will gain control.)

(continued on next page)

Often, but not always, *unless* has the same meaning as *if…not*.

Unless you vote, you won't have a say in the future of our city.

OR

If you **don't** vote, you won't have a say in the future of our city.

FOCUSED PRACTICE

1. Discover the Grammar

Match the conditions with their results.

	Condition	Result
g	1. If Ibarguen wins, she	a. will improve housing.
_____	2. If we lower taxes, businesses	b. will be more jobs.
_____	3. If businesses move back to the city, there	c. won't have a say in government.
_____	4. If the education system improves, we	d. will be more garbage in the streets.
_____	5. Unless you register, you	e. will have an educated work force.
_____	6. Unless you vote, you	f. won't be able to vote.
_____	7. If the sanitation workers strike, there	g. will be the first female mayor.
_____	8. If crime decreases, this	h. will move back to the city.
_____	9. If Baker wins, he	i. will be a safer place to live.

2. Meet the Press

Complete this interview with another mayoral candidate, Herb Tresante.
Use the correct form of the verbs in parentheses.

Interviewer: Election day is just around the corner. Polls indicate that you have a pretty good

chance of winning. What's the first thing you _____'ll do_____ if you
1. (do)

_____get_____ elected?
2. (get)

Tresante: Well, it's been a long, hard campaign. If I _____, I _____ a
3. (win)   4. (take)

short vacation with my family.

Interviewer: Sounds good. Where to?

Tresante: To be perfectly honest, I'd rather not say. If I _____ mayor, I

5. (become)

_____ to keep my private life private.

6. (try)

Interviewer: I can understand that. Now, every election has a winner and a loser. What _____

you _____ if you _____?

7. (do)   8. (lose)

Tresante: Well, let's hope that won't happen. But, if I _____ this election, I

9. (not win)

_____ to be active in politics. Unless both parties _____, this

10. (continue)   11. (cooperate)

city _____ as great as it can be. If my opponent _____ my

12. (not be)   13. (accept)

help, I _____ to improve the school system. And last, but not least, if the

14. (work)

people _____ me to office this time, I _____ back in four

15. (not elect)   16. (be)

years to try again!

3. False Promises

The president of Eastward, Inc., is trying to convince a job candidate to work for him. All of his statements are false. Correct them, using the words in parentheses.

1. If you work for Eastward, you'll be very happy.

    _____ If you work for Eastward, you won't be very happy. _____

    _____ You'll be miserable. _____

(miserable)

2. If you take the job, you'll have the chance to travel a lot.

    _____

    _____

(never leave the office)

3. If you become an employee of Eastward, you'll get a raise every year.

    _____

    _____

(every two years)

4. If you join Eastward, you'll receive wonderful benefits.

    _____

    _____

(terrible benefits)

5. If you accept Eastward's offer, it will be the best career move of your life.

    _____

    _____

(the worst)

4. A Taxing Issue

There is more than one tax rate for federal income taxes. Look at the tax tables for next year's rates and write sentences using the words below.

Married Filing Together and Surviving Spouses (widows and widowers):

Bracket	Tax Rate
$0 to $29,750	15%
over $29,750	28%

Married Filing Separately:

Bracket	Tax Rate
$0 to $14,875	15%
over $14,875	28%

Single:

Bracket	Tax Rate
$0 to $17,850	15%
over $17,850	28%

1. (single/$15,000)

   If you are single and earn $15,000 this year, you will pay a tax rate of 15% next year.

2. (married and filing separately/$15,000)

3. (married and filing together/$15,000)

4. (widowed/$30,000)

5. (single/$18,000)

6. (married and filing separately/$13,000)

5. At the Polls

Complete these conversations with **if** *or* **unless.**

1. **A:** Oh, no. I can't find my voter registration card.

   B: That's OK. _____If_____ you don't have it, they'll look your name up in the registration book.

2. **A:** I've never voted before. I hope I can figure out how to use the voting machine.

   B: Don't worry. _____ you have trouble, they'll show you what to do.

3. **A:** I really didn't feel like coming out tonight.

   B: Me neither. But we won't have any say at all _____ we vote.

4. **A:** I've got to make a phone call. Would you mind holding my place in line?

   B: Sure. _____ it gets close to your turn, I'll come get you.

   A: Thanks.

5. **A:** Hi, Alicia. This is Manuel. I'm calling from the polling place. Where are you?

   B: I'm getting ready to leave now.

   A: Better hurry. They close the doors at nine o'clock. You won't get here in time _____ you leave right away.

6. **A:** I really hope Baker wins.

   B: Me too. I'm going to be *very* unhappy _____ he loses.

   A: Well, it's going to be a close race. Keep your fingers crossed.

7. **B:** Why?

   A: _____ you cross your fingers, you'll have good luck.

   B: I didn't know you were superstitious.

COMMUNICATION PRACTICE

6. Practice Listening

Gabriela Ibarguen is talking about her political platform. Listen to the interview. Then read the list of issues. Listen again and check the things that Ibarguen promises to do if she is elected.

1. ☑ hold neighborhood meetings   4. ☐ raise teachers' salaries

2. ☐ open recreation centers   5. ☐ raise taxes

3. ☐ close health centers at six o'clock   6. ☐ improve public transportation

7. Solutions

Work in pairs. Read these problems and think of possible solutions. Use **if, if . . . not,** *or* **unless.**

1. Your neighbors are always playing music so loud that you can't fall asleep.

    Example:
    If they don't stop, I'll call the police.
    Unless they stop, I'll call the landlord.
    If they continue to bother me, I'll consider moving.

(continued on next page)

2. You've had a headache every day for a week. You can't concentrate.

3. You keep phoning your boyfriend or girlfriend, but there is no answer. It's now midnight.

4. You like your job, but you just found out that other workers are making much more money than you are.

5. You live in an apartment building. It's winter and the building hasn't had any heat for a week. You're freezing.

6. You're ten pounds overweight. You've been trying for months to lose weight, but so far you haven't lost a single pound.

7. You bought a radio in a local store. It doesn't work, but when you tried to return it, the salesclerk refused to take it back.

8. Superstitions

Read the following superstitions. Work in a small group and discuss similar superstitions that you know about.

If you cross your fingers, you'll have good luck.

Example:
In Germany, people believe that if you press your thumbs, you will have good luck.

If you touch blue, your dreams will come true.

If you break a mirror, you will have seven years of bad luck.

If you put on a piece of clothing inside out, you will have good luck.

If your palm itches, you're going to find some money soon.

With your group, make a list of superstitions. Use the following ideas or your own.

getting married	knocking on wood
finding money	sneezing
losing money	whistling
having good luck	dropping or spilling something
having bad luck	taking the last piece of food

Example:
If you take the last piece of food on a plate, you won't get married.

Share your list of superstitions with the whole class.

9. Vote for Me

Listen again to the candidate in exercise 6. Imagine you are running for the position of class or school president. Write five campaign promises. In small groups, read your promises and elect a candidate. Then hold a general class election.

Example:
If I become school president, I will buy ten new computers.
If you elect me, I'll…

INTRODUCTION

▼

🔲 *Read and listen to this version of a famous fairy tale.*

The Fisherman and His Wife

nce upon a time there was a poor fisherman and his wife who lived in a pigsty near the sea. Every day the man went to fish. One day, after waiting a very long time, he caught a very big fish. The fish said, "Please let me live. I'm not a regular fish—I'm an enchanted prince. **It wouldn't do you any good if you killed me. If you ate me, I wouldn't even taste right.**" The fisherman agreed, threw the fish back into the clear water, and went home to his wife.

"Husband," said the wife, "didn't you catch anything today?"

"I caught a fish, but it said it was an enchanted prince, so I let it go."

"You mean you didn't wish for anything?" asked the wife.

"No," said the fisherman. "What do I need to wish for?"

"Just look around you," said the wife. "We live in a pigsty. **I wish we had a nice little cottage. If we had a cottage, I would be a lot happier.** You saved the prince's life. Go back and ask him for it."

The fisherman didn't want to go, but he did. He was afraid that **if he asked for a cottage, the fish would be angry.** But he was also afraid that **if he didn't ask, his wife would be even angrier.**

When he got to the sea, it was all green and yellow. **"My wife wishes we had a cottage,"** said the fisherman.

"Just go on back," said the fish. "She already has it."

When he returned home, the fisherman found his wife sitting outside a lovely little cottage. The kitchen was filled with food and all types of cooking utensils. Outside was a little garden with vegetables, fruit trees, hens, and ducks.

Things were fine for a week or two. Then the wife said, "This cottage is much too crowded. **I wish we lived in a bigger house. If we lived in a big stone castle, I would be much happier.** Go and ask the fish for it."

The fisherman didn't want to go, but he did. When he got to the sea, it was dark blue and gray. **"My wife wishes we lived in a big stone castle,"** he said to the fish.

"Just go on back. She's standing in front of the door," said the fish.

When he returned home, the fisherman found his wife on the steps of a great big stone castle. The inside was filled with beautiful gold furniture, chandeliers, and carpets, and there were servants everywhere.

The next morning the wife woke up and said, **"I wish I were King of all this land."**

"What would you do if you were King?" asked her husband.

"If I were King, I would own all this land. Go on back and ask the fish for it."

This time, the sea was all blackish gray, and the water was rough and smelled terrible. "What does she want now?" asked the fish.

"She wants to be King," said the embarrassed fisherman.

"Just go on back. She already is."

When the fisherman returned home, he found an enormous palace. Everything inside was made of marble and pure gold, and it was surrounded by soldiers with drums and trumpets. His wife was seated on a throne, and he said to her, "How nice for you that you are King. Now we won't need to wish for anything else."

But his wife was not satisfied. **"If I were Emperor, I would be much happier,"** she said. "I am King and I command you to go back and ask the fish to make me Emperor."

Reluctantly, the fisherman went back to the fish, and again the wish was granted. Next, his wife wanted to be Pope, and that wish, too, was granted. "Wife, now be satisfied," said the fisherman. "You're Pope. You can't be anything more."

The wife, however, wasn't convinced. She kept thinking and thinking about what more she could be. **"I wish I were like the Lord of the universe,"** she finally said. **"If I were like the Lord, I could make the sun rise and set.** Then **I would be much happier.** Go right now and tell the fish that I want to be like the Lord."

"Oh, no," said the fisherman. "The fish can't do that. **If I were you, I wouldn't ask for anything else."** But his wife got so furious that the poor fisherman ran back to the fish. There was a terrible storm, and the sea was pitch black with waves as high as mountains. "Well, what does she want now?" asked the fish.

"She wishes she were like the Lord of the universe," said the fisherman.

"Just go on back. She's sitting in the pigsty again."

And they are still sitting there today.

UNREAL CONDITIONALS: PRESENT

AFFIRMATIVE STATEMENTS	
IF CLAUSE	**RESULT CLAUSE**
IF + SUBJECT + SIMPLE PAST FORM	**SUBJECT + *WOULD* + BASE FORM OF VERB**
If I **had** time, **were*** a parent,	I **would read** fairy tales.

*Note that *were* is used for all persons of *be*.

NEGATIVE STATEMENTS	
IF CLAUSE	**RESULT CLAUSE**
IF + SUBJECT + SIMPLE PAST FORM	**SUBJECT + *WOULD NOT* + BASE FORM OF VERB**
If I **didn't have** time, **weren't** a parent,	I **would not read** fairy tales.

CONTRACTIONS		
I would	=	I'd
you would	=	you'd
he would	=	he'd
she would	=	she'd
we would	=	we'd
they would	=	they'd
would not	=	wouldn't

YES/NO QUESTIONS	
RESULT CLAUSE	**IF CLAUSE**
***WOULD* + SUBJECT + BASE FORM OF VERB**	***IF* + SUBJECT + SIMPLE PAST FORM**
Would you **read** fairy tales	**if** you **had** time? **were** a parent?

SHORT ANSWERS	SHORT ANSWERS
AFFIRMATIVE	**NEGATIVE**
Yes, I **would.**	**No,** I **wouldn't.**

WH- QUESTIONS	
RESULT CLAUSE	**IF CLAUSE**
***WH- WORD* + *WOULD* + SUBJECT + BASE FORM OF VERB**	***IF* + SUBJECT + SIMPLE PAST FORM**
What **would** you **do**	**if** you **had** more time? **were** a parent?

Grammar Notes

1. Use present unreal conditional sentences to talk about unreal, untrue, imagined, or impossible conditions and their results. Notice that the *if* clause presents the unreal condition. The result clause presents the unreal result of that condition.

> **If** I **lived** in a large house, I **would have** a lot of room. (But I don't live in a large house, so I don't have a lot of room.)
> **If** they **had** children, they **would read** them fairy tales. (But they don't have children.)
> **If** you **were** the fisherman's wife, **would** you **be** happy with your life?
> (You aren't the fisherman's wife.)

Be careful! The *if* clause uses the simple past tense form, but the meaning is not past.

> If I **had** more money **now,** I would take a trip around the world.

Use *were* for all persons when the verb in the *if* clause is a form of *be.*

> If I **were** King, I would rule the land.
> NOT ~~If I was King, I would rule the land.~~

Usage note: You will sometimes hear native speakers use *was* in the *if* clause. However, many people still feel that this is not completely correct.

2. Be careful! Don't use *would* in the *if* clause in present unreal conditional sentences.

> If she **knew** the answer, she would tell you. NOT ~~If she would know the answer, she would tell you.~~

3. If the result is not certain, use *might* or *could* in the result clause to express possibility.

If I had time, I **might/could read** more fairy tales. (It's possible I would read them.)

You can also use *could* in the result clause to express ability.

> If you **knew** German, you **could translate** this story for me.

4. Remember that you can negate either or both clauses of conditional sentences.

> If I caught a fish, I would be happy.
> If I **didn't** catch a fish, I would be unhappy.
> If I caught a fish, I **wouldn't** be unhappy.
> If I **didn't** catch a fish, I **wouldn't** be happy.

5. Statements beginning with *If I were you . . .* are often used to give advice.

> **If I were you,** I wouldn't ask the fish for anything else. He could get angry.

6. Use *wish* and the simple past tense to talk about things that you want to be true <u>now</u>, but that are not true.

> I **wish** I **lived** in a castle. (I don't live in a castle, but I want to live in one.)
> I **wish** I **were** King. (I'm not King, but I want to be.)

Use *could* or *would* after *wish*. Don't use *can* or *will*.

> I wish she **would be** less demanding.
> NOT ~~I wish she will be less demanding.~~

Remember to use *were* instead of *am, is,* or *are* in the *if* clause.

> I **wish** I **were** Emperor. NOT ~~I wish I was Emperor.~~

FOCUSED PRACTICE

1. Discover the Grammar

Read the first sentence in each set. Then mark the other sentences
true (T) *or false* (F).

1. If I had time, I would read fairy tales in English.
   ___F___ a. I have time.
   ___F___ b. I'm going to read fairy tales in English.

2. If it weren't so cold, I would go fishing.
   _____ a. It's cold.
   _____ b. I'm going fishing.

3. If I caught an enchanted fish, I would make three wishes.
   _____ a. I believe I'm going to catch an enchanted fish.
   _____ b. I'm going to make three wishes.

4. If I had three wishes, I wouldn't ask for a palace.
   _____ a. I have three wishes.
   _____ b. I don't want a palace.

5. If my house were too small, I would try to find a bigger one.
   _____ a. My house is big enough.
   _____ b. I'm not looking for a bigger house right now.

6. If we won the lottery, we would buy a new car.
   _____ a. We recently won the lottery.
   _____ b. We want a new car.

7. If we didn't earn enough money, I would train for a better job.
   _____ a. We don't earn enough money.
   _____ b. I'm training for a better job.

8. Your friend tells you, "If I were you, I wouldn't change jobs."
   _____ a. Your friend is giving you advice.
   _____ b. Your friend thinks you shouldn't change jobs.

2. Abracadabra!

Complete this article from a popular psychology magazine. Use the correct form of the verbs in parentheses.

Marta Hijab has always wanted to invite her whole family over for the holidays, but her apartment is small, and her family is very large. "If I _____invited_____ them all
1. (invite)
for dinner, there _____ enough room for everyone to sit down," she told a
2. (not be)
friend. If Marta _____ a complainer, she _____ about the
3. (be)   **4. (moan)**
size of her apartment and spend the holiday at her parents' house. But Marta is a problem

solver. This year she is hosting an open house. People can drop in at different times

during the day, and there will be room for everyone.

"If life _____ a fairy tale, we _____ problems away,"
5. (be)   **6. (can / wish)**
noted Joel Grimes, a practicing Los Angeles therapist. "This is what complainers are

trying to do when they moan about a problem. What they are really saying is, 'If I

_____ a magical solution, I _____ deal with this myself.'
7. (have)   **8. (not have to)**
I wish it _____ that easy," says Grimes, "but unfortunately it's not." He
9. (be)
gives the example of one of his clients, a very wealthy man who complains constantly

about his limited time for his family. "He's waiting for a miracle to give him the time he

needs to get to know his children. But if he _____ about the problem
10. (think)
creatively, he _____ time," says Grimes.
11. (can / find)
Resources (time, money, space) always have limits, even for the rich. If complainers

_____ this, then they _____ that there will always be
12. (realize)   **13. (understand)**
problems. They could then stop using these limitations as excuses and concentrate on

solutions. Marta is a student and works only part-time. If she _____
14. (insist)
on a bigger apartment for her party, she _____ wait for years before
15. (may / have to)
having her whole family over for dinner. Instead, she is using her actual resources

creatively and solving her problems right now.

There's an old saying: "If wishes _____ horses, then beggars
16. (be)
_____." But wishes aren't horses. We have to learn to create our own
17. (can / ride)
good fortune and not wait for a powerful genie with three wishes to come along and

solve our problems.

3. Making Excuses

In his practice, psychologist Joel Grimes hears all types of excuses from his clients. Rewrite these excuses, using present unreal conditional sentences.

1. I'm so busy. That's why I don't read bedtime stories to my little girl.

   If I weren't so busy, I would read bedtime stories to my little girl.

2. My husband's not ambitious. That's why he doesn't ask for a raise.

   _____

3. I'm not in shape. That's why I don't play sports.

   _____

4. I don't have enough time. That's why I'm not planning to study for the exam.

   _____

5. I'm too old. That's why I'm not going back to school.

   _____

6. My boss doesn't explain things properly. That's why I can't do my job.

   _____

7. I'm not good at math. That's why I don't balance my checkbook.

   _____

8. I feel nervous all the time. That's why I can't stop smoking.

   _____

4. The Fish's Wishes

Remember the fish from the fairy tale on pages 211 and 212? Now read his regrets. Rewrite them with **wish.**

1. I'm a fish.

   I wish I weren't a fish.

2. I'm not a handsome prince.

   _____

3. I live in the sea.

   _____

4. I don't live in a castle.

   _____

5. I have to swim all day long.

   _____

(continued on next page)

6. I don't have a princess.

_____

7. The fisherman comes here every day.

_____

8. His wife always wants something.

_____

9. She isn't satisfied.

_____

10. They don't leave me alone.

_____

5. What If?

Marta is having her open-house holiday party. Her nieces and nephews are playing a fantasy question game. Complete their questions with the words below.

1. What/you/do/if/you/be a millionaire?

What would you do if you were a millionaire?
_____

2. What/you/do/if/you/be the leader of this country?

_____

3. How/you/feel/if/you/never/need to sleep?

_____

4. What/you/do/if/you/have more free time?

_____

5. What/you/do/if/you/can swim like a fish?

_____

6. What/you/do/if/you/not have to work?

_____

7. Where/you/travel/if/you/have a ticket for anywhere in the world?

_____

8. If/you/can build anything/what/it/be?

_____

6. The Disappearance

Read part of a book report that Marta's niece wrote. There are six mistakes in the use of the present unreal conditional. Find and correct them.

What would happen to the women if all the men
in the world ~~would disappear~~? What would happen
disappeared
to the men when there were no women? Philip Wiley's
1951 science-fiction novel, *The Disappearance*,
addresses these intriguing questions.

According to Wiley, if men and women live
in different worlds, the results would be
catastrophic. Wiley thinks that men are too
aggressive to survive on their own. If women
didn't control them, men will start more wars.
He also believes that women wouldn't have the
technological skills to survive in their own
world. If men aren't there to pump gas and run
the businesses, women wouldn't be able to manage.

Many people disagree with Wiley's visions. In
fact, they think the book is sexist. They don't
think men are more warlike than women, and they
don't believe that women are more helpless
than men. I think if men and women learned to
cooperate more, the world will be a much better
place.

COMMUNICATION PRACTICE

7. Practice Listening

You are going to listen to a modern fairy tale about Cindy, a clever young girl, and a toad. Before you listen, read the statements. Then listen again and mark each statement true (T) or false (F).

___F___ 1. Cindy wishes she had a new soccer ball.

_____ 2. The toad wishes Cindy would marry him.

_____ 3. If Cindy married the toad, he would become a prince.

_____ 4. Cindy wishes she could become a beautiful princess.

_____ 5. If Cindy became a princess, she'd have plenty of time to study science.

_____ 6. The toad doesn't know how to use his powers to help himself.

_____ 7. Cindy wants to become a scientist and help the prince.

_____ 8. Cindy and the prince get married and live happily ever after.

8. Just Imagine

Work in small groups. Answer the questions in exercise 5. Discuss your answers with your classmates.

Example:
A: What would you do if you were a millionaire?
B: If I were a millionaire, I would donate half my money to charity.

9. If I Were You . . .

Work in pairs. You have a problem. Your classmate gives advice beginning with **If I were you, I would/wouldn't . . .**

1. You need $500 to pay this month's rent. You only have $300.

   Example:
   If I were you, I'd try to borrow the money.

2. You are lonely. You work at home and never meet new people.

3. You never have an opportunity to practice English outside of class.

4. You have been invited to dinner. You know that the main dish is going to be shrimp. You hate shrimp.

Add problems of your own. Ask your partner for advice.

5. _____

6. _____

10. Just Three Wishes

In fairy tales people are often granted three wishes. Imagine you had just three wishes. What would they be? Write them down. Discuss them with a classmate.

   Example:
   I wish I were famous.
   I wish I spoke perfect English.
   I wish I knew how to fly a plane.

There is an old saying: "Be careful what you wish for; it may come true." Look at your wishes again. Discuss what negative results might happen if they came true.

   Example:
   If I were famous, I would have no free time. I wouldn't have a private life . . .

11. Different Worlds

Reread the book report on page 219. In groups, discuss the question: **What would happen if men and women lived in separate worlds?** *Decide if the results would be positive or negative. Give some examples to support your ideas. Then write two paragraphs about your opinion.*

INTRODUCTION

Read and listen to this video review from the entertainment section of a newspaper.

BEST BETS FOR HOLIDAY VIEWING

It's a Wonderful Life (1946)****
What would have happened if you had never been born? George Bailey (played by Jimmy Stewart) learns the answer in Frank Capra's movie classic.

When the film opens, George Bailey, the president of a small-town building-and-loan association, is in desperate trouble with his business. Unable to see a way out, he is about to commit suicide by jumping off a bridge. In a long flashback, we see George as a boy, playing on a frozen pond with his brother and friends. Suddenly his brother falls through the ice. Without thinking of his own safety, George pulls him out of the water. **If George hadn't been there, his brother Harry would have drowned.** We later learn that Harry went on to become a war hero. **If he had died that day, he wouldn't have saved hundreds of other lives in battle.**

The scene is typical of George's life. As the flashback continues, we see George as a young man, bursting to do great things in the world outside his hometown of Bedford Falls. However, each time he starts to fulfill his own dreams, someone needs him at home. George always stays, even though he feels frustrated and somewhat bitter. **He wishes he could have gone to college**, like his brother. **He wishes he had traveled around the world and built great buildings.** But George can't refuse the people who need him.

Now, with his business in ruin and facing a possible jail sentence because of misplaced money, George needs a miracle to save him from suicide. The miracle appears in the form of Clarence, a pudgy, middle-aged, "second-class angel" sent down from Heaven to rescue George.

"I suppose **it would have been better if I had never been born at all,**" George bitterly tells his genial rescuer.

Clarence then teaches George a hard lesson. In a series of painful episodes, he shows him what life would have been like in Bedford Falls without George Bailey. George goes back to the site of his mother's home. He finds, instead, a depressing boarding house. **If George had not supported his mother after his father's death, she would have become an embittered, overworked boarding-house owner.** George's own home is a ruin, and his wife Mary is living a sad life of isolation. **If she had not married George, she would not have had a happy family life. She wouldn't have converted the crumbling old mansion into a beautiful home.** Each vignette is more disturbing than the last, until finally we see the graves of hundreds of soldiers who died because George's brother had not been there to save them.

At that point, George is desperate to return to his own life, no matter how different it is from his boyhood fantasies. He returns home and joyfully announces that he is going to jail. However, the real ending brings a heartwarming holiday message. *It's a Wonderful Life* shows us the importance of each person's life and how each of our lives touches those of others. We see through George's eyes how **the lives of those around him would have been different if George hadn't known them.** If I had only one movie to watch this holiday season, I would choose this movie.

Highly recommended.

Unreal Conditionals: Past

AFFIRMATIVE STATEMENTS	
If Clause	**Result Clause**
If + Subject + Past Perfect	**Subject + *Would have* + Past Participle**
If I had had time,	I **would have watched** the movie.

NEGATIVE STATEMENTS	
If Clause	**Result Clause**
If + Subject + Past Perfect	**Subject + *Would not have* + Past Participle**
If George **had not stayed** home,	he **would not have married** Mary.

CONTRACTIONS		
I had	=	I'd
you had	=	you'd
he had	=	he'd
she had	=	she'd
we would	=	we'd
they would	=	they'd
would have	=	would've
would not have	=	wouldn't have

(continued on next page)

YES/NO QUESTIONS		SHORT ANSWERS	SHORT ANSWERS
RESULT CLAUSE	**IF CLAUSE**	**AFFIRMATIVE**	**NEGATIVE**
WOULD + SUBJECT + *HAVE* + PAST PARTICIPLE	*IF* + SUBJECT + PAST PERFECT	**Yes,** I would have.	**No,** I wouldn't have.
Would you **have watched** it	**if** you **had had** time?		

WH- QUESTIONS	
RESULT CLAUSE	**IF CLAUSE**
WH- WORD + *WOULD* + SUBJECT + *HAVE* + PAST PARTICIPLE	*IF* + SUBJECT + PAST PERFECT
What **would** you **have done**	**if** you **had had** more time?

Grammar Notes

1. Use past unreal conditional sentences to talk about past unreal, untrue, or imagined conditions and their results. As in present unreal conditional sentences, the *if* clause presents the condition and the result clause presents the result.

> **If** George **hadn't been born**, many people's lives **would have been** worse. (But George was born, so people's lives were better.)
>
> **If** George's brother **had died**, he **wouldn't have become** a war hero. (But he didn't die, so he went on to become a hero.)

2. Remember that you can begin conditional sentences with the *if* clause or the result clause. The meaning is the same.

> **If he had had a million dollars,** he would have traveled around the world.
> OR
> He would have traveled around the world **if he had had a million dollars.**

Be careful! Use a comma between the two clauses only when the *if* clause comes first.

3. Usage note: Although some native speakers use *would* in the *if* clause, this is still not the preferred written form.

> If she **had known** the answer, she would have told you. NOT ~~If she would have known the answer, she would have told you.~~

4. If the result is not certain, use *might have* or *could have* in the result clause to express possibility.

> If I had been home last night, I **might have watched** *It's a Wonderful Life.* (It's possible—but not certain—I would have watched it.)
>
> If George had gone into business with his brother, he **could have made** a lot of money. (It's possible—but not certain—he would have made a lot of money.)

Pronunciation note: In informal speech, *have* in *would have, could have,* and *might have* is often pronounced like the word *of.*

> **would have** /wʊdəv/

Be careful! Do not write *of* instead of *have.*

He **could have** made a lot of money.
NOT He ~~could of~~ made a lot of money.

5. Remember that you can negate either or both clauses of conditional sentences.

If it had rained, they would have stayed home.
If it **hadn't** rained, they would have gone out.
If it had rained, they **wouldn't** have gone out.
If it **hadn't** rained, they **wouldn't** have stayed home.

6. Past unreal conditional statements are often used to express regret about what really happened in the past.

If I had known she was in town, I would have invited Mary to the party. (I regret that I didn't invite Mary to the party.)

7. You can also use *wish* and the past perfect to express regret or sadness about things in the past that you wanted to be true, but that weren't true.

George **wishes** he **had studied** architecture. (He didn't study architecture, and now he thinks that was a mistake.)

FOCUSED PRACTICE

1. Discover the Grammar

Read the first sentence in each set. Then mark the other sentences true (T) *or false* (F), *based on the information in the first sentence.*

1. If I had had time, I would have watched *It's a Wonderful Life.*
   __T__ a. I didn't have time to watch *It's a Wonderful Life.*
   __F__ b. I watched *It's a Wonderful Life.*

2. I would have taped the movie if my VCR hadn't broken.
   _____ a. I taped the movie.
   _____ b. My VCR broke.

3. If George Bailey hadn't been depressed, he wouldn't have wanted to jump off the bridge.
   _____ a. George was depressed.
   _____ b. George wanted to jump off the bridge.

4. If George hadn't saved his little brother's life, his brother wouldn't have become a war hero.
   _____ a. George didn't save his brother's life.
   _____ b. George's brother became a war hero.

5. George wouldn't have met Mary, his future wife, if he hadn't gone to his brother's graduation party.
   _____ a. George met Mary.
   _____ b. George didn't go to the party.

6. George would have been happy if he had liked his job.
   _____ a. George wasn't happy.
   _____ b. George liked his job.

(continued on next page)

7. George says, "I wish I had traveled around the world."
_____ a. George feels sad that he hasn't traveled around the world.
_____ b. George has traveled around the world.

2. George's Thoughts

Complete George's thoughts about the past. Use the correct form of the words in parentheses.

1. I didn't go into business with my brother. If I ____had gone____ into business with him, I
   ___would have become___ a success.
   (go)
   (become)

2. I couldn't go into the army because I was deaf in one ear. I _____ into the army if I
   (go)
   _____ my hearing in that ear.
   (not lose)

3. My uncle lost $8,000 of the company's money. I _____ so desperate if he
   (not feel)
   _____ the money.
   (find)

4. I'm so unhappy. I wish I _____ never _____ born.
   (be)

5. Clarence showed me how the world would look without me. I _____ that I was so
   (not know)
   important if Clarence _____ me.
   (not show)

6. My brother became a hero. If I _____ him, he _____ all those lives.
   (not rescue)
   (not save)

7. My old boss, Mr. Gower, once almost made a terrible mistake. If I _____ him, he
   (not help)
   _____ to jail.
   (go)

8. Mary _____ happy if she _____ me.
   (not be)
   (not meet)

9. Many people _____ buy homes if we _____ in business.
   (not be able to)
   (not stay)

10. Life in Bedford Falls really _____ different if I _____.
    (be)
    (not live)

3. Regrets and Wishes

These people in the movie feel bad about some things. Read their regrets. Then write their wishes.

1. Clarence (the angel): I wasn't a first-class angel then. I didn't have much self-confidence.

   _____I wish I had been a first-class angel then._____

   _____I wish I had had more self-confidence._____

2. Mr. Gower (George's childhood employer): I hit little George when he was trying to help me. I wasn't nice to him.

   _____

   _____

3. George: My father had a heart attack. I had to stay and run the business.

_____

_____

4. Mary (George's wife): We weren't able to go on our honeymoon. We needed the money to save the business.

_____

_____

5. Mr. Potter (the town villain): I wasn't able to trick George out of his business. He didn't accept my offer to buy his business.

_____

_____

6. Billy (George's uncle): I lost $8,000. George got into trouble with the law because of me.

_____

_____

7. George's daughter: Daddy was upset about the business. He yelled at us on Christmas Eve.

_____

_____

8. George's friends: We didn't know about George's troubles earlier. We didn't have enough money to help him.

_____

_____

4. The Lost Wallet

_In_ It's a Wonderful Life, _George's uncle loses $8,000. Mean Mr. Potter finds it and doesn't give it back. Complete this conversation about a lost wallet. Use the correct form of the verbs in parentheses and short answers._

Emily: Did you hear what happened to Lauren? She was walking down the street and found a

wallet with just a hundred dollar bill and a library card.

Diane: Did she call the owner?

Emily: If she ____had had____ the phone number, she _____, of course, but the
                 1. (have)   2. (call)
library card only had the person's name.

Diane: Well, what did she do?

Emily: She took it to the police.

Diane: Oh, I _____ it to the police if I _____ it.
                      3. (not take)   4. (find)

(continued on next page)

Emily: Why not? What _____ you _____ if you _____ the wallet?
5. (do)   6. (find)

Diane: I _____ to find the owner myself.
7. (try)

Emily: How? _____ you _____ a notice in the newspaper?
8. (put)

Diane: No, I _____. That would be silly. Anyone _____ it.
9.   10. (can / answer)

Emily: Well, it _____ easy if there _____ more identification in the wallet.
11. (be)   12. (be)
But there was only the person's name on the card.

Diane: Well, I _____ in the phone book.
13. (look)

Emily: She did look in the phone book. The name wasn't there. At least now that the police have it, the owner can try to get it back.

COMMUNICATION PRACTICE

5. Practice Listening

Some friends are discussing a party. Listen to their short conversations. Then listen again and circle the letter of the sentence you heard.

1. a. If I had her number, I would call her.
   b. If I'd had her number, I would've called her.

2. a. I would've invited him if he'd been in town.
   b. I wouldn't have invited him if he'd been in town.

3. a. If he changed jobs, he would've gotten the same benefits.
   b. If he'd changed jobs, he wouldn't have gotten the same benefits.

4. a. I liked it better on a big screen.
   b. I would've liked it better on a big screen.

5. a. I wish David had invited her.
   b. I wish David hadn't invited her.

6. a. I would have.
   b. I wouldn't have.

7. a. If I'd invited Holly, I would've invited Greg.
   b. If I'd invited Holly, I wouldn't have invited Greg.

8. a. If the party had been on a Saturday, they could've come.
   b. If the party hadn't been on a Saturday, they could've come.

6. What Would You Have Done?

Read the following situations. In small groups discuss what you would have done for each situation.

1. George's business was going to fail. He had no money. He went to a bridge and was going to jump.

   Example:
   I would have tried to borrow the money. I wouldn't have tried to kill myself.

2. A man was walking down the street when he found ten $100 bills lying on the ground. There was no one else around. He picked them up and put them in his pocket.

3. A woman came home late and found her apartment door unlocked. She was sure she had locked it. No one else had the keys. She went inside.

4. A teenage boy was walking home when he saw two men fighting. One had a knife. The other was screaming "Help!" The teenager ran away.

7. If Only . . .

With a partner discuss a situation in your life that you have regrets about. Describe the situation and talk about what you wish had happened and why.

Example:
Someone asked me to go to a party the night before a test. I didn't like the course, and I didn't feel like studying, so I decided to go to the party. The next day, I failed the test, and I had to repeat the course. I wish I hadn't gone to the party. If I had stayed home, I would have studied for the test. If I had been prepared, I would have passed.

8. Life without George

Work in pairs. Look at the pictures. They show life with George Bailey and how life would have been without him. Discuss the pictures.

Life with George:

1.

Life without George:

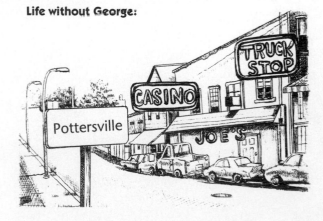

Example:
If George hadn't lived, mean Mr. Potter would've owned the town. They would've called the town Pottersville, not Bedford Falls. The town wouldn't have been . . .

(continued on next page)

Life with George: **Life without George:**

2.

3.

Mary   Mary

4.

Mr. Gower   Mr. Gower

5.

6.

Life with George:

Life without George:

Mom

9. | If I Hadn't Been Born

Think about all the things that would have been different if you hadn't been born. Tell a classmate.

Example:

If I hadn't been born, my son wouldn't have been born either.

I. *Circle the letter of the correct words to complete each conversation.*

1. **A:** These buses are so undependable. I _____ 'll be _____ late

       a. am   ©'ll be
       b. was   d. 've been

   for work if the Number Four doesn't arrive pretty soon.

   B: Would you like to share a cab with me? I'm going to the airport, too.

   A: You're a flight attendant, aren't you?

   B: Yes, I am.

   A: What do you do when your bus _____ late? Do

       a. was   c. had been
       b. wasn't   d. is

   you ever miss a flight?

   B: Oh, no. I can't miss a flight. If it _____ ten

       a. wasn't   c. 's
       b. was   d. has been

   minutes late, I take a cab. Always.

2. **A:** Some of us are stopping for coffee after work. Can you come?

   B: Maybe. I have a class, but the teacher was sick last time. If he

   _____class again today, I can join you.

       a. cancels   c. would cancel
       b. 'll cancel   d. had canceled

   A: Great. And if class meets today, then _____

       a. you come   c. comes
       b. will come   d. come

   with us tomorrow.

3. **A:** I'm sorry, sir. This flight is overbooked. _____ some-

       a. If   c. When
       b. Unless d. Where

   one volunteers to give up a seat, you might not get on this flight.

   B: That's outrageous. I have a confirmed reservation.

   A: I know, but you've got to check in early. If you

   _____ early enough, we can't save a seat for you.

       a. 'll check in   c. don't check in
       b. check in   d. have checked in

4. **A:** How did you get interested in being a pilot?

   B: My brother Harry's hobby was building model airplanes.

   Funny—if he hadn't been fascinated with flying, I

   _____ to become a pilot.

       a. would decide   c. won't decide
       b. decided   d. wouldn't have decided

A: Does he fly?

B: No, and I'm glad. We're really competitive. If he _____ a pilot, I think I would

  a. becomes   c. became
  b. had become   d. 'll become

have tried to become an astronaut.

5. **A:** You seem upset. What's wrong?

  B: I have this silly problem. Gerry's invited me to have Thanksgiving dinner with his family, but I

  can't stand turkey. What _____ if that happened to you?

    a. would you do   c. do you do
    b. did you do   d. had you done

  A: _____ I were you, I'd just go for dessert.

    a. Whenever   c. If
    b. Unless   d. When

  B: That's brilliant.

6. **A:** I'm so busy these days. I wish I _____ more free time.

    a. had had   c. had
    b. have   d. 'll have

  B: Really? What _____ if you didn't have to work for six months?

    a. would you do   c. did you do
    b. will you do   d. have you done

  A: That's easy. If I were free for six months, I _____ around the world.

    a. traveled   c. travel
    b. 'd travel   d. 'll travel

  B: But you do that for a living!

7. **A:** The passenger in seat 13F has a bad headache.

  B: If she drinks some juice, she _____ better. You can get awfully dehydrated

    a. feels   c. might feel
    b. felt   d. has felt

  on a long flight.

8. **A:** I think it's going to get bumpy up here.

  B: Yuck. I _____ sick whenever there's turbulence.

    a. would get   c. 'll get
    b. get   d. had gotten

  A: If you _____ some deep breaths, you'll be fine.

    a. take   c. took
    b. had taken   d. should take

9. **A:** Did you hear that the Internat Air flight attendants just got a big raise?

  B: That does it. Unless North American _____ us a raise, I'm going to apply for a

    a. doesn't give   c. would give
    b. gave   d. gives

  job with Internat.

10. **A:** My roommate is driving me crazy. He eats all our food and doesn't replace anything.

  B: If I _____ with someone like that, I'd talk to him about the problem

    a. live   c. lived
    b. 'll live   d. to live

  right away.

  A: Well, what would you do if he refused to change?

  B: If he _____ soon, I'd probably move.

    a. didn't change   c. had changed
    b. doesn't change   d. changed

(continued on next page)

11. **A:** Why are the flaps on the wing going up like that?

    B: The pilot uses them to control the airplane. Whenever the flaps on that wing

    _____ up, the wing goes down a little. That turns the plane.
        a. go   c. can go
        b. went   d. will go

12. **A:** My lottery ticket had three out of the six winning numbers this week.

    B: Wow. The prize was a million dollars. What would you have done if you

    _____?
        a. win   c. 'll win
        b. 'd won   d. 've won

    A: I don't know. Nothing different for a while anyway.

II. *Complete the conversation with the correct form of the verbs in parentheses.*

A: Where were you Sunday night?

B: Home. I had to study for Spanish.

A: If you _____ had come _____ with us, you _____
                1. (come)   2. (see)

an awesome movie.

B: Yeah? What?

A: *Back to the Future.* It's about a kid who time-travels back to his parents' high-school days. He

changes his own future. It's so cool. At the end, his parents . . .

B: Wait–don't tell me. If you _____ me the ending, you
                                        3. (tell)

_____ it for me. I want to see it myself.
    4. (spoil)

A: OK. But have you ever thought about that?

B: About what?

A: About how things could be different. You grew up here in Baileyville, and you're almost an

adult now. But what _____ your childhood _____ like if
                                                     5. (be)

you _____ in a different family?
    6. (be born)

B: Let's see. If I _____ a different family, I
                        7. (have)

_____ here in Baileyville.
    8. (not grow up)

A: Right. And if you _____ here, I

9. (not grow up)

_____ you.

10. (not meet)

B: That's true. But getting back to the here-and-now, how did you do on the Spanish test?

A: I flunked. I wish I _____ that course. I'm afraid I'm going to fail.

11. (not take)

B: You just don't study enough. If you _____, you

12. (study)

_____ this course easily this semester.

13. (pass)

A: That's easy for you to say. You always get A's.

B: Sometimes I don't. It's not automatic. I _____ A's unless I

14. (not get)

_____.

15. (study)

III. *Complete the news article with the correct form of the verbs in parentheses. Choose the affirmative or the negative form of the verb.*

Imagine that you are unemployed and have a family to support. What _____ *would* _____ you

_____ *do* _____ if you _____ a wallet in the street?

1. (do)   2. (find)

_____ you _____ the money if you _____ no one would

3. (keep)   4. (know)

ever find out?

When Lara Williams faced that situation last week, she brought the wallet to the police, who

traced it to Mr. and Mrs. Asuki, tourists from Japan. The Asukis were pleasantly surprised to see the

wallet—and their money—again. "If we _____ the money back, we

5. (get)

_____ money for our return tickets. It _____ a long time to pay

6. (borrow)   7. (take)

back that debt," beamed Mrs. Asuki.

The police officer who handled the situation was not surprised, however. "Most people are

honest," commented Lieutenant Kronsky. "If they _____, our job

8. (be)

_____ even harder than it is."

9. (be)

Did Mrs. Williams have a hard time making her decision? "Frankly, yes. We need the money. I

_____ Mr. Asuki's wallet in the gutter unless I _____ down just at

10. (see)   11. (glance)

that moment. For a little while, it seemed like fate had sent it to us. But whenever I

_____ a difficult decision to make, I always _____ the problem

12. (have)   13. (discuss)

with my husband. We both knew what was right in this situation. We always tell our kids, if something

_____ to you, _____ it. Our kids _____ the

14. (belong)   15. (return)   16. (follow)

(continued on next page)

rules unless we _____ the rules ourselves."
                        17. (obey)

   The Asukis have offered the Williamses a reward, and a friendship has sprung up between

the two families. "If the Williams family ever _____ to Japan, they
                                                      18. (come)

_____ our guests," said Mr. and Mrs. Asuki.
      19. (be)

IV. *Rewrite each sentence or group of sentences as a wish.*

   1. I want spring vacation to last six months.

       _____ I wish spring vacation lasted six months. _____

   2. I didn't buy business-class tickets. I'm sorry I didn't.

       _____

   3. Oh, no. The in-flight movie is *Back to the Future IV.* I hate that one.

       _____

   4. Carrie just asked the flight attendant for a soda, and soda makes her sick.

       _____

   5. I'm sorry that we went to Disneyland on vacation.

       _____

   6. The beach is a better place to go.

       _____

   7. Florida's nice. I'd like to live there.

       _____

   8. Maybe my office can transfer me to Orlando.

       _____

V. *Read this student's essay. There are five mistakes with conditionals. Find and correct them.*

                         get
   Whenever we ~~will get~~ a long holiday, my family goes somewhere. We usually visit someplace

close to home, but this year we went to Disneyland on our spring vacation. We camped out and

went to the park every day. The weather was great, but even if it had rained the whole time, we've had fun. There are so many things to do. If you like rides, you can do that all day. You can visit Universal Studios and look at movie sets and special effects unless you're interested in the movies. There are other places to visit nearby, too, like Sea World. If you stayed a month, you still wouldn't run out of things to do.

I wish my family lives closer to Florida. Then we could go more often. If I am an adult, I would try to get a job there.

VIII

▼

Adjective
Clauses

INTRODUCTION

Read and listen to the article about friendship.

A Word
with Many Meanings

Almost everyone has at least one. Most people have several. But definitions of *friend* vary from person to person. For some, a friend is someone **who plays cards with you** every Friday night. For others, a friend is someone **who has known you all your life.** Someone **whose family knows you, too.**

Others reserve the term for someone **who knows your innermost secrets.** What one person defines as a friend, another calls an acquaintance, and vice versa.

If definitions of friendship can vary so much within a single culture, imagine the differences between cultures. But interestingly, there have

been very few cross-cultural studies on the topic. Writing in 1970, anthropologist Margaret Mead compared notions of friendship in the United States, France, Germany, and Great Britain. She says:

> For the French, friendship is a one-to-one relationship **that demands a keen awareness of the other person's intellect, temperament, and particular interests.** A friend is someone **who draws out your own best qualities.** . . . Your political philosophy assumes more depth, appreciation of a play becomes sharper, taste in food is accentuated . . . enjoyment of a sport is intensified.

In contrast to the French, says Mead, friendship in Germany has more to do with feelings. Young Germans form bonds early and usually incorporate their friends into their family life. According to Mead:

Between French friends, **who have chosen each other for the congeniality of their point of view,** lively disagreement and sharpness of argument are the breath of life. But for Germans, **whose friendships are based on mutuality of feeling,** deep disagreement on any subject **that matters to both** is regarded as a tragedy.

As a result of their expectations of friendship, young Germans **who come to the United States** often have difficulty making friends with Americans, **"who view friendship more tentatively . . . ,"** reports Mead. These friendships are "subject to changes in intensity as people move, change their jobs, marry, or discover new interests."

The British follow another pattern. According to Mead, the basis for friendship among the British is shared activity. Unlike German relationships, British friendships usually remain outside the family. Mead compares this type of friendship to a dance **whose partners must stay in step with each other.**

Americans **who have made English friends** comment that, even years later, "you can take up just where you left off." Meeting after a long interval, friends are like a couple **who begin to dance again** when the orchestra strikes up after a pause.

Studies of American friendships indicate that, like the French and British, people in the United States often form friendships around interests. They have friends **who enjoy sports,** friends **who go shopping with them,** friends **who share a hobby.** However, like the Germans, they also form long-lasting friendships **which are based on feelings.** In fact, the variety of relationships **that Americans call friendships** can confuse people from other cultures, especially when Americans say things like, "I just made a new friend yesterday."

However, the term does not seem to confuse Americans, **who know very well the difference between friends and acquaintances.** According to a 1970 survey in a U.S. magazine, *Psychology Today,* those **who answered the survey** "find it easy to distinguish between close and casual friends and reported they have more close friends than casual ones."

Although different people and cultures emphasize different aspects of friendship, there is one element **which is always present,** and that is the element of choice. We may not be able to select our families, our co-workers, or even the people **that ride the bus with us,** but we can pick our friends. As Mead puts it, "A friend is someone **who chooses and is chosen."** It is exactly this freedom of choice, without the legal ties of marriage, **that makes friendship such a special and unique relationship.**

Sources: Margaret Mead and Rhoda Metraux, *A Way of Seeing* (New York: McCall, 1970); *Psychology Today,* October, 1979

ADJECTIVE CLAUSES WITH SUBJECT RELATIVE PRONOUNS

ADJECTIVE CLAUSES THAT DESCRIBE A NOUN IN THE PREDICATE OF THE MAIN CLAUSE

MAIN CLAUSE			ADJECTIVE CLAUSE		
SUBJECT	VERB	NOUN/PRONOUN	RELATIVE PRONOUN AS SUBJECT	VERB	
I	read	a book	**that**	**discusses**	**friends.**
A friend	is	someone	**who**	**knows**	**you well.**

			WHOSE + NOUN		
I	have	a friend	**whose home**	**is**	**in Boston.**

ADJECTIVE CLAUSES THAT DESCRIBE THE SUBJECT OF THE MAIN CLAUSE

MAIN CLAUSE	ADJECTIVE CLAUSE			MAIN CLAUSE (CONTINUED)	
SUBJECT	RELATIVE PRONOUN AS SUBJECT	VERB		VERB	
A friend	**who**	**knows**	**you**	can give	you advice.
The book	**that**	**discusses**	**friends**	is	by Ruben.

	WHOSE + NOUN				
My friend	**whose sister**	**writes**	**books**	lives	in Boston.

Grammar Notes

1. Use <u>adjective clauses</u> (also called <u>relative clauses</u>) to identify or give information about nouns (people, places, or things).

> The woman **who lives across the street** is a good neighbor. (**Who lives across the street** identifies the woman we are talking about.)
> Boston, **which is my hometown,** is still my favorite city. (**Which is my hometown** gives information about Boston.)
> The job **that was most interesting to me** was in the marketing department. (**That was most interesting to me** identifies which job the speaker means.)

In most cases the adjective clause directly follows the noun it is describing.

2. Sentences with adjective clauses can be seen as a combination of two sentences.

> I have a friend. + She loves to shop. = I have a friend **who loves to shop.**
> Tom calls often. + He lives in Boston. = Tom, **who lives in Boston,** calls often.
> Sylvia has a colleague. + The colleague's son is her student. = Sylvia has a colleague **whose son is her student.**

3. Adjective clauses are introduced by <u>relative pronouns</u>. Relative pronouns that can be the subject of the clause are *who, that, which,* and *whose.*

a. Use *who* or *that* to refer to people.

> That's the boy **who** plays basketball with us.
>
> OR
>
> That's the boy **that** plays basketball with us.

Usage note: When referring to people, *that* is less formal than *who.*

b. Use *that* or *which* to refer to places or things.

> New York is a city **that** attracts a lot of tourists.
>
> OR
>
> New York is a city **which** attracts a lot of tourists.
> I read a book **that** talks about friendship.
>
> OR
>
> I read a book **which** talks about friendship.

Usage note: *That* and *which* can be used interchangeably except in certain cases. See Be careful note 6.

c. Use *whose* to refer to people's possessions.

> The man **whose friend** is an author lives across the hall.

Be careful! When the relative pronoun is the subject of an adjective clause, do not use a subject pronoun (*I, you, he, she, it, we, they*) too.

> Scott is someone who never forgets a friend's birthday. NOT Scott is someone ~~who he never forgets~~ a friend's birthday.

4. Relative pronouns have the same form when they refer to singular and plural nouns and to masculine and feminine nouns.

> That's the man **who** lives next door.
> That's the woman **who** lives next door.
> Those are the people **who** live next door.

5. The verb in the adjective clause is singular if the subject relative pronoun refers to a singular noun. It is plural if it refers to a plural noun.

> Ben is my friend who **lives** in Boston.
> Jane and Mary are my friends who **live** in Boston.

Be careful! When *whose* + noun is the subject of an adjective clause, the verb agrees with the subject of the adjective clause.

Marla is a person **whose friends are** important to her. NOT Marla is a person ~~whose friends is important to her.~~

Arif and Yusef are the students **whose friend comes** from Cyprus. NOT Arif and Yusef are the students ~~whose friend come from Cyprus.~~

6. There are two kinds of adjective clauses: <u>identifying</u> and <u>nonidentifying</u>.

a. Use an <u>identifying adjective clause</u> (also called a <u>restrictive</u> or <u>defining clause</u>) to identify which member of a group the sentence talks about.

I have a lot of friends. My friend **who lives in Chicago** visits me once a year. (The adjective clause is necessary to identify which friend is meant.)

Barbara knows a lot of the students in the program, but she doesn't know any students **who started the program this year.** (Barbara knows some, but not all, of the students. The adjective clause identifies which ones she doesn't know.)

Notice that commas are not used to separate an identifying adjective clause from the rest of the sentence.

b. Use a <u>nonidentifying adjective clause</u> (also called a <u>nonrestrictive</u> or <u>nondefining clause</u>) to give additional information about the noun it refers to. This information is not necessary to identify the noun.

I have a lot of friends. My best friend, **who works for a florist,** always sends me flowers on my birthday. (The friend has already been identified. He or she is my best friend. The adjective clause adds additional information, but it isn't needed to identify the friend.)

Mrs. Santini, **who owns the house across the street,** has lived here for thirty years. (There is only one Mrs. Santini in the neighborhood. The adjective clause gives more information about her, but it is not necessary to identify her. Her name identifies her.)

Notice that commas are used to separate a nonidentifying adjective clause from the rest of the sentence.

Be careful! Do not use *that* to introduce nonidentifying adjective clauses. Use *who* for people and *which* for places and things.

Marielle, **who** introduced us at the party, called me last night. NOT Marielle, ~~that introduced us at the party,~~ called me last night.

San Diego, **which** reminds me of home, is my favorite vacation spot. NOT San Diego, ~~that reminds me of home,~~ is my favorite vacation spot.

Pronunciation note: There is a brief pause before and after a nonidentifying adjective clause.

Identifying Adjective Clause

My sister **who lives in Seattle** came to visit me this year. (I have several sisters. One of them lives in Seattle.)

Nonidentifying Adjective Clause

My sister, **who lives in Seattle**, came to visit me this year. (I have only one sister. She lives in Seattle.)

FOCUSED PRACTICE

1. Discover the Grammar

Read the article about different types of friends. First circle the relative pronouns and underline the adjective clauses. Then draw an arrow from the relative pronoun to the noun or pronoun that it describes.

Most of us have very few "best friends." These are friends who stand by us through thick and thin. They are people who accept us completely (warts and all) and who know our most secret thoughts. But our lives crisscross with many others whose relationships with us may be less deep but are still important. What would our lives be without these acquaintances, buddies, and dear old friends?

ACQUAINTANCES. These are people whose paths often cross ours. We attend the same school committee meetings or share a car pool with them. Acquaintances may exchange favors easily. The neighbor who borrows your chairs for a big party or the colleague who waters your plants while you're on vacation fit this category. But we usually don't get too intimate with them. One woman commented; "Our next-door neighbor, who car pools with us, is very nice. But we don't have anything in common. We never get together for anything but car pool."

BUDDIES. A lot of people have a friend who shares a particular activity or interest. These usually aren't close relationships, but they're important ones that keep us connected to our interests and hobbies. Because they're based on activities rather then feelings, it's relatively easy to make a new buddy. One foreign-exchange student reported;"For the first two months, I didn't have any real friends. My table-tennis partner, who's from Beijing, was my only social contact. We couldn't communicate in English very well, but we had a good time anyway. Without him, I would have been completely isolated."

OLD FRIENDS. "Delores knew me when I worked in the mailroom," recalls an advertising executive. "I'll never forget this day. The vice president who promoted me called me for an interview. I didn't have the right clothes, and Delores was the one who came with me to buy my first business suit." We all have old friends who knew us "back when." They keep us in touch with parts of ourselves which are easy to lose as we move through life. "Whenever I go home, I always visit Delores," recalls the executive. "We look through old albums and talk about experiences that have helped form us. She always reminds me how shy I used to be. I agree with George Herbert, who said that the best mirror is an old friend."

Now reread this information from the article. Then write true (T) *or false* (F) *for each statement.*

1. The colleague who waters your plants while you're on vacation is your acquaintance.

   The writer believes that you have more than one colleague. ___T___

2. Our next-door neighbor, who car pools with us, is very nice.

   The speaker may have only one next-door neighbor. _____

3. My table-tennis partner, who was from Beijing, was my only social contact.

   The speaker probably had only one table-tennis partner. _____

4. The vice president who promoted me called me for an interview.

   The company has only one vice president. _____

2. Definitions

First, match the words on the left with the descriptions on the right.

Word	Description
__e__ 1. acquaintance	a. This person is married to you.
_____ 2. album	b. This event brings people together after a long separation.
_____ 3. alter ego	c. This relationship exists between friends.
_____ 4. colleague	d. This person is a relative.
_____ 5. confidant	e. This person knows you but is not a close friend.
_____ 6. empathy	f. This feeling lets you experience another person's feelings.
_____ 7. friendship	g. This person is very similar to you in thought and feeling.
_____ 8. kin	h. This book has pages for saving photos.
_____ 9. reunion	i. This person listens to your private feelings and thoughts.
_____ 10. spouse	j. This person has the same job or profession as you.

Now, write definitions for the words on the left. Use the correct description on the right and appropriate relative pronouns.

1. _____ An acquaintance is a person who knows you but is not a close friend. _____

2. _____

3. _____

4. _____

(continued on next page)

5. _____

6. _____

7. _____

8. _____

9. _____

10. _____

3. Survey Results

In 1979, a U.S. magazine, Psychology Today, *conducted a national survey on friendship. Below are some of the results. Complete the sentences with an appropriate relative pronoun and the correct form of the verbs in parentheses.*

1. People ___who___ ___have___ moved a lot have fewer casual friends.
   (have)

2. People _____ _____ lived in the same place have more casual friends.
   (have)

3. The qualities _____ _____ most important in a friend are loyalty, warmth, and the
   (be)
   ability to keep secrets.

4. People _____ _____ a crisis turn first to their friends for help, not to their families.
   (face)

5. Betrayal is the cause _____ _____ most responsible for ending a friendship.
   (be)

6. Most people can maintain friendships with friends_____ _____ become more successful
   (have)
   than they are.

7. A few people want friends _____ _____ their alter egos.
   (be)

8. Many people have friends _____ social or religious backgrounds _____ different from
   (be)
   theirs.

9. Most people _____ friends _____ members of the opposite sex say that these
   (include)
   relationships are different from relationships with the same sex.

10. This survey, _____ _____ in *Psychology Today* in 1979, was completed by typical readers
    (appear)
    of this magazine.

11. Someone _____ _____ *Psychology Today* might have different ideas about friendship.
    (not read)

4. Between Friends

Read these conversations between friends. Then use the first sentence in each conversation to help you write a summary. Use adjective clauses. Remember to use commas where necessary.

1.   **A:** This article is really interesting.

      B: What's it about?

      A: It discusses the different types of friendship.

   SUMMARY: *This article, which discusses the different types of friendship, is really interesting.*

2.   **A:** So, they'll meet us at the restaurant, OK?

      B: Which restaurant?

      A: You know the one. It's across the street from the library.

   SUMMARY: _____

3.   **A:** The navy blue suit looked the best.

      B: Which navy blue suit?

      A: The one on sale.

   SUMMARY: _____

4.   **A:** Bill and Sue aren't close friends with the Swabodas, are they?

      B: Well, the Swabodas' interests are very different from theirs.

   SUMMARY: _____

5.   **A:** The neighbors came by while you were gone.

      B: Do you know what they wanted?

      A: They wanted to borrow some folding chairs.

   SUMMARY: _____

6.   **A:** I was just laughing at an old picture.

      B: Which one? You have hundreds.

      A: You know the one—it's in my high-school yearbook.

   SUMMARY: _____

7.   **A:** My boyfriend left me a lot of plants to water.

      B: How come?

      A: He took a group of students to Venezuela for two weeks.

   SUMMARY: _____

5. New Friends

Read this student's essay about a friend. There are ten mistakes in adjective clauses. Find and correct them. Each incorrectly punctuated clause counts as one mistake.

A writer once said that friends are born, not made. I think he meant that friendship is like love at first sight— we become friends immediately with people who ~~They~~ are compatible with us. I don't agree with this writer. Last summer I made friends with some people who's completely different from me.

In July, I went to Mexico City to study Spanish for a month. In our group, there were five adults, which were all language teachers from our school. Two teachers stayed with friends in Mexico City, and we only saw those teachers during the day. But we saw the teachers, who stayed with us in the dormitory, both day and night. They were the ones who they helped us when we had problems. Bob Taylor who is much older than I am became a really good friend. In my first week, I had a problem that was getting me down. Mexico City, that is a very exciting place, was too distracting. I went out all the time, and I stopped going to my classes. Bob, who have studied abroad a lot, helped me get back into my studies. After the trip I kept writing to Bob, who's letters are always interesting and encouraging. Next summer, he's leading another trip what sounds interesting. It's a three-week trip to Spain, a place he knows a lot about. I hope I can go.

COMMUNICATION PRACTICE

6. Practice Listening

Some friends are at a high school reunion. They haven't seen one another for twenty-five years. Listen to the friends talk about the people at the table below. Then listen again and label the people with their correct names.

| Ann | ~~Bob~~ | John | Pat | Pete | Sue |

Bob

7. A Friend Is Someone Who . . .

Complete the questionnaire. Check all the items that you believe are true.

A friend is someone who . . .

☐ 1. always tells you the truth.
☐ 2. has known you for a very long time.
☐ 3. cries with you.
☐ 4. lends you money.
☐ 5. talks to you every day.
☐ 6. helps you when you are in trouble.
☐ 7. listens to your problems.
☐ 8. does things with you.
☐ 9. respects you.
☐ 10. supports you.
☐ 11. is loyal.
☐ 12. accepts you the way you are.
☐ 13. understands you.
☐ 14. gives you advice.
☐ 15. keeps your secrets.
☐ 16. cares about you.

Other: _____

Now, work with a partner and compare questionnaires. Discuss the reasons for your choices.

Example:
A: I think a friend is someone who always tells you the truth.
B: I don't agree. Sometimes the truth can hurt you.

After your discussion, tally the results of the whole class.

8. Quotable Quotes

Work with a group and choose five of the quotations about friendship to discuss. Talk about what the quotations mean. Give examples from your own experience to support your ideas.

Chance makes our relatives, but choice makes our friends.
> —*Jacques Delille (French poet, 1738–1813)*

> **Example:**
> **A:** I think this means that we don't choose our families, but we do choose our friends.
> **B:** I agree. When I was in high school my best friend was someone who was completely different from my family. . . .

He is wise who can make a friend of a foe.
> —*Scottish proverb*

In life it is difficult to say who do you the most mischief, enemies with the worst intentions, or friends with the best.
> —*Edward Bulwer Lytton (English novelist, 1831–1891)*

Show me a friend who will weep with me; those who will laugh with me I can find myself.
> —*Yugoslav proverb*

A friend in need is a friend indeed.
> —*English proverb*

It is in the character of very few men to honor without envy a friend who has prospered.
> —*Aeschylus (Greek playwright, 525–456 B.C.)*

The one absolutely unselfish friend that man can have in this selfish world, the one that never deserts him, the one that never proves ungrateful or treacherous, is his dog. . . . When all other friends desert, he remains.
> —*George Graham Vest (U.S. Senator, 1830–1904)*

The best mirror is an old friend.
> —*George Herbert (English poet and novelist, 1593–1633)*

Each friend represents a world in us, a world possibly not born until they arrive, and it is only by this meeting that a new world is born.
> —*Anaïs Nin (U.S. writer, 1903–1977)*

[A friend is] another I.
> —*Zeno (Greek philosopher, 335–263 B.C.)*

Wherever you are it is your own friends who make your world.
> —*Ralph Barton Perry (U.S. philosopher, 1876–1957)*

Friendship is a plant which we must often water.
> —*German proverb*

A good man finds all the world friendly.
> —*Hindustan proverb*

One friend in a lifetime is much; two are many; three are hardly possible.

Friends are born, not made.
> —*Henry Brooks Adams (U.S. writer and historian, 1838–1918)*

Have no friends not equal to yourself.
> —*Confucius (Chinese philosopher, 551–479 B.C.)*

A true friend is somebody who can make us do what we can.
> —*Ralph Waldo Emerson (U.S. writer, 1803–1882)*

9. My Friend

Write an essay of two paragraphs about a friend. You may want to begin your essay with one of the quotations from exercise 8. You can use the student's essay in exercise 5 as a model.

10. What's the Difference?

Work in small groups. Discuss the differences between:

a friend and an acquaintance

a friend and a best friend

a friend and a colleague

a friend and a buddy

Now discuss these questions:

What is the word for *friend* in your first language?

Is it used the same as the Engish word?

Can men and women be friends?

What about people of different ages?

People from different religious, social, or economic backgrounds?

INTRODUCTION

▼

🔊 *Read and listen to a review of two autobiographies.*

TORN
Between Two Worlds

I'm filled to the brim with what I'm about to lose—images of Cracow, **which I loved as one loves a person**, of the sun-baked villages **where we had taken summer vacations**, of the hours **I spent poring over passages of music** with my music teacher, of conversations and escapades with friends.

So writes Eva Hoffman, author of *Lost in Translation: A Life in a New Language* (New York: Penguin, 1989). Hoffman, whose early childhood was spent in Cracow, moved with her family to Vancouver, Canada when she was thirteen. Her autobiography relates her experiences as she is uprooted from her beloved Cracow and as she struggles to understand her surroundings and herself in a new language.

In spite of poverty, a cramped apartment, and her parents' wartime memories, home to Ewa Wydra (Hoffman's Polish name) had seemed a paradise. Cracow was a city of "shimmering light and shadow," a place **where life was lived intensely**. As a child, she had visited its cafes with her father, **who she watched in lively conversations with his friends**. Her mother, she recalls, also took her to cafes **where they ate ice cream from tall, elegant glasses.** Hoffman remembers neighbors, "people **between whose apartments there's constant movement with kids, sugar, eggs, and teatime visits.**" By the age of seven, Ewa was able to travel to some places alone. Her friendship with Marek, **whose apartment she visited almost daily**, deepened, and the two grew up assuming that they would be married.

At eight, Ewa and Marek began piano lessons together, and Ewa's musical talent became apparent to her teachers and her family. When she was twelve, a new teacher was found for her, one **with whom some well-known young pianists had studied.** At music school, Ewa developed her other deep friendship, with Basia, another music student. Pani

253

Witeszczak, Ewa's teacher, was the last person **Ewa said good-bye to** before she left Poland. "What do you think you'll miss most?" her teacher asked.

"Everything. Cracow. The School. Basia. You. Everything . . ." It turns out that this is the person and the room **I can least bear to leave**; after all, it's here **that I've felt most intimately understood**; it's here **that I've felt most intensely all my hopes for the future**. . . .

At her new school in Vancouver, Ewa is given her English name, Eva, **which her teachers find easier to pronounce.** Eva, however, feels no connection to the name, or to the English name of anything **that she feels is important**. All her memories and feelings are still in her first language, Polish. The story of Eva as she grows up and comes to terms with her new identity and language is fascinating and moving. *Lost in Translation* is highly recommended reading.

Also recommended is *The Rice Room*, by Ben Fong-Torres (New York: Hyperion, 1994). Unlike Hoffman, a first-generation immigrant, Fong-Torres was born in the United States of parents who had emigrated from China. Many of the problems **that he faces**, however, are similar to Hoffman's. Fong-Torres must try to reconcile his family's culture with his new culture. To do this, he must grapple with a language barrier. A successful radio announcer and journalist, Fong-Torres describes the frustration of trying to communicate with his parents, **for whom English is still a foreign language**.

Over the years, I've talked with my parents many times, but we've never really communicated. . . . When we talk, it sounds like baby talk—at least my half of it. . . . I don't know half the words **I need**; I either never learned them, or I heard but forgot them. The Chinese language is stuck in its own place and time. When we were growing up, we learned to say *police* in Chinese: *look yee*. That means "green clothes," which referred, we'd learn years later, to the uniforms worn by the police in Canton. There are no Chinese words for "computer," "laser," "Watergate," "annuity," "AIDS," or "recession." When the telephone was invented, the Chinese, who concocted so many things **that the rest of the world has to find words for,** simply called it "electric line."

. . . What we have here is a language barrier as formidable, to my mind, as the Great Wall of China.

The barrier has stood . . . through countless moments **when we needed to talk with each other**, about the things **parents and children usually discuss:** jobs and careers; marriage and divorce; health and finances; history, the present, and the future.

This is one of the great sadnesses of my life. How ironic, I would think. . . . I'm a journalist and a broadcaster—my *job* is to communicate—and I can't with the two people **with whom I want to most.**

First- or second-generation immigrant—the issues persist. These two books eloquently describe the lives of people trying to bridge the gap between the worlds that were left behind and the worlds **that they now call home.**

ADJECTIVE CLAUSES WITH OBJECT RELATIVE PRONOUNS, *WHEN,* AND *WHERE*

ADJECTIVE CLAUSES THAT DESCRIBE A NOUN IN THE PREDICATE OF THE MAIN CLAUSE

MAIN CLAUSE			ADJECTIVE CLAUSE		
SUBJECT	VERB	NOUN/PRONOUN	(RELATIVE PRONOUN)	SUBJECT	VERB
I	know	the author	(who[m])	you	mean.
He	read	the book	(that)	she	recommended.

			WHOSE + NOUN		
That	is	the author	whose book	I	read.

			WHERE/(WHEN)		
She	describes	the city	where	she	grew up.
They	remember	a time	(when)	life	was easier.

ADJECTIVE CLAUSES THAT DESCRIBE A NOUN IN THE SUBJECT OF THE MAIN CLAUSE

MAIN CLAUSE	ADJECTIVE CLAUSE			MAIN CLAUSE (CONTINUED)	
SUBJECT	(RELATIVE PRONOUN)	SUBJECT	VERB	VERB	
The book	(that)	I	'm reading	is	by Hoffman.
The woman	(who[m])	you	met	is	an author.

	WHOSE + NOUN				
The man	whose sister	you	know	writes	for the *Times.*

	WHERE/(WHEN)				
The library	where	I	work	has	videos.
The summer	(when)	she	graduated	passed	slowly.

Grammar Notes

1. In Unit 19, you learned about adjective clauses in which the relative pronoun was the subject of the clause.

> Eva Hoffman is a famous author. +
> **She** wrote *Lost in Translation.* =
> Eva Hoffman, **who wrote *Lost in Translation,*** is a famous author.

Relative pronouns can also be the object of an adjective clause.

> Eva Hoffman writes about Poland. +
> I saw **her** on TV. =
> Eva Hoffman, **who(m) I saw on TV**, writes about Poland.

Notice that even when the relative pronoun is the object, it comes at the beginning of the adjective clause.

Remember: Relative pronouns have the same form for singular and plural nouns and for masculine and feminine nouns.

> That's the man **who(m)** I met.
>
> That's the woman **who(m)** I met.
>
> Those are the people **who(m)** I met.

2. The verb in the adjective clause agrees with the subject of the adjective clause.

> I'm reading the book. +
> He recommends it. =
> I'm reading the book which **he recommends.**
> I'm reading the books. +
> He recommends them. =
> I'm reading the books which **he recommends.**
> I'm reading the book. +
> They recommend it. =
> I'm reading the book which **they recommend.**
> I'm reading the books. +
> They recommend them. =
> I'm reading the books which **they recommend.**

3. Remember: There are two kinds of adjective clauses: identifying and nonidentifying. (See Unit 19, page 243.)

In identifying relative clauses, object relative pronouns are often deleted. The meaning is the same.

> She's the writer **who(m) I met**.
> OR
> She's the writer **I met**.

Usage note: It is very common in everyday spoken English to delete relative pronouns in identifying adjective clauses.

Be careful! You cannot delete relative pronouns in nonidentifying adjective clauses.

> She remembers Marek, **who she visited often.** NOT She remembers Marek, ~~she visited often.~~

4. Object relative pronouns are *who(m)*, *that*, *which*, and *whose*. In an identifying adjective clause, you can delete *who(m)*, *that*, and *which*, but not *whose*.

a. To refer to people, use *whom, who,* or *that,* or delete the relative pronoun.

More Formal/Written

> She's the writer **whom I met.**
> OR
> She's the writer **who I met.**
> OR
> She's the writer **that I met.**
> OR
> She's the writer **I met.**

Less Formal/Spoken

Usage note: *Whom* is very formal. Most speakers do not use *whom* in everyday speech. *That* is less formal than *who.* The most common spoken form is the one with no relative pronoun.

b. To refer to things, use *that* or *which* or delete the relative pronoun.

More Formal/Written

I read the book **which** you recommended.

OR

I read the book **that** you recommended.

OR

I read the book you recommended.

Less Formal/Spoken

c. Use *whose* to refer to people's possessions. You cannot delete *whose.*

That's the author **whose** book I read.

5. The same object relative pronouns can be the object of a preposition. They can also be deleted. Note that in everyday spoken English, we place the preposition at the end of the clause.

He's the writer. + I work **for him.** =

More Formal/Written

He's the writer **whom** I work **for.**

OR

He's the writer **who** I work **for.**

OR

He's the writer **that** I work **for.**

OR

He's the writer I work **for.**

Less Formal/Spoken

That's the book. + I told you **about it.** =

More Formal/Written

That's the book **which** I told you **about.**

OR

That's the book **that** I told you **about.**

OR

That's the book I told you **about.**

Less Formal/Spoken

Usage note: In very formal English and in written English, we put the

preposition at the beginning of the clause. In this case, use only *whom* (not *who* or *that*) to refer to people, and use only *which* (not *that*) to refer to things.

He's the writer **for whom** I work.
That's the book **about which** I told you.

Be careful! Do not use an object pronoun (*me, you, him, her, it, us, them*) together with an object relative pronoun in an adjective clause.

She is the writer who I saw on TV. NOT She is the writer ~~who I saw her on TV.~~
This is the book I talked about. NOT This is the book ~~I talked about it.~~

6. *When* and *where* can also be used to introduce adjective clauses.

a. *Where* refers to a place.

That's the library. +
My sister works **there.** =
That's the library **where my sister works.**

b. *When* or *that* refers to a time.

I remember the afternoon. +
I met Ben Fong-Torres **then.** =
I remember the afternoon **when I met Ben Fong-Torres.**

OR

I remember the afternoon **that I met Ben Fong-Torres.**

You can delete *when* in identifying adjective clauses.

I remember the afternoon **I met Ben Fong-Torres.**

FOCUSED PRACTICE

1. Discover the Grammar

The excerpt below comes from Eva Hoffman's book, Lost in Translation. *It describes Hoffman's home in Cracow, Poland. First circle all the words that introduce adjective clauses (relative pronouns,* **when,** *and* **where***) and underline the adjective clauses. Then draw a line from the relative pronoun to the noun or pronoun that it refers to.*

> The kitchen is usually steamy with large pots of soup cooking on the wood stove for hours, or laundry being boiled in vats for greater whiteness; behind the kitchen, there's a tiny balcony, barely big enough to hold two people, on (which) we sometimes go out to exchange neighborly gossip with people peeling vegetables, beating carpets, or just standing around an adjoining balconies. Looking down, you see a paved courtyard, in which I spend many hours bouncing a ball against the wall with other kids, and a bit of garden, where I go to smell the few violets that come up each spring and climb the apple tree, and where my sister gathers the snails that live under the boysenberry bushes, to bring them proudly into the house by the bucketful. . . .
>
> . . . Across the hall from us are the Twardowskis, who come to our apartment regularly. . . . I particularly like the Twardowskis' daughter, Basia, who is several years older than I and who has prettiest long braids, which she sometimes coils around her head. . . .

Now read this excerpt about Hoffman's music school. There are four adjective clauses in which the relative pronouns are deleted. Find these four clauses and underline them.

> Pani Konek teaches at the Cracow Music School, which I've been attending for two years—ever since it has been decided that I should be trained as a professional pianist. I've always liked going to school. At the beginning of the year, I like buying smooth navy blue fabric from which our dressmaker will make my school uniform—an anonymous overdress we are required to wear over our regular clothes in order to erase economic and class distinctions; I like the feel of the crisp, untouched notebook . . . and dipping my pen into the deep inkwell in my desk, and learning how to make oblique letters. It's fun to make up stories about the eccentric characters I know, or about the shapes icicles make on the winter windows, and to try to outwit the teacher when I don't know something, and to give dramatic recitations of poems we've memorized . . . .

Source: Eva Hoffman, *Lost in Translation: A Life in a New Language* (New York: Penguin, 1989)

2. First Impressions

Complete this interview from a school newspaper. Use a relative pronoun,
when, *or* **where** *and the correct form of the verbs in parentheses.*

Maniya, _____*who*_____ a lot of our readers already _____*know*_____, has been at
                                                        1. (know)
Grover High for three years now. We interviewed Maniya about her experiences coming to the
United States.

Interviewer: How did your family choose Atlanta, Maniya?

Maniya: My cousin, _____ we _____ with at first,
                                        2. (stay)
lives here in Atlanta. She said it was a good place to settle.

Interviewer: What were your first impressions?

Maniya: At first it was fun. We got here in the summer, _____ there
_____ no school, so I didn't feel much pressure to
        3. (be)
speak English.

Interviewer: What was the most difficult thing about going to school?

Maniya: Of course, the class in _____ I _____ the
                                                    4. (have)
biggest problems at first was English. It was so hard for me to write com-
positions or to say the things _____ I _____
                                                    5. (want)
to say. Now it's much easier.

Interviewer: What was the biggest change for you when you got here?

Maniya: In the Philippines, we lived in a big house, _____ there
_____ always a lot of people. Here I live with my mother
        6. (be)
and father and my sister, _____ I _____
                                            7. (take care of)
after school. We're by ourselves in the afternoon until my parents get home
from work. Sometimes it feels a little lonely.

Interviewer: How does your sister like Atlanta?

Maniya: She doesn't speak much English yet. She can understand a lot, but she doesn't
have anyone else _____ she can _____ to
                                            8. (talk)
about her feelings. So she depends on me.

How did you learn English so quickly?

I have a study system. At night, I write words and idioms on a piece of paper,
_____ I _____ in my shirt pocket. Then I
                    9. (put)
study them at school whenever I have a chance.

Interviewer: Is there anything you still have trouble with?

Maniya: One thing _____ I still _____ hard to do is
                                        10. (find)
make jokes in English. Some things are funny in Tagalog but not in English.

Interviewer: Do you still write to your friends in the Philippines?

Maniya: Yes. I write to my old classmate, Julie. She's the person _____
friendship I _____ the most now. I hope I can go back
                11. (miss)
and visit her someday.

Interviewer: You'll graduate in June. Are you planning to go to college?

Maniya: Yes. The school _____ I _____ isn't far, so
                                        12. (attend)
I plan to live at home.

3. Memories

Combine the pairs of sentences, using adjective clauses. Make any other necessary changes.

1. That's the house. I grew up in the house.

   That's the house that I grew up in.

2. I lived with my parents and my siblings. You've met my parents.

3. I had two sisters and an older brother. I got along well with my sisters.

4. My sisters and I shared a room. We spent nights talking there.

5. My brother slept on the living room couch. I hardly ever saw him.

6. It was a large old couch. My father had made the couch himself.

7. My best friend lived across the hall. I saw her every day.

8. We went to the same school. We both studied English there.

9. Mr. Robinson was our English teacher. Everyone was a little afraid of Mr. Robinson.

10. After school I worked in a bakery. My aunt and uncle owned it.

11. They sold delicious bread and cake. People stood in line for hours to buy the bread and cake.

12. I took piano lessons from a woman. The woman's sister worked in the bakery.

13. I remember one summer. The whole family went to the lake then.

14. It was a great summer. I'll never forget that summer.

15. My brother and sisters live far away now. I miss them.

16. When we get together we like to reminisce about the old days. We were all together then.

4. Home

Read this student's essay. First put commas where necessary. (Remember: Nonidentifying adjective clauses need commas.) Then delete the relative pronouns where possible.

Tai Dong, where I grew up, is a small city on the southeast coast of Taiwan. My family moved there from Taipei the summer ~~when~~ I was born. I don't remember our first house which we rented from a relative, but when I was two, we moved to the house that I grew up in. This house where my parents still live is on a main street in Tai Dong. To me, this was the best place in the world. My mother had a food stand in our front courtyard where she sold omelettes early in the morning. All her customers whom I always chatted with were very friendly to me. On the first floor, my father conducted his tea business in the front room. After school, I always went straight to the corner where he sat drinking tea with his customers. In the back was our huge kitchen with its stone floor and brick oven. I loved dinnertime because the kitchen was always full of relatives and the customers that my father had invited to dinner. It was a fun and noisy place to be. Next to the kitchen, there was one small bedroom. My oldest cousin whose father wanted him to learn the tea business slept there. Our living room and bedrooms were upstairs. My two sisters slept in one bedroom, and my older brother and I slept in the other. My younger sister shared a room with my grandmother who took care of her a lot of the time.

COMMUNICATION PRACTICE

5. Practice Listening

Listen to a woman describe the room of her childhood. Then listen again and choose the correct picture.

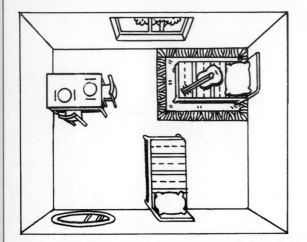
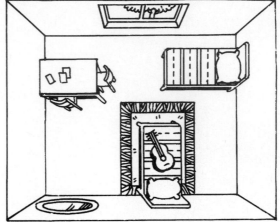

Listen again. Decide if the description is in formal or informal English.

6. Information Gap: Biography

Work with a partner. You are each going to read some biographical information about Ben Fong-Torres, author of The Rice Room. *Each of your biographies is missing some information. Your task is to get the missing information from your partner.*

Student A, read the biographical data about Ben Fong-Torres. Then ask Student B questions about him in order to fill in the missing information. Answer Student B's questions.

Student B, turn to the Information Gap for Unit 20 on page IG 3 in the back of the book, and follow the instructions there.

Example:
A: When was the Exclusion Act still in effect?
B: In 1929.
Where did his father obtain a birth certificate?
A: In the Philippines.

Ben Fong-Torres was born in Alameda, California, in 1945. He was the son of first-generation Chinese parents. His father had emigrated to the United States _____in 1929_____, when the Exclusion Act, which limited the number of Chinese entering the country, was still in effect. To avoid this obstacle, his father first went to the Philippines, where he obtained a birth certificate and added Torres to his name. Ben's mother came to the United States _____, when their marriage was arranged by relatives. Ben, along with his brother and sister, grew up in Oakland, California, where there was a large Chinese community. His family owned _____, in which all the children worked when they were not in school. Ben's parents, whose views were quite traditional, were a little surprised and concerned by their children's love for U.S. culture. Ben was an enthusiastic reader of cartoons and a listener of popular music, which he heard on the radio. At the age of twelve, Ben went with his father to _____, where they opened another Chinese restaurant. It was a difficult time for Ben, among people who had had no previous contact with Asians. Back in Oakland, after the failure of the restaurant, Ben got jobs writing for various magazines and newspapers. After graduation from college in 1966, he wrote for *Rolling Stone* magazine, which covered stories about contemporary U.S. political and cultural life. His interviews with hundreds of famous musicians included the Beatles, the Rolling Stones, Grace Slick, and an interview with _____, for which he won the Deems Taylor award. Fong-Torres was also a DJ for San Francisco radio station KSAN, which plays rock music, and in 1976 he won an award for broadcasting excellence. Today Fong-Torres lives in San Francisco with Diane Sweet, who he married in 1976.

Compare texts with your partner. Are they the same?

7. I Remember

Write about a place you remember from your childhood. Use adjective clauses to help you explain where things were and why they were important. Use exercise 4 as a model.

8. People and Places

Bring in some family photographs to share with your classmates. They can be recent photographs or ones taken some time ago. Work in a small group. Explain the people and places in your photographs.

Example:
A: This is the street where we lived before we moved here.
B: Is that the house you grew up in?
A: Yes, it is. I lived there until I was ten.

P A R T

VIII

Review
or
SelfTest

I. *Complete the sentences by circling the correct words.*

1. The neighborhood (that)/who I grew up in was very friendly.

2. There were a lot of people <u>who/which</u> liked to do things together.

3. Mrs. Morris, <u>that/who</u> lived across the street, was one of my mother's closest friends.

4. She lived in a large old house <u>where/which</u> I spent many happy hours.

5. I played there every day with her daughter, <u>which/whose</u> name was Katy.

6. Katy had a little dog to <u>which/that</u> I was very attached.

7. We took the dog for walks in the park <u>where/which</u> was down the block.

8. There we met other children <u>who/whose</u> we knew from school.

9. The classmate <u>that/which</u> I remember best was Rosa.

10. She had beautiful long hair, <u>that/which</u> she wore in braids.

11. I remember the summer <u>when/which</u> the whole community had a big picnic in the park.

12. I like to think back on the "good old days" <u>when/which</u> people seemed to have more time for one another.

II. *Combine these pairs of sentences, using adjective clauses. Use a relative pronoun,* **when,** *or* **where.** *Make any other necessary changes.*

1. That's my neighbor. I water her plants.

     That's my neighbor whose plants I water.

2. She lives in the house. The house is across the street.

     _____

3. This is the time of the year. She always goes away now.

     _____

4. She travels with her older sister. Her sister lives in Connecticut.

     _____

5. This year they're taking a trip with the car. She just bought the car.

     _____

6. They're going to Miami. They grew up there.

     _____

(continued on next page)

265

7. They have a lot of relatives in Florida. They haven't seen them in years.

   _____

8. The family is going to have a reunion. They've been planning the reunion all year.

   _____

9. They'll be staying with their Aunt Sonya. Her house is right on a canal.

   _____

10. They really need this vacation. They've been looking forward to it all year.

    _____

III. *Read the postcard. Complete it with relative pronouns,* **where,** *or* **when,** *and the correct form of the verbs in parentheses.*

Dear Jessie,

After a week on the road, we finally got to Miami, __where__ my aunt __lives__. It's the first
                                                      1.   2. (live)
time we've seen her new house, _____ _____ right next to a beautiful canal
                                    3.   4. (be)
_____ we _____ swimming and boating every day. Our nephews, _____
    5.   6. (go)   7.
_____ five and seven, are great. By the way, they love the t-shirts _____ you
 8. (be)   9.
_____ me pick out.
 10. (help)

The family reunion is tomorrow. The hotel in _____ it _____ is gorgeous. It's right
                                                  11.   12. (take place)
on the beach _____ I used to play on when I was a kid. My great aunt and uncle, _____
                 13.   14.
_____ in Texas, _____ last night, and my nephew, _____ _____ in England,
 15. (live)   16. (arrive)   17.   18. (live)
_____ tomorrow. I can't wait.
 19. (arrive)

How are you? Please remember to give my plants enough water, especially the one

_____ _____ the purple flowers.
   20.   21. (have)

See you soon.

Carol

IV. *Read the sentences. Cross out the relative pronouns and* **when** *wherever possible.*

Things to Do

1. Bring in the roll of film ~~that~~ Uncle Pete took at the reunion.

2. Send copies of the pictures to the man who wants to write the article for the local paper.

3. Send thank-you notes to the relatives who John received gifts from.

4. Pay all the bills that came in last week.

5. Call the woman who I met at lunch.

6. Call Mr. Jones, who I met at the pool.

7. Buy the book that Mr. J. recommended.

8. Buy a gift for the neighbors who watered our plants.

9. Buy Annie the t-shirt that she wanted from the hotel gift shop.

10. Try to agree on a time when we can all get together again.

V. *Read this student essay. There are seven mistakes related to the use of adjective clauses. Find and correct them.*

       There is an old German proverb that says "Friendship is a plant ~~what~~ *which* we must often water." This means that we have to nurture our relationships to make them grow and flourish. A relationship that you neglect will wilt and die.

       When I was ten, my family moved from Germany to the United States. There I had a "friend" (whom I will call Jack) who he never invited me to do things with him. Jack lived in a house where I never got to see even though it was just a few blocks away from mine. He had family and friends whom I never met. Of course, today I realize that Jack really wasn't a friend at all. He was what in Germany is called a *Bekannter*—someone who you knows, an acquaintance. And for an acquaintance his behavior was fine. I got confused on the day where Jack referred to me as his friend.

       "Friend" is a word that has a different set of expectations for me. In Germany, that word is reserved for people with that one is really close. I learned through the experience with Jack that although you can translate a word from one language to another, the meaning can still be different. Today I have friends from many countries. I also have many acquaintances who friendships I have learned to value, too.

Indirect Speech and Embedded Questions

INTRODUCTION

Read and listen to this excerpt from an article about lying.

THE TRUTH
About Lying

THE CHECK IS IN THE MAIL...

TILT

At 9:00 Dick Spivak's bank telephoned and said **his credit card payment was late.** "**The check is in the mail,**" Dick replied quickly. At 11:45 Dick left for a 12:00 meeting across town. Arriving late, he told his client **that traffic had been bad.** That evening, Dick's fiancée wore a new dress. Dick hated it. "**It looks just great on you,**" he said.

Three lies in one day! Yet Dick Spivak is just an ordinary guy. Each time, he told himself **that sometimes the truth causes too many problems.** Most of us tell similar white lies, harmless untruths that help us avoid trouble. In fact, everyone probably recognizes these four most frequent reasons people tell lies:

1. To get something more quickly or to avoid unpleasant situations: "**I have to have that report by 5:00 today,**" or "**I tried to call you, but your line was busy.**"

2. To appear more acceptable to a new friend or to feel better about yourself: "**I run a mile every day,**" or "**I'm looking better these days.**"

3. To make a polite excuse: "**I'd love to go to your party, but I have to work this evening.**"

4. To protect someone else's feelings: **"That tie looks great on you."**

Like Dick, almost everyone lies sometimes. How often depends in part on our age, education, gender, and even where we live. According to one U.S. survey, young, college-educated men from New England lie the most, while elderly, high-school-educated women from the South are the most truthful. In general, women are more truthful than men (57 percent report **that they always tell the truth),** and honesty increases as we get older.

While most people use little white lies to make life easier, the majority of Americans are concerned about honesty in both public and personal life. In a recent survey, seven out of ten people said **that they were dissatisfied with current standards of honesty.** The majority told interviewers **that people today are less honest than they were ten years ago.** However, in spite of our belief that things are getting worse, lying seems to be an age-old human problem. The French philosopher Vauvenargues, writing in the eighteenth century, touched on the truth when he wrote, **"All men are born truthful and die liars."**

DIRECT AND INDIRECT SPEECH

DIRECT SPEECH

SUBJECT	REPORTING VERB	DIRECT SPEECH
He	said,	**"The check is in the mail."** **"The dress looks good on you."** **"The traffic was bad."**

INDIRECT SPEECH

SUBJECT	REPORTING VERB	NOUN OR PRONOUN	(THAT)	INDIRECT SPEECH
He	**told** **said**	her Jennifer his client	**(that)**	**the check was in the mail.** **the dress looked good on her.** **the traffic had been bad.**

Grammar Notes

1. Speech may be reported in two ways, directly or indirectly. <u>Direct speech</u> (also called <u>quoted speech</u>) states or writes a speaker's exact words, that is, the words he or she said. When writing direct speech, put quotation marks before and after the speech you are quoting.

> **"The check is in the mail,"** he said.

See Appendix 22 on page A16 for the punctuation rules for direct speech.

<u>Indirect speech</u> (also called <u>reported speech</u>) reports some, most, or all of what a speaker said without using the exact words the speaker used. Do not use quotation marks when writing indirect speech.

> He said **the check was in the mail.** *

2. We usually use the past tense of reporting verbs such as *say* or *tell* to report speech. When these verbs are in the past tense, the tense of the verbs in indirect speech changes from the one the speaker actually used. For example, if the speaker made a statement using the simple present tense, the indirect speech uses the simple past tense.

Direct Speech

"It**'s** a great dress," he said.

Indirect Speech

He said (that) it **was** a great dress.

Likewise, if the speaker made a statement in the simple past tense, the indirect speech usually uses the past perfect.

Direct Speech

She said, "It **was** on sale."

Indirect Speech

She told him (that) it **had been** on sale.

See Unit 23 for additional tense changes in indirect speech.

3. There are times when it is not necessary to use a different verb tense in indirect speech from the one actually used by the speaker. In the following cases, the verb tense change is optional:

a. when reporting something someone has just said

> Mandy: I**'m** tired from all that shopping.
> Dick: What did you say?
> Mandy: I said I**'m** tired.
> OR
> I said I **was** tired.

b. when reporting something that is still true

> Dick said that the bank **wants** the payment this week.
> OR
> Dick said that the bank **wanted** the payment this week.

c. when reporting a general truth or scientific law

> Vauvenargues wrote that all men **are** born truthful.
> Mrs. Smith told her students that water **freezes** at 0° Celsius.
> OR
> Vauvenargues wrote that all men **were** born truthful.
> Mrs. Smith told her students that water **froze** at 0° Celsius.

4. When the reporting verb is in the present tense, do not change the verb tense in the indirect speech.

> She **says** that she **runs** a mile every day.

Note that in newspaper and magazine articles, reporting verbs are often in the present tense.

> Fifty-seven percent of women **report** that they always **tell** the truth.

(continued on next page)

---

*Notice that *the check was in the mail* is a noun clause. Noun clauses perform the same functions as nouns. Like nouns, they can function as subjects and objects. Here the noun clause is the object of the reporting verb *said*. He said SOMETHING.

5. In indirect speech, make changes in pronouns and possessives to keep the speaker's original meaning.

> Dick told Mandy, "I like **your** new dress."

> Dick told Mandy that **he** liked **her** new dress.

6. When you mention the listener, it is preferable to use the verb *tell* in both direct and indirect speech. The verb *say* can also be used in these cases.

> "I'm sorry to be so late," Dick **told Ms. Adams.**
> Dick **told his client** that he was sorry to be so late.
> Dick **told her** he was sorry to be so late.

OR

> Dick **said to Ms. Adams,** "I'm sorry to be so late."
> Dick **said to his client** that he was sorry to be so late.
> Dick **said to her** that he was sorry to be so late.

Be careful! When you don't mention the listener, you cannot use the verb *tell*.

> He said he had come as fast as he could.
> NOT ~~He told he had come as fast as he could.~~

See Appendix 13 on page A8 for a list of verbs used to report speech.

FOCUSED PRACTICE

1. Discover the Grammar

Read this magazine article. First circle the reporting verbs. Then underline once all the examples of direct speech and underline twice all the examples of indirect speech.

Lying on the Job

"Lying during a job interview is risky business," says Martha Toledo, director of the management consulting firm Maxwell Enterprises. "The truth has a funny way of coming out." Toledo tells the story of one woman applying for a job as an office manager. The woman told the interviewer that she had a B.A. degree. Actually she was eight credits short. She also said that she had made $30,000 at her last job. The truth was about $5,000 less. "Many firms really do check facts," warns Toledo. In this case, a call to the applicant's company revealed the discrepancies.

Toledo relates a story about another job applicant, Gloria. During an interview, Gloria reported that she had quit her last job. Gloria landed the new job and was doing well until the company hired another employee, Pete. Gloria and Pete had worked at the same company. Pete eventually told his boss that his old company had fired Gloria. In spite of the fact that the new employer was very pleased with Gloria's job performance, he felt that he just couldn't trust her anymore. Gloria got fired—again. "It's a small world," says Toledo. "When it comes to a business interview, it's best to stick to the facts."

2. Confessions

Complete this student's essay with the correct words.

Once when I was a teenager, I went to a party at my Aunt Leah's house. Leah collected pottery, and as soon as I got there, she _____told_____ me she _____ to show me
1. (said / told)   2. (wants / wanted)

_____ new bowl. She _____ she _____ just bought it. It was
3. (my / her)   4. (said / told)   5. (has / had)

beautiful, and after I heard the price, I knew why. When Leah went to answer the door, I picked up the

bowl. It slipped from my hands and smashed to pieces on the floor. As Leah walked back into the

room, I screamed and _____ that the cat had just broken _____ new bowl.
6. (said / told)   7. (her / your)

Leah got this funny look on her face and _____ me that it _____ important.
8. (said / told)   9. (isn't / wasn't)

I didn't sleep at all that night, and the next morning, I called my aunt and _____ her
10. (said / told)

that I had broken _____ bowl. She said _____'d known that all along. We still
11. (her / your)   19. (I / she)

laugh about the story today. When we talk about it, Leah always reminds me that people

_____ more important than things.
13. (are / were)

3. To Be Honest

*Look at the pictures. Rewrite the statements as indirect speech. Use **said** as the reporting verb and make necessary changes in verbs and pronouns.*

1.

   It looks great on you.

   <u>She said it looked great on her.</u>

2.

   It's my own recipe.

   Clara Lee

   _____

3.

   I have to drive my aunt to the airport.

   _____

4.

   my car broke down.

   _____

5.

_____

6.

_____

7.

_____

4. Then She Said

Report the conversation between Ben and Lisa. Use the reporting verbs in parentheses. Make necessary changes in verbs and pronouns.

1. **Lisa:** I just heard about a job at Biodata, a scientific research company.

   (tell) She told him she had just heard about a job at Biodata, a scientific research company.

2. **Ben:** Oh, I majored in science at Florida State.

   (say) He said that he had majored in science at Florida State.

3. **Lisa:** They want someone with some experience as a programmer.

   (say) _____

4. **Ben:** Well, I work as a programmer for Data Systems.

   (tell) _____

5. **Lisa:** Oh—they need a college graduate.

   (say) _____

6. **Ben:** Well, I graduated from Florida State.

   (tell) _____

7. **Lisa:** But they don't want a recent graduate.

   (say) _____

8. **Ben:** I got my degree two years ago.

   (tell) _____

9. **Lisa:** It sounds like the right job for you.

   (tell) _____

10. **Ben:** I think so too.

    (say) _____

COMMUNICATION PRACTICE

5. Practice Listening

Read Lisa's weekly planner. Then listen to the conversations. Lisa wasn't always honest. Listen again and note the differences between what Lisa said and the truth.

SATURDAY		MONDAY
Morning		Morning
Afternoon		Afternoon
Evening *6:00 date with Ben!*	*6:00 vegetarian cooking class*	Evening
	7:30 dinner with Chris	
SUNDAY		TUESDAY
Morning *9:00 aerobics class* *sleep late!*		Morning
Afternoon	*4:00 weekly staff meeting — present sales report*	Afternoon
Evening		Evening

Now write sentences about Lisa's white lies.

1. _____ She said her parents were in town, but she has a date with Ben. _____
2. _____
3. _____
4. _____

6. Why Lie?

Review the four types of lies described on pages 269 and 270. Work in small groups and discuss Lisa's lies in exercise 5. Why did she lie? Is it OK to lie in these circumstances? Give examples from your own experience to support your ideas.

Example:
Once my friend told me that my haircut looked great, but it really looked awful. I think she should have told me the truth. Now it's hard for me to believe anything she says.

| 7. | **Honesty Questionnaire** |

Complete the questionnaire about yourself. Then work in groups. Report your group's results to the rest of the class.

	Always	Usually	Sometimes	Rarely	Never
1. I tell the truth to friends.					
2. I tell the truth to my family.					
3. It's OK to lie on the job.					
4. "White lies" are necessary to protect people's feelings.					
5. Most people are honest.					
6. It's best to tell the truth.					
7. I tell people my real age.					
8. My friends are honest with me.					
9. It's difficult to tell a convincing lie.					
10. Politicians are honest.					
11. Doctors tell their patients the whole truth.					
12. I answer questionnaires honestly.					

Example:
Five of us said that we usually told the truth.
Only one of us said it was always best to tell the truth.

8. To Tell the Truth

Play this game with the whole class. Three "contestants" leave the room. They choose one experience to report to the class. Only one contestant has actually had the experience. The other two must tell convincing lies to make the class believe that they are the ones who have had the experience.

After the contestants choose the experience they will relate, they go back into the room and sit in front of the class. Each contestant states the experience. Then class members ask each contestant detailed questions about it.

Example:
Contestant A: Once I climbed a 10,000-meter-high mountain.
Contestant B: Once I climbed a 10,000-meter-high mountain.
Contestant C: Once I climbed a 10,000-meter-high mountain.
Class member: Contestant A, how long did it take you to climb the mountain?
Contestant B, how long did it take *you* to climb the mountain?
Contestant C, how many people were with you when you climbed the mountain?

After each contestant has answered questions, decide which contestant is telling the truth. Explain which statements convinced you that someone was lying or telling the truth.

Example:
I believed Contestant A because she said that it had taken her two days to get to the top.
I think Contestant C was lying because he said he'd climbed the mountain by himself.

9. Quotable Quotes

*In a group, discuss these famous quotations about lying. Do you agree with them? Give examples to support your opinion. Use **says** to report the proverbs and **said** to report the ideas of individuals.*

All men are born truthful and die liars.
   —*Vauvenargues (French philosopher, 1715–1747)*

Example:
Vauvenargues said that all men are born truthful and die liars.
I agree because babies don't lie, but children and adults do.

A half truth is a whole lie.
   —*Jewish proverb*

A little inaccuracy saves tons of explanation.
   —*Saki (British short-story writer, 1870–1916)*

A liar needs a good memory.
   —*Quintilian (First-century Roman orator)*

The man who speaks the truth is always at ease.
   —*Persian proverb*

The cruelest lies are often told in silence.
   —*Robert Louis Stevenson (Scottish novelist, 1850–1894)*

INTRODUCTION

Read and listen to this excerpt from an article about Hurricane Andrew.

FORCE **FiVE**

*I*n late August, 1992, meteorologists from the National Hurricane Center in Florida noticed a small tropical storm over West Africa. When the storm grew stronger and moved west, they named it Andrew. A few days after that, Lixion Avila of the National Hurricane Center, who had been tracking Andrew all night, called his boss at 3:00 A.M. and told him **that they had a hurricane.** Andrew quickly grew to a force four, and the National Hurricane Center went on the air to warn Florida residents **that a giant storm was coming.** They said **Andrew might even be a force five**—the most powerful class of hurricanes.

Government workers told people **that they had to leave homes near the coast,** and television reporters announced **that everyone should buy extra food and water.** As Floridians prepared for Hurricane Andrew, stores and gas stations reported **that they could not keep up with demands for gasoline, canned food, and bottled water.**

In spite of their preparation, Andrew's 170-mile-an-hour winds caused terrible damage. After the storm, officials at the National Hurricane Center reported **that the electricity had gone out and the radar had been torn off the roof of the twelve-story center.**

Those in private homes and trailer parks suffered most. One family said **they had run from room to room with windows exploding around them.** Jim Jenkins, who had just moved to Florida in June, told a reporter **that if he had known what a force-five hurricane was like, he would have left immediately.** He said **that he and his family had spent a terrifying night in a closet after a trailer had blown through the house.** Jim said, "I'm from New Jersey, and I've seen hurricanes. But there are no words to describe this storm."

After the terror came the realization of loss. In one trailer park, a young woman held her baby as she sifted through the scraps of metal that had been their home. Her husband, still dazed, told us he **had lost his home, his job, and his dog in just two hours.** While the government struggled to provide emergency services for the victims, officials predicted **it would cost at least $20 billion to rebuild after Andrew.**

INDIRECT SPEECH: TENSE CHANGES

DIRECT SPEECH

SUBJECT	REPORTING VERB	DIRECT SPEECH
		STATEMENTS
He	said,	"I **live** in Miami."
		"I **moved** here in June."
		"I**'m looking** for an apartment."
		"I**'ve started** a new job."
		"I**'m going to** stay here."
		"I**'ll invite** you for the holidays."
		"We **can go** swimming."
		"I **may look** for a roommate."
		"I **should get** back to work."
		"I **have to finish** my report."
		"You **must come** to visit."
		"We **ought to see** each other more often."

INDIRECT SPEECH

SUBJECT	REPORTING VERB	NOUN/ PRONOUN	(THAT)	INDIRECT SPEECH
				STATEMENTS
He	told	me	(that)	he **lived** in Miami.
		you		he **had moved** there in June.
		him		he **was looking** for an apartment.
		her		he **had started** a new job.
		us		he **was going to** stay there.
		them		he **would invite** me for the holidays.
		the reporter		we **could go** swimming.
				he **might look** for a roommate.
	said			he **should get** back to work.
				he **had to finish** his report.
				I **had to come** to visit.
				we **ought to see** each other more often.

Grammar Notes

1. As you learned in Unit 21, verb tenses often change in indirect speech when the reporting verb is in the past tense. Note how the present progressive and present perfect change in indirect speech.

	Direct Speech		**Indirect Speech**
Present progressive	"am," "is," "are" ("doing")	⟶	was, were (doing)
Present perfect	"has," "have" ("done")	⟶	had (done)

Direct Speech
"A hurricane **is coming**," she said.
"I**'ve heard** the reports," he told her.

Indirect Speech
She said a hurricane **was coming.**
He told her that he **had heard** the reports.

2. Note how these modals change in indirect speech:

Direct Speech		**Indirect Speech**
"will"	⟶	would
"can"	⟶	could
"may"	⟶	might
"must"	⟶	had to

Direct Speech
They said, "The winds **will be** strong."
"You **can stay** with us," they told us.
He said, "The storm **may last** all night."
"You **must leave** right away," he told us.

Indirect Speech
They said that the winds **would be** strong.
They told us we **could stay** with them.
He said the storm **might last** all night.
He told us that we **had to leave** right away.

3. Some verbs do not change in indirect speech. Do not change *should, could, might,* and *ought to* in indirect speech.

Direct Speech
"You **should listen** to the weather report," he said.
"You **ought to buy** water," he said.

Indirect Speech
He said that I **should listen** to the weather report.
He said we **ought to buy** water.

Do not change the past perfect in indirect speech.

Direct Speech
"I **had** just **moved** here a week before the hurricane," she said.

Indirect Speech
She said she **had** just **moved** here a week before the hurricane.

Do not change verbs in present and past unreal conditional sentences in indirect speech.

Direct Speech
Jim said, "If I knew, I**'d tell** you."
Jim said, "If I **had known,** I **would have told** you."

Indirect Speech
Jim said that if he **knew,** he**'d** tell me.
Jim said that if he **had known,** he **would have told** me.

Do not change past modals in indirect speech.

Direct Speech
"We **should have gone** to California."

Indirect Speech
They told me that they **should have gone** to California.

4. Change time phrases in indirect speech to keep the speaker's original meaning. Here are some possible changes:

Direct Speech	Indirect Speech
"now" ⟶	then
"today" ⟶	that day, yesterday (*depending on the meaning*)
"yesterday" ⟶	the day before
"tomorrow" ⟶	the next day
"this week"/"month"/"year" ⟶	that week/month/year
"last week"/"month"/"year" ⟶	the previous week/month/year
"next week"/"month"/"year" ⟶	the following week/month/year

> **Sam** (to Kate): I just got home **yesterday**. I'll start cleaning up **tomorrow**.
> **Kate** (to Rick a few days later): He said that he had just gotten home **the day before**. He said he would start cleaning up **the next day**.

5. Change "*here*" to *there* and "*this*" to *that* in indirect speech to keep the speaker's original meaning.

> **Jim** (in Florida) to Erica (in New Jersey): I love it **here**. **This** climate is great for my allergies.
> **Erica** to Susan (both in New Jersey): He said he loved it **there**. He told me that **that** climate was great for his allergies.

FOCUSED PRACTICE

1. Discover the Grammar

Read the indirect speech. Then circle the letter of the direct speech that is being reported.

1. The local weather forecaster said that it was going to be a terrible storm.

    a. "It was going to be a terrible storm."

    b. "It's going to be a terrible storm." *(circled)*

    c. "It was a terrible storm."

2. She said the winds might reach 170 miles per hour.

    a. "The winds reached 170 miles per hour."

    b. "The winds would reach 170 miles per hour."

    c. "The winds may reach 170 miles per hour."

3. She said there would be more rain the next day.

    a. "There will be more rain the next day."

    b. "There would be more rain tomorrow."

    c. "There will be more rain tomorrow."

(continued on next page)

4. She told people that they should try to leave the area.

    a. "You should try to leave the area."

    b. "You should have tried to leave the area."

    c. "You would leave the area."

5. She reported that people were leaving the coastal towns.

    a. "People are leaving the coastal towns."

    b. "People were leaving the coastal towns."

    c. "People left the coastal towns."

6. She said that they could expect a lot of damage.

    a. "We could expect a lot of damage."

    b. "We could have expected a lot of damage."

    c. "We can expect a lot of damage."

7. She said that Andrew was the worst hurricane they had had there.

    a. "Andrew is the worst hurricane we have here."

    b. "Andrew is the worst hurricane we have had here."

    c. "Andrew is the worst hurricane we have had there."

8. She told them that the Red Cross had arrived the day before.

    a. "The Red Cross arrived the day before."

    b. "The Red Cross arrived yesterday."

    c. "The Red Cross arrived today."

9. She reported that the president would be there to inspect the damage.

    a. "The president will be here to inspect the damage."

    b. "The president will be there to inspect the damage."

    c. "The president would be there to inspect the damage."

10. She said that if they hadn't had time to prepare, the danger would have been even greater.

    a. "If we hadn't had time to prepare, the danger would have been even greater."

    b. "If we don't have time to prepare, the danger will be even greater."

    c. "If we didn't have time to prepare, the danger would be even greater."

2. Rumors

You are in Florida. Imagine you heard these rumors yesterday, and you are reporting them today. Use **They said** *to report the rumors.*

1. "The hurricane changed direction last night."

   They said that the hurricane had changed direction the night before.

2. "It's going to pass north of here."

   _____

3. "The Texaco station ran out of gas this afternoon."

   _____

4. "It's not really a hurricane, just a tropical storm."

   _____

5. "They've closed the bridge because of high tides."

   _____

6. "They won't restore the electricity until tomorrow."

   _____

7. "They can't reopen the schools for at least a week."

   _____

8. "You ought to use bottled water for a few days."

   _____

3. Hurricane

Read the interview with meteorologist Ronald Myers.

Interviewer: A hurricane is just a bad storm, right?

Myers: No, a hurricane is much more than just a bad storm.

Interviewer: What's the technical definition? When is a storm a hurricane?

Myers: To be called a hurricane, a tropical storm must have winds of at least 73 miles per hour. Hurricane winds often exceed 150 miles per hour near the center, or eye, of the storm.

Interviewer: How often do these killer storms develop?

Myers: Until recently, storms like Andrew have been rare. But that may be changing. We've had three major hurricanes since 1988, and two of them have been force five. Meteorologists are predicting an increase in big storms.

Interviewer: Why is that?

Myers: As you know, the planet may be getting warmer. Warmer temperatures could cause more severe storms.

Interviewer: You mean we'll see more storms like Andrew?

Myers: Yes, I think so. Force five storms will probably become more common. Of course, not everyone agrees with me.

Interviewer: What can we do?

Myers: Well, we can't do anything about the weather. But we have to have a better emergency relief program.

Interviewer: What's the upside to all of this?

Myers: I guess it's weather satellites. If we didn't have weather satellites. we wouldn't be able to warn people about approaching storms.

Interviewer: You're saying things could have been worse in Florida?

Myers: Oh, sure. After all, before Andrew hit, people had had several days to get ready or to leave the area.

Now read the following statements.
For each statement write **That's right** *or* **That's wrong**
and report what Dr. Myers said.

1. A hurricane is just a bad storm.

   That's wrong. He said a hurricane was much more than just a bad storm.
   _____

2. Hurricane winds often exceed 150 miles per hour.

   _____

3. Until recently, force-five hurricanes have been rare.

_____

4. We've had two major hurricanes since 1988.

_____

5. Meteorologists are predicting an increase in big storms.

_____

6. Warmer temperatures could cause more severe storms.

_____

7. Force-five storms will probably become more common.

_____

8. We can do something about the weather.

_____

9. We have to have a better emergency relief program.

_____

10. If we didn't have weather satellites, we wouldn't be able to warn people.

_____

11. Things could have been worse in Florida.

_____

12. Before Andrew hit, people in Florida had had no time to leave the area.

_____

4. Weather Reports

Jim and Rita live in Florida. Read the information that Jim got during the day. Then write as direct speech the things that people said.

Jim's mother told him that she was listening to the weather report. She said that she was worried about Jim and Rita. She told him that if they weren't so stubborn they'd pack up and leave right then.

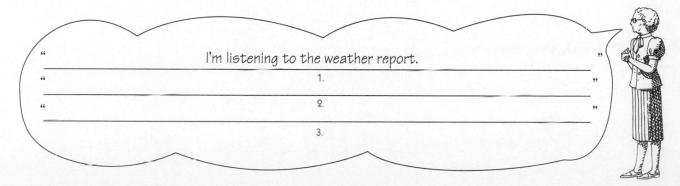

" I'm listening to the weather report. "

" 1. "

" 2. "

3.

(continued on next page)

Jim's father gave him some good advice. He said he'd had a lot of experience with hurricanes. He told Jim he had to put tape on all their windows. He also told him that Jim and his wife ought to fill the sinks and bathtubs with water. He said they should buy a lot of batteries.

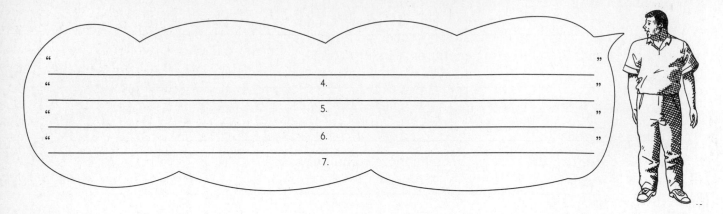

" _____
" _____ 4. _____ "
" _____ 5. _____ "
" _____ 6. _____ "
    7.

Paz and Sara called. Their place is too close to the coast. They said that they couldn't stay there, and they told Jim that they wanted to stay with him and Rita. They said they were leaving that night. They told Jim they should have called him and Rita sooner.

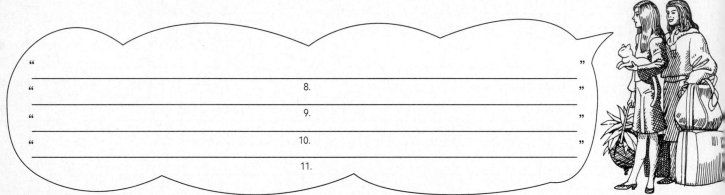

" _____
" _____ 8. _____ "
" _____ 9. _____ "
" _____ 10. _____ "
    11.

Jim listened to the weather advisory in the afternoon. The forecaster said the storm would hit the coast that night. She warned that the eye of the hurricane was going to pass over that area, and she said that the storm might last for several hours.

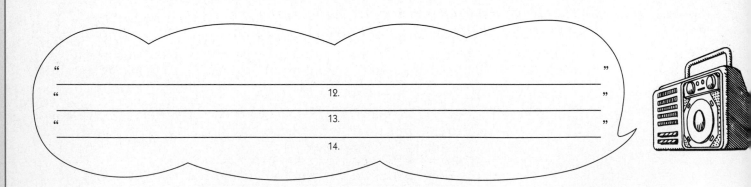

" _____
" _____ 12. _____ "
" _____ 13. _____ "
    14.

COMMUNICATION PRACTICE

5. Practice Listening

Work in groups of four. Listen to the weather advisory. Listen again and check the correct information. It's all right to leave something blank. You're not expected to answer every question. After you listen, you will pool your information.

Schools

1. Today, schools — ☑ closed at 10:00. ☐ will close at 1:00.
2. Students and teachers — ☐ should stay at school. ☐ should go home immediately.
3. Tomorrow, schools — ☐ will open. ☐ may stay closed.

Roads

4. Road conditions — ☐ are safe. ☐ are dangerous.
5. Drivers must — ☐ drive slowly. ☐ pick up passengers on the road.
6. Everyone should — ☐ avoid driving. ☐ continue driving.

Public Offices

7. Libraries — ☐ will stay open. ☐ will close at 1:00.
8. Post offices — ☐ will stay open until 5:00. ☐ will close early.
9. Government offices — ☐ will stay closed. ☐ will remain open tomorrow.

Businesses

10. Banks — ☐ will close at noon. ☐ will stay open until 3:00.
11. Gas stations — ☐ will close at noon. ☐ will stay open until evening.
12. Supermarkets — ☐ are open now. ☐ are closed now.

Now compare your information with what other group members heard. Complete any missing information in your chart. Then listen again and check your work.

Example:
A: She said that schools would close at 1:00.
B: That's not right. She said that schools had closed at 10:00.

6. Telephone

Play this game in groups of seven or eight students. One student whispers something in the ear of another student. That student reports (in a whisper) what he or she heard to the next student. Each student must report to the next student in a whisper and may only say the information once. Expect some surprises—people often hear things inaccurately or report them slightly differently from what was actually said. The last student to hear the reported information tells the whole group what he or she heard.

Example:
A: There won't be any class tomorrow.
B: He said that there wouldn't be any class tomorrow.
C: She said that there'd be a guest in class tomorrow.

7. Interview

Use the questions below to interview three people in your class about their experiences. Report your findings to the class.

Have you ever experienced an extreme weather condition or other natural phenomenon such as the following?

a hurricane or typhoon

very hot weather

very cold weather

a drought

a flood

a sandstorm

an earthquake

Other: _____

How did you feel?

What did you do to protect yourself?

What advice would you give to someone in the same situation?

Example:
Arielle told me she had experienced a very hot summer when temperatures were over 40° C. She told me that she had felt sick a lot of the time. She said she had stayed indoors until evening every day. Arielle told me that everyone should move slowly and drink a lot of liquids in hot weather.

INTRODUCTION

▼

▶ *Read and listen to a radio interview with the director of a sleep clinic.*

Connie: Good morning! This is Connie Sung, bringing you "Here's to Your Health!," a program about modern health issues. Today **we've invited Dr. Ray Thorpe to talk to us** about insomnia. Dr. Thorpe is the director of the U.S. Sleep Disorders Clinic and he has just written a book, *Night Shift,* which will be coming out shortly. Dr. Thorpe, welcome to "Here's to Your Health!"

Dr. Thorpe: Thanks, Connie. It's great to be here.

Connie: In your book, **you tell people to pay more attention to sleep disorders.** What's the big deal about losing a little sleep?

Dr. Thorpe: Whenever people ask me that, Connie, **I tell them to think of the biggest industrial disaster they've ever heard about.** It usually turns out that it was caused at least in part by sleep deprivation. On a personal level, think about what can happen if you drive when you're tired. Did you know that every year, up to 200,000 automobile accidents are caused by drowsy drivers?

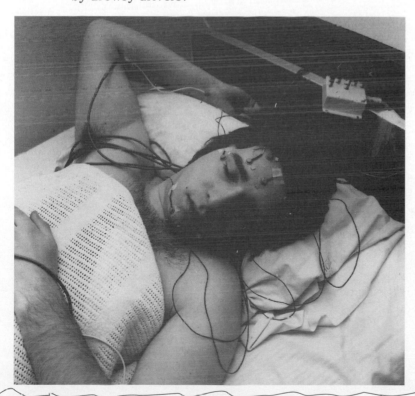

Indirect Instructions, Commands, Requests, and Invitations

▼

Connie: Wow. That *is* a big problem.

Dr. Thorpe: Yes, and it adds up. Besides the price in human misery, we figure that fatigue costs U.S. businesses about $70 billion a year.

Connie: Now I see why we should be paying more attention to sleep. . . . But let's bring this back to the personal level. Say that I'm suffering from insomnia. I come to your clinic. What advice would you give me?

Dr. Thorpe: First, I would find out about some of your habits. If you smoked or drank alcohol, **I would tell you to stop.**

Connie: Really? A lot of people have a drink to relax.

Dr. Thorpe: Bad idea. Both habits are not only bad for your general health, but they interfere with sleep.

Connie: What about the old-fashioned remedies like warm milk? Are those mistakes too?

Dr. Thorpe: Actually, a lot of home remedies do make sense. **We tell patients to have a high-carbohydrate snack like a banana before they retire for the night.** Warm milk works too. But **I'd advise you not to eat a heavy meal before bed.**

Connie: Does exercise help?

Dr. Thorpe: Yes, if you exercise regularly, you'll sleep better. But **we always ask patients not to exercise within three hours of bedtime.**

Connie: **My mother always said to get up and scrub the floor** when I couldn't sleep.

Dr. Thorpe: That works. **I advised one patient to balance his checkbook.** He went right to sleep, just to escape from the task.

Connie: Besides insomnia, what other problems do you treat?

Dr. Thorpe: Many people say that they get to sleep with no trouble, but that they wake up feeling exhausted.

Connie: You know, that happens to me. What's that all about?

Dr. Thorpe: You sleep in cycles of light sleep and deep slumber. If you feel tired after a night's sleep, you could have a problem with the sleep cycles. **We often ask patients with this problem to spend a night at our sleep clinic.**

Connie: What happens there?

Dr. Thorpe: We have electronic equipment that permits us to monitor the patient through the night. In fact, if you're interested, why don't you come and spend a night in the clinic?

Connie: Maybe I should do that. . . .

INDIRECT INSTRUCTIONS, COMMANDS, REQUESTS, AND INVITATIONS

	DIRECT SPEECH	
SUBJECT	**REPORTING VERB**	**DIRECT SPEECH**
He	said,	"Drink warm milk." "Don't drink alcohol before bed." "Can you please turn out the light?" "Why don't you visit the sleep clinic?"

	INDIRECT SPEECH		
SUBJECT	**REPORTING VERB**	**NOUN/ PRONOUN**	**INDIRECT SPEECH**
He	told	her	**to drink** warm milk.
	advised		**not to drink** alcohol.
	asked	Connie	**to turn out** the light.
	said		
	invited	her	**to visit** the sleep clinic.

Grammar Notes

1. Use the infinitive to report instructions and commands.

   Dr. Thorpe told Lois **to go** to bed at the same time every night.
   The doctors told me **to come** to the sleep clinic at 8:00.

2. Report a negative instruction or command by adding *not* before the infinitive.

   They said **not to worry** about sleep.

   Be careful! Notice the different meanings when the reporting verb is negative and when the verb in the indirect instruction is negative.

   The doctor **didn't tell** Matthew **to exercise** before bedtime. (The doctor said nothing about this.)
   The doctor **told** Matthew **not to exercise** before bedtime. (The doctor told Matthew he should not exercise before bedtime.)

3. You can also report requests and invitations with the infinitive.

Direct Speech	Indirect Speech
"Can you shut the door, please?" she requested.	She **asked** Michael **to shut** the door.
"Could you have dinner with us on Friday?" they asked.	They **invited** us **to have dinner** with them on Friday.

   See Appendix 13 on page A8, for a list of verbs used to report instructions, commands, requests, and invitations.

FOCUSED PRACTICE

1. Discover the Grammar

Connie Sung decided to write an article about her visit to Dr. Thorpe's clinic. Read her notes for the article. Circle the reporting verbs and underline the indirect commands, instructions, requests, and invitations.

12:00 Noon the day of my visit. The clinic calls and (asks) me <u>to arrive</u> at 8:30 that night. They tell me to bring my nightshirt and toothbrush. They tell me people also like to bring their own pillow, but I decide to travel light.

8:30 P.M. I arrive on schedule. My room is small but cozy. Only the video camera and cable tell me I'm in a sleep clinic. Juan Estrada, the technician on duty, tells me to relax and watch TV for an hour.

9:30 P.M. Juan comes back and gets me ready to sleep. He pastes twelve small metal disks to my face, legs, and stomach. I ask him to explain, and he tells me that the disks, called electrodes, will be connected to a machine that records electrical activity in my brain. I feel like a Martian in a science fiction movie.

11:30 P.M. Juan comes back and asks me to get into bed. After he hooks me up to the machine, he instructs me not to leave the bed any more that night. I fall asleep easily.

7:00 A.M. Juan comes to awaken me and to disconnect the wires. He invites me to join him in the next room, where he had spent the night monitoring the equipment. I look at the pages of graphs and wonder aloud whether Juan and Dr. Thorpe will be able to read my weird dream of the night before. Juan laughs and tells me not to worry. "These are just electrical impulses," he assures me.

8:00 A.M. Dr. Thorpe reviews my data with me. He tells me I have healthy sleep patterns, except for some leg movements during the night. He tells me to get more exercise, and I promise I will.

2. Dear Helen

*Read the questions to Helen, a newspaper columnist, and report her
instructions. Use the reporting verbs in parentheses.*

Many minor ailments that readers ask about will respond to easy home
remedies. Here are a few treatments that really work. IMPORTANT: CALL
YOUR DOCTOR ABOUT ANY CONDITION THAT DOESN'T IMPROVE OR
GETS WORSE.

Q: I have trouble getting to sleep every night.
MIKE LANDERS, DETROIT

A: Don't drink anything with caffeine after 2:00 P.M. Try exercising regularly, early in the day. Read
Dr. Thorpe's new book, *Night Shift,* for more tips.

1. (tell) _____ She told him not to drink anything with caffeine after 2:00 P.M. _____

2. (say) _____ She said to try exercising regularly. _____

3. (tell) _____

Q: Is there anything I can do to soothe a sore throat? I don't like over-the-counter medicines.
ANNE BOYLE, MIAMI

A: Sip some hot herbal tea with honey. But don't drink black tea. Regular black tea contains a
chemical that will dry out your throat.

4. (say) _____

5. (tell) _____

Q: I have cramps in my legs every night. They wake me up, and I have trouble getting back to
sleep.
LOUISE RICH, DALLAS

A: The next time you feel a cramp, do this: Pinch the place between your upper lip and your nose.
The cramp should stop right away.

6. (say) _____

Q: Do you know of any way to remove stains on teeth?
PETE LEE, BROOKLYN

A: Make a toothpaste of one tablespoon of baking soda and a little water.

7. (tell) _____

Q: What can I do to ease an itchy poison ivy rash?
MARVIN SMITH, HARTFORD

A: Spread cool, cooked oatmeal over the rash. Also, try soaking the rash in a cool bath with one-
fourth cup baking soda. Don't scratch the rash. That will make it worse.

8. (tell) _____

(continued on next page)

9. (say) _____

10. (tell) _____

Q: Bugs seems to love me. Mosquitoes and gnats bite me much more than other people.
ED SMALL, WASHINGTON, D.C.

A: There are a couple of things you can do to keep the pests away. Eat onions or garlic every day. Your skin will have a slight odor which bugs hate. Or ask your doctor about a vitamin B supplement.

11. (say) _____

12. (tell) _____

Q: What makes a sunburn feel better?
PAM LUKAS, LOS ANGELES

A: Dissolve one-fourth cup of cornstarch in a lukewarm bath. Don't rub your skin with the towel when drying off. Don't use anything containing alcohol on your skin. Alcohol dries skin and makes a sunburn feel worse.

13. (tell) _____

3. Connie's Dream

Connie had a dream at the sleep clinic. She wrote about it in her journal. Read her account of the dream and underline the indirect commands, instructions, requests, and invitations. Then complete the cartoon by writing what each character said.

I dreamed that a Martian came into my room. He told me to get up. Then he said to follow him. There was a space ship outside the clinic. I asked the Martian to show me the ship, so he invited me to come aboard. Juan, the lab technician, was on the ship. Suddenly, Juan told me to pilot the ship. He ordered me not to leave the controls. Then he went to sleep. Next, Dr. Thorpe was at my side, giving me instructions. He told me to slow down. Then he said to point the ship towards the earth. There was a loud knocking noise as we hit the ground, and I told everyone not to panic. Then I heard Juan tell me to wake up. I opened my eyes and saw him walking into my room at the sleep clinic.

COMMUNICATION PRACTICE

4. Practice Listening

🔊 *Juan went to a headache clinic. Listen to the conversation to find out what he learned there. Then listen again and check the appropriate column to show what they told him to do, what they told him not to do, and what they didn't mention.*

	Do	Don't Do	Not Mentioned
1. Get regular exercise.	✔	☐	☐
2. Get eight hours of sleep.	☐	☐	☐
3. Take pain killers.	☐	☐	☐
4. Use an ice pack.	☐	☐	☐
5. Massage around your eyes.	☐	☐	☐
6. Eat three big meals a day.	☐	☐	☐
7. Eat chocolate.	☐	☐	☐
8. Avoid cheese.	☐	☐	☐

5. Simple Remedies

What advice have you heard for the following ailments? Work with a partner and tell what to do and what not to do about these problems. Then report to the class.

> minor kitchen burns
> insomnia
> insect bites
> headaches
> snoring
> hiccups
> Other: _____

Example:
A: My mother always told me to hold a burn under cold water.
B: They say not to put butter on a burn.

6. Home Alone

Jeff's parents went out for the evening and left a list of instructions for him. Work with a partner. Read the list and look at the picture. Talk about which instructions he followed and which ones he didn't follow. Use indirect instructions.

> Dear Jeff,
>
> We'll be home late. Please follow these instructions:
>
> Don't stay up after 10:00.
>
> Take the garbage out.
>
> Wash the dishes.
>
> Do your homework.
>
> Let the cat in.
>
> Don't watch any horror movies.(They give you nightmares—remember?)
>
> Please don't invite your friends in tonight.
>
> > Love,
> >
> > Mom and Dad

Example:

His parents told him not to stay up after 10:00, but it's 11:30 and he's still awake.

7. Dreaming

Use the paragraph from Connie's journal in exercise 3 as a model and write an account of a dream. It can be a dream you had, or one that someone has told you about. You can even invent a dream. Use indirect instructions, commands, requests, and invitations in your writing.

Exchange your paragraph with a partner. Make a sketch of your partner's dream and write the direct speech in speech bubbles. Discuss your drawing with your partner to make sure you understood the story and the indirect speech in your partner's dream.

INTRODUCTION

▼

●● *Read and listen to this excerpt from an article about job interviews.*

THE
STRESS
INTERVIEW

> How much experience have you had?

> How old are you?

> What was your starting salary?

> Are you a citizen?

A few weeks ago, Melissa Morrow had an unusual job interview. First, the interviewer asked Melissa **why she couldn't work under pressure.** Before she could answer, he asked **if she had cleaned out her car recently.** Then he wanted to know **who had written her application letter for her.** Melissa was shocked, but she handled herself well. She asked the interviewer **whether he was going to ask her serious questions.** Then she politely ended the interview.

Melissa had had a stress interview, a type of job interview that features tough, tricky questions, long silences, and negative evaluations of the candidate. To the candidate, this strategy may seem like unnecessary nastiness on the part of the interviewer. However,

some positions require an ability to handle just this kind of pressure. If there is an accident in a nuclear power plant, for example, the plant's public relations officer must remain poised when unfriendly reporters ask **how the accident could have occurred.**

The hostile atmosphere of a stress interview gives the employer a chance to watch a candidate react to pressure. In one case, the interviewer ended each interview by telling the candidate, "We're really not sure that you're the right person for this job." One very promising candidate asked the interviewer angrily **if he was sure he knew how to conduct an interview.** She clearly could not handle the pressure she would encounter as a television news anchor—the job she was interviewing for.

Stress questioning has its limitations, however. It's an appropriate technique only for positions which feature extreme on-the-job pressure. Accountants, secretaries, and computer programmers all experience job pressures, but not enough to merit a stress interview. Even when the job warrants it, this strategy can backfire and alienate good candidates. Melissa Morrow came through her interview with flying colors but later asked herself **if she really wanted to work for that company.** Her answer was no.

A word of warning to job candidates: Not all tough questioning constitutes a legitimate stress interview. Some questions are just illegal unless the answers are directly related to the job. If your interviewer asks **how old you are, whether you are married,** or **how much money you owe,** you can refuse to answer. If you think a question is improper, you should ask the interviewer **how the answer specifically relates to that job.** If you don't get a satisfactory explanation, you don't have to answer the question.

When an interviewer introduces pressure to create a reaction, it's easy to lose your composure. Remember that all interviews create stress. If you expect it and learn to control your response, you can remain poised, even in a stress interview.

INDIRECT QUESTIONS

DIRECT SPEECH: *YES/NO* QUESTIONS		
SUBJECT	**REPORTING VERB**	**DIRECT SPEECH**
He	asked,	"Do you have any experience?" "Can you use a computer?" "Will you stay for a year?"

INDIRECT SPEECH: *YES/NO* QUESTIONS				
SUBJECT	**REPORTING VERB**	**NOUN/PRONOUN**	***IF/WHETHER***	**INDIRECT SPEECH**
He	asked	her Melissa	**if** **whether**	**she had any experience.** **she could use a computer.** **she would stay for a year.**

DIRECT SPEECH: *WH-* QUESTIONS ABOUT THE SUBJECT		
SUBJECT	**REPORTING VERB**	**DIRECT SPEECH**
He	asked,	"Who told you about this job?" "What happened on your last job?"

INDIRECT SPEECH: *WH-* QUESTIONS ABOUT THE SUBJECT				
SUBJECT	**REPORTING VERB**	**NOUN/PRONOUN**	**QUESTION WORD**	**INDIRECT SPEECH**
He	asked	him Bob	**who**	**had told him about the job.**
			what	**had happened on his last job.**

DIRECT SPEECH: *WH-* QUESTIONS ABOUT THE PREDICATE		
SUBJECT	**REPORTING VERB**	**DIRECT SPEECH**
He	asked,	"Who(m) did you work for?" "What did you do there?" "When did you leave?" "Where do you work now?" "How are you going to get to work?" "Why have you decided to change jobs?"

INDIRECT SPEECH: *WH-* QUESTIONS ABOUT THE PREDICATE				
SUBJECT	**REPORTING VERB**	**NOUN/PRONOUN**	**QUESTION WORD**	**INDIRECT SPEECH**
He	asked	her Melissa	who(m)	she had worked for.
			what	she had done there.
			when	she had left.
			where	she worked now.
			how	she was going to get to work.
			why	she had decided to change jobs.

Grammar Notes

1. Use *if* or *whether* in indirect *yes/no* questions.

Direct Question	Indirect Question
"Can you type?" she asked.	She asked me **if** I could type.
"Do you know how to use a fax machine?" he asked.	He wanted to know **whether** I knew how to use a fax machine.

People often use *whether or not* to report *yes/no* questions.

> He wanted to know **whether or not** I knew how to use a fax machine.

Usage note: *Whether* is considered more formal than *if*.

2. Use question words in indirect *wh-* questions.

Direct Question	Indirect Question
"Where is your office?" I asked.	I asked **where** his office was.
I asked, "How much is the salary?"	I asked **how much** the salary was.

3. Be careful! Use statement word order, not question word order, for indirect *yes/no* questions and for indirect *wh-* questions about something in the predicate.

Direct Question	Indirect Question
He asked, "**Does the company provide** good benefits?"	He asked whether **the company provided** good benefits. NOT ~~He asked does the company provide good benefits.~~

Direct Question	Indirect Question
"**Have you started** working there yet?" Sylvia asked.	Sylvia asked whether **I had started** working there yet. NOT ~~Sylvia asked have I started working there yet.~~
"Why **did you leave** your previous job?" she asked.	She asked me why **I had left** my previous job. NOT ~~She asked me why did I leave my previous job.~~
"How long **had you worked** there?" she asked.	She asked how long **I had worked** there. NOT ~~She asked how long had I worked there.~~

Notice that the indirect questions in the examples above end with a period (rather than a question mark) and do not use the auxiliary *do, does,* or *did.*

4. For indirect *wh-* questions about the subject, keep the same word order as direct questions.

Direct Question	Indirect Question
"**Who got** the job?" I asked.	I asked **who had gotten** the job.
"**What caused** the problem?" I asked.	I asked **what had caused** the problem.

5. The same verb tense changes and other changes occur in indirect questions as in indirect statements. See Units 21 and 22.

See Appendix 13 on page A8 for a list of verbs used to report questions.

FOCUSED PRACTICE

1. | Discover the Grammar

Melissa Morrow is telling a friend about her job interview. Underline the indirect questions in the conversation.

Don: So, how did the interview go?

Melissa: It was very strange.

Don: What happened?

Melissa: Well, it started off like a normal interview. He asked me <u>how much experience I had had,</u> and I told him I had been a public relations officer for ten years. Let's see. . . . He also asked what I would change about my current job. That was a little tricky.

Don: What did you say?

Melissa: Well, I didn't want to say anything negative, so I told him that I was ready for more responsibility.

Don: Good. What else did he ask?

Melissa: Oh, you know, the regular things. He asked when I had been most successful, and how much money I was making.

Don: Sounds like a normal interview to me. What was so strange about it?

Melissa: Well, at one point, he just stopped talking for a long time. Then he asked me all these bizarre questions that weren't even related to the job.

Don: Like what?

Melissa: He asked me if I had cleaned out my car recently.

Don: You're kidding.

Melissa: No, I'm not. Then he asked me why my employer didn't want me to stay at my job.

Don: That's crazy. I hope you told him that you hadn't been fired.

Melissa: Of course. Oh, and he asked if I was good enough to work for such an important company.

Don: What did you tell him?

Melissa: I told him that with my skills and experience I was one of the best in my field.

Don: That was a great answer. It sounds like you handled yourself very well.

Melissa: Thanks. But now I'm asking myself if I really want this job.

Don: Take your time. Don't make any snap decisions.

Now check the direct questions that Melissa was asked.

☑ 1. How much experience have you had?

☐ 2. What would you change about your current job?

(continued on next page)

☐ 3. Are you ready for more responsibility?

☐ 4. When were you most successful?

☐ 5. How much are you making now?

☐ 6. Was it a normal interview?

☐ 7. Have you cleaned out your car recently?

☐ 8. Have you been fired?

☐ 9. Are you good enough to work for such an important company?

☐ 10. Do you ever make any snap decisions?

2. Nosy Neighbor

Claire has an interview next week. Her neighbor, Jaime, wants to know all about it. Report Jaime's questions, using the words in parentheses.

Jaime: I heard you're going on an interview next week. What kind of job is it?

Claire: It's a secretarial job.

1. _____ He asked what kind of job it was. _____
(kind of job / what / was / it)

Jaime: Oh, really? When is the interview?

Claire: It's on Tuesday at 9:00.

2. _____
(the interview / was / when)

Jaime: Where's the company?

Claire: It's downtown on the west side.

3. _____
(was / where / the company)

Jaime: Do you need directions?

Claire: No, I know the way.

4. _____
(needed / if / she / directions)

Jaime: How long does it take to get there?

Claire: About half an hour.

5. _____
(to get there / it / takes / how long)

Jaime: Are you going to drive?

Claire: I think so. It's probably the fastest way.

6. _____
(was going / if / she / to drive)

Jaime: Who's going to interview you?

Claire: Uhmm. I'm not sure. Probably the manager of the department.

7. _____
(was going / her / who / to interview)

Jaime: Well, good luck. When will they let you know?

Claire: It will take a while. They have a lot of candidates.

8. _____

(her / they / would / when / let / know)

3.   Who's Asking

Read the following questions, which were asked during Claire Yang's interview. Some were asked by Claire, and some were asked by the manager, Pete Stollins. Decide who asked each question. Then rewrite each question as indirect speech.

1. "What type of training is available for the job?"

_____ Claire asked what type of training was available for the job. _____

2. "What kind of experience do you have?"

_____ Pete asked what kind of experience she had. _____

3. "Is there opportunity for promotion?"

_____

4. "Are you interviewing with other companies?"

_____

5. "What will my responsibilities be?"

_____

6. "How is job performance rewarded?"

_____

7. "What was your starting salary at your last job?"

_____

8. "Did you get along well with your last employer?"

_____

9. "Do you hire many women?"

_____

10. "Were you fired from your last job?"

_____

11. "Why did you apply for this position?"

_____

12. "Have you had any major layoffs in the past few years?"

_____

4. Reports

Read part of a memo an interviewer wrote after an interview. Correct five mistakes in indirect questions.

May 15,1995

To: Francesca Giuffrida

From: Bob Marley

Subject: Interview with Carl Treng

    This morning I interviewed Carl Treng for the secretarial position. Since this position requires a lot of contact with the public, I did some stress questioning. I asked Mr. Treng why ~~couldn't he~~ *he couldn't* work under pressure. I also asked him why his supervisor disliked him. Finally, I inquired when he would quit the job with our company?

    Mr. Treng kept his poise throughout the interview. He answered all my questions calmly, and he had some excellent questions of his own. He asked "if we expected changes in the job." He also wanted to know how often do we evaluate employees. I was quite impressed when he asked why did I decide to join this company.

COMMUNICATION PRACTICE

5. Practice Listening

You are going to hear a job interview that takes place in the United States. Before you listen, read the chart about equal employment opportunity laws in the United States. Then listen to the interview and check the topics the interviewer asks about. The interviewer asks seven illegal questions. Listen again and note the illegal questions.

Equal Employment Opportunity
Topics You Can Be Asked about During a Job Interview

OK		Not OK (if not directly related to the job)	
☐	Name	☐	Age
☐	Address	☐	Race
☐	Work experience	☐	Sex
☑	Reason for leaving job	☐	Religion
☐	Reason for seeking position that is open	☐	National origin
☐	Salary	☐	Height
☐	Education	☐	Weight
☐	Professional organizations	☐	Marital status
☐	Convictions for crimes	☐	Information about spouse
☐	Skills	☐	Arrest record
☐	Job performance	☐	Physical disabilities
☐	Permission to work in the United States	☐	Children
		☐	Citizenship
		☐	English language skill
		☐	Financial situation

The illegal questions:

1. _____ How old are you? _____
2. _____
3. _____
4. _____
5. _____

(continued on next page)

6. _____

7. _____

Report the illegal questions to your classmates.

Example:
He asked her how old she was.

Discuss with the class: Do you think this was a stress interview? Why or why not?

6. Role Play

Work in groups. Using the ad and the résumé, develop questions for a job interview. Half of the group should write questions for the interviewer, and the other half should write questions for the candidate. Then select two people in your group to act out the interview for the whole class.

Pat Rogers
215 West Hill Drive
Baltimore, MD 21233
Telephone: (410) 555-7777

EDUCATION	**Taylor Community College** Associate's Degree (Business), 1988
	Middlesex High School High school diploma, 1985
EXPERIENCE **1989–1995** **Patients Plus** **Baltimore, MD**	**Medical receptionist** Responsibilities: Greeted patients, made appointments, answered telephones, typed medical records using computer.
1985–1989 **Union Hospital** **Baltimore, MD**	**Admitting clerk, hospital admissions office** Responsibilities: Interviewed patients for admission, entered information in computer, answered telephones.

MEDICAL RECEPTIONIST for busy doctor's office. Mature individual needed to answer phones, greet patients, make appointments, some filing and billing. Similar experience preferred. Computer skills a plus.

After each role play, discuss the interview as a class. Use the following questions to guide your discussion. Support your ideas by reporting questions that were asked in the interview.

1. Was it a stress interview? Why or why not?

2. Did the interviewer ask any illegal questions? Which ones were illegal?

3. Which of the candidate's questions were the most useful in evaluating the job? Explain your choices.

4. Which of the interviewer's questions gave the clearest picture of the candidate? Explain your choices.

5. If you were the interviewer, would you hire this candidate? Why or why not?

6. If you were the candidate, would you want to work for this company? Why or why not?

Example:
I think it was a stress interview because the interviewer asked him why he couldn't find a job.
The interviewer asked two illegal questions. She asked when the candidate was born. She also asked where the candidate was from.

7. In Your Experience

In small groups, discuss a personal experience with a school or job interview. It could be your own experience, or the experience of someone you know. Talk about these questions:

What did the interviewer want to find out?
What was the most difficult question to answer? Why?
Were there any questions that you didn't want to answer? What did you say?
What did you ask the interviewer?

Embedded Questions

INTRODUCTION

▶▶ *Read and listen to this magazine article and interview.*

The Tip

In China it's illegal. In Australia it's not customary. In Germany it's included in the bill. In the United States and Canada it's common but follows no logical pattern: You tip the person who delivers you flowers, but not the person who delivers you a package. And in restaurants, you tip according to the amount of your bill, but not according to the amount of labor involved in bringing you your meal.

So, what's a person to do?

Our correspondent, Marjorie Fuchs, interviewed Irene Frankel, author of *Tips on Tipping* (New Jersey, 1990), to help sort through the tipping maze.

Fuchs: Tell me **why you decided to write a book about tipping.**

Frankel: Well, I was working with a lot of people who were living here from abroad and who I thought needed to have a book on tipping because they had come from cultures where tipping wasn't a custom. But when I started talking to people about the book, I found that the people I was speaking to, who were mostly Americans, had a lot of questions about tipping also. So what started out as a book primarily for

people living here from abroad became a book primarily for anybody living here.

Fuchs: That's very interesting. It's true that a lot of people get very nervous when it comes to tipping. Does your book explain **who to tip?**

Frankel: Oh, absolutely. It tells you **who to tip** in a variety of situations: in restaurants, hotels, taxis. It also tells you **how much to tip** and **when to tip.** Equally important, it tells you **when not to tip.**

Fuchs: Yes. That *is* important to

know. Now, I've always wondered **when the custom of tipping began.**

Frankel: Well, actually it's a very old custom, and it started in England in the late 1700s. There was a box in coffee houses that was labeled *TIP. TIP* stood for "to insure promptness," and the box was placed by the door to let people put money in before they got service to ensure that they got good service. So it used to be that tipping was done *before* service was given, and then gradually it became reversed so that today tipping is done afterwards.

Fuchs: Now, what about bad service? I'd really like to know **what to do** when I get bad service. Should I still tip?

Frankel: I recommend that you tip *something* when you get bad service so that the person who gave you the bad service is aware that you didn't just forget to leave a tip. But I don't think you should tip the ordinary amount.

Fuchs: Now, suppose I don't know **whether to tip someone,** and I left your book at home. Is it OK to ask?

Frankel: Absolutely. If you don't know **whether or not to tip someone,** the best thing to do is to ask. Most people will probably say, "It's up to you." They won't tell you exactly **what to do,** but they *will* tell you **what most people do.**

Fuchs: Is there any reason **why we tip a restaurant server but not a flight attendant?**

Frankel: The rules for tipping in this country are very illogical, and there are often contradictions in **who we tip.** A flight attendant serves beverages and meals, just like a server in a restaurant. But we tip only the servers. In fact, flight attendants aren't allowed to accept tips.

Fuchs: I see. Now, when the waiter or waitress brings me my change, I never know **if it's OK to leave pennies.** What's the word

on pennies?

Frankel: Well, there are a couple of things about pennies. If you're taking a taxi somewhere and you want to know **how much to tip the taxi driver,** you don't figure out 15 percent to the penny and then tip with pennies. But if you're in a restaurant, and the change comes back with some pennies, it's fine to leave them as part of the tip.

Fuchs: Before we leave the topic of restaurants, can you explain **why a restaurant tip is tied to the amount of the bill rather than the amount of labor involved?** After all, bringing out a $10 dish of food involves the same amount of work as carrying out a $2 plate.

Frankel: Can I explain why? No. And you're right. It makes no sense. It's just the way it is. But, I guess you could look at other occupations and compare the amount of labor somebody does in two occupations, and there are inequities in those kinds of things as well. So, the answer is: Nothing is fair.

Fuchs: One last question. Suppose I'm planning a trip to, let's say, Egypt, for example. Tell me **how I can learn about tipping customs in that country**—or any other country, for that matter.

Frankel: OK. Well, as you know, tipping isn't international, and so it's really important to find out before you go abroad **what the tipping customs are.** Usually travel agents are aware of **what the rules are for tipping in each country,** or you can get the information from a travel book. If you're really not sure, and you don't have a travel agent or you don't want to buy a book or go to the library, you can call up the consulate and they'll let you know.

Fuchs: Well, thanks for all the good tips. I know our readers will find them very helpful. I certainly did.

Frankel: Thank you.

EMBEDDED QUESTIONS

MAIN CLAUSE	EMBEDDED QUESTION
I'm not sure He wondered	**if I left the right tip.** **whether five dollars was enough.**
Can you remember	**how much our bill was?**

	WH- WORD + INFINITIVE
I don't know	**how much to tip.**
Do you know	**where to leave the tip?**

Grammar Notes

1. In Unit 24, you learned to use indirect questions to report another person's words.

   Direct Question

   Did you leave a tip, Steven?

   How much do you tip a taxi driver, Irene?

   Indirect Question

   I asked if he had left a tip.

   I asked her how much she tipped a taxi driver.

   Indirect questions are a kind of <u>embedded question.</u> An embedded question is a question that is included within another sentence. This unit discusses embedded questions that do not report another person's words. We often use these kinds of embedded questions to ask politely for information or to express something we do not know.

   Direct Question

   Is the tip included?

   Why didn't he tip the mechanic?

   Embedded Question

   Can you tell me **if the tip is included?**

   I wonder **why he didn't tip the mechanic.**

   Usage note: When we approach people we don't know, or in formal situations, it is considered more polite to use an embedded question than a direct question.

	More Polite
Does our bill include a service charge?	Can you tell me **if our bill includes a service charge?**

2. Introduce embedded *yes/no* questions with *if* or *whether*.

   Do you know **if** they delivered the pizza?
   OR
   Do you know **whether** they delivered the pizza (or not)?

   Introduce embedded *wh-* questions with a question word.

   Many tourists wonder **how much** they should tip their restaurant servers.

3. Remember: Use statement word order, not question word order in embedded *yes/no* questions and embedded *wh-*questions about the predicate.

   Direct

   What time is it?

   Embedded

   Could you tell me **what time it is?** NOT Could you tell me ~~what time is it?~~

Be careful! Do not use the auxiliary verbs *do, does,* or *did* in embedded questions.

> I don't know when the pizza came.
> NOT I don't know ~~when did the pizza come.~~

4. You can also use the infinitive after a question word.

> Could you explain **how I should figure out the tip?**
>
> OR
>
> Could you explain **how to figure out the tip?**

> I don't know **whether I should leave a tip.**
>
> OR
>
> I don't know **whether to leave a tip.**

Be careful! Do not use the infinitive after *why.*

> I don't understand **why I should tip.**
> NOT I don't understand ~~why to tip.~~

5. Embedded questions often follow these phrases:

> I don't know . . .
> I'd like to know . . .
> Do you know . . . ?

Can you tell me . . . ?
I can't remember . . .
Can you remember . . . ?
Let's ask . . .
We need to find out . . .
I'd like to find out . . .
I wonder . . .
I'm not sure . . .
It doesn't say . . .
Could you explain . . . ?
I can't imagine . . .

Be careful! If the embedded question is in a statement, use a period at the end of the sentence.

> I don't know **who our waiter is.**
> NOT I don't know ~~who our waiter is?~~
> (The main sentence is the statement *I don't know.* . . . Therefore, it ends in a period.)

If the embedded question is in a question, use a question mark at the end of the sentence.

> Do you know **who our waiter is?**
> (The main sentence is the question *Do you know . . . ?* Therefore, it ends with a question mark.)

FOCUSED PRACTICE

1. Discover the Grammar

Read the ad for Tips on Tipping. *Underline the embedded questions.*

Tips on Tipping
This book is for you if . . .

. . . you've ever avoided a situation just because you didn't know <u>how much to tip</u>.

. . . you've ever realized (too late) that you were supposed to offer a tip.

. . . you've ever given a huge tip and then wondered if a tip was necessary at all.

. . . you've ever needed to know how to calculate the right tip instantly.

. . . you're new to the United States and you're not sure who you should tip here.

. . . you'd like to learn how tipping properly can get you the best service for your money.

Send for the ultimate guide to tipping and have all these questions answered.

— —

Yes! I want to learn who to tip, when to tip, and how much to tip. Please send me _____ copies of *Tips on Tipping*. I'm enclosing $4.95 plus $1.50 postage and handling for each book. (New Jersey residents: Add sales tax.) Don't forget to include your address and ZIP code.

I've enclosed my check or money order for $_____ made payable to:

Martin Unlimited, Inc.
P.O. Box 2075
Hoboken, New Jersey 070730

2. Service Charges

Complete the travel column about international tipping customs. Change the direct questions in parentheses to embedded questions. Use correct punctuation.

Tipping customs vary all over the world, so travelers should find out who, where, and how much to tip in countries they plan to visit. Here are some questions our readers often ask.

Q: Can you tell me whether _____ I should tip in Canada?
1. (Should I tip in Canada?)

A: Yes. Tipping practices in Canada are very similar to those in the United States.

Q: I know that some places in France include a service charge. Could you explain

_____
2. (How can I tell if the tip is included in the bill?)

A: A service charge is usually added to the bill in France. To make sure, look for the phrase *service compris* (service included) on the bill.

Q: I'm going to China next month on business. I understand that tipping is illegal. Please suggest

_____
3. (What can I do instead?)

I'll be staying at a hotel, and I like to show that I appreciate good service.

A: You can express appreciation for good service by giving a small gift. A picture album of your hometown, a pen, or a dictionary would all be good choices.

Q: On a recent trip to Iceland I found that service people refused tips. Could you explain

_____
4. (Why did this happen?)

A: In Iceland people often feel insulted by tips. Just say thank you—that's enough.

Q: Our family is planning a trip to Norway to visit my in-laws. My daughter wants to take some skiing lessons while we're there. I'd like to know _____
5. (Should I tip her instructor?)

A: It's not customary to tip a ski instructor in Norway. In fact, tipping is rare all over Scandinavia. Take the instructor to lunch instead.

Q: I'm going to work in Japan for a year. I'm bringing a lot of luggage. Could you tell me

_____
6. (How much should I tip the airport and train porters?)

A: There's a fixed fee of ¥200 per bag for airport porters. No tipping is expected for train porter .

Q: My husband and I are planning a trip to Australia. Please tell us

_____
7. (Who expects a tip and who doesn't?)

A: This is in the process of changing, but tipping is not yet customary "Down Under." Tip someone who gives you very special treatment. Otherwise, just say thanks.

(continued on next page)

Q: My family hosted a Russian exchange student for a year. Now the student's family has invited me to visit in St. Petersburg. Is tipping customary? For example, I don't know

_____
                              8. (Can I tip taxi drivers on my trip?)

A: Taxi drivers in Russia now expect a tip of 10 percent of the fare.

3. Tourists

Two foreign exchange students are visiting Washington, D.C. Complete their conversations. Choose the appropriate questions from the box and change them to embedded questions. Remember to correctly punctuate the sentences.

> How much are we supposed to tip the taxi driver?
>
> Could we rent a car and drive there?
>
> Do they have tour buses that go there?
>
> How much does the metro cost?
>
> How long will it take?
>
> How far are you going?
>
> How are we going to choose?
>
> How much does a bus tour cost?
>
> What did they put in the sauce?
>
> What's wrong with it?
>
> Where are you?
>
> Where is the Smithsonian Museum?
>
> ~~Where is it?~~
>
> Where do they sell them?

1. **Martina:** Taxi! Taxi!

   Driver: Where do you want to go? Airport?

   Martina: The Hotel Edison. Do you know _____*where it is?*_____
                                                              a.

   Driver: Sure, South Dakota. Get in and I'll take you there.

   Martina: (whispering to Miuki) Do you know _____
                                                                    b.

   Miuki: According to the book, we're supposed to leave 10–15 percent. Don't worry. I've got it.

2. **Martina:** There's so much to see in Washington. I don't know _____

a.

   Miuki: We could take a bus tour of the city first, and then decide.

   Martina: Does the guidebook say _____

b.

   Miuki: Yeah. About $15 per person, plus tips for the guide and the driver.

3. **Martina:** That was delicious.

   Miuki: Let's try to find out _____

a.

   Martina: It tasted like it had garlic and ginger.

   Miuki: I'll ask the waiter.

4. **Martina:** This map is useless. I'm totally lost.

   Miuki: There's a police officer. Let's ask.

   Martina: Excuse me. Can you tell me _____

a.

   Officer: Sure. Just turn right at the corner and go straight. It's about a twenty-minute walk from here.

5. **Martina:** I'm tired. Let's take the metro.

   Miuki: OK. Do you know _____

a.

   Martina: It's not expensive. I think it depends on _____

b.

   But we have to get tickets, and I'm not sure _____

c.

   Miuki: Oh. Probably right in the station.

6. **Martina:** I'd like to visit Williamsburg, Virginia, while we're here.

   Miuki: I wonder _____

a.

   Martina: I'm sure they do, but do you think _____

b.

   It isn't that far to Virginia.

   Miuki: Let's do that. We can drive back along the shore.

7. **Clerk:** RAC Rent-a-Car. How can I help you?

   Miuki: Our rental car just broke down on the expressway. I don't know _____

a.

   Clerk: Can you tell me _____

b.

   Miuki: I'm calling from the tollbooth at Exit 57 on Route 95.

   Clerk: OK. We'll send a tow truck right away, and we'll also send someone to pick you up.

   Miuki: Do you know _____

c.

   Clerk: It shouldn't be too long.

   Miuki: Thanks.

4. Asking for Advice

Complete the conversation. Use a question word and the infinitive form of the verbs in the box.

figure out	get	go	invite	leave	~~wear~~

Martina: I'm going out to dinner with Janek when we get back Friday night. I can't decide
_____ what to wear _____. Any ideas?
1.

Miuki: Your red dress. You always look great in it. By the way, where are you going?

Martina: John's Grill. Have you ever been there?

Miuki: No, but I hear it's good. Where is it located?

Martina: It's down by the river at Tenth and Water Streets.

Miuki: Oh, that's right. You know _____ there, don't you?
2.

Martina: I think so. I take the number six bus. But I'm not sure _____.
3.
I'm meeting him there at 7:00.

Miuki: Well, it takes about forty-five minutes to get there from our place.

Martina: So, I guess I'll leave at 6:00. That'll give me plenty of time. You know, I'd like to take Janek
someplace for dessert afterwards, but I don't know _____. Any ideas?
4.

Miuki: Well, there are quite a few cafes in that area, but the desserts at John's are supposed to be
pretty good.

Martina: Oh. By the way, it's Janek's birthday, so I'm paying. But I'm never quite sure
_____ the tip. I usually just let the person I'm with do it.
5.

Miuki: Just double the tax. That comes to about 15 percent. And, you know, you can always take a
calculator with you.

Martina: That's true.

Miuki: By the way, how old is Janek going to be?

Martina: Twenty-one. I thought about asking a few people to join us, but I really didn't know
_____.
6.

Miuki: Don't worry. I'm sure it will be fine with just the two of you.

COMMUNICATION PRACTICE

5. Practice Listening

A travel agent is being interviewed on a call-in radio show. The topic is tipping. Listen to the callers' questions. Then listen again and for each question decide on an appropriate response.

1. a. Between 15 and 20 percent of the total bill.
   b. The waiter.
2. a. About 15 percent of the fare.
   b. Only if you are happy with the ride.
3. a. Before you leave.
   b. On the table.
4. a. The person who takes you to your seat.
   b. 20 francs.
5. a. The manager.
   b. Don't leave a tip.
6. a. $1.00.
   b. At the cashier.

6. Information Gap: Eating Out

Work in groups of three. Students A and B are customers in a restaurant. Look at the menu below. Student C, turn to the Information Gap for Unit 25 on page IG 4 and follow the instructions there.

John's Grill

Starters
Soup of the Day	$2.95
Caesar Salad	$3.25
John's Salad	$2.95

MAIN DISHES

Fish
Catch of the Day (please ask waiter)	price varies
Filet of Sole with Sauce Dijon	$8.95
Fried Shrimp	$9.95

Chicken
Chicken à la John	$7.95
Half Roast Chicken	$6.95

Beef
Steak Frites	$8.95
John's Hamburger Deluxe	$5.95

Pasta—made daily at John's
Macaroni and Cheese	$5.95
Spaghetti à la John	$6.95

All main courses (except pasta) come with your choice of baked potato or fries and the vegetable of the day

Desserts
Fruit Pie (in season)	$1.95
à la mode	$2.25
Chocolate Cake	$1.95
Fresh Fruit Salad	$2.95
Dessert of the Day (ask your waiter)	

Beverages
Soda	$ .95
Coffee or tea	$1.15

Prices include tax. Service not included.

Student A, you are allergic to tomatoes and dairy products. Student B, you don't eat meat or chicken. Discuss the menu with your partner. Then ask your server about items on the menu and order a meal. When you get the check, figure out a 15 percent tip.

Example:
- **A:** I wonder what the soup of the day is.
- **B:** Me too. Do you know what's in a Caesar salad?
- **A:** Not really. We'll have to ask the server.
  Excuse me. Can you tell us what's in the Caesar salad?
- **C:** Sure. It has lettuce, parmesan cheese, and croutons.
- **A:** Croutons? I don't know what they are.
- **C:** They're toasted cubes of bread.

7. The First Time's Always the Hardest

Think about the first time you did something, for example, the first time you:

drove a car
went on a job interview
traveled to a foreign country
became a parent

What problems did you have? Tell a classmate.

Example:
I remember the first time I drove a car. I didn't know how to start it. I didn't know which gear to use. I even had to ask someone how to turn the windshield wipers on. . . .

8. Tipping

Work in small groups. Discuss these questions.

1. Do you think tipping is a good system? Why or why not?

2. Were you ever in a situation where you didn't know what to do about a tip?

3. How is tipping different in the United States and other countries you know?

Example:
- **A:** I'm not sure whether tipping is good or not. I think people should get paid enough so that they don't have to depend on tips.
- **B:** I wonder if you would still get good service if the tip were included.
- **C:** Sure you would. A service charge is included in a lot of countries, and the service is still good.

I. Karen and Jon had a party a week ago. Karen is telling a friend about the conversations she had before the party. Read what people actually said. Then circle the correct words to complete each reported sentence.

1. "We'd like you and Bill to come to a party at our apartment this Friday."

   I invited Maria and Bill came/to come to a party at our apartment last/this Friday.

2. "It'll be a housewarming for our new apartment."

   I told them it would be/will be a housewarming for our/their new apartment.

3. "We'll be a little late."

   They said/told me that they/we would be a little late.

4. "What time is your party going to start?"

   Sheila said/asked what time our party is/was going to start.

5. "Should I bring something?"

   She asked if I/she should bring/should have brought something.

6. "Thanks, but that's OK. Don't bring anything."

   I thanked her, but I told/said her not to bring/didn't bring anything.

7. "I've been planning to call you for a long time."

   Tory told me he 's been planning/'d been planning to call us/you for a long time.

8. "I don't know how to get to your place."

   He said he didn't know how/doesn't know how to get to your/our place.

9. "Is there a bus stop nearby?"

   He said/asked was there/if there was a bus stop nearby.

10. "Don't be afraid of getting lost."

    I said not to be/be afraid of getting lost.

11. "Take the Woodmere Avenue bus."

    I invited/told him take/to take the Woodmere Avenue bus.

12. "I can't come tomorrow night."

    Nita said that she can't/couldn't come the following night/tomorrow night.

13. "My cousin from Detroit is arriving today."

    She told me her cousin from Detroit is/was arriving today/that day.

14. "Bring your cousin along."

    I said/told her to bring her/your cousin along.

15. "The weather bureau has issued a storm warning for tonight."

    Jon told me that the weather bureau has issued/had issued a storm warning for tonight/that night.

16. "Schools will close early today."

The forecaster said that schools <u>would/will</u> close early <u>today/that day</u>.
_{a.} _{b.}

17. "Motorists must drive with extreme caution."

She said that motorists <u>must have driven/had to drive</u> with extreme caution.
_{a.}

18. "I love snow."

Jon always <u>tells/says</u> that he <u>loves/loved</u> snow.
_{a.} _{b.}

19. "Would you please shovel the driveway?"

The next morning I asked <u>you/him</u> <u>to shovel/if he had shoveled</u> the driveway.
_{a.} _{b.}

20. "Where are my boots?"

He <u>told/asked</u> me where <u>were his boots/his boots were</u>.
_{a.} _{b.}

II. *One of the guests is getting ready for the party. Complete the sentences with embedded questions.*

1. I don't know _____ if it's a formal party. _____
(Is it a formal party?)

2. I wonder _____
(What should I wear?)

3. I'd like to know _____
(Who's going to be there?)

4. I'd like to find out _____
(Did they invite Tory?)

5. I'm not sure _____
(Will I be able to find a cab?)

6. Do you know _____
(How do you get to Woodmere Avenue?)

7. I don't know _____
(How far is it?)

8. Now I've got to figure out _____
(How much should I tip the driver?)

9. The street sign doesn't say _____
(Is this Woodmere Avenue?)

10. Could you tell me _____
(What time is it?)

III. *Complete the reported comments made the day after the party. Use the correct verb form.*

1. "You look beautiful in that dress."

She said that I ____looked____ beautiful in that dress.

2. "Have you met Bill and Maria yet?"

Harry asked me if I _____ Bill and Maria yet.

3. "Is Troy coming tonight?"

I asked Jon whether Tory _____ last night.

4. "I'm not sure."

He told me he _____ sure.

5. "Why don't you ride home with us?"

Bill invited me _____ home with them.

(continued on next page)

6. "It may snow tonight."

   He said that it _____ that night.

7. "Call me tomorrow."

   Karen told me _____ her the next day.

8. "We ought to get together more often."

   We all said that we _____ more often.

9. "Drive carefully."

   Jon told Bill and Maria _____ carefully.

10. "Don't worry."

    They told him _____ .

IV. *Report the conversation that Nita and Jon had at the party last week.*

1. **Nita:** How long have you and Karen been living here?

   (ask) _____ Nita asked how long Jon and Karen had been living there. _____

2. **Jon:** We moved in three weeks ago.

   (tell) _____

3. **Nita:** Do you like this place better than your old apartment?

   (ask) _____

4. **Jon:** We like it a lot more.

   (say) _____

5. **Jon:** When did your cousin arrive from Detroit?

   (ask) _____

6. **Nita:** He just came yesterday.

   (tell) _____

7. **Jon:** It's been an incredible winter.

   (say) _____

8. **Nita:** The roads may close again with this storm.

   (say) _____

9. **Jon:** Don't drive tonight.

   (say) _____

10. **Jon:** Stay here with your cousin.

    (say) _____

11. **Nita:** We should try to make it home.

(tell) _____

12. **Nita:** I have to walk my dog early tomorrow morning.

(say) _____

V. *Read this draft of a news story. There are nine mistakes with direct and indirect speech and embedded questions. Find and correct them.*

Motorists returning home during last night's snow storm were pleasantly surprised. Early

yesterday afternoon, forecasters had predicted that Route 10 ~~will~~ *would* close because of high winds.

However, all major highways remained open last night. One woman, stopping for a newspaper on

Woodmere Avenue at about midnight, told this reporter that she and her cousin have almost decided

to stay with a friend tonight, rather than drive home. Her cousin told me that I had just arrived from

Detroit, where the storm hit first. He said "that it had been a big one." School children seemed

especially pleased Yesterday morning, most schools announced that they will close at 1:00 P.M. Several

kids at James Fox Elementary reported that they are planning to spend that afternoon sledding and

having snowball fights.

Many people are wondering how could weather forecasters make such a big mistake. Carla

Donati, the weather reporter for WCSX, said that they were not sure why this had happened? The

National Weather Service has not commented.

PART

X

Pronouns and Phrasal Verbs

INTRODUCTION

Read and listen to this excerpt from a psychology magazine.

Self-Talk

Recent studies show that self-talk, or the way we explain a problem to **ourselves**, can affect our performance and even our health. To illustrate, one researcher tells the story of co-workers Tom and Sara. Both lost their jobs last fall, but their responses to this loss were very different. Before they left the job, they took **each other's** telephone numbers so that they could keep in touch during the winter. Sara called Tom and other friends often, continued her leisure-time activities, and kept **herself** fit. She encouraged Tom to do the same, but he couldn't take her advice. In fact, if Sara hadn't kept in touch with him, Tom would have had almost no contact with friends. He isolated **himself**, deprived **himself** of his hobbies, and even made **himself** sick with a bad cold all winter.

> I'll never find another job.

> I really made a mess of that.

> It was all my fault.

What made their responses so different from **one another**? Since both Tom and Sara were laid off, the job loss **itself** can't explain Tom's problems. One major difference was the way Tom and Sara explained the problem to **themselves**. Sara told **herself** that her problem was temporary and that she **herself** could change it. Tom saw **himself** as helpless and permanently unemployed.

> I'm the best worker they had.

In the spring, Tom and Sara both got their jobs back. Their responses when they talked to **each other** were similar to the way they explained things to **themselves**. "They finally realized that they needed me," said Sara the optimist. Tom grumbled, "I guess they were really desperate."

> Fred messed up the account, not me.

> I'll find a better job soon.

REFLEXIVE AND RECIPROCAL PRONOUNS

REFLEXIVE PRONOUNS

SUBJECT PRONOUN		REFLEXIVE PRONOUN	
I		**myself**	
You		**yourself**	
He		**himself**	
She	looked at	**herself**	in the mirror.
It (The cat)		**itself**	
We		**ourselves**	
You		**yourselves**	
They		**themselves**	

RECIPROCAL PRONOUNS

SUBJECT PRONOUN		RECIPROCAL PRONOUN
We You They	looked at	**each other.** **one another.**

Grammar Notes

1. Use a <u>reflexive pronoun</u> when the subject and object of a sentence refer to the same person or thing.

> Subject = Object
> **Sara** looked at **herself** in the mirror. (Sara looked at her own face.)
> **Tom** cut **himself** shaving. (Tom cut his own face.)

2. In imperative sentences, the subject is understood to be *you*. When you use reflexive pronouns in imperative sentences, remember to use *yourself* when the subject is singular and *yourselves* when the subject is plural.

> Don't be so hard on **yourself,** Tom. You're too impatient.
> "Don't push **yourselves** so hard," Sara told the people in her office.

3. Use a reflexive pronoun to emphasize a noun. A reflexive pronoun used for emphasis often follows the noun directly.

> Tom was upset when he lost his job. The **job itself** wasn't important to him, but he needed the money for school. (Tom didn't care about the job; he just needed the money.)
> The instructions for the new computers were very confusing. The **computer operators themselves** had trouble understanding them. (Even the computer operators had trouble understanding the instructions.).

4. *By* + a reflexive pronoun means *alone* or *without any help*.

> Sara lives **by herself,** but she has a lot of friends nearby.
> The kids painted their apartment **by themselves** last winter. They didn't hire painters.

Be + a reflexive pronoun means *act in a typical way*.

> Relax and **be yourself** on your interview.
> Tom hasn't **been himself** since he lost his job.

See Appendix 14 on page A9 for a list of verbs and expressions that are commonly used reflexively.

5. We also use <u>reciprocal pronouns</u> when the subject and object of a sentence refer to the same person or thing. Notice the meaning of reciprocal pronouns in these sentences.

> Tom and Sara met **each other** at an office party last year. (Tom met Sara, and Sara met Tom.)
> There were twenty people at the office party. We all told **one another** about our families and jobs. (Each person exchanged news with all the other people.)

Usage note: Some people use *each other* when the subject consists of two people and *one another* when the subject consists of more than two people. However, not everyone follows this rule.

Be careful! Reciprocal pronouns and plural reflexive pronouns have different meanings.

> Tom and Sara talked to **each other** about the news. (Tom talked to Sara; Sara talked to Tom.)

> Tom and Sara talked to **themselves** about the news. (Tom talked to himself; Sara talked to herself.)

6. Reciprocal pronouns have possessive forms.

> Tom and Sara decided to keep in touch with each other.
> They took **each other's** telephone number.

FOCUSED PRACTICE

1. Discover the Grammar

Read the rest of the article about self-talk. Underline the reflexive pronouns once and the reciprocal pronouns twice. Draw an arrow to the words that these pronouns refer to.

Winning athletes have known about self-talk for a long time. Golf pro Jack Nicklaus used to imagine <u>himself</u> making a winning shot just before he played. Olympic swimmer Summer Sanders prepares herself for a race by smiling. Now sports psychologists actually train athletes to use positive self-talk. For example, when things go wrong, athletes remind themselves of past successes.

At the Olympics, where competition is the most intense, positive self-talk can make the difference between winning and losing. In fact, one sports psychologist believes that Olympic athletes are not very different from <u>one another</u> — they are all the best in their sports. When two top athletes compete against each other, The winner is the one with the most powerful positive "mental movies."

Psychologists say that ordinary people can use these techniques as well. We ourselves can create the "mental movies" that help us succeed in difficult situations.

2. The Office Party

Tom and Sara's company had an office party. Choose the correct reflexive or reciprocal pronouns to complete the conversations.

1. **A:** Listen, guys! The food and drinks are over here. Please come and help

   _____yourselves_____.
   (yourselves / themselves)

   B: Thanks. We will.

2. **A:** Isn't that the new head of the accounting department over there?

   B: I think so. Have you met him yet?

   A: Not yet. Let's go over and introduce _____.
   (himself / ourselves)

3. **A:** I'm really nervous about my date with Nicole after the party. I cut

   _____ twice while shaving, and then I lost my car keys.
   (herself / myself)

   B: Come on. This is a party. Just relax and be _____. You'll do fine.
   (yourself / yourselves)

4. **A:** Did you hear that Erika's sales team won the award this year?

   B: I know. They were all surprised. In fact, Erika _____ didn't know
(themselves / herself)
her team had won.

5. **A:** What are you giving your boss for the holidays this year?

   B: We always give _____ the same holiday gifts. Every year I give
(ourselves / each other)
him a book and he gives me a scarf.

6. **A:** What do you think of the new computer program?

   B: I like it. It's so easy to use, it seems to work by _____.
(itself / themselves)

   A: Really? In our department, we're still teaching _____ how to
(ourselves / themselves)
use it.

7. **A:** Jessica looks upset. Didn't she get the promotion?

   B: No, and she keeps blaming _____. She should read that article
(herself / himself)
you showed me about self-talk.

8. **A:** The Aguayos are going to Japan on vacation this year.

   B: Are they going by _____ or with a tour group?
(each other / themselves)

9. **A:** This was a great party.

   B: Yeah. We really enjoyed _____.
(ourselves / myself)

3. We Learn from One Another

Read this interview with George Prudeau, a high-school French teacher.
Complete the interview with the correct reflexive or reciprocal pronouns.

Interviewer: What do you like best about your profession?

George: One of the great things about teaching is the freedom I have. I run the class

    _____myself_____ —just the way I want to. I also like the way my students
          1.

    and I learn from _____. My students have taught me a lot.
                2.

Interviewer: What about discipline? Is that a problem?

George: We have just a few rules. I tell my students, "Keep _____ busy. Discuss
                                   3.

    the lessons, but don't interfere with _____'s work."
                                  4.

Interviewer: What do you like to teach best?

George: I've taught French, geography, history—the subject _____ isn't that
                                   5.

    important. A good teacher helps students learn by _____ and encourages
                                   6.

    them not to give up when they have problems. John just taught _____
                                             7.

(continued on next page)

how to bake French bread. The first few loaves were failures, and he had to use some positive self-talk to keep going.

Interviewer: What materials do you use?

George: Very simple ones. I pride _____ on the fact that I could teach
8.
anywhere, even on a street corner.

Interviewer: What do you like least about your job?

George: The salary. I teach culture, and I really need to be in contact with the places and people _____. But I can't travel much on this salary.
9.

4. Friends

Find and correct six mistakes in this woman's diary.

>   Jan's birthday was Wednesday, and I forgot to call him. I know his
>
> birthday is important to him because he told me so ~~hisself~~. On
>   *himself*
>
> Tuesday I wrote a note to remind me, but then I got busy and forgot
>
> to read it. I felt terrible. My sister Anna said, "Don't be so hard on
>
> yourself," but that didn't really help. She's so forgetful herself! Then
>
> I remembered that article on self-talk. It said that people can
>
> change the way they explain problems to theirselves. Well, I listened
>
> to my own self-talk, and it sounded really insulting, a lot like the way
>
> our high-school math teacher used to talk to ourselves. I thought,
>
> Jan myself wouldn't talk to me that way. In fact, he had already
>
> forgiven me for my mistake. And I forgave him for forgetting our
>
> dinner date two weeks ago. Friends can forgive themselves, so I
>
> guess I can forgive myself.

COMMUNICATION PRACTICE

5. Practice Listening

Listen to the conversations at the office party. Then listen again and circle the pronouns that you hear.

1. **A:** Mark's department did a great job this year.

   B: I know. They should be really proud of <u>themselves</u>/<u>each other</u>.

2. **A:** What's wrong? You look upset.

   B: I just heard Ed and Jeff talking. You know Ed blames <u>him/himself</u> for everything.

3. **A:** I hear you're going to Japan on vacation this year. Are you going by <u>yourself/yourselves</u> or with a tour?

   B: Oh, with a tour.

4. **A:** Hillary looks happy tonight. Did Meredith give her the promotion?

   B: No, not yet. Meredith keeps asking <u>herself/her</u> if she can do the job.

5. **A:** How do you like the new computer system?

   B: I'm not sure. In our department, we're still teaching <u>each other/ourselves</u> how to use it.

6. **A:** So long, now. Thanks for coming. It was good to see you.

   B: Oh, it was a great party.

   A: I'm glad you enjoyed <u>yourself/yourselves</u>.

6. The Optimist Test

Are you an optimist or a pessimist? Test yourself by completing the questionnaire.

What do you tell yourself when things go wrong? Check your most likely self-talk for each situation. below. then find out if you're an optimist or pessimist.

1. Your boss doesn't say good morning to you.

_____ a. She wasn't herself today.
_____ b. She doesn't like me.

2. Your family forgot your birthday.

_____ a. Next year we should keep in touch with one
   another more.
_____ b. They only think about themselves.

3. You gain ten pounds.

_____ a. I promise myself to eat properly from now on.
_____ b. Diets never work for me.

4. Your romantic partner decides to go out with other people.

_____ a. We didn't spend enough time with each other.
_____ b. We're wrong for each other.

5. You're feeling tired lately.

_____ a. I pushed myself too hard this week.
_____ b. I never take care of myself.

6. Your friend forgets an appointment with you.

_____ a. He sometimes forgets to read his appointment book.
_____ b. He never reminds himself about important things.

Score your questionnaire . . .
Optimists see bad situations as temporary or limited. Pessimists see them as permanent. All the *a* answers are optimistic, and all the *b* answers are pessimistic. Give yourself 0 for every a answer and 1 for every b answer.

If You Scored	You Are
0–2	very optimistic
3–4	somewhat optimistic
5–6	pessimistic

Now interview five classmates and find out how they answered the questions. Report the results to another group. Use reflexive and reciprocal pronouns in your descriptions.

Example:
For question 5, three people said they pushed themselves too hard. Two people said they never take care of themselves. . . .

7. The Memory Game

Work with a partner. First look at the picture carefully for thirty seconds. Then shut your books. Tell your partner as many things as you can remember about what people in the picture are doing. Use reciprocal and reflexive pronouns in your description.

Example:
Two people are waving at each other.

Compare your answers with those of another pair. Who remembered the most?

INTRODUCTION

Read and listen to the magazine article.

Eureka!

Say *inventor*, and many people **think of** a professional scientist working in a laboratory full of modern equipment. However, creativity is a universal quality. We are all potential inventors, regardless of age, education, or situation. Inventions have been **dreamed up** and developed in kitchens as well as in laboratories, by elementary school children as well as by trained scientists. The first personal computer was **put together** in a garage by two young college students who had **dropped out of** school.

If higher education and an expensive laboratory aren't required, what is? People who **come up with** new ideas do have some special qualities. Curiosity comes first. Inventors are people who want to **find out** why things happen the way they do. For example, when George de Mestrel, a Swiss inventor, took his dog for walks in the mountains, burrs would get stuck in the dog's coat. De Mestrel wondered why they were so hard to remove. Acting on his curiosity, he examined the burrs through a microscope. When he saw the many tiny hooks on each burr, he realized that he was looking at the perfect fastener. Years later, de Mestrel developed this idea into Velcro®, now used to fasten everything from sneakers to space suits.

Imagination is also crucial for an inventor. This quality helps inventors **put** things **together** in a new way. One U.S. sixth grader invented a solar-powered light by combining solar cells and a bicycle. When he rides his bike during the day, the sunlight **charges up** two batteries. Then at night, when he needs the light, he **switches** it **on**. Imagination can also mean seeing a new use for a common object. The original Frisbee® was a pie pan that two truck drivers were tossing to each other in a parking lot. As he watched the two men **playing around**, Walter Morrison **came up with** his idea for a new toy that became popular all over the world.

Inventors are often problem solvers. When fifteen-year-old Chester Greenwood's ears got frostbitten during Maine's bitter winters, he didn't **give up** and stay indoors. Instead, he attached fur cups to the ends of a piece of wire, and wrapped the wire around his head. His friends made fun of him at first, but soon the idea **caught on**, and they wanted earmuffs too. The Greenwood family had to work hard to **keep up with** the orders. Chester patented his invention when he was only nineteen.

After an inventor says "Eureka!" (Greek for "I've found it!"), there's still a lot of work to do. Another quality found in successful inventors is tenacity—the ability to **stick with** a project until it is com-pleted. This usually involves **looking up** information related to the idea. George Eastman, inventor of the Kodak® camera and film, spent years researching chemicals and photography. Tenacity also involves **trying out** different materials and designs. De Mestrel experimented with many kinds of materials before he perfected Velcro.®

Finally, inventors need a lot of self-confidence. They have to believe in their ideas and be willing to learn from their failures. Gail Borden, who developed a process for condensing and canning milk, was **turned down** when he first applied for a patent. He **kept on** trying to perfect his method and after years he finally succeeded. His invention probably saved many lives at a time when there was no way to refrigerate milk. Borden's motto is engraved on his tombstone: "I tried and failed; I tried again and again and succeeded."

PHRASAL VERBS

SUBJECT	VERB	PARTICLE	DIRECT OBJECT
She	**turned**	**on**	the machine.
He	**ran**	**into**	the teacher.
They	**sat**	**down.**	

SUBJECT	VERB	DIRECT OBJECT	PARTICLE
She	**turned**	it the machine	**on.**

Grammar Notes

1. A phrasal verb (also called a <u>two-part</u> or <u>two-word verb</u>) consists of a verb + particle.*

Verb	+	Particle	=	Phrasal Verb
think		up		**think up**
talk		over		**talk over**
call		off		**call off**

2. The verb and particle are usually common words, but their separate meanings may not help you guess the meaning of the phrasal verb.

Phrasal Verb	Meaning	Example
turn down	reject	They **turned down** his application for a patent.
turn off	extinguish	She **turned off** the light before leaving the room.
turn up	appear	Velcro® **turns up** in thousands of products.

Usage note: Phrasal verbs are much more common in everyday speech than their one-word equivalents.

> Please **turn off** the light before you leave.
> NOT Please ~~extinguish~~ the light before you leave.

Be careful! Like other verbs, phrasal verbs often have more than one meaning.

> Please **turn down** the radio. It's too loud. (Please lower the volume.)
> Bill didn't get the job. They **turned down** his application. (They rejected his application.)

3. Many phrasal verbs are transitive (they take direct objects).

Phrasal Verb	Meaning	Example
dream up	invent	Edison **dreamed up** many new ideas.
look up	try to find in a book	Inventors **look up** informaton about their ideas.
get on	board	I never **get on** a plane without my Walkman®.

*Particles can also be adverbs or prepositions in other sentences.

Verb	Preposition	
He walked	up	the hill.

Phrasal Verb	Meaning	Example
put together	assemble	Two young men **put together** the first personal computer.
stick with	persevere	Borden **stuck with** his idea until he succeeded.
try out	see if something works	Morrison **tried out** several designs for the Frisbee®.
run into	meet accidentally	We **ran into** an old friend recently.

See Appendix 15 on pages A9 and A10 for a list of more transitive phrasal verbs.

4. Transitive verbs can be <u>separable</u> or <u>inseparable</u>.

a. Most transitive phrasal verbs are separable. This means that noun objects can go after the particle (look up *a word*) or between the verb and the particle (look *a word* up). The following transitive phrasal verbs from grammar note 3 are separable.

Phrasal Verb	Example
dream up	I just **dreamed up** a new idea.
	OR
	I just **dreamed** a new idea **up.**
look up	He **looked up** information in the library.
	OR
	He **looked** information **up** in the library.
put together	It's time to **put together** the project.
	OR
	It's time to **put** the project **together.**
try out	We want to **try out** the invention.
	OR
	We want to **try** the invention **out.**

Notice that when the noun object is part of a long phrase, we do not separate the phrasal verb.

> She **tried out** a new and complicated device for developing photographs. NOT She ~~tried a new and complicated device for developing photographs out~~.

Be careful! If the direct object is a pronoun, it must go between the verb and the particle.

> There were a lot of new words. We **looked them up** in the dictionary. NOT We ~~looked up them~~ in the dictionary.

b. For inseparable phrasal verbs, objects always go after the particle. You can not separate the verb from its particle.

> She **ran into her science teacher** in the library. NOT She ~~ran her science teacher into~~ in the library.
> She **ran into him** in the library. NOT She ~~ran him into~~ in the library.

The following transitive phrasal verbs from grammar note 3 are inseparable.

Phrasal Verb	Example
get on	We couldn't **get on** the bus this morning. It was too crowded.
stick with	At first her idea failed, but she **stuck with** it until it worked.
run into	I hadn't seen Professor Mederi for years, and then I **ran into** him in the supermarket.

See Appendix 15 on pages A9 and A10 for a list of more inseparable transitive phrasal verbs.

5. A small group of phrasal verbs must be separated. Following are some examples.

(continued on next page)

Phrasal Verb	Meaning	Example
see (something) **through**	complete	Eastman worked for years to **see his ideas through.** NOT Eastman worked for years to see through his ideas.
keep (something) **on**	not remove	**Keep** your earmuffs **on.** It's very cold outside. NOT Keep on your earmuffs.
get (something) **out of**	benefit from	I **got** a lot **out of** this course. NOT I get out of a lot . . .

6. Some transitive phrasal verbs are used in combination with certain prepositions. A phrasal verb + preposition combination (also called a three-part or three-word verb) is usually inseparable.

The following are some common phrasal verb + preposition combinations.

Phrasal Verb + Preposition	Meaning	Example
come up with	imagine	She **came up with** a brilliant idea.
drop out of	quit	They **dropped out of** school and got jobs.
keep up with	go as fast as	The class went too quickly for me to **keep up with.**

See Appendix 15 on pages A9 and A10 for a list of common phrasal verbs + prepositions.

7. Phrasal verbs can also be intransitive. (They don't take an object.) The following phrasal verbs are intransitive.

Phrasal Verb	Meaning	Example
catch on	become popular	His earmuffs **caught on.** Everyone wanted a pair.
give up	quit	Don't **give up.** Keep trying.

See Appendix 16 on page A11 for a list of more intransitive phrasal verbs.

FOCUSED PRACTICE

1. Discover the Grammar

Underline the phrasal verbs in this article about a recent invention that has changed the world.

If you are looking at a modern laptop computer, it's hard to believe that computers were once huge devices available only to government or big businesses. Today's computers are often not much bigger than a typewriter and are taken for granted in homes, schools, and offices. Technological advances made the small personal computer possible, but two electronic whiz kids working in a garage actually <u>brought</u> it <u>about</u>.

Steven Jobs and Stephen Wozniak first met at Hewlett-Packard, an electronics firm in California. Jobs was a high-school student when William Hewlett, the president, took him on as a summer employee. Wozniak, a college dropout, was also working there, and the two got along right away.

Jobs and Wozniak went separate ways in 1972. When they got together again in 1974, Wozniak was spending a lot of time with a local computer club, and he convinced Jobs to join the group. Jobs immediately saw the potential for a small computer. He teamed up with Wozniak, a brilliant engineer, to build one.

The two designed the Apple I computer in Jobs's bedroom, and they put the prototype together in his garage. With $1,300 in capital raised by selling Jobs's car and Wozniak's scientific calculator, they set up their first production line.

Apple I, which they brought out in 1976, had sales of $600, a promising beginning. By 1980, Apple Computers, which had started four years earlier as a project in a garage, had a market value of $1.2 billion.

Now write down each phrasal verb from the article next to its meaning.

Phrasal Verb	Meaning
1. _____set up_____	started
2. _____	started working (with)
3. _____	introduced
4. _____	reunited
5. _____	made something happen
6. _____	hired
7. _____	assembled
8. _____	related well

2. Edison, Thomas Alva (1847–1931)

Read about one of the greatest inventors in history. Complete the information with the appropriate form of the correct phrasal verbs in the boxes.

drop out of	grow up	think back on	~~try out~~

Thomas Alva Edison was born on February 11, 1847. A curious child, he _____tried out_____
1.
almost anything he had read about or seen. His parents liked to _____ the time they
2.
found young Thomas sitting on a number of eggs. He had recently seen a goose hatch eggs and wanted to
see if it would work for him, too.

Edison _____ in the midwestern part of the United States. When he was seven, his
3.
family moved from Ohio to Michigan. He was a poor student and _____ school after
4.
just a few months. From then on, he received his education from his mother. An avid reader, he read—
and remembered—everything he could get his hands on.

break out	carry out	fill up	keep away	set up

When he was twelve, he started to work, selling newspapers, candy, and sandwiches on trains. With the
money he saved, he _____ a laboratory in the basement of his home. He had collected
5.
hundreds of bottles from junk heaps and _____ them _____
6.
with chemicals he needed to _____ his experiments. He
7.
labeled all his bottles "poison" to _____ his family _____ from
8.
them. Soon, Edison moved his lab to the baggage car of the train. As the result of an overturned bottle of
chemicals, a fire _____ in the car, putting an end to his career on the rails.
9.

break down	bring about	carry on	find out	pay back	set up

At age of fifteen, he saved the life of a child who had been playing on the railroad tracks. The grateful
father, a telegraph operator, _____ Edison _____ by teaching
10.
him the skill of telegraphy. For the next five years, Edison earned money as a telegraph operator working
in various cities in the United States and Canada. He worked nights so that he could
_____ his experiments. In 1868, he built his first patented invention, a vote recorder.
11.
No one wanted it. From that point on, he never worked on a project before _____
12.
first if there was a need for it.

In 1869, he went to New York City. Trying to find work, he walked into a company which supplied
quotations on gold prices by wire. The electrical device for sending the prices to brokers had just
_____. Edison repaired it and was hired on the spot. This incident _____
13. 14.
his first useful invention—the stock ticker—for which he recieved $40,000. With the money,
he _____ a workshop in Newark, N.J. and began his career as a
15.
professional inventor. He was just twenty-two.

| carry out | come up with | give up | keep on |

During the next sixty years, Edison patented over a thousand inventions, among them the electric light-bulb, record player, storage battery, movie camera, and projector, and telephone transmitter. He worked tirelessly—often more than eighteen hours a day. He frequently had to be reminded to eat and sleep. Whenever he _____ a new idea he read everything he could about it. Then he
16.
_____ test after test. He never _____ or became discouraged. If
17.   18.
an experiment failed, he _____ trying new approaches until he found the one that
19.
worked. Ten thousand tests were required before he succeeded in developing the storage battery. Edison once said,"Genius is 1 percent inspiration and 99 percent perspiration."

Source: *The World Book Encyclopedia*, 1958

3. In the Lab

Complete these conversations that take place in a school lab. Use phrasal verbs and pronouns.

1. **A:** Please put on your lab coats.

   B: Do we really have to _____ put them on _____? It's hot in here.

   A: Sorry. You know the rules. I'll open a window if you'd like.

2. **A:** I can't figure out this problem.

   B: I know what you mean. I can't _____ either.

3. **A:** Remember to fill out these forms.

   B: Can we _____ at home, or do we have to do it right now?

4. **A:** Are you going to hand out the next assignment today?

   B: I _____ a few minutes ago. You must have been out of the room.

5. **A:** I can't get this to work. I think we'd better do the whole procedure over again.

   B: We don't have time to _____. Class is over in ten minutes.

6. **A:** Please remember to turn off your Bunsen burner before you leave the lab.

   B: I've already _____.

7. **A:** Are we supposed to turn in our lab reports today?

   B: No. Please _____ next week.

8. **A:** You left your safety goggles on.

   B: Thanks. I _____ last week too. I couldn't figure out why everyone on the bus was staring at me.

4. Creativity

Complete the article about creativity with the phrasal verbs and objects in parentheses. Place the object between the verb and the particle whenever possible.

There are two parts to creativity: _____*dreaming an idea up*_____ and

1. (dream up / an idea)
_____. Remember, anyone can invent new things. Here are

2. (follow through / it)
some ways to get started.

Getting an Idea

Practice creativity. Make a list of common objects. _____ and have a

3. (Pick out / one)
brainstorming session. _____. Give yourself five minutes

4. (Think up / uses for the object.)
and don't _____. _____

5. (throw away / any ideas) 6. (Write down / them)
and _____ with another person.

7. (talk over / them)

Ask around. Another way to get ideas is to talk to people about things that they use every day.

_____ someone has with a common, everyday object, and then

8. (Find out about / a problem)
_____. If you can _____, then you'll

9. (work out / a solution) 10. (come up with / one)
have something that people really need.

Developing the Idea

After you get your idea, _____. Learn all you can about everything

11. (stick with / it)
related to your invention. Write to manufacturers or _____ in a

12. (look up / information)
library. _____ until you find the best ones. You will

13. (Try out / different materials)
_____ every failure. Remember Edison's words: "Results! Why, man, I

14. (get out of / something)
have plenty of results. I know a thousand things that won't work."

5. Eureka!

Susan DuLac is inventing a new product. Like many inventors, she keeps a notebook to record her progress. Find and correct seven mistakes with phrasal verbs in her notes.

May 3, 1995. Today, I came up ~~with~~ a good idea ~~with~~— a jar of paint with an applicator like the kind used for shoe polish. It can be used to paint dirty spots or nicks on a wall after a paint job, when people don't want to do a whole room.

Market: Homeowners, renters, anyone who paints a home or apartment.

Idea for product design:

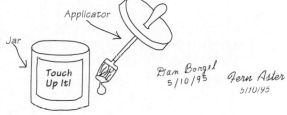

Jar

Applicator

Touch Up It!

Dam Borgel 5/10/95   Fern Aster 5/10/95

May 10. I went to five paint stores today and asked the owners about my idea. I found out that nothing like this is on the market right now. They seemed to be excited by this idea. I asked two of them to sign my notebook. That way I can prove that the idea was actually mine.

May 12. I found a manufacturer of applicators. I called up them and ordered several types.

June 10. The applicators finally arrived. I tried in several and found one that worked well. I'm going to have about two dozen samples made.

August 4. I filled down an application for a patent and mailed it yesterday. I'll be able to set a strong and convincing demonstration of the product up soon.

August 30. I demonstrated the product at a decorator's exhibition yesterday. I wanted to point out that it's very neat and easy to use, so I put white gloves and evening clothes for the demonstration. It went over very well.

COMMUNICATION PRACTICE

6. Practice Listening

🔲🔲 *Listen to a teacher explain how to make a simple camera. Then listen again and in the boxes number the pictures to show the correct order. Listen a third time and complete each caption with the correct phrasal verb.*

flaps

🔲 Use tape to _____ the tissue paper _____.

🔲 _____ them _____.

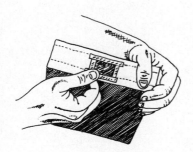

🔲 _____ the hole _____ with foil.

1 <u>Empty</u> it <u>out</u>.

top

bottom

🔲 _____ the box _____.

🔲 _____ something _____ and look at it.

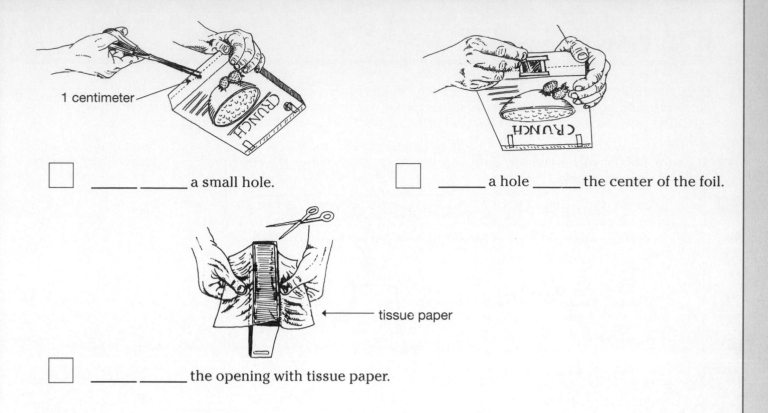

□ _____ _____ a small hole.

□ _____ a hole _____ the center of the foil.

tissue paper

□ _____ _____ the opening with tissue paper.

7. Matching Sets

Work with a partner. Read each set of words. Decide on a phrasal verb that can be used with every word in the set. Then compare your answers with those of your classmates. There may be more than one right answer!

1. balloon   photograph   dynamite   firecracker

   Example:
   A: You can blow up a balloon. And dynamite and firecrackers
       blow up. But what about a photograph?
   B: When you enlarge a photograph it's called blowing it up.

2. car   plane   bus   boat
3. tax   problem   puzzle   bill
4. answer   word   phone number   address
5. lipstick   glasses   shoes   clothes
6. light   stereo   oven   TV

Can you make up your own set? Use the lists of phrasal verbs beginning on page A9 in Appendices 15 and 16 for help. Then see if your classmates can come up with the answer.

8. Crazy Inventions

Rube Goldberg was a cartoonist who became famous in the early twentieth century for his cartoons of crazy inventions. His drawings became so popular that people now use the term "a Rube Goldberg machine" to describe any gadget that peforms a simple task in a very complicated way.

Prepare to invent your own Rube Goldberg machine. Work with a partner to do the following puzzle. Look at one of Goldberg's inventions. Complete the description of how the machine works with the appropriate phrasal verbs in the box.

Simple Way to Open an Egg

Reprinted with special permission of King Features Syndicate.

come off	end up	get out	go off
jump up	~~pick up~~	push up	set off

Steps

1. When you ___pick up___ your morning paper (A), the string (B) opens the door of the birdcage (C).

2. The bird (D) can now _____ of the cage.

3. The bird follows the bird seed (E) up the platform (F).

4. The bird falls over the edge of the platform and _____ in the pitcher of water (G).

5. The water splashes on the flower (H).

6. The flower grows and _____ the rod (I).

7. The rod causes the string (J) to _____ the pistol (K).

8. The pistol _____ and scares the monkey (L).

9. The monkey _____, hitting its head against the bumper (M).

10. The bumper forces the razor (N) into the egg (O).

11. The broken shell _____ and falls into the saucer (P).

Now make up your own crazy invention. Think of a way to

swat a fly
water the flowers
open a window
shut a door

scratch your back
put a stamp on a letter
or perform another simple task:
_____.

9. Quotable Quotes

Work in small groups. Read what people have said about imagination, inventiveness, and discovery. Discuss the quotes. What do they mean? Which do you agree with?

Genius is one percent inspiration and ninety-nine percent perspiration.
—*Thomas Alva Edison (U.S. inventor, 1847–1931)*

Example:
I think this means that it's easier to come up with an idea than to carry it out. But I don't know if I agree with it. I think Edison was just being modest.

Necessity is the mother of invention.
—*Latin saying*

I don't think necessity is the mother of invention—invention, in my opinion, arises directly from idleness, possibly also from laziness. To save oneself trouble.
—*Agatha Christie (British detective-story writer, 1891–1986)*

Invention breeds invention.
—*Ralph Waldo Emerson (U.S. writer, 1803–1882)*

Name the greatest of all inventors: Accident.
—*Mark Twain (U.S. writer, 1835–1910)*

Discovery consists of seeing what everybody has seen and thinking what nobody has thought.
—*Albert Szent-Gyorgyi (U.S. chemist, 1893–1986)*

Imagination grows by exercise and, contrary to common belief, is more powerful in the mature than in the young.
—*W. Somerset Maugham (British writer, 1874–1965)*

Sit down before facts as a little child, be prepared to give up every preconceived notion, follow humbly wherever and to whatever abyss nature leads, or you shall learn nothing.
—*Thomas Huxley (British biologist, 1825–1895)*

10. What the World Needs Now

Now work in small groups. Brainstorm ideas for inventions that you would like to see. Choose your top three ideas and share them with the rest of the class.

Example:
I think we need a solar-powered car. It wouldn't use up resources, and it wouldn't pollute the atmosphere.

I. *Circle the words to complete these classroom guidelines.*

1. Fill (out)/up the school questionnaire. If you have any questions, I myself/yourself will be glad to help you.

2. Answer all the questions. Don't leave anything out/off.

3. Clear up/away any questions you have about your homework assignment before you begin.

4. If you make a lot of mistakes, do the assignment over/after.

5. Look over/up your homework before submitting it.

6. Please hand in/out all your homework on time.

7. It is recommended that you exchange phone numbers with several classmates. Having each other's/ourselves phone numbers will be useful if you miss a class or need to discuss an assignment.

8. You must come up with/to an idea for your science project by March 2.

9. During the second week of class, I will pass out/up a list of suggested topics for your science project.

10. Pick up/out one of the suggested topics or select one by yourself/itself.

11. If you have an idea for a topic, please make an appointment to talk it over/into with me.

12. If you are having trouble with your project, don't give up/away. Come speak to me.

13. If your project topic is turned down/off, I will help you think up/back another one.

14. You can discuss your projects with each other/yourselves, but please work on them by themselves/yourselves.

15. Please don't cross things out/on. If you make a mistake, erase or retype it. The writing process itself/himself is important.

16. If you don't know how to spell a word, look it over/up in the dictionary. Spelling counts!

17. All projects must be turned in/up on time. There will be no extensions and no exceptions!

18. If you are having touble keeping after/up with the class, let me know. Additional help can be arranged for you.

19. There are extra handouts in the back of the room. Supplies are limited. Please take one before they run <u>out/into</u>.

20. The Learning Center is open from 10:00 A.M. to 3:00 P.M. Students should avail <u>themselves/each other</u> of this important resource.

21. All tests will be graded and given <u>back/up</u> on the next day of class.

22. The final exam is scheduled for May 15 and cannot be put <u>off/away</u>.

23. If you get <u>through/over</u> with the exam early, you may leave.

24. Last semester two students hurt <u>themselves/yourselves</u> while carrying <u>off/out</u> a lab experiment. Be sure to follow all safety rules and regulations.

25. Please put <u>away/off</u> all test tubes and chemicals. The students <u>themselves/yourselves</u> are responsible for keeping the work area neat.

26. Please shut <u>up/off</u> all lights and equipment before leaving the room. Help conserve electricity!

27. Please straighten <u>up/over</u> your desks before the break so we have a neat room to return to.

28. David M. Adams, the principal <u>himself/herself</u>, will visit our class on April 13 to look at your science projects.

II. *Complete the conversations with reflexive and reciprocal pronouns.*

1. **A:** Could you help me with the first problem?

   B: Sorry. I don't understand it very well _____myself_____.

2. **A:** Hey. You forgot to turn off the water.

   B: It's automatic. It turns _____ off after ten seconds.

3. **A:** Who's Barry talking to?

   B: I don't see anyone around. He must be talking to _____.

4. **A:** Can you explain why you and Sadie had exactly the same answers on yesterday's quiz?

   B: No. I can't. We didn't look at _____ answers. We each worked on the problems by _____.

5. **A:** I'm so worried about this science project. I'm actually making _____ sick.

   B: Just keep telling _____ that you can do it.

   A: The project _____ isn't the problem. I'm just too busy to work on it.

6. **A:** Want to study together tonight?

   B: I'm putting together my science project.

   A: Let's both work on our projects at my house. When we run into problems, we can talk them over with _____.

(continued on next page)

7. **A:** Gina dropped out of school.

   B: Why? She was doing so well.

   A: She didn't think so. She never believed in _____.

8. **A:** Are Len and Marta working together? I thought they were supposed to do that

   project by _____.

   B: They're just proofreading _____ reports.

9. **A:** What did you do in class today?

   B: We displayed our science projects. Then we all explained our projects to _____.

10. **A:** What was your project?

    B: Volcanoes.

    A: Great idea.

    B: Well, I didn't really come up with it _____. The teacher suggested it.

III. *Complete these conversations. Use phrasal verbs and pronouns.*

1. **A:** I'm thinking over a possible topic for my project.

   B: Well, don't _____ *think it over* _____ too long. It's almost the end of the semester.

2. **A:** I heard that they called off the last class.

   B: Really? Why did they _____?

3. **A:** Today we're going to carry out an experiment.

   B: What materials do we need to _____?

4. **A:** Could you switch on the light?

   B: I've already _____.

5. **A:** Do you get along with John?

   B: Sure. I _____. Why do you ask?

6. **A:** Keep away from those chemicals! They're dangerous.

   B: Don't worry! I'll _____.

7. **A:** Could you put back that book when you're done?

   B: Sure. I'll _____.

8. **A:** You can take off your safety goggles now.

   B: We've already _____.

9. **A:** Will someone please wake Alice up? She's fallen asleep again.

   B: I'll _____.

10. **A:** We have three problems to work out before our next class.

    B: When are you going to _____?

IV. *Rewrite these sentences. Use appropriate phrasal verbs in the box to replace the underlined words.*

blow up	~~come up~~	give up	go after
hand out	leave out	let down	light up
point out	show up	talk over	throw away
turn down	turn in	turn off	

1. A question <u>arose</u> about the science project.

   _____A question came up about the science project._____

2. The students didn't understand one of the problems. They <u>discussed</u> it thoroughly.

   _____

3. Keep all your old notes. Please don't <u>discard</u> them.

   _____

4. The teacher <u>rejected</u> my topic proposal.

   _____

5. All forms must be <u>submitted</u> by April 8.

   _____

6. Please <u>extinguish</u> all lights upon leaving the room.

   _____

7. Exercise great caution when working with these chemicals. They could <u>explode</u>.

   _____

8. Don't <u>abandon</u> hope. Keep trying.

   _____

9. Your homework assignment will be <u>distributed</u> at the end of the class.

   _____

10. What happened to the last problem? You <u>omitted</u> it.

    _____

11. The test grades were very low. They <u>disappointed</u> me.

    _____

12. That corner is too dark. Can someone take this flashlight and <u>illuminate</u> it?

    _____

13. There's something wrong with that equation. Can someone <u>indicate</u> what the mistake is?

    _____

(continued on next page)

14. Everyone has goals. You must <u>pursue</u> them with diligence.

_____

15. Please make an appointment to see me. Don't just <u>appear</u> without one.

_____

V. *Read this science report. There are eight mistakes in phrasal verbs and pronouns. Find and correct them.*

    For this science project, Jason and I teamed ~~out~~ up and decided to find out about volcanoes. First we went to the library and looked up some basic information about volcanoes. Then we talked over it and decided to set a model volcano with explanations and charts up. We divided up the tasks, but we cooperated and helped ourselves out when we had problems. For my part, I taught myself how to use the computer encyclopedia in the library. I printed out explanations and charts. The volcano itself wasn't easy to make. Jason found a volcano kit in a store, but he decided to make it hisself. He covered up a wire cone with wet papier mâché, leaving a hole in the center for the lava. When our two parts of the projects were finished, we put together them. We pasted the charts onto cardboard and placed the model in the center. Just before we turned it in, we ran an article across that showed how to make the volcano erupt. We put baking soda in a dish and placed it inside the cone. When we displayed the model, we poured vinegar over the baking soda. The mixture blew over and poured out of the volcano. It was a great success.

Information Gaps

Unit 3, page 48

Read the story. Answer Student A's questions. Get information from Student A and fill in the blanks.

Example:
A: What had the woman been doing?
B: She had been driving all night.
What had the woman been drinking?
A: She'd been drinking coffee.

She was tired. She had been driving all night. She had been drinking cup after cup of

_____coffee_____, but it hadn't helped. The radio was on loud. She had been listening to

_____ when they interrupted the program with a special news bulletin. The police had

been looking for a man since 3:00 P.M. The man had robbed a bank. He was dangerous.

The woman shivered. The streets were slippery and wet. It had been snowing for more than an

hour. She wasn't sure where she was. She had been looking for her _____ when suddenly

she saw something ahead on the road. It was a man. She hadn't noticed him at first because he had

been standing behind a tree. The woman stepped on the brakes. The man opened the door and got in.

The woman smiled and breathed a sigh of relief. She had been expecting _____ .

When you are finished, compare your two versions. Are they the same?

*Now discuss the following questions: Who do you think the woman was? Who was
the man? What do you think their relationship was?*

Unit 6, page 86

Read about Los Angeles and answer Student A's questions.

Los Angeles

Although Los Angeles isn't the capital of California, it is the state's largest
city and the third largest city in the United States. Located on the Pacific
Ocean, L.A. is famous for its climate and its beaches. Tourists are also
attracted to Hollywood, a section of L.A. which is home to many movie
studios. Unfortunately, L.A. is also famous for its smog—air pollution
caused by the city's large number of cars.

(continued on next page)

Now look at the questions below. What do you know about New York City?
Circle the correct words and complete the tag questions.

Example:
B: New York City (is)/isn't the largest city in the United States, <u>isn't it?</u>
A: Yes, it is.

1. New York City <u>is/isn't</u> located on a river, _____?

2. It consists of <u>five/two</u> separate "boroughs," or parts, _____?

3. It <u>has/doesn't have</u> over ninety universities and colleges, _____?

4. It played a <u>small/big</u> role in U.S. history, _____?

5. <u>Many/Not many</u> tourists visit New York, _____?

Ask Student A the same questions. He or she will read a paragraph about New York City and tell you if your information is correct or not.

Unit 10, page 141

Look at the map of Mindanao. Complete the chart for Mindanao. Answer Student A's questions. Then ask Student A questions about Luzon. Write Y for yes and N for no.

Example:
A: Is tobacco grown in Mindanao?
B: No, it isn't.
Is it grown in Luzon?
A: Yes, it is. It's grown in the north and central part of the island.

			Mindanao	Luzon
G R O W		tobacco	N	Y
		corn		
		bananas		
		coffee		
		pineapples		
		sugar		
R A I S E		cattle		
		pigs		
M I N E		gold		
		manganese		
P R O D U C E		cotton		
		rubber		
		lumber		

MINDANAO

Now compare charts with Student A. Are they the same?

Unit 20, page 263

Read the biographical data about Ben Fong-Torres. Then ask Student A questions about him in order to fill in the missing information. Answer Student A's questions.

Example:
A: When was the Exclusion Act still in effect?
B: In 1929.
Where did his father obtain a birth certificate?
A: In the Philippines.

Ben Fong-Torres was born in Alameda, California, in 1945. He was the son of first-generation Chinese parents. His father had emigrated to the United States in 1929, when the Exclusion Act, which limited the number of Chinese entering the country, was still in effect. To avoid this obstacle, his father first went to ___the Philippines___, where he obtained a birth certificate and added Torres to his name. Ben's mother came to the United States ten years later, when their marriage was arranged by relatives. Ben, along with his brother and sister, grew up in _____, where there was a large Chinese community. His family owned a Chinese restaurant, in which all the children worked when they were not in school. Ben's parents, whose views were quite traditional, were a little surprised and concerned by their children's love for U.S. culture. Ben was an enthusiastic reader of cartoons and a listener of _____, which he heard on the radio. At the age of twelve, Ben went with his father to Texas, where they opened another Chinese restaurant. It was a difficult time for Ben, among people who had had no previous contact with Asians. Back in Oakland, after the failure of the restaurant, Ben got jobs writing for various magazines and newspapers. After graduation from college in 1966, he wrote for _____, which covered stories about contemporary U.S. political and cultural life. His interviews with hundreds of famous musicians included the Beatles, the Rolling Stones, Grace Slick, and an interview with Ray Charles, for which he won the Deems Taylor award. Fong-Torres was also a DJ for San Francisco radio station KSAN, which plays rock music, and in 1976 he won an award for broadcasting excellence. Today Fong-Torres lives in San Francisco with _____, who he married in 1976.

Compare texts with your partner. Are they the same?

Unit 25, page 322

You are a server at John's Grill. Read these notes about today's menu. Answer your customers' questions. When they are done ordering, look at the menu on page 322 and write a check.

Starters

Soup of the Day

Monday:	vegetable soup (carrots, peas, string beans in a tomato broth)
Tuesday:	tomato soup
Wednesday:	pea soup
Thursday:	onion soup
Friday:	fish soup
Saturday:	potato soup

Caesar Salad (lettuce, parmesan cheese, croutons—toasted bread cubes)

John's Salad (spinach, mushrooms, tomatoes, onions)

MAIN DISHES

Catch of the Day: broiled flounder ($6.95)
    Sauce Dijon (mustard sauce)

Chicken à la John (chicken baked in a cream sauce with olives and nuts)

Steak Frites (steak cooked in pan with butter, served with french fried potatoes)

John's Hamburger Deluxe (hamburger with tomatoes, onions, mushrooms, and cheese)

Spaghetti à la John (spaghetti with spinach, fresh tomatoes, and mushrooms in a light cream sauce)

Vegetable of the Day: broccoli

Desserts

Pies (cherry, apple, blueberry)

Ice Cream (chocolate, strawberry, vanilla)

Fruit Salad (apples, bananas, and strawberries)

Dessert of the Day: strawberry shortcake (yellow cake with fresh strawberries and whipped cream)

Example:

    A: I wonder what the soup of the day is.

    B: Me too. Do you know what's in a Caeser salad?

    A: Not really. We'll have to ask the server.
        Excuse me. Can you tell us what's in the Caeser salad?

    C: Sure. It has lettuce, parmesan cheese, and croutons.

    A: Croutons? I don't know what they are.

    C: They're toasted cubes of bread.

Appendices

1. Irregular Verbs

Base Form	Simple Past	Past Participle
arise	arose	arisen
awake	awoke	awoken
be	was/were	been
beat	beat	beaten
become	became	become
begin	began	begun
bend	bent	bent
bet	bet	bet
bite	bit	bitten
bleed	bled	bled
blow	blew	blown
break	broke	broken
bring	brought	brought
build	built	built
burn	burned/burnt	burned/burnt
burst	burst	burst
buy	bought	bought
catch	caught	caught
choose	chose	chosen
cling	clung	clung
come	came	come
cost	cost	cost
creep	crept	crept
cut	cut	cut
deal	dealt	dealt
dig	dug	dug
dive	dived/dove	dived
do	did	done
draw	drew	drawn
dream	dreamed/dreamt	dreamed/dreamt
drink	drank	drunk
drive	drove	driven
eat	ate	eaten
fall	fell	fallen
feed	fed	fed
feel	felt	felt
fight	fought	fought
find	found	found
fit	fit	fit
flee	fled	fled
fling	flung	flung
fly	flew	flown

(continued on next page)

Base Form	Simple Past	Past Participle
forbid	forbade/forbad	forbidden
forget	forgot	forgotten
forgive	forgave	forgiven
freeze	froze	frozen
get	got	gotten/got
give	gave	given
go	went	gone
grind	ground	ground
grow	grew	grown
hang	hung	hung
have	had	had
hear	heard	heard
hide	hid	hidden
hit	hit	hit
hold	held	held
hurt	hurt	hurt
keep	kept	kept
kneel	knelt	knelt
knit	knit/knitted	knit/knitted
know	knew	known
lay	laid	laid
lead	led	led
leap	leapt	leapt
leave	left	left
lend	lent	lent
let	let	let
lie (lie down)	lay	lain
light	lit/lighted	lit/lighted
lose	lost	lost
make	made	made
mean	meant	meant
meet	met	met
pay	paid	paid
prove	proved	proved/proven
put	put	put
quit	quit	quit
read /riʸd/	read /rɛd/	read /rɛd/
ride	rode	ridden
ring	rang	rung
rise	rose	risen
run	ran	run
say	said	said
see	saw	seen
seek	sought	sought
sell	sold	sold
send	sent	sent
set	set	set
sew	sewed	sewn/sewed
shake	shook	shaken
shave	shaved	shaved/shaven
shine	shone	shone
shoot	shot	shot

Base Form	Simple Past	Past Participle
show	showed	shown
shrink	shrank/shrunk	shrunk/shrunken
shut	shut	shut
sing	sang	sung
sink	sank	sunk
sit	sat	sat
sleep	slept	slept
slide	slid	slid
speak	spoke	spoken
speed	sped	sped
spend	spent	spent
spill	spilled/spilt	spilled/spilt
spin	spun	spun
spit	spat	spat
split	split	split
spread	spread	spread
spring	sprang	sprung
stand	stood	stood
steal	stole	stolen
stick	stuck	stuck
sting	stung	stung
stink	stank/stunk	stunk
strike	struck	struck
swear	swore	sworn
sweep	swept	swept
swim	swam	swum
swing	swung	swung
take	took	taken
teach	taught	taught
tear	tore	torn
tell	told	told
think	thought	thought
throw	threw	thrown
understand	understood	understood
upset	upset	upset
wake	woke	woken
wear	wore	worn
weave	wove	woven
weep	wept	wept
win	won	won
wind	wound	wound
withdraw	withdrew	withdrawn
wring	wrung	wrung
write	wrote	written

2. Verbs that Are Commonly Used as Non-action (Stative) Verbs

Emotions

adore
appreciate
care
detest
dislike
doubt
envy
fear
hate
hope
like
love
regret
respect

Mental States

agree
assume
believe
consider
disagree
disbelieve
estimate
expect
feel (believe)
find
guess
hesitate
hope
imagine
know
mean
mind
presume
realize
recognize
remember
see (understand)
suppose
suspect
think (believe)
understand
wonder

Wants and Preferences

desire
need
prefer
want
wish

Perception and the Senses

feel
hear
notice
observe
perceive
see
smell
taste

Appearance and Value

appear
be
cost
equal
feel
look
matter
represent
resemble
seem
signify
smell
sound
taste
weigh

Possession and Relationship

belong
contain
have
own
possess

3. Common Verbs Followed by the Gerund (Base Form of Verb + -*ing*)

acknowledge
admit
advise
appreciate
avoid
can't help
can't stand
celebrate
consider
delay
deny
detest
discontinue
discuss
dislike

endure
enjoy
escape
explain
feel like
finish
forgive
give up (stop)
imagine
justify
keep (continue)
mention
mind (object to)
miss
postpone

practice
prevent
prohibit
propose
quit
recall
recommend
report
resent
resist
risk
suggest
support
tolerate
understand

4. Common Verbs Followed by the Infinitive (*To* + Base Form of Verb)

agree	expect	pretend
appear	fail	promise
ask	hesitate	refuse
arrange	hope	request
attempt	learn	seem
begin	manage	struggle
can('t) afford	mean	swear
can('t) wait	need	volunteer
choose	offer	want
consent	pay	wish
decide	plan	would like
deserve	prepare	

5. Verbs Followed by Objects and the Infinitive

advise	forbid	remind
allow	force	request
ask*	get	require
cause	hire	teach
challenge	invite	tell
choose*	need*	urge
convince	order	want*
enable	pay*	warn
encourage	permit	wish*
expect*	persuade	would like*

*These verbs can also be followed by the infinitive without an object (example: *ask to leave* or *ask someone to leave*).

6. Common Verbs Followed by the Gerund or the Infinitive

begin	intend	remember*
can't stand	like	start
continue	love	stop*
forget*	prefer	try*
hate		

*These verbs can be followed by either the gerund or the infinitive but there is a big difference in meaning.

7. Common Verb + Preposition Combinations

advise against
apologize for
approve of
believe in
choose between/among
complain about

deal with
dream about/of
feel like
insist on
look forward to
object to

plan on
rely on
resort to
succeed in
think about

8. Common Adjective + Preposition Expressions

afraid of
amazed at/by
angry at
ashamed of
aware of
awful at
bad at
bored with/by
capable of
careful of
content with
curious about
different from

excited about
famous for
fed up with
fond of
glad about
good at
happy about
interested in
nervous about
opposed to
pleased about
ready for
responsible for

sad about
safe from
satisfied with
shocked at/by
sick of
slow at
sorry for/about
surprised at/about/by
terrible at
tired of
used to
worried about

9. Common Adjectives that Can Be Followed by the Infinitive*

afraid
alarmed
amazed
angry
anxious
ashamed
curious
delighted
depressed
determined
disappointed
distressed

disturbed
eager
embarrassed
encouraged
excited
fortunate
glad
happy
hesitant
lucky
pleased
proud

ready
relieved
reluctant
sad
shocked
sorry
surprised
touched
upset
willing

*Example: *I'm happy to hear that.*

10. Irregular Comparisons of Adjectives and Adverbs

Adjective	Adverb	Comparative	Superlative
bad	badly	worse	worst
far	far	farther/further	farthest/furthest
good	well	better	best
little	little	less	least
many	—	more	most
much	much	more	most

11. Common Participial Adjectives

alarmed	alarming	fascinated	fascinating
amazed	amazing	frightened	frightening
amused	amusing	horrified	horrifying
annoyed	annoying	inspired	inspiring
astonished	astonishing	interested	interesting
bored	boring	irritated	irritating
confused	confusing	moved	moving
depressed	depressing	paralyzed	paralyzing
disappointed	disappointing	pleased	pleasing
disgusted	disgusting	relaxed	relaxing
distressed	distressing	satisfied	satisfying
disturbed	disturbing	shocked	shocking
embarrassed	embarrassing	surprised	surprising
entertained	entertaining	terrified	terrifying
excited	exciting	tired	tiring
exhausted	exhausting	touched	touching

12. Some Adjectives that Form the Comparative and Superlative in Two Ways

Adjective	Comparative	Superlative
common	commoner/more common	commonest/most common
cruel	crueler/more cruel	cruelest/most cruel
deadly	deadlier/more deadly	deadliest/most deadly
friendly	friendlier/more friendly	friendliest/most friendly
handsome	handsomer/more handsome	handsomest/most handsome
happy	happier/more happy	happiest/most happy
likely	likelier/more likely	likeliest/most likely
lively	livelier/more lively	liveliest/most lively
lonely	lonelier/more lonely	loneliest/most lonely
lovely	lovelier/more lovely	loveliest/most lovely
narrow	narrower/more narrow	narrowest/most narrow
pleasant	pleasanter/more pleasant	pleasantest/most pleasant
polite	politer/more polite	politest/most polite
quiet	quieter/more quiet	quietest/most quiet
shallow	shallower/more shallow	shallowest/most shallow
sincere	sincerer/more sincere	sincerest/most sincere
stupid	stupider/more stupid	stupidest/most stupid
true	truer/more true	truest/most true

13. Common Reporting Verbs

Statements		Instructions, Commands, Requests, and Invitations	Questions
acknowledge	indicate	advise	ask
add	maintain	ask	inquire
admit	mean	caution	question
answer	note	command	want to know
argue	observe	instruct	wonder
assert	promise	invite	
believe	remark	order	
claim	repeat	say	
complain	report	tell	
conclude	say	urge	
confess	state	warn	
declare	suggest		
deny	tell		
exclaim	warn		
explain			

14. Verbs and Expressions Commonly Used Reflexively

amuse oneself	cut oneself	look after oneself
ask oneself	deprive oneself of	look at oneself
avail oneself of	dry oneself	pride oneself on
be hard on oneself	enjoy oneself	push oneself
be oneself	feel sorry for oneself	remind oneself
be pleased with oneself	help oneself	see oneself
be proud of oneself	hurt oneself	take care of oneself
behave oneself	imagine oneself	talk to oneself
believe in oneself	introduce oneself	teach oneself
blame oneself	kill oneself	tell oneself

15. Some Common Transitive Phrasal Verbs*

Phrasal Verb	Meaning	Phrasal Verb	Meaning
ask over	invite to one's home	empty out	empty
blow out	stop burning by blowing	figure out	solve
		fill in	complete with information
blow up	1. explode 2. enlarge (a photograph)	fill out	complete (a form)
		follow through	complete
bring about	cause to happen	fool around with*	be playful
bring out	introduce, present	get along with*	relate well
bring up	raise (children)	get back from*	return
burn down	burn completely	get in*	enter (a car, taxi)
call back	return a phone call	get off*	leave (a plane, train, bus, bike)
call off	cancel		
call on*	visit	get on*	enter (a plane, train, bus, bike)
call up	telephone		
carry on	continue	get out of*	leave (a car, taxi)
carry out	conduct	get out of	get a benefit from
charge up	charge electrically	get over*	recover from an illness or bad experience
clear up	clarify		
close down	close by force		
come up with	imagine	get through with*	finish
cover up	cover completely	give back	return something
cross out	draw a line through	give up	quit, abandon
cut off	remove with a knife or scissors	go after*	pursue
		hand in	give some work to a teacher or boss
cut out	remove by cutting		
do over	do again	hand out	distribute
dream up	invent	hand over	submit
dress up	put on special clothes	hang up	end a phone conversation
drink up	drink completely		
drop in on*	visit unexpectedly	hold back	prevent
drop off	1. deliver 2. allow someone to get out of a car	hold on	keep attached
		keep away from*	avoid
		keep away from	prevent
drop out of*	quit	keep on*	continue

*Indicates that the phrasal verb is inseparable.

(continued on next page)

Phrasal Verb	Meaning	Phrasal Verb	Meaning
keep on	not remove	straighten up	make neat
keep up with*	go as fast as	switch on	start a machine or light
lay off	end someone's employment	take back	return something
leave on	not remove	take off	remove
leave out	omit	take on	hire
let down	disappoint	talk into	persuade
let in	permit to enter	talk over	discuss
let off	allow to leave (a bus, train, or car)	team up with*	begin working together
light up	illuminate	tear down	destroy
look out for*	be careful	tear off	remove by tearing
look over	examine	tear out of	remove a piece of paper from a book
look up	try to find in a book		
make up	invent	tear up	tear into small pieces
pass out	distribute	think back on*	remember
pass up	not use	think up	invent
pay back	repay	throw away/out	discard
pick out	select	touch up	improve by making small changes
pick up	lift		
point out	indicate	try on	put clothing on to see if it fits
punch out	make a hole		
push up	cause to rise	try out	see if something works
put away	return to its proper place	turn down	1. reject
			2. lower the volume
put back	return to its original place	turn in	submit
put down	stop holding	turn off	1. extinguish
put off	postpone		2. stop a machine
put on	cover the body with clothes	turn on	start a machine or light
put together	assemble	turn up	1. raise in volume
put up	erect		2. turn so that the top side is on top
put up with*	tolerate		
run into*	meet accidentally	use up	consume
run out of*	not have enough of a supply	wake up	awaken
		watch out for*	be careful
see through	complete	work out	solve
set off	cause to explode	write down	write on a piece of paper
set up	establish		
shut off	stop a machine or light		
start over	start again		
stay up*	not go to bed		
stick with*	persevere		

*Indicates that the phrasal verb is inseparable.

16. Some Common Intransitive Phrasal Verbs

Phrasal Verb	Meaning	Phrasal Verb	Meaning
ask around	question many people	go on	continue
blow up	explode	go over	create an impression
break down	stop working	grow up	become an adult
break out	occur suddenly	hold on	wait
burn down	burn completely	jump up	jump
call back	return a phone call	keep away	stay at a distance
catch on	become popular	keep on	continue
clear up	become clear	keep up	go as fast as
close down	stop operating	lie down	recline
come about	happen	light up	illuminate
come in	enter	look out	be careful
come off	become unattached	make up	reconcile
come out	appear	pass out	lose consciousness
come up	arise	play around	have fun
cut in	interrupt	run out	not have enough of a supply
dress up	put on special or formal clothes	show up	appear
drop in	visit unexpectedly	sit down	take a seat
drop out	quit	stand up	rise
eat out	eat in a restaurant	start over	start again
empty out	empty	stay up	remain awake
end up	end	straighten up	make neat
follow through	complete	take off	depart (a plane)
fool around	be playful	team up	begin working together
get along	relate well		
get back	return	turn up	appear
get together	meet	wake up	arise after sleeping
get up	rise from bed	watch out	be careful
give up	quit	work out	1. be resolved
go off	explode		2. exercise

17. Spelling Rules for the Present Progressive

1. Add *-ing* to the base form of the verb.

   read   read*ing*
   stand   stand*ing*

2. If a verb ends in a silent *-e*, drop the final *-e* and add *-ing*.

   leave   leav*ing*
   take   tak*ing*

3. In a one-syllable word, if the last three letters are a consonant-vowel-consonant combination (CVC), double the last consonant before adding *-ing*.

   CVC
   ↓↓↓
   s i t   sit*ting*

   CVC
   ↓↓↓
   r u n   run*ning*

   However, do not double the last consonant in words that end in *w*, *x*, or *y*.

   sew   sew*ing*
   fix   fix*ing*
   enjoy   enjoy*ing*

4. In words of two or more syllables that end in a consonant-vowel-consonant combination, double the last consonant only if the last syllable is stressed.

   admít   admit*ting*   (The last syllable is stressed.)
   whísper   whisper*ing*   (The last syllable is not stressed, so don't double the *-r*.)

5. If a verb ends in *-ie*, change the *ie* to *y* before adding *-ing*.

   die   d*ying*

18.

Spelling Rules for the Simple Present Tense: Third-Person Singular *(he, she, it)*

1. Add *-s* for most verbs.

work	work*s*
buy	buy*s*
ride	ride*s*
return	return*s*

2. Add *-es* for words that end in *-ch, -s, -sh, -x,* or *-z.*

watch	watch*es*
pass	pass*es*
rush	rush*es*
relax	relax*es*
buzz	buzz*es*

3. Change the *y* to *i* and add *-es* when the base form ends in a consonant + *y.*

study	stud*ies*
hurry	hurr*ies*
dry	dr*ies*

   Do not change the *y* when the base form ends in a vowel + *y.* Add *-s.*

play	play*s*
enjoy	enjoy*s*

4. A few verbs have irregular forms.

be	is
do	does
go	goes
have	has

19. Spelling Rules for the Simple Past Tense of Regular Verbs

1. If the verb ends in a consonant, add *-ed.*

   return   return*ed*
   help   help*ed*

2. If the verb ends in *-e,* add *-d.*

   live   live*d*
   create   create*d*
   die   die*d*

3. In one-syllable words, if the verb ends in a consonant-vowel-consonant combination (CVC), double the final consonant and add *-ed.*

   CVC
   ↓↓↓
   h o p   hop*ped*

   CVC
   ↓↓↓
   r u b   rub*bed*

   However, do not double one-syllable words ending in *-w, -x,* or *-y.*

   bow   bow*ed*
   mix   mix*ed*
   play   play*ed*

4. In words of two or more syllables that end in a consonant-vowel-consonant combination, double the last consonant only if the last syllable is stressed.

   prefér   prefer*red*   (The last syllable is stressed.)
   vísit   visit*ed*   (The last syllable is not stressed, so don't double the *t.*)

5. If the verb ends in a consonant + *y,* change the *y* to *i* and add *-ed.*

   worry   worr*ied*
   carry   carr*ied*

6. If the verb ends in a vowel + *y,* add *-ed.* (Do not change the *y* to *i.*)

   play   play*ed*
   annoy   annoy*ed*

   Exceptions: pay—paid, lay—laid, say—said

20. Spelling Rules for the Comparative (-er) and Superlative (-est) of Adjectives

1. Add -er to one-syllable adjectives to form the comparative. Add -est to one-syllable adjectives to form the superlative.

| cheap | cheaper | cheapest |
| bright | brighter | brightest |

2. If the adjective ends in -e, add -r or -st.

| nice | nicer | nicest |

3. If the adjective ends in a consonant + y, change y to i before you add -er or -est.

| pretty | prettier | prettiest |

| Exception: | shy | shyer | shyest |

4. If the adjective ends in a consonant-vowel-consonant combination (CVC), double the final consonant before adding -er or -est.

CVC
↓↓↓
| big | bigger | biggest |

However, do not double the consonant in words ending in -w or -y.

| slow | slower | slowest |
| coy | coyer | coyest |

21. Spelling Rules for Adverbs Ending in -ly

1. Add -ly to the corresponding adjective.

nice	nicely
quiet	quietly
beautiful	beautifully

2. If the adjective ends in a consonant + y, change the y to i before adding -ly.

| easy | easily |

3. If the adjective ends in -le, drop the e and add -y.

| possible | possibly |

However, do not drop the e for other adjectives ending in -e.

| extreme | extremely |

| Exception: | true | truly |

4. If the adjective ends in -ic, add -ally.

| basic | basically |
| fantastic | fantastically |

22. Punctuation Rules for Direct Speech

Direct speech may either follow or precede the reporting verb. When direct speech follows the reporting verb,

a. Put a comma after the reporting verb.
b. Use opening quotation marks (") before the first word of the direct speech.
c. Begin the quotation with a capital letter.
d. Use the appropriate end punctuation for the direct speech. It may be a period (.), a question mark (?), or an exclamation point (!).
e. Put closing quotation marks (") after the end punctuation of the quotation.

Examples:

He said, "I had a good time."
She asked, "Where's the party?"
They shouted, "Be careful!"

When direct speech precedes the reporting verb,

a. Begin the sentence with opening quotation marks (").
b. Use the appropriate end punctuation for the direct speech.
    If the direct speech is a statement, use a comma (,).
    If the direct speech is a question, use a question mark (?).
    If the direct speech is an exclamation, use an exclamation point (!).
c. Use closing quotation marks after the end punctuation for the direct speech (").
d. Begin the reporting clause with a lower-case letter.
e. Use a period at the end of the main sentence (.).

Examples:

"I had a good time," he said.
"Where's the party?" she asked.
"Be careful!" they shouted.

23. Pronunciation Table

These are the pronunciation symbols used in this text. Listen to the pronunciation of the key words.

VOWELS	
SYMBOL	**KEY WORD**
iʸ	beat
ɪ	bit
eʸ	bay
ɛ	bet
æ	bat
ɑ	box, car
ɔ	bought, horse
oʷ	bone
ʊ	book
uʷ	boot
ʌ	but
ə	banana, sister
aɪ	by
aʊ	bound
ɔɪ	boy
ɜr	burn
ɪər	beer
ɛər	bare
ʊər	tour

CONSONANTS	
SYMBOL	**KEY WORD**
p	pan
b	ban
t	tip
d	dip
k	cap
g	gap
tʃ	church
dʒ	judge
f	fan
v	van
θ	thing
ð	then
s	sip
z	zip
ʃ	ship
ʒ	measure
h	hot
m	sum
n	sun
ŋ	sung
w	wet
hw	what
l	lot
r	rot
y	yet

/t̬/ means that the /t/ sound is said as a voiced sound (like a quick English /d/).

From *Longman Dictionary of American English*, © 1983.

24. Pronunciation Rules for the Simple Present Tense: Third-Person Singular *(he, she, it)*

1. The third person singular in the simple present tense always ends in the letter *-s*. There are, however, three different pronunciations for the final sound of the third person singular.

/s/	/z/	/ɪz/
talks	loves	dances

2. The final sound is pronounced /s/ after the voiceless sounds /p/, /t/, /k/, and /f/.

top	tops
get	gets
take	takes
laugh	laughs

3. The final sound is pronounced /z/ after the voiced sounds /b/, /d/, /g/, /v/, /ð/, /m/, /n/, /ŋ/, /l/, and /r/.

describe	describes
spend	spends
hug	hugs
live	lives
bathe	bathes
seem	seems
remain	remains
sing	sings
tell	tells
lower	lowers

4. The final sound is pronounced /z/ after all vowel sounds.

agree	agrees
try	tries
stay	stays
know	knows

5. The final sound is pronounced /ɪz/ after the sounds /s/, /z/, /ʃ/, /ʒ/, /tʃ/, and /dʒ/. /ɪz/ adds a syllable to the verb.

relax	relaxes
freeze	freezes
rush	rushes
massage	massages
watch	watches
judge	judges

6. *Do* and *say* have a change in vowel sound.

say	/seʸ/	says	/sɛz/
do	/duʷ/	does	/dʌz/

25. Pronunciation Rules for the Simple Past Tense of Regular Verbs

1. The regular simple past always ends in the letter -*d*. There are, however, three different pronunciations for the final sound of the regular simple past.

/t/	/d/	/ɪd/
raced	lived	attended

2. The final sound is pronounced /t/ after the voiceless sounds /p/, /k/, /f/, /s/, /ʃ/, and /tʃ/.

hop	hopped
work	worked
laugh	laughed
address	addressed
publish	published
watch	watched

3. The final sound is pronounced /d/ after the voiced sounds /b/, /g/, /v/, /z/, /ʒ/, /dʒ/, /m/, /n/, /ŋ/, /l/, /r/, and /ð/.

rub	rubbed
hug	hugged
live	lived
surprise	surprised
massage	massaged
change	changed
rhyme	rhymed
return	returned
bang	banged
enroll	enrolled
appear	appeared
bathe	bathed

4. The final sound is pronounced /d/ after all vowel sounds.

agree	agreed
play	played
die	died
enjoy	enjoyed

5. The final sound is pronounced /ɪd/ after /t/ and /d/. /ɪd/ adds a syllable to the verb.

start	started
decide	decided

Answer Key

Note: In this answer key, where the contracted form is given, the full form is also correct, and where the full form is given, the contracted form is also correct.

PART I Present and Past

UNIT 1 Review and Integration: Present, Past, Present Perfect

Section One

1.

Underlined verbs: are waiting, giving, seeking, looking
Circled verbs: need, are, take, has

2.

1. b. does...come c. means d. do...do e. sell
f. 'm working g. owns h. 're joking i. guess j. influence
2. a. 'm trying b. Do...know c. mean d. calls e. always wins *or* 's always winning
3. a. hear b. 're expecting c. 're thinking of d. do...think about e. do...spell f. does...mean g. like h. sounds
4. a. Are...leaving b. 're making c. smells d. want
e. Do...know f. 's teaching g. believe h. is taking
i. does...look j. call
5. a. don't drink b. makes c. 's boiling d. teach
e. does...boil f. boils

3.

a. Alex b. Karl c. Mehmet d. "Sunshine" f. Vicki, Bertha

4.

Answers will vary.

Section Two

5.

2. F
3. ?
4. T
5. T
6. T
7. ?
8. F
9. F
10. T

6.

1. b. were sleeping c. Did...write down d. met e. was working f. nicknamed g. was always eating *or* always ate
h. made i. got used to
2. a. were...living b. was born c. had d. moved
e. were...doing f. was taking g. met h. married
3. a. did...get b. was born c. were going to name d. liked
e. wanted f. was born g. was raining *or* rained
h. changed i. named j. did...decide k. was growing up
l. was asked *or* were always asking m. decided
4. a. fell b. hurt c. was playing d. pushed e. got
5. a. looked b. were...doing c. struck d. was sleeping
e. happened f. began g. jumped up h. ran i. did...do
j. stopped k. ran l. was still sleeping

7.

c.

8.

Answers will vary.

Section Three

9.

Underlined verbs: has chosen, has been, has taught, has been studying, has been
Circled verbs: performed, graduated, received, owned, managed, graduated, worked, ended

2. F
3. T
4. F
5. F
6. T
7. F
8. F
9. F

10.

2. have thought *or* have been thinking
3. has been
4. began
5. have changed *or* have been changing
6. lost
7. came
8. have adopted *or* have been adopting
9. traced
10. appeared
11. has become
12. changed
13. made
14. assigned
15. could
16. created
17. turned
18. have reclaimed *or* have been reclaiming
19. has published *or* has been publishing
20. has always hated
21. 's thought *or* 's been thinking
22. hasn't made up
23. have disguised *or* have been disguising
24. had
25. decided

11.

Checked items: pick up plane tickets, read travel guide, stop mail for two weeks

12.

Answers will vary.

Integration

13.

2. T	9. T
3. T	10. F
4. F	11. F
5. T	12. T
6. F	13. T
7. T	14. T
8. F	

14.

1. b. worked   c. started   d. sings   e. Are you crying
f. is wearing   g. water
2. a. are you eating   b. looks   c. haven't tried   d. Do you
want   e. 've had   f. 've been eating   g. got
3. a. has Matt known   b. met   c. 've been seeing
d. started   e. asked   f. wasn't going to invite   g. had
h. didn't think   i. could
4. a. 've worked   b. 's mentioned   c. Do you do   d. pay
e. Have you worked   f. 're playing   g. 've been taking
5. a. are you going   b. came   c. Didn't you talk   d. were
dancing   e. came

15.

They named me John ➜ They were going to name me John
is coming ➜ comes
have called ➜ called
have started ➜ started
was sounding ➜ sounded
prefer ➜ preferred
was deciding ➜ decided
is calling ➜ calls
expect ➜ are expecting
don't decide ➜ haven't decided
consider ➜ are considering
haven't been deciding ➜ haven't decided

16.

2. b
3. a
4. a
5. a
6. a
7. b

17.–20.

Answers will vary.

UNIT 2 ▼ Past Perfect

1.

2. b
3. b
4. b
5. a
6. a
7. b
8. b

2.

2. hadn't yet entered
3. hadn't yet gotten
4. had already gotten
5. hadn't yet been
6. had already begun
7. hadn't yet gotten
8. had already been

3.

2. had brought
3. had lost
4. had left
5. had had
6. had become
7. had hurt
8. had arrested
9. had recommended

4.

2. my father had beaten me for the third time, I was afraid to stay there.
3. I left home, I had arranged to stay with a friend in Miami.
4. had saved enough money from my allowance, I paid for my ticket.
5. I got to Miami, I had already spent all my money.
6. I had hardly eaten on the trip…I had very little money.

5.

2. Had he seen
   Yes, he had.
3. Had he written
   Yes, he had.
4. Had he met with
   No, he hadn't.
5. Had he reported
   Yes, he had.
6. Had he eaten *or* Had he had
   No, he hadn't.

6.

Correct order:

___2___ moved to Chicago

___1___ got married

___4___ sold an article to a magazine

___5___ got a job as a newspaper reporter

___3___ found an apartment

7.–9.

Answers will vary.

UNIT 3 Past Perfect Progressive

1.

Underlined words: had been raining, 'd been working, hadn't been exercising, 'd been training, hadn't been spending, Had…been running, 'd been selling

2. F
3. T
4. F
5. T

2.

2. had been trailing
3. had been trying
4. had been running
5. had been training
6. had been leading
7. had been waiting

3.

2. How long had you been living
3. How long had you been studying
4. How long had you been dating
5. How long had you been running

4.

2. had been planning
3. had been joking and laughing
4. had been practicing
5. had been running
6. had been trailing
7. had been looking forward
8. had been waiting

5.

2. F
3. T
4. F
5. T

6.–8.

Answers will vary.

PART I Review or SelfTest

I.

2. Are you thinking 3. barbecue 4. cooks 5. dispute
6. continues 7. claim 8. comes 9. refers 10. used
11. believe 12. means 13. roasted 14. is 15. had become
16. stood 17. drank 18. was 19. sounds 20. is

II.

Conversation 1
b. 's been happening c. Haven't you heard d. moved
e. bought f. had been looking g. were going to move
h. decided i. is j. Have you ever been k. have

Conversation 2
a. tried b. 've already eaten c. smell d. 'm thinking
e. saw f. looked

Conversation 3
a. Have you met b. calls c. What does she do d. was
working e. laid off f. lost g. have been cutting h. liked
i. trying

Conversation 4
a. Have b. got c. 're staying d. sounds e. need f. haven't
been g. met h. are they doing i. 're taking j. have been
learning

Conversation 5
a. 've been considering b. haven't decided c. were going
d. have you been doing e. 'd been having f. turned
g. had gotten h. gave i. sounds j. don't

Conversation 6
a. are driving b. found c. 've been swatting d. attracts
e. don't f. did you read g. heard h. turned on i. were
interviewing j. did you learn

III.

2. mentioned 3. don't look 4. guess 5. did...decide 6. was
7. loved 8. was 9. had read 10. knew 11. was going to go
or would go 12. grew 13. 're attending *or* 've been
attending 14. got 15. didn't mind 16. was 17. met
18. 've wanted 19. understand 20. have...had 21. 've been
following 22. haven't been able to 23. worry

IV.

I was taking scuba lessons ➔ I've been taking scuba
                                lessons
Yesterday, I am going ➔ Yesterday, I was going
the weather has changed ➔ the weather had changed
We were deciding ➔ We decided
So we've rented ➔ So we rented
They aren't having any ➔ They don't have any
we've been driving ➔ we had been driving
When we were first seeing ➔ When we first saw
Jack gets ready to go ➔ Jack is getting ready to go

PART II Future

UNIT 4 Future Progressive

1.

2. F
3. F
4. T
5. F
6. T
7. F
8. T

2.

2. At 9:00 Robo will (or he'll) be paying bills.
3. At 10:00 Robo will (or he'll) be vacuuming.
4. At 11:00 Robo (or he) won't be doing laundry. He'll be dusting.
5. At 12:00 Robo (or he) won't be making lunch. He'll be doing laundry.
6. At 12:30 Robo will (or he'll) be making lunch.
7. At 1:00 Robo will (or he'll) be shopping for food.
8. At 2:00 Robo will (or he'll) be recycling garbage.
9. At 3:00 Robo will (or he'll) be giving Mr. Granite a massage.
10. At 5:00 Robo will (or he'll) be making dinner.
11. At 6:00 Robo (or he) won't be playing cards with Karen and Danny. He'll be playing chess with them.

3.

1. 'll be going
2. Will . . . be joining.   Yes, I will.
3. are . . . going to be leaving
4. will be starting   're going to be hearing
5. are . . . going to be making   No, we're not.

4.

2. is
3. 'll be defying
4. 'll be floating
5. offers
6. 'll be reading
7. rocks
8. 'll be getting ready
9. won't be thinking

5.

Name	Time Not Free
Brian	second and third weeks of July
Lorna	first and second weeks of July
Tranh	second, third, and fourth weeks of July, and second, third, and fourth weeks of August

The time that they're all available: first week in August

6.–7.

Answers will vary.

UNIT 5 ▼ Future Perfect and Future Perfect Progressive

1.

2. b   3. b   4. a   5. a   6. a

2.

2. By 2010 Tom won't have graduated from college.
3. By 2010 he'll have gotten married.
4. By 2010 he'll have become a parent.
5. By 2010 he'll have bought a car.
6. By 2010 he won't have bought a house.
7. By 2010 he won't have moved to Phoenix.
8. By 2010 he won't have started his own business.

3.

2. By the time Tom graduates from college, he'll have already become a parent.
3. By the time Tom buys a car, he won't have graduated from college yet.
4. By the time Tom moves to Phoenix, he won't have graduated from college yet.
5. By the time Tom buys a house, he'll have already gotten married.
6. By the time Tom moves to Phoenix, he won't have started his own business yet.
7. By the time Tom starts his own business, he'll have already graduated from college.

4.

2. By February 18, how much will she have saved?
   Answer: By February 18, she'll have saved $35.00.
3. By June 16, how many books will Tom have read?
   Answer: By June 16, he'll have read fifteen books.
4. Will she have lost ten pounds by October 6?
   Answer: Yes, she will (have).
5. How long will Don have been running by December 29?
   Answer: By December 29, he'll have been running for five weeks.
6. How many miles will Tania have run by December 29?
   Answer: By December 29, she'll have run seventy miles.
7. Will Rick have saved $100 by July 1?
   Answer: No, he won't (have).
8. How many apartments will Tim have painted by October 25?
   Answer: By October 25, he'll have painted six apartments.
9. Will Tim have finished by November 15?
   Answer: Yes, he will (have).

5.

food	$ 500
clothing	$ 550
transportation	$1,000
entertainment	$ 420
Total:	$2,470
Where they can go:	1, 2, and 3

6.–7.

Answers will vary.

PART II Review or SelfTest

I.

2. 'll have been studying
3. 'll have graduated
4. 'll you be doing
5. 'll be looking
6. won't have graduated
7. 'm going to be getting ready
8. 'll be sitting
9. 'll still be sitting
10. get
11. 'll have found
12. 'm learning
13. 'll be starting

II.

2. a 3. d 4. c a 5. c 6. a 7. c 8. c

III.

2. won't be driving
3. 'll have finished
4. won't be polluting
5. won't be spending
6. will . . . be going
7. 'll be working
8. 'll have finished
9. 'll have been telecommuting *or* 'll have telecommuted
10. 'll be sleeping

IV.

We'll be travel ➔ We'll be traveling
we'll staying ➔ we'll be staying
I finished school by then ➔ I will have finished school by then
you'll been studying ➔ you'll have been studying
We'll be having a great time ➔ We'll have a great time

PART III Tag Questions, Additions, and Responses

UNIT 6 Tag Questions

1.

Underlined words: do you?, is it?, does he?, can't he?

2.

2. e 3. h 4. f 5. b 6. g 7. k 8 c. 9. j 10. l 11. a 12. d

3.

2. did you
3. doesn't it
4. haven't they
5. aren't you
6. don't you
7. isn't it

4.

2. You grew up in Burbank, didn't you?
3. You've always loved horror films, haven't you?
4. They didn't like your work, did they?
5. You weren't satisfied with *Batman*, were you?
6. You liked *Batman Returns* better, didn't you?
7. You don't like publicity, do you?
8. You aren't planning to leave the business, are you?

5.

Expect an answer: 2, 3, 6
Don't expect an answer: 4, 5, 7, 8

6.–8.

Answers will vary.

UNIT 7 Additions and Responses with *So, Too, Neither, Not either,* and *But*

1.

2. F
3. T
4. F
5. T
6. T
7. F
8. T
9. T
10. F

2.

2. did I
3. can I
4. do too
5. do I
6. do I
7. do I
8. do I

3.

2. but Bob Phillips isn't.
3. and so does Bob Phillips *or* and Bob Phillips does too.
4. and so does Bob Phillips *or* and Bob Phillips does too.
5. and neither does Bob Phillips *or* and Bob Phillips doesn't either.
6. and so does Bob Phillips *or* and Bob Phillips does too.
7. but Bob Phillips didn't.
8. and so has Bob Phillips *or* and Bob Phillips has too.
9. but Bob Phillips didn't.
10. and neither does Bob Phillips *or* and Bob Phillips doesn't either.

4.

and he too ➔ and he does too *or* and so does he
either can he ➔ neither can he
but I don't ➔ but I do
but he not ➔ but he isn't

5.

2. cooks	[X]	[✓]
3. eats out a lot	[✓]	[✓]
4. enjoys old movies	[✓]	[✓]
5. reads biographies	[✓]	[✓]
6. enjoys fiction	[X]	[X]
7. plays sports	[X]	[✓]
8. watches sports on TV	[X]	[X]
9. watches news programs	[✓]	[✓]
10. wants to see the documentary	[✓]	[✓]

6.–11.

Answers will vary.

PART III Review or SelfTest

I.

2. isn't he
3. do they
4. haven't they
5. did they
6. didn't they
7. wasn't he
8. had he
9. aren't we
10. shouldn't we
11. will it
12. won't we

II.

2. isn't
3. exports
4. produces
5. are . . . planting
6. hasn't . . . been
7. didn't build
8. named
9. doesn't use
10. speak

III.

2. b 3. b 4. a 5. b 6. a 7. a 8. b 9. c 10. b

IV.

2. Neither does
3. So does
4. did too
5. I was
6. So would

7. am too
8. doesn't either
9. Neither should
10. So am

V.

but so do I ➔ and so do I
neither don't I ➔ neither do I
she does either ➔ she does
do you? ➔ don't you?

PART IV Gerunds and Infinitives

UNIT 8 Gerunds and Infinitives: Review and Expansion

1.

Underlined words: requiring, allowing, living, banning, handling, purchasing, stopping, controlling
Circled words: to carry, to prevent, to make, to keep, to enforce, to pass, to ban, to purchase, to work, to stop, to pass, to complete, to sign, to enclose, to get

2.

2. hunting
3. collecting
4. shooting
5. to protect
6. to control
7. to buy
8. to get
9. to carry
10. protecting
11. imposing

12. to find
13. to solve
14. Blaming
15. to have
16. to bear
17. interfering
18. to seek
19. to curb
20. to handle
21. to lock up

3.

2. hesitated to ask
3. stopped to drink
4. considered (or had considered) inviting
5. agreed to answer
6. denied wearing
7. suggesting having
8. promised to hire
9. volunteered to patrol
10. appreciated . . . attending

4.

2. He urged her to vote for stricter gun-control legislation.
3. She discussed the officer's teaching personal safety.
4. They convinced him to take up rock climbing.
5. He feels nervous about his keeping a handgun in his apartment.
6. She appreciated his telling her about it.
7. He warned them to resolve their problems right away.
8. He's surprised at his not supporting gun control.

5.

it was necessary own ➔ it was necessary to own
to defending ➔ to defend
we need keeping ➔ we need to keep
stop to use violence ➔ stop using violence
recommend start ➔ recommend starting
prevent they learning ➔ prevent their learning *or* them from learning
remember to watch ➔ remember watching
ways solving ➔ ways to solve *or* ways of solving
eager graduating ➔ eager to graduate

6.

	Sen. Lois Blake	Sen. Tom Wilson
2. Banning assault weapons	✔	✔
3. Prohibiting hunting	☐	✔
4. Limiting the number of guns an individual may buy within a specific time period	✔	✔
5. Making the production of real-looking toy guns illegal	☐	✔
6. Holding parents responsible if their children find and use a gun	✔	✔
7. Applying the death penalty for criminals who use a gun to commit a crime	☐	☐

7.–9.

Answers will vary.

UNIT 9 Verbs Followed by Objects and the Base Form: Make, Have, Let, Help

1.

2. a
3. b
4. b
5. b
6. a

2.

2. made, d
3. got, a
4. let, f
5. had, b
6. had, h
7. let, c
8. made, e

3.

2. made them work
3. didn't let them use
4. had him (*or* Fernando) clean
5. let her (*or* Yasuko) leave
6. got him (*or* Uri) to pronounce
7. had him (*or* Hector) ask
8. let them record
9. made her (*or* Greta) speak
10. helped them find (*or* to find)

4.

made me helping ➔ made me help
let me to have ➔ let me have
have my child learns ➔ have my child learn
let he or she have fun ➔ let him or her have fun
makes Jack to become ➔ makes Jack become

5.

2. F
3. F
4. F
5. T
6. T

6.–9.

Answers will vary.

PART IV Review or SelfTest

I.

2. b
3. c
4. b
5. b
6. b
7. a
8. b
9. a
10. c
11. c
12. b
13. c
14. b
15. a
16. c
17. a
18. b
19. a
20. c

II.

2. driving
3. suspending
4. to drive
5. to drive
6. being
7. passing
8. not to take
9. to instill
10. pay
11. to be
12. obeying
13. having to
14. feeling
15. to prevent (*or* prevent)
16. not to use
17. to buckle up
18. ride
19. driving
20. to behave
21. saving
22. to make

III.

2. is letting *or* is going to let *or* will let Caryn use
3. afford to buy
4. persuaded Caryn to take
5. invited Jason to join them
6. quit eating
7. offered to lift
8. suggested turning on
9. made Dan show him *or* her
10. denied calling Caryn

IV.

2. urges Alicia to ask
3. lets students stay
4. doesn't mind my daughter's *or* daughter taping
5. appreciates the teacher's *or* teacher being
6. are used to Mrs. Allen's *or* Allen demanding
7. makes them take
8. gets them to help
9. wants them to do
10. are happy with her teaching

PART V Passive

 UNIT 10 The Passive: Overview

1.

2. P
3. A
4. P
5. P
6. P
7. P
8. A
9. P
10. P
11. P
12. A
13. A
14. P
15. P

2.

2. speak Ho.
3. Tagalog is spoken
4. is spoken by 371 million people
5. 65 million people speak
6. Arabic is spoken by
7. speak English
8. Swahili is spoken *or* They speak Swahili

V.

stop to smoke ➜ stop smoking
object to have to ➜ object to having to
imagine to work ➜ imagine working
refuse working ➜ refuse to work
make more smokers to give up ➜ make more smokers
give up
give up to smoke ➜ give up smoking

3.

2. No, it wasn't.
3. was . . . created
4. Is . . . grown
5. No, it isn't.
6. is . . . spelled
7. are . . . used
8. are . . . raised
9. is . . . mined
10. are grown
11. is found
12. are . . . spoken
13. Yes, they are.
14. Are . . . seen
15. Yes, they are.
16. are . . . made

4.

2. were bought
3. were built
4. were published
5. was discontinued
6. was replaced
7. were reduced
8. were increased
9. were appreciated

5.

2. Quinoa isn't spelled with a *k*.
   It's spelled with a *q*.
3. Llamas aren't raised only for transportation.
   They're raised for many uses.
4. Llamas aren't raised for meat in the lowlands.
   Cattle are raised for meat in the lowlands.
5. Rubber isn't found in that region.
   Oil is found in that region.
6. The parrot isn't seen in the highest mountains.
   The condor is seen in the highest mountains.
7. A great civilization wasn't created on the shores of the Pacific.
   It was created on the shores of Lake Titicaca.
8. Portuguese isn't spoken in the government.
   Spanish is spoken in the government.
9. Traditional textiles aren't woven by machine.
   They're woven by hand.

6.

3. are not allowed
4. is controlled by the feet, the head, and the body
5. wasn't played
6. was made popular by Pelé and other international stars
7. was enjoyed
8. was banned by King Edward III of England
9. were played
10. are held

7.

2. a
3. b
4. a
5. b
6. a

8.

1. Chinese
2. German
3. Spanish
4. Portuguese
5. Hindi
6. Korean
7. Russian
8. Hungarian
9. Swedish
10. French
11. Finnish
12. Czech

9.

		Mindanao	Luzon
GROW	tobacco	N	Y
	corn	Y	N
	bananas	Y	N
	coffee	N	Y
	pineapples	N	Y
	sugar	Y	Y
RAISE	cattle	Y	Y
	pigs	Y	Y
MINE	gold	Y	Y
	manganese	N	Y
PRODUCE	cotton	N	Y
	rubber	Y	N
	lumber	Y	N

10.

1. a
2. a
3. b
4. a
5. c
6. c
7.–10. (answers will vary)

11.–12.

Answers will vary.

UNIT 11 The Passive with Modals

1.

Underlined words: can be overcome, could be removed, could . . . be provided, should be investigated, should be done, could be frozen . . . brought, should be provided, ought to be done

2.

2. should be kept   will be designed   can be removed
3. could be given   should be given
4. ought to be carried out
5. will be done   may be stored . . . removed . . . brought   has to be solved

3.

2. Will . . . be prepared
3. squeezed
4. will be prepackaged
5. 'll . . . be warmed up
6. should . . . be selected
7. have to be offered
8. should be filled out
9. can be selected
10. Will . . . be used
11. Will . . . be shared
12. must be provided
13. can be learned
14. Could . . . be provided
15. ought to be placed
16. can be met

4.

can be misunderstanding ➜ can be misunderstood
can actually been tasted ➜ can actually be tasted
the clouds can see ➜ the clouds can be seen
It simply have to be experienced ➜ It simply has to be experienced
I think the next crews will be better train ➜ I think the next crews will be better trained

5.

2. could
3. must
4. They'll be picked up by the radar
5. grown
6. repaired

6.–8.

Answers will vary.

UNIT 12 Passive Causatives

1.

2. F
3. F
4. T
5. T
6. F
7. T
8. T

2.

2. He's going to get (*or* He's getting) his address changed at the post office on the twenty-fourth.
3. He got the carpet cleaned on the sixteenth.
4. He got his locks changed on the fifth.
5. He's going to have (*or* He's having) his shelves put up on the twenty-sixth.
6. He's going to get (*or* He's getting) the hall light repaired on the twenty-second.
7. He had the house painted the second week in April *or* from the eighth to the twelfth.
8. He's going to have (*or* He's having) furniture moved in on the twenty-ninth.

3.

2. have *or* get it dry cleaned
3. had *or* got them cleaned
4. 'm going to have *or* get it cut
5. have *or* get it colored
6. 've . . . had *or* gotten it repaired
7. Did . . . have *or* get it painted
8. have *or* get them developed
9. Have *or* Get them delivered
10. have *or* get it made

4.

Art did the job himself: 2, 6
Art hired someone to do the job: 3, 4, 5, 7

5.

They had:
the roof repaired
the antenna fixed
the broken window fixed
the windows cleaned
the house painted
the grass cut
an air conditioner installed
the garage enlarged
the driveway paved
the tree cut down
bushes planted
a porch built
a fence put up

6.

Answers will vary.

PART V Review or SelfTest

I.

2. leave
3. were mailed
4. have
5. were made
6. were confirmed
7. need
8. be met
9. rent
10. just handed
11. were sent
12. was done

II.

2. might be delivered
3. 'll be read
4. 'll be satisfied
5. have to be packed
6. ought to be told
7. could be extended
8. should be painted
9. has to be serviced
10. can be arranged

III.

2. is celebrated
3. are enjoyed
4. was established
5. are attended
6. is used
7. is exported
8. is produced
9. was settled
10. is spoken
11. were brought
12. is visited

IV.

2. have *or* get . . . cleaned
3. have *or* get . . . looked at
4. have *or* get . . . painted
5. had *or* got . . . designed
6. have *or* get . . . delivered
7. have *or* get . . . made up
8. 'll have *or* 'll get . . . catered
9. Have *or* Get . . . sent

V.

2. is grown
3. are employed by the sugar industry
4. is exported
5. is struck by hurricanes
6. was popularized by Bob Marley
7. 's listened to

VI.

They will corrected ➔ They will be corrected
it's printed by the printer. ➔ it's printed.
A funny thing was happened ➔ A funny thing happened
estimates . . . was left on my desk ➔ estimates . . . were left
on my desk
should make by all of us ➔ should be made by all of us

PART VI Modals

UNIT 13 Advisability and Obligation in the Past: Should have, Ought to have, Could have, Might have

1.

2. b
3. a
4. a
5. b
6. a
7. b
8. b

2.

2. should have
3. shouldn't have refused
4. shouldn't have taken
5. should . . . have done
6. might have asked
7. could have paid
8. ought to have worn
9. should . . . have fired
10. shouldn't have
11. should . . . have handled
12. ought to have warned
13. shouldn't have . . . fired

3.

2. I might have warned him.
3. I shouldn't have eaten all the chocolate.
4. She might have called.
5. He could have lent me some money.
6. I shouldn't have jogged five miles.
7. They shouldn't have charged me for the bag.
8. I ought to have done the laundry.
9. I should have invited her to the party.

4.

he might has talked to her ➜ he might have talked to her
I ought a have confronted him ➜ I ought to have confronted him
Should I of told ➜ Should I have told
I should handle things ➜ I should have handled things
should never has hired ➜ should never have hired

5.

Items checked:
Walk to work
Buy coat
Call Ron

6.–8.

Answers will vary.

UNIT 14 Speculations and Conclusions about the Past: May have, Might have, Could have, Must have, Had to have

1.

2. a
3. h
4. c
5. f
6. b
7. d
8. g

2.

2. could not have erected
3. had to have gotten
4. could . . . have planned
5. might have developed
6. may have drawn
7. could have designed
8. Could . . . have cut
9. could . . . have moved
10. must not have known
11. could have carved
12. transported
13. might have been
14. may have supported
15. Could . . . have helped
16. could . . . have visited
17. (have) written
18. could have explored
19. developed
20. must have had

3.

2. Dinosaurs must not have survived the cold.
3. A huge meteor might have hit the Earth.
4. Dust from the impact may have blocked the sun for a long time.
5. A Bigfoot couldn't have kidnapped Ostman.
6. Ostman must have seen a bear.
7. Ostman may have dreamed (or dreamt) it.
8. He could have thought his dream was real.
9. The photograph must have been a fake.
10. The man might have seen a large fish.
11. It may have been a dead tree trunk.
12. He couldn't have seen a dinosaur.

4.

2. They might have been.
3. They couldn't have been.
4. They might have.
5. He couldn't have.
6. They may have.
7. He might not have been.
8. He must have.

5.

1. c
2. f
3. e
4. b
5. d

6.

1. It's a ceramic pillow. Many of these have been found in the sleeping area of Chinese houses, and some have the Chinese character for pillow written on them.
2. It's a kind of ornamental safety pin. This one is from Hungary and dates from about 50 B.C. Men and women used them to fasten their woolen cloaks. Archaeologists know this because they have found these iron brooches on clothing in graves.
3. This is part of a book from the Mayan culture in Central America. It was found in Spain in 1860. Another Mayan book was found in the Bibliothèque Nationale in Paris. Archaeologists can now read a lot of the Mayan script, so they know that books like these recorded stories from Mayan literature, told about the gods, and gave information about agriculture, pottery, astronomy, and other arts and sciences.
4. No one knows where or when this object was found, so archaeologists have no clues to help them identify it. Some experts think it may have been a curler, used to curl hair in Egyptian wigs.
5. These are ice cleats. Inuits used them to walk on ice or snow. Scientists in early expeditions to the Arctic saw Inuits using them, and many Inuits still recognize them.

7.–8.

Answers will vary.

PART VI Review or SelfTest

I.

2. could have
3. shouldn't have
4. had to have
5. should have
6. might have
7. must not have
8. might have
9. shouldn't have
10. ought not to have

II.

2. may not have been
3. might have been
4. couldn't have been
5. should have studied
6. could . . . have done
7. could have read
8. shouldn't have missed
9. ought to have copied
10. must have come

III.

2. I should've watched the show about von Däniken.
3. It must've been very interesting.
4. The library ought to have had his books.
5. Sara should've reminded me about it.
6. John could've told me about it.
7. He must not have remembered our conversation about it.
8. My roommate might've invited me to the party.
9. John might not have gotten an invitation.
10. He couldn't have forgotten our date.

IV.

could of gotten ➔ could have gotten
had to has been ➔ had to have been
should have stay ➔ should have stayed

PART VII Conditionals

UNIT 15 Factual Conditionals: Present

1.

Condition (Underlined Twice)	Main (Underlined Once)
if a flight is unduly delayed	the airline provides meals and hotel rooms
If the delay is caused by overbooking	the airline owes you a lot more
If all the passengers actually show up	then the flight is overbooked
if no one volunteers	your flight may be delayed
Whenever the delay is over four hours	you receive 200 percent of the cost of your ticket
if your luggage is delayed	Ask for funds to buy clothing or toiletries
If the airline actually loses your suitcase	then it must pay you the value of its contents

2.

2. If you're traveling with your children, take them to Lai Chi Kok Amusement Park in Kowloon.
3. If you need a moderate-priced hotel, I suggest Harbour View International House.
4. If you like seafood, there are wonderful seafood restaurants on Lamma Island.
5. If you're fascinated by Chinese opera, you might like the street opera in the Shanghai Street Night Market.
6. If you'd like to get a good view of Hong Kong, you should take the funicular to the Peak.
7. If you're interested in buying some traditional Chinese crafts, then you ought to visit the Western District on Hong Kong Island.
8. If you're looking for a good dim sum restaurant, try Luk Yu Teahouse on Stanley Street.

3.

3. If I stay with friends, I spend time with them.
4. It's not so nice if I get a Dracula.
5. If you have three roommates, you don't have trouble finding dogwalkers.
6. It's very rewarding if you don't mind hard work.
7. If a flight has an empty seat, I ride for free.
8. If flight is completely booked, you can't get on it.

4.

2. If you heat the air in a balloon, the balloon rises.
3. If you boil water, the water evaporates.
4. If you put an empty glass upside down in a basin of water, the air in the glass keeps the water out.
5. If you attach an object to a parachute, the object falls slowly.
6. If you suck on a straw, liquid replaces the air that has been sucked out.

5.

2. F
3. T
4. F
5. T
6. F

6.–7.

Answers will vary.

8.

1. If you blow across the top of a strip of paper, the strip rises. Moving air has less air pressure than still air. If you blow across the top of a strip of paper, you lower the air pressure above the strip. The stronger air pressure under the strip of paper pushes it up.
2. If you pinch a straw tightly, you can push it through an apple. As you push the straw into an apple, you squash the air inside the straw. The compressed air makes the straw very strong, and you can push it right through the apple.
3. If you drop a small object and a large object from the same height, they hit the floor at the same time. In the sixteenth century, Galileo experimented by dropping objects from the tower of Pisa. He observed that if you drop objects of different sizes at the same time from the same height, they hit the ground at about the same time.
4. If you blow between two sheets of paper, the sheets move together. The reason is the same as for experiment number 1: Moving air has lower air pressure than still air. If you blow between the sheets, you lower the air pressure between them. The higher air pressure on the outside pushes the sheets of paper together.

9.

Answers will vary.

UNIT 16 Factual Conditionals: Future

1.

2. h
3. b
4. e
5. f
6. c
7. d
8. i
9. a

2.

3. win
4. 'll take *or* 'm going to take
5. become
6. 'll try *or* 'm going to try
7. will . . . do *or* are . . . going to do
8. lose
9. don't win
10. 'll continue *or* 'm going to continue
11. cooperate
12. won't be *or* isn't going to be
13. accepts
14. 'll work *or* 'm going to work
15. don't elect
16. 'll be *or* 'm going to be

3.

2. If you take the job, you won't have the chance to travel a lot. You'll never leave the office.
3. If you become an employee of Eastward, you won't get a raise every year. You'll get one (*or* You'll get a raise) every two years.
4. If you join Eastward, you won't receive wonderful benefits. You'll receive terrible benefits.
5. If you accept Eastward's offer, it won't be the best career move of your life. It will be the worst.

4.

2. If you are married and filing separately and earn $15,000 this year, you will pay (*or* you are going to pay) a tax rate of 28% next year.
3. If you are married and filing together and earn $15,000 this year, you will pay (*or* you are going to pay) a tax rate of 15% next year.
4. If you are widowed and earn $30,000 this year, you will pay (*or* you are going to pay) a tax rate of 28% next year.
5. If you are single and earn $18,000 this year, you will pay (*or* you are going to pay) a tax rate of 28% next year.
6. If you are married and filing separately and earn $13,000 this year, you will pay (*or* you are going to pay) a tax rate of 15% next year.

5.

2. If
3. unless
4. If
5. unless
6. if
7. If

6.

Items checked: 2, 4, 6

7.–9.

Answers will vary.

UNIT 17 Unreal Conditionals: Present

1.

2.	a. T	b.	F
3.	a. F	b.	F
4.	a. F	b.	T
5.	a. T	b.	T
6.	a. F	b.	T
7.	a. F	b.	F
8.	a. T	b.	T

2.

2. wouldn't be
3. were
4. would moan
5. were
6. could wish
7. had
8. wouldn't have to
9. were
10. thought
11. could find
12. realized
13. would understand
14. insisted
15. might have to
16. were
17. could ride

3.

2. If he were ambitious, he would ask for a raise.
3. If I were in shape, I'd play sports.
4. If I had enough time, I would (plan to) study for the exam.
5. If I weren't too old, I would go back to school.
6. If my boss explained things properly, I could (would be able to) do my job.
7. If I were good at math, I would balance my checkbook.
8. If I didn't feel nervous all the time, I could (would be able to) stop smoking.

4.

2. I wish I were a handsome prince.
3. I wish I didn't live in the sea.
4. I wish I lived in a castle.
5. I wish I didn't have to swim all day long.
6. I wish I had a princess.
7. I wish the fisherman didn't come here every day.
8. I wish his wife didn't always want something.
9. I wish she were satisfied.
10. I wish they left me alone.

5.

2. What would you do if you were the leader of this country?
3. How would you feel if you never needed to sleep?
4. What would you do if you had more free time?
5. What would you do if you could swim like a fish?
6. What would you do if you didn't have to work?
7. Where would you travel if you had a ticket for anywhere in the world?
8. If you could build anything, what would it be?

UNIT 18 Unreal Conditionals: Past

1.

2.	a.	F	b.	T
3.	a.	T	b.	T
4.	a.	F	b.	T
5.	a.	T	b.	F
6.	a.	T	b.	F
7.	a.	T	b.	F

2.

2. would have gone . . . hadn't lost
3. wouldn't have felt . . . had found
4. had . . . been
5. wouldn't have known . . . hadn't shown
6. hadn't rescued . . . wouldn't have saved
7. hadn't helped . . . would have gone
8. wouldn't have been . . . hadn't met
9. wouldn't have been able to . . . hadn't stayed
10. would have been . . . hadn't lived

6.

when there were no women ➔ if there were no women
if men and women live ➔ if men and women lived
men will start more wars ➔ men would start more wars
If men aren't there ➔ If men weren't there
the world will be ➔ the world would be

7.

2. T
3. T
4. F
5. F
6. T
7. T
8. F

8.–11.

Answers will vary.

3.

2. I wish I hadn't hit little George when he was trying to help me. I wish I had been nice to him.
3. I wish my father hadn't had a heart attack. I wish I hadn't had to stay and run the business.
4. I wish we had been able to go on our honeymoon. I wish we hadn't needed the money to save the business.
5. I wish I had been able to trick George out of his business. I wish he had accepted my offer to buy his business.
6. I wish I hadn't lost $8,000. I wish George hadn't gotten into trouble with the law because of me.
7. I wish Daddy hadn't been upset about the business. I wish he hadn't yelled at us on Christmas Eve.
8. We wish we had known about George's troubles earlier. We wish we had had enough money to help him.

4.

2. would have called
3. wouldn't have taken
4. had found
5. would . . . have done
6. had found
7. would have tried
8. Would . . . have put
9. wouldn't have
10. could have answered
11. would have been
12. had been
13. would have looked

5.

2. a
3. b
4. b
5. a
6. a
7. b
8. b

6.–9.

Answers will vary.

PART VII Review or SelfTest

I.

1. d, c
2. a, d
3. b, c
4. d, b
5. a, c
6. c, a, b
7. c
8. b, a
9. d
10. c, a
11. a
12. b

II.

2. would have seen
3. tell
4. 'll spoil
5. would . . . have been
6. had been born
7. had had
8. wouldn't have grown up
9. hadn't grown up
10. wouldn't have met
11. hadn't taken
12. studied
13. 'd pass
14. don't get
15. study

III.

2. found
3. Would . . . keep
4. knew
5. hadn't gotten
6. would have borrowed
7. would have taken
8. weren't
9. would be
10. wouldn't have seen
11. had glanced
12. have
13. discuss
14. doesn't belong
15. return
16. won't follow
17. obey
18. comes
19. 'll be

IV.

2. I wish I had bought business-class tickets.
3. I wish the in-flight movie weren't *Back to the Future IV*.
4. I wish Carrie hadn't asked the flight attendant for a soda.
5. I wish we hadn't gone to Disneyland on vacation.
6. I wish we had gone to the beach.
7. I wish I *or* we lived in Florida.
8. I wish my office could transfer me to Orlando.

V.

we've had fun ➔ we would have had fun
unless you're interested ➔ if you're interested in the
  in the movies   movies
I wish my family lives closer ➔ I wish my family lived
                                                      closer
If I am an adult ➔ If I were an adult

PART VIII Adjective Clauses

 UNIT 19 Adjective Clauses with Subject Relative Pronouns

1.

Paragraph 1

people (who) accept us completely (warts and all) and
(who) know our most secret thoughts

others (whose) relationships with us may be less deep
but are still important

Acquaintances

people (whose) paths often cross ours

The neighbor (who) borrows your chairs for a big party or
the colleague (who) waters your plants while you're
on vacation

"Our next-door neighbor, (who) car pools with us

Buddies

a friend (who) shares a particular activity or interest

important ones (that) keep us connected to our interests
and hobbies

My table-tennis partner, (who's) from Beijing

Old Friends

The vice president (who) promoted me

Delores was the one (who) came with me

old friends (who) knew us "back when"

parts of ourselves (which) are easy to lose as we move
through life

experiences (that) have helped form us

George Herbert, (who) said that the best mirror is an old
friend

2. T
3. T
4. F

2.

2. h
3. g
4. j
5. i
6. f
7. c
8. d
9. b
10. a

2. An album is a book which (*or* that) has pages for saving photos.
3. An alter ego is a person who (*or* that) is very similar to you in thought and feeling.
4. A colleague is a person who (*or* that) has the same job or profession as you.
5. A confidant is a person who (*or* that) listens to your private feelings and thoughts.
6. Empathy is a feeling which (*or* that) lets you experience another person's feelings.
7. Friendship is a relationship which (*or* that) exists between friends.
8. Kin is a person who (*or* that) is a relative.
9. A reunion is an event which (*or* that) brings people together after a long separation.
10. A spouse is the person who (*or* that) is married to you.

3.

2. who (*or* that) have
3. which (*or* that) are
4. who (*or* that) face
5. which (*or* that) is
6. who (*or* that) have
7. who (*or* that) are
8. whose . . . are
9. whose . . . include
10. which appeared
11. who (*or* that) doesn't read

4.

2. They'll meet us at the restaurant which is (*or* that's) across the street from the library.
3. The navy blue suit which (*or* that) was on sale looked the best.
4. Bill and Sue aren't close friends with the Swabodas, whose interests are very different from theirs.
5. The neighbors, who wanted to borrow some folding chairs, came by while you were gone.
6. I was just laughing at an old picture which (*or* that) is in my high-school yearbook.
7. My boyfriend, who took a group of students to Cuba for two weeks, left me a lot of plants to water.

5.

some people who's completely → some people who are (*or* were) completely

adults, which were → adults, who were

the teachers, who stayed → the teachers who stayed with
with us in the dormitory,   us in the dormitory

ones who they helped us → ones who helped us

Bob Taylor who is much → Bob Taylor, who is much older
older than I am became   than I am, became

Mexico City, that is a very → Mexico City, which is a very

Bob, who have studied → Bob, who has studied

Bob, who's letters → Bob, whose letters

trip what sounds interesting → trip that sounds interesting

6.

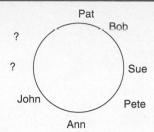

7.–10.

Answers will vary.

UNIT 20 Adjective Clauses with Object Relative Pronouns, When, and Where

1.

Looking down, you see a paved courtyard, in which I spend
many hours . . . and a bit of garden, where I go to smell the
few violets that come up each spring . . . and where my
sister gathers the snails that live

. . . the Twardowskis, who come to our apartment
regularly. . . . I particularly like the Twardowskis' daughter,
Basia, who is several years older than I and who has the
prettiest long braids, which she sometimes coils around her
head

. . . about the eccentric characters (who, whom, that)
I know

. . . about the shapes (that, which) icicles make

. . . dramatic recitations of the poems (that, which) we've
memorized

2.

2. who(m) . . . stayed
3. when . . . was
4. which . . . had
5. which *or* that . . . wanted
6. where . . . were
7. who(m) . . . take care of
8. who(m) . . . talk
9. which . . . put
10. which *or* that . . . find
11. whose . . . miss
12. which *or* that . . . 'll attend *or* 'm going to attend

3.

2. I lived with my parents, who(m) you've met, and my
    siblings.
3. I had two sisters, who(m) I got along well with (*or* with
    whom I got along well), and an older brother.
4. My sisters and I shared a room, where we spent nights
    talking.
5. My brother, who(m) I hardly ever saw, slept on the
    living room couch.
6. It was a large old couch, which my father had made
    himself.
7. My best friend, who(m) I saw every day, lived across
    the hall.
8. We went to the same school, where we both studied
    English.
9. Mr. Robinson, who(m) everyone was a little afraid of (*or*
    of whom everyone was a little afraid), was our English
    teacher.
10. After school I worked in a bakery which (*or* that) my
    aunt and uncle owned.
11. They sold delicious bread and cake, which people stood
    in line for hours to buy.
12. I took piano lessons from a woman whose sister worked
    in the bakery.
13. I remember one summer when the whole family went to
    the lake.
14. It was a great summer, which I'll never forget.
15. My brother and sisters, who(m) I miss, live far away
    now.
16. When we get together we like to reminisce about the old
    days when we were all together.

4.

I don't remember our first house, which we rented from a
   relative,
we moved to the house ~~that~~ I grew up in
This house, where my parents still live, is on
in our front courtyard, where she sold omelettes
All her customers, whom I always chatted with, were
straight to the corner where he sat drinking tea
and the customers ~~that~~ my father had invited to dinner
My oldest cousin, whose father wanted him to learn the tea
   business, slept there
a room with my grandmother, who took care of her a lot of
   the time

5.

Room: b
The description is in formal English.

6.–8.

Answers will vary.

PART VIII Review or SelfTest

I.

2. who
3. who
4. where
5. whose
6. which
7. which
8. who
9. that
10. which
11. when
12. when

II.

2. She lives in the house which (*or* that) is across the
   street.
3. This is the time of year when (*or* that) she always goes
   away.
4. She travels with her older sister, who lives in
   Connecticut.
5. This year they're taking a trip with the car that (*or*
   which) she just bought.
6. They're going to Miami, where they grew up.
7. They have a lot of relatives in Florida, who(m) they
   haven't seen in years.
8. The family is going to have a reunion, which they've
   been planning all year.
9. They'll be staying with their Aunt Sonya, whose house is
   right on a canal.
10. They really need this vacation, which they've been
    looking forward to all year.

III.

3. which
4. is
5. where
6. go
7. who
8. are
9. that *or* which
10. helped
11. which
12. will take place *or* 's going to take place *or* 's taking place
13. that *or* which
14. who
15. live
16. arrived
17. who
18. lives
19. is arriving *or* arrives *or* will arrive *or* is going to arrive
20. which *or* that
21. has

IV.

**Sentences where you can delete the relative pronoun or
when:**
3. Send thank-you notes to the relatives John received
   gifts from.
5. Call the woman I met at lunch.
7. Buy the book Mr. J. recommended.
9. Buy Annie the t-shirt she wanted from the hotel gift
   shop.
10. Try to agree on a time we can all get together again.

V.

who he never invited me ➔ who never invited me
where I never got to see ➔ that (*or* which) I never got to see
someone who you knows ➔ someone who you know
the day where ➔ the day when (*or* that)
people with that ➔ people with whom
who friendships ➔ whose friendships

PART IX Indirect Speech and Embedded Questions

 UNIT 21 Direct and Indirect Speech

1.

"Lying during a job interview is risky business," (says) Martha Toledo, director of the management consulting firm Maxwell Enterprises. "The truth has a funny way of coming out." Toledo tells the story of one woman applying for a job as an office manager. The woman (told) the interviewer that she had a B.A. degree. Actually, she was eight credits short. She also (said) that she had made $30,000 at her last job. The truth was about $5,000 less. "Many firms really do check the facts," (warns) Toledo. In this case, a call to the applicant's company revealed the discrepancies.

Toledo relates a story about another job applicant, Gloria. During an interview, Gloria (reported) that she had quit her last job. Gloria landed the new job and was doing well until the company hired another employee, Pete. Gloria and Pete had worked at the same company. Pete eventually (told) his boss that his old company had fired Gloria. In spite of the fact that the new employer was very pleased with Gloria's job performance, he felt that he just couldn't trust her anymore, Gloria got fired–again. "It's a small world," (says) Toledo. "When it comes to a business interview, it's best to stick to the facts."

2.

2. wanted
3. her
4. said
5. had
6. said
7. her
8. told
9. wasn't
10. told
11. her
12. she
13. are

3.

2. She said it was her own recipe.
3. He said he had to drive his aunt to the airport.
4. He said his car had broken down *or* He said his car broke down.
5. She said she exercised every day.
6. He said he'd just mailed the check.
7. He said he was 35.

4.

(Note: Both the name and pronoun are acceptable.)

3. She (*or* Lisa) said (that) they wanted someone with some experience as a programmer.
4. He told her (that) he worked as a programmer for Data Systems.
5. She said (that) they needed (*or* need) a college graduate.
6. He told her (that) he (had) graduated from Florida State.
7. She said (that) they didn't want a recent graduate.
8. He told her (that) he had gotten his degree two years ago.
9. She told him (that) it sounded like the right job for him.
10. He said (that) he thought so too.

5.

2. She said that she never missed an aerobics class, but she slept late on Sunday.
3. She said the weekly staff meeting was on Monday, but it's on Tuesday.
4. She said she loved the meat sauce, but she's a vegetarian.

6.–9.

Answers will vary.

UNIT 22 Indirect Speech: Tense Changes

1.

2. c
3. c
4. a
5. a
6. c
7. b
8. b
9. a
10. a

2.

2. They said (that) it was going to pass north of here (*or* there).
3. They said (that) the Texaco station had run out of gas that afternoon (*or* yesterday afternoon).
4. They said (that) it wasn't really a hurricane, just a tropical storm.
5. They said (that) they had closed the bridge because of high tides.
6. They said (that) they wouldn't restore the electricity until today.
7. They said (that) they couldn't reopen the schools for at least a week.
8. They said (that) we ought to use bottled water for a few days.

3.

2. That's right. He said (that) hurricane winds often exceeded (*or* exceed) 150 miles per hour.
3. That's right. He said (that) until recently, force-five hurricanes had been rare.
4. That's wrong. He said (that) we'd had three major hurricanes since 1988.
5. That's right. He said (that) meteorologists were (*or* are) predicting an increase in big storms.
6. That's right. He said (that) warmer temperatures could cause more severe storms.
7. That's right. He said (that) force-five storms would probably become more common.
8. That's wrong. He said (that) we couldn't (*or* can't) do anything about the weather.
9. That's right. He said (that) we had to have a better emergency relief program.
10. That's right. He said (that) if we didn't have weather satellites, we wouldn't be able to warn people.
11. That's right. He said (that) things could have been worse in Florida.
12. That's wrong. He said (that) people in Florida had had time to leave the area.

4.

2. I'm worried about you and Rita.
3. If you weren't so stubborn you'd pack up and leave right now.
4. I've had a lot of experience with hurricanes.
5. You have to put tape on all your windows.
6. You (*or* You and Rita) ought to fill the sinks and bathtubs with water.
7. You should buy a lot of batteries.
8. We can't stay here.
9. We want to stay with you (*or* you and Rita).
10. We're leaving tonight.
11. We should have called you and Rita sooner.
12. The storm will hit the coast tonight.
13. The eye of the hurricane is going to pass over this area.
14. The storm may (*or* might) last for several hours.

5.

Items checked:
2. should go home immediately
3. may stay closed
4. are dangerous
5. drive slowly
6. avoid driving
7. will close at 1:00
8. will stay open until 5:00
9. will stay closed
10. will close at noon
11. will stay open until evening
12. are open now

6.–7.

Answers will vary.

UNIT 23 Indirect Instructions, Commands, Requests, and Invitations

1.

(tell) to bring

(tells) to relax and watch TV

(ask) to explain

(asks) to get into the bed

(instructs) not to leave

(invites) to join him

(tells) not to worry

(tells) to get more exercise

2.

3. She told him to read Dr. Thorpe's new book, *Night Shift*, for more tips.
4. She said to sip some hot herbal tea with honey.
5. She told her not to drink black tea.
6. She said to pinch the place between your (*or* her) upper lip and your (*or* her) nose.
7. She told him to make a toothpaste of one tablespoon of baking soda and a little water.
8. She told him to spread cool, cooked oatmeal over the rash.
9. She said to try soaking the rash in a cool bath with one-fourth cup baking soda.
10. She told him not to scratch the rash.
11. She said to eat onions or garlic every day.
12. She told him to ask his doctor about a vitamin B supplement.
13. She told her to dissolve one-fourth cup of cornstarch in a lukewarm bath.
14. She said not to rub your (*or* her) skin with the towel when drying off.
15. She told her not to use anything containing alcohol on her skin.

3.

Underlined indirect commands, instructions, requests, and invitations:
to follow him
to show me the ship
to come aboard
to pilot the ship
not to leave the controls
to slow down
to point the ship towards the earth

2. Follow me.
3. Please show me the ship.
4. Come aboard! *or* Why don't you come aboard? *or* Please come aboard!
5. Pilot the ship.
6. Don't leave the controls.
7. Slow down.
8. Point the ship towards the earth.
9. Don't panic.
10. Wake up.

4.

2. Do
3. Don't do
4. Do
5. Not mentioned
6. Don't do
7. Don't do
8. Not mentioned

5.–7.

Answers will vary.

UNIT 24 Indirect Questions

1.

Indirect questions underlined:

what I would change about my current job

when I had been most successful

how much money I was making

if I had cleaned out my car recently

why my employer didn't want me to stay at my job

if I was good enough to work for such an important company

if I really want this job

Direct questions checked:

2., 4., 5., 7., 9.

2.

2. He asked when the interview was.
3. He asked where the company was.
4. He asked if she needed directions.
5. He asked how long it takes (or took) to get there.
6. He asked if she was going to drive.
7. He asked who was going to interview her.
8. He asked when they would let her know.

3.

3. Claire asked if there was opportunity for promotion.
4. Pete asked if she (or Claire) was interviewing with other companies.
5. Claire asked what her responsibilities would be.
6. Claire asked how job performance was rewarded.
7. Pete asked what her (or Claire's) starting salary at her last job had been.
8. Pete asked if she (or Claire) had gotten along well with her last employer.
9. Claire asked if they hired many women.
10. Pete asked if she (or Claire) had been fired from her last job.
11. Pete asked why she (or Claire) had applied for this position.
12. Claire asked if they had had any major layoffs in the past few years.

4.

with our company? → with our company.

asked "if we expected → asked if we expected
changes in the job"   changes in the job

how often do we evaluate → how often we evaluated

asked why did I decide → asked why I (had) decided

5.

Questions checked:

OK	Not OK
Reason for leaving job	Age
Reason for seeking position	National origin
Skills	Height
Job performance	Marital status
	Information about spouse
	Arrest record
	Financial situation

Illegal questions:

2. What nationality are you?
3. How tall are you?
4. Are you married?
5. What does your husband do?
6. Have you ever been arrested?
7. Do you owe anyone any money?

6.–7.

Answers will vary.

UNIT 25 Embedded Questions

1.

Underlined phrases:
if a tip was necessary at all
how to calculate the right tip instantly
who you should tip here
how tipping properly can get you the best service for your money
who to tip
when to tip
how much to tip

2.

2. how I can tell if the tip is included in the bill?
3. what I can do instead.
4. why this happened?
5. if (*or* whether) I should tip her instructor.
6. how much I should tip the airport and train porters?
7. who expects a tip and who doesn't.
8. if (*or* whether) I can tip taxi drivers on my trip.

3.

1. b. how much we are supposed to tip the taxi driver?
2. a. how we are going to choose.
   b. how much a bus tour costs?
3. a. what they put in the sauce.
4. a. where the Smithsonian Museum is?
5. a. how much the metro costs?
   b. how far you're going.
   c. where they sell them.
6. a. if (*or* whether) they have tour buses that go there.
   b. we could rent a car and drive there?
7. a. what's wrong with it.
   b. where you are?
   c. how long it will take?

4.

2. how to get
3. when (*or* what time) to leave
4. where to go
5. how to figure out
6. who(m) to invite

5.

2. a   5. b
3. b   6. b
4. a

6.–8.

Answers will vary.

PART IX Review or SelfTest

I.

1. b. last
2. a. would be   b. our
3. a. told   b. they
4. a. asked   b. was
5. a. she   b. should bring
6. a. told   b. not to bring
7. a. 'd been planning   b. us
8. a. didn't know how   b. our
9. a. asked   b. if there was
10. a. not to be
11. a. told   b. to take
12. a. couldn't   b. the following night
13. a. was   b. that day
14. a. told   b. her
15. a. had issued   b. that night
16. a. would   b. that day
17. a. had to drive
18. a. says   b. loves
19. a. him   b. to shovel
20. a. asked   b. his boots were

II.

2. what I should wear.
3. who's going to be there.
4. if (*or* whether) they invited Tory.
5. if (*or* whether) I'll be able to find a cab.
6. how to get (*or* how you get) to Woodmere Avenue?
7. how far it is.
8. how much I should tip the driver.
9. if (*or* whether) this is Woodmere Avenue.
10. what time it is?

III.

2. had met
3. was coming
4. wasn't
5. to ride
6. might snow
7. to call
8. ought to get together
9. to drive
10. not to worry

IV.

2. Jon told her (that) they had moved in three weeks before.
3. Nita asked if (or whether) they liked (or like) that place better than their old apartment.
4. Jon said (that) they liked (or like) it a lot more.
5. Jon asked when her cousin had arrived from Detroit.
6. Nita told him (that) he had just come the day before.
7. Jon said (that) it had been (or has been) an incredible winter.
8. Nita said (that) the roads might close again with that storm.
9. Jon said not to drive that night.
10. Jon said to stay there with her cousin.
11. Nita told him (that) they should try to make it home.
12. Nita said (that) she had to walk her dog early the next morning.

V.

she and her cousin have almost decided	➔	she and her cousin had almost decided
to stay with a friend tonight	➔	to stay with a friend that night
told me that I had just arrived	➔	told me that he had just arrived
He said "that it had been a big one."	➔	He said that it had been a big one.
that they will close at 1:00 P.M.	➔	that they would close at 1:00 P.M.
reported that they are planning	➔	reported that they were planning
how could weather forecasters	➔	how weather forecasters could
they were not sure why this had happened?	➔	they were not sure why this had happened.

PART X Pronouns and Phrasal Verbs

U N I T 26 Reflexive and Reciprocal Pronouns

1.

Pronoun	Refers to
herself	Summer Sanders
themselves	athletes
each other	athletes
ourselves	We

2.

2. ourselves
3. myself, yourself
4. herself
5. each other
6. itself, ourselves
7. herself
8. themselves
9. ourselves

3.

2. one another or each other
3. yourselves
4. one another or each other
5. itself
6. themselves
7. himself
8. myself
9. themselves

4.

to remind me ➜ to remind myself
theirselves ➜ themselves
talk to ourselves ➜ talk to us
Jan myself ➜ Jan himself
forgive themselves ➜ forgive each other

5.

2. himself
3. yourself
4. herself
5. ourselves
6. yourselves

6.–7.

Answers will vary.

UNIT 27 Phrasal Verbs

1.

took him on as a summer employee
and the two got along right away
When they got together again
He teamed up with Wozniak
they put the prototype together
they set up their first production line
which they brought out in 1976

Phrasal Verb
2. teamed up (with)
3. brought out
4. got together
5. brought about
6. took on
7. put together
8. got along

2.

2. think back on
3. grew up
4. dropped out of
5. set up
6. filled . . . up
7. carry out
8. keep . . . away
9. broke out
10. paid . . . back
11. carry on
12. finding out
13. broken down
14. brought about
15. set up
16. came up with
17. carried out
18. gave up
19. kept on

3.

2. figure it out
3. fill them out
4. handed it out
5. do it over
6. turned it off
7. turn them in
8. left them on

4.

2. following it through
3. Pick one out
4. Think up uses for the object
5. throw any ideas away
6. Write them down
7. talk them over
8. Find out about a problem
9. work a solution out
10. come up with one
11. stick with it
12. look information up
13. Try different materials out
14. get something out of

5.

Touch Up It! ➜ Touch It Up!
called up them ➜ called them up
tried in several ➜ tried out several
filled down an application ➜ filled out an application
set a strong and convincing ➜ set up a strong and
 demonstration up   convincing demonstration
so I put ➜ so I put on

6.

Pictures numbered in the following sequence:
8, 6, 3, 1, 5, 9, 2, 4, 7

Use tape to hold the tissue paper on.
Cut them off.
Cover the hole up with foil.
Turn the box up.
Light something up and look at it.
Cut out a small hole.
Punch a hole through the center of the foil.
Cover up the opening with tissue paper.

7.

2. get out
4. ends up
6. pushes up
7. set off
8. goes off
9. jumps up
11. comes off

8.

Possible Answers:
2. get on, get off, break down
3. figure out
4. look up, write down
5. put on, take off
6. turn on, turn off, turn up, turn down

9.–10.

Answers will vary.

PART X Review or SelfTest

I.

1. myself
2. out
3. up
4. over
5. over
6. in
7. each other's
8. with
9. out
10. out, yourself
11. over
12. up
13. down, up
14. each other, yourselves
15. out, itself
16. up
17. in
18. up
19. out
20. themselves
21. back
22. off
23. through
24. themselves, out
25. away, themselves
26. off
27. up
28. himself

II.

2. itself
3. himself
4. each other's, ourselves
5. myself, yourself, itself
6. each other
7. herself
8. themselves, each other's
9. each other
10. myself

III.

2. call it off
3. carry it out
4. switched it on
5. get along with him
6. keep away from them
7. put it back
8. taken them off
9. wake her up
10. work them out

IV.

2. They talked it over thoroughly.
3. Please don't throw them away.
4. The teacher turned down my topic proposal (*or* turned my topic proposal down).
5. All forms must be turned in by April 8.
6. Please turn off all lights (*or* turn all lights off) upon leaving the room.
7. They could blow up.
8. Don't give up hope.
9. Your homework assignment will be handed out at the end of the class.
10. You left it out.
11. They let me down.
12. Can someone take this flashlight and light it up?
13. Can someone point out what the mistake is?
14. You must go after them with diligence.
15. Don't just show up without one.

V.

talked over it ➔ talked it over
set a model volcano with explanations ➔ set up a model . . . and charts up
helped ourselves ➔ helped each other
hisself ➔ himself
put together them ➔ put them together
ran an article across ➔ ran across an article
blew over ➔ blew up

Index